WILDLANDS AND WOODLOTS

FUTURES OF NEW ENGLAND

WILDLANDS AND WOODLOTS

The Story of New England's Forests

LLOYD C. IRLAND

University Press of New England
Hanover and London, 1982

University Press of New England

Brandeis University

Brown University

Clark University

Dartmouth College

University of New Hampshire

University of Rhode Island

Tufts University

University of Vermont

Photographs by Chris Ayres © Chris Ayres

Library of Congress Catalogue Card Number 81-69943

International Standard Book Number 0-87451-227-1

Library of Congress Cataloging in Publication Data will be found on the last printed page of this book.

To my teachers

Trees both in hills and plaines, in plenty be,
The long liv'd Oake, and mournefull Cypris tree,
Skie towring pines, and Chesnuts coated rough,
The lasting Cedar, with the Walnut rough:
The rozin dropping Firre for masts in use,
The boatmen seeke for Oares light, neate growne sprewse,
The brittle Ash, the ever trembling Aspes,
The broad-spread Elme, whose concave harbours waspes,
The water spungie Alder good for nought,
Small Elderne by th' *Indian* Fletchers sought,
The knottie Maple, pallid Birtch, Hawthornes,
The Horne bound tree that to be cloven scornes;
Which from the tender Vine oft takes his spouse,
Who twinds imbracing armes about his boughes.
Within this *Indian* Orchard fruites be some,
The ruddie Cherrie, and the jettie Plumbe,
Snake nurthering Hazell, with sweet Saxaphrage,
Whose spurnes in beere allayes hot fevers rage.
The Diars Shumach, with more trees there be,
That are both good to use, and rare to see.

from William Wood,
New England's Prospect (1634)

CONTENTS

PREFACE

This is a book about New England, my adopted home region. It is a story of the region's forests, of how they have changed, and of what they can mean to New England's future. The attitudes about the forest expressed by the impersonal market and by public policy have altered, but the importance of forests in New England life has never changed.

I am an office forester: my lungs have never choked with smoke while fighting a forest fire, nor have my pants ever been spattered with tree-marking paint. My view of the forest has mostly been acquired from the office window of the research station, the university, and the bureaucracy, and from official reports, statistics, history books, and talking with colleagues. I am indebted to the dozens of New England foresters who have shown me their work as we walked in the woods.

This book is full of numbers, most of them estimates. Before the 1950s no serious sampling of the forest was done; few aerial photos were available. Foresters offered their best judgments on forest area, volume cut and grown. Census enumerators did their best, but there are inevitable gaps in the data. In this book, I refrain from detailed comment on the accuracy of the figures. I draw frequent historical comparisons, using employment, production, and wage figures, but recognizing that data from before 1950 must be used with special care. Changing definitions, different standards of accuracy, and the frequent guesswork of early estimates must be remembered.

I offer many numbers that are purely personal estimates. This book is a general essay and not a report of an extensive and costly research project. I usually offer my estimates in very round terms, so that readers will not be tempted to rely overmuch on their precision. Many of the things I define (the suburban forest, the area regrown after farm abandonment) are difficult to measure precisely, and basic data do not exist. Other readers may well prefer their guesswork to mine. While I do not think that slightly different numbers would change the story, I hope that these rough estimates will challenge others to refine them by detailed local and regional studies.

This is a book about forests, by a forester, written for nonforesters. It tries to identify those themes about New England's great forest that may interest the general public. Stories of technical forestry do not fit here, nor do details of silviculture, taxation, pest and fire control, forest land use planning, forest research, and administrative policy. These subjects have been my daily concerns as a forestry administrator and civil servant, but they interest, I suspect, few New England citizens.

Other topics have been omitted, not because they are unimportant, but because they are more distant from my main focus. I do not discuss the region's wildlife resource and its management, though New England's sportsmen have been important conservation leaders. There is nothing on presettlement forest history and on the role of science and education, and little on federal policies and the federal land managing agencies. Nor do I consider the literary, artistic, and cultural history and values of the region's forests. These topics are also part of the story, but they are not the central concern of this book.

I would like to acknowledge the assistance given by all of my teachers, who equipped me for this work. More particularly, I owe thanks to friends and colleagues who, in reviewing this and other works, have helped me: Ernie Gould of the Harvard Forest, who patiently read several drafts of the entire manuscript, testing and challenging ideas; Neal Kingsley and Steve Boyce of the United States Department of Agriculture Forest Service; David Field of the School of Forestry, University of Maine at Orono; Philip Conkling of Cushing, Maine; Al Worrell and Clark Binkley of the Yale School of Forestry and Environmental Studies; Tom Rumpf, Dick Arbour, and Ellen Baum of the Maine Forest Service; and Tim Glidden and Chuck Hewett of the Resource Policy Center, Thayer School of Engineering, Dartmouth College. Many of my associates in the Maine Department of Conservation, the region's forest products companies, and New England's forestry community have taught me things without even realizing it. As editor of the Futures of New England series, Carl Reidel of the University of Vermont read several drafts and gave suggestions and encouragement as the book developed.

Lauren Brown prepared most of the maps and charts; the balance were done by Bob Johnson. Chris Ayres supplied several of the photos and skillfully prepared prints from borrowed negatives for others.

Many people helped by supplying photos: the Maine Department of Conservation; the Maine State Library; Paula Broydrick of the International Paper Company; Paul McCann of the Great Northern Paper Company; Keith Ruff and Ray Kozen of Georgia-Pacific Corporation; Bill Leak, U.S.D.A. Forest Service, Durham, New Hampshire, and Charles Gill, U.S.D.A. Forest Service, Milwaukee, Wisconsin; the Architect of the Capitol, Washington, D.C.; Lester DeCoster, American Forest Institute; John Lawrence, Rhode Island Division of Forest Environment; Tom Siccama, Yale School of Forestry; Bill Gove, Vermont Division of Forests, Parks, and Recreation; Mary Henley, Trustees of Reservations; Ellie Horwitz, Massachusetts Division of Fish and Wildlife; and Greg Gurdel, Vermont Agency of Development and Community Affairs. Priscilla Bickford, Maine Department of Conservation librarian, obtained for me many of the sources used in this book.

For encouragement, discussion, and tolerance while this book was being written, as well as for a helpful reading of an early draft, I am indebted to my wife, Connie.

CHAPTER 1

Forests In New England Life

he forest sets the stage for New England life. Forests provided colonists with masts and staves for exports, with
fuel, and with game; with raw materials for their distinctive architecture and their principal industries. New England is full
of Sawmill Roads, Papermill Roads, Clapboard Hills, and Mill
Rivers.

For much of this century, New England forests were of little concern to legislators and the public. But during the 1970s, a series of
dramatic changes swept over the region. A new investment boom in
paper and sawmills boosted wood use in northern New England, at
the same time that a spruce budworm outbreak threatened the softwood timber supply. Rising land prices prompted legislative clashes
over forest taxation in every New England state. A wave of land
speculation hit rural areas, converting woodlots to subdivisions.
Controversy erupted over the proper management of state forests,
over wilderness areas in the national forests, and over management
of the region's water supply protection forests. Finally, an increasing harvest of fuelwood in the late 1970s rapidly approached the
level of current growth in parts of southern New England, raising
once again the specter of overcutting. Concerned people toyed with
municipal regulations, public subsidies, and a spate of education
programs to cope with this dizzying increase in cut, unequaled since
the 1890s.

By 1980 it was clear to thoughtful observers that a new age was
dawning for New England's forests. The forest values of aesthetics,
watershed protection, wildlife, recreation, and timber production
are increasing in importance to the region's residents. All of these
values are threatened by careless cutting, land posting, suburban
sprawl, speculative rural subdividing, and landowner indifference
to sound land stewardship. These trends are no longer of concern
only to foresters, paper companies, and government planners. They
concern all of us.

It was also clear that the policies of the past will not meet the
needs of the future for protecting and nurturing the diverse values

Old growth oak, Massachusetts, represents the forest values threatened today. *Courtesy of Bill Leak, USDA Forest Service.*

of the forest. This book is the story of changes, of conflicts, and of policies. It provides a basis for my own prescriptions for forest policies for New England's future.

New England is today about 75 percent forested. A century ago, there was far less forest in New England—about 58 percent of the land, or 23 million acres. Farm abandonment has released enough land so that, despite the inroads of suburbia, there are still 31 million acres of forest (table 1). Today's forestry needs and opportunities emerge from the consequences of these past cycles of land use change.

The forest sets the visual tone of New England. It is difficult to find a place outside of a central city where a woodlot or wooded hillside is not in view. The pine-lined lakeshores and the stone walls rambling through the woods are essential ingredients of New England's scenery and quality of life, which are in turn key attractions for the region's bustling tourist trade. The institutions related to ownership and management of New England forest are rooted in colonial times, and in the history of a region dominated by private landownership. Only 6 percent of the New England forest is publicly owned. The agencies, nonprofit groups, corporations, and laws that are the fabric of the region's forestry institutions emerged in the conservation movement of 1890–1910, during the Great Depression, and in the 1950s and 60s.

The early colonists discovered a forest abounding in useful trees and game. They quickly found uses for many of these trees and considered it necessary to regulate carefully forest utilization and product trade.[1]

Today, 100,000 jobs depend directly on the region's forest industry, and additional employment relies on these industries. Roughly 60,000 of these jobs depend directly on timber produced in New England. In the 1950–70 period, many New Englanders placed a higher value on the forest as a green backdrop for subdivisions than as a source of useful products. Under pressure of the current fuelwood boom, this attitude is changing.

By the close of the American Revolution, the region's population was only 600,000 persons. Most of New England remained an untouched and unexplored wilderness. The forests were diminished only slightly by settlement and were invaded only along a few coastal and inland streams for the largest trees. At times, such as the 1730s and 1780s, waves of speculation in wildland townships occurred, though very little was settled. After 1790, it took forty

Table 1. Farm and Forest Land Use in New England, 1770–1979.

	1770	1880	1940	1979
Population (millions)	0.5	4.0	8.4	12.2
Number of farms	80,000	200,000	135,000	25,570
Acres in farms (thousands)	3,000	20,725	13,800	5,100
Woodland	–	7,155	6,950	2,400
Tillable	2,000	6,790	4,850	1,700
Pasture	–	6,780	2,000	1,000
Total acres in forested land, including farms (thousands)	36,400	23,536	29,762	30,984
Urban and developed acres (thousands)	100	500	2,000	5,000

SOURCES: Author estimates, based heavily on the following: J. D. Black, *The rural economy of New England* (Cambridge: Harvard Univ. Press, 1950), p. 449; for land in farms and number of farms. 1979, USDA, *Agricultural statistics, 1979* (Washington, D.C.: GPO); for forested land, 1880 and 1940, H. I. Baldwin, *Forestry in New England* (Boston: National Resources Planning Board, 1942), 1976, U.S.D.A. Forest Service, *Analysis of the timber situation, 1952-2030,* Review Draft (Washington, D.C.: GPO, 1980), App. 3, p. 20; for detailed data for 1974, H. T. Frey, *Major uses of land in the U.S., 1974,* USDA, Econ. Stat. and Coop Serv., Agr. Econ. Rept. 440, 1979, p. 28; USDA Soil Conservation Service, *1980 Appraisal, part I* (Washington, D.C.: GPO, 1981), p. 73. The 1974 figures are not comparable to those for 1880 and 1940. (Note that this estimate of forest land in farms is lower than the U.S. Forest Service estimate reported in ch. 8.)

Forest landscape in the southern White Mountains, New Hampshire. *Courtesy of Bill Leak, USDA Forest Service.*

years for the region's population to double to 2 million persons, and farms were appearing even in remote corners of New England's hills. At the peak of land clearing, in 1880, only 4 million people lived in New England's mostly rural society.

The period from 1880 to the 1920s was one of slow, steady decline of farming. During the same time, the lumber industry reached an all-time high production level, and a new paper industry, based on wood pulp, emerged.

From 1920 to the 1940s, the automobile changed the face of New England. As more and more farms "went back" to forest, cottages and camps sprang up along rural and northwoods lakesides. The seacoast was dotted with recreational developments. From the late 40s to the 1980s, the landscape again changed dramatically. While total forest acreage remained stable, farm acreage plummeted. Suburban sprawl on a massive scale engulfed millions of southern New England acres in an unprecedented wave of land use change. Farmers sold off land by millions of acres. In the 1970s, an explosion in recreational land speculation converted large areas to partially built, partially sold, and occasionally bankrupt subdivisions.

Today, 12 million people live in New England. Their landscape has only a fraction of the farmland that it had a century ago—they eat food grown elsewhere. The area devoted to urban, suburban, and industrial uses exceeds crop and pasture land. The area of untouched virgin forest is nominal, as is the acreage of artificial forest plantations. There is a far larger area of land purposely growing commercial wood crops than is devoted to farming, housing, office buildings, and factories. Clearly, woodgrowing is, by acreage, New England's dominant land use.

Patterns of wood use in New England have changed significantly over the centuries. In colonial times, fuelwood was dominant. Its abundance, by allowing warmer homes, has even been credited with fostering a higher level of health than existed in Europe in those times. Despite its commercial importance, I doubt that the colonial export trade in lumber, masts, staves, and other products equaled the wood consumption of fuelwood and locally used lum-

Table 2. New England's Five Forests and
Nonforest Land, 1980

Forest Land	Acres (millions)
Industrial	13
Recreational	3
Suburban	3
Wild	1
Rural	11
Total forest	31
Nonforest Land	
Cropland and pasture	2.7
Unproductive woodland, marsh, and other nonforest	1.4
Developed	5.0
Total nonforest	9.0
Total land area	40.1

SOURCE: Author estimates, based on following sources: USDA Forest Service, *Analysis of the timber situation in the U.S. 1952–2030*, Review Draft, Appendix 3: 1977 Forest Statistics, Washington, D.C., 1980.

NOTE: The industrial forest includes industrially owned land plus an estimated 3.2 million acres owned by families and trusts managed for timbergrowing. The recreational forest is a judgment estimate. The suburban forest acreage is based on studies showing that about 5 million acres of land in New England are developed and that 50 percent or more of the land in the urbanized regions remains undeveloped. The wild forest is an estimate of designated wilderness plus designated watershed protection lands and estimated nonprofit organization holdings. The rural forest is a residual. Data on cropland, marsh and other, and developed land are based on Frey, *Major uses of land*, p. 26. Another data set on land use (for 1976) may be found in Council on Environmental Quality, *National Agricultural Lands Study* (Washington, D.C.: GPO, 1981).

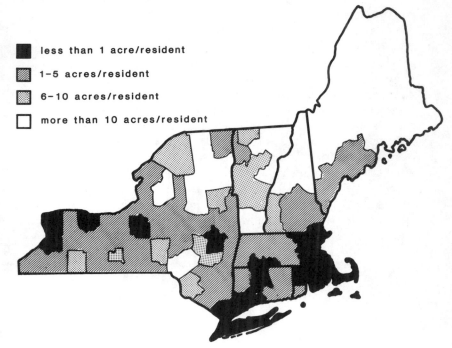

Figure 1. Forest land per capita, 1970s. *Courtesy of Professor E. M. Gould.*

ber. Throughout the nineteenth century, fuelwood and charcoal for industry remained key forest uses, except in the north, where lumbering dominated and people were few. Wood pulp paper arrived in 1880, but it was not until the mid twentieth century that its wood use exceeded fuelwood. After its peak in 1909, lumber output fell, until its regional recovery in the 1970s. Today, fuelwood use is rising dramatically and will catch up with pulpwood again in a few years if its growth continues at recent rates.

New England's Five Forests

This book is the story of New England's five forests—industrial, recreational, suburban, wild, and rural (table 2). These forests are defined by distinctive economic and geographic traits (fig. 1). They are not divided by clear boundaries but intermingle. Some individ-

Fields, woods, brushland, and houselots present a panorama of land use change. *Photo by Chris Ayres.*

ual ownerships are part of more than one of the five forests. For example, the White Mountain National Forest contains bits of wild forest, industrial forest, and recreational forest. Forest industry lands in Maine commonly include inholdings of recreational and wild forest.

The forests do not follow municipal boundaries. Many southern New England towns include bits of suburban, rural, industrial, and wild forest. But the forests usually occupy general regions, in which a single type sets the overall tone of the region's landscape (fig. 2). The acreages in table 2 are estimates. They are not based on detailed statistics tabulated according to rigorous definitions, which are beyond the scope of this work.

About three-fourths of the region's forest is in industrial and the rural forests. These provide the timber for the region's mills and fireplaces, and a wide range of hunting, fishing, watershed protection, and aesthetic benefits. The remaining forests are devoted to more specialized uses, but still provide diverse benefits.

A sixth forest, very important to most New Englanders, is not discussed in this book. This is the urban forest, consisting of for-

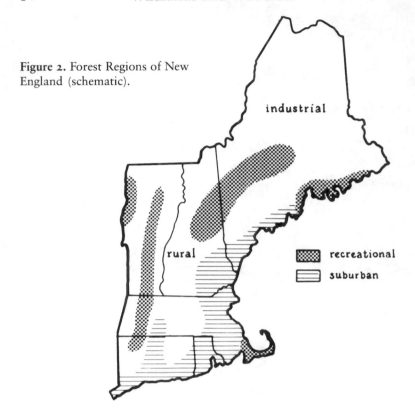

Figure 2. Forest Regions of New England (schematic).

ested parks and parkways in the region's cities and suburbs. These forests exist for their amenity values, and the financial values that real estate markets attribute to them are extremely high. The management problems of this forest are distinctive and have produced a new academic subdiscipline and a series of bureaucratic programs—urban forestry.

The New England Region

Though it is not a distinctive botanical or economic unit, New England recommends itself as the scope of this work for several reasons. The region, comprising Maine, New Hampshire, Vermont, Massachusetts, Rhode Island, and Connecticut, shares a common heritage of town government, a unique pattern of industrial forest ownership, and a strong sense of itself as a region. Moreover, I know New England well. I suspect, though, that residents of New York and Pennsylvania will find New England's forestry conditions familiar.

Is the story of New England's forests of interest to persons concerned with forest conservation elsewhere? I believe it is.

New England has been ahead of the rest of the nation in many ways in its forestry trends and concerns. Farmland abandonment, returning land to forest, occurred early in the nineteenth century. Later, New England was the first region to "cut out," to exhaust pine and spruce for lumber. It then made a transition—pioneering in the nation—to a pulp economy. During the same period, private initiative prompted government conservation efforts in land acquisition for national, state, and local forests.

Since then, New England has led, during the 1960s and 1970s, in developing town and state land conservation groups, such as land trusts and conservation commissions. These groups and a few wealthy individuals have created the bulk of New England's wild forest. Such groups play a leading role in public policy at the local and state levels.

New England was a region of pulpmills and tiny sawmills until the boom of the 1970s, when large spruce-fir sawmills, particleboard plants, and hardwood pulp mills arrived. The region never fully abandoned the woodstove, and the recent growth in wood energy has nearly returned its wood use pattern to the position of the turn of the century, when fuelwood exceeded pulpwood in wood consumption.

New England is a region of private forests. Its forest future depends almost entirely on what private owners and land markets do. Its wood economy is scarcely influenced by federal timber policy, over which loud debates constantly rage in Oregon. The United States Department of Agriculture Forest Service expects private lands to be the principal source of growth in future wood production and other forest services. As the region already most dependent on private land, New England will lead in responding to the trend toward more timber output from private land. Its rich diversity of forestry and conservation organizations provides an excellent base for progress.

Government agencies face severe inflation and public resistance to higher budgets. In coming decades, the ability of government to meet land conservation needs will decline. By land conservation

Maine log drive, Penobscot River, 1920s. This was the dominant mode of log transportation in New England for three centuries. *Courtesy of Maine State Library, Myron H. Avery Collection.*

needs, I mean wise land use as well as preservation. New England, which already relies heavily on private action and initiative, is well placed to meet future challenges, at a time when governments must retrench.

New England differs from other major regions in that its forest management concerns are not dominated by plantations. Elsewhere, major debates over plantation forestry are underway. Here, natural forests, often of poor or degraded quality, are the basis for management. We will grow wood with the trees we have, by managing natural stands, not by planting new forests.

Public Concerns and Policies

Public concerns with the forest have evolved slowly over New England's history. During colonial times, the forests were seen as indispensable raw material sources. Their use was a critical concern, and public authorities regulated everything from roadside trees to grazing to promotion of mills, as well as pricing and the export of products. During the nineteenth century, however, public regulations vanished and the forests were seen as significant assets by individual citizens but as wastelands by public policy. What few laws about fires and taxes existed were not implemented by administrative organizations, and forest policy was dormant. During this period, certain areas were used for recreation, hunting, and fishing. Traditional rights of public use of the land were respected, though recreational use of the forest was limited. Thoreau rarely met other casual strollers in the Concord woods.

As suburbs spread, New England community leaders began to work for preserving patches of forest through public and nonprofit groups. Their efforts were based on interest in preserving forests from despoliation, or on preserving future timber supply. The rest of the forest landscape was ignored by public policy, though its use for timber continued.

The principal area of public and government concern with forests from the 1950s to the early 70s was the value of the forest as a "green backdrop," a wooded setting for houses or parks. Open space was the perceived public need. Many suburban residents saw harvesting timber products as a threat to higher forest values. The green backdrop emphasis in land policy is typical of suburbia and is often more concerned with preventing development than with positive values of wildland.

Today, active interest has revived in a host of problems that would have been recognized by colonial town selectmen. Planners attempt to identify and conserve prime farmland for future crop production. They work to preserve forests for watershed protection and to conserve recharge areas. Faced with increasing timber cutting, some southern New England towns are considering zoning restrictions on logging. The booming fuelwood market has revived not only an active concern with the ability of the forest to provide timber but also the old New England custom of timber stealing. The king's timber agents would feel at home with today's trespass situation and would feel just as helpless as they were in their own time.[2]

Two concerns, however, are new. First is the concern over continued public access to the forest, particularly in the suburban, rural, and recreational forests. This problem is a product of modern social conflicts, of higher use pressures, and of the suburban attitude toward land—as a commodity for private use and not as a community asset.

Second is the concern, familiar from the turn of this century, over the future forest land base. The loss of productive forest land through recreational subdividing and suburban speculation, the fragmentation and inundation by land-hungry, inefficient development, have turned the tide after a century of increases in woodland area. Future trends raise the possibility of dramatic reductions in forest area, especially considering how difficult it is to manage for timber, wildlife, and recreation on tiny parcels. This trend is especially acute in the suburban forests, highly valuable for open space, wildlife, aquifer and watershed protection, and amenity. The suburban forest could be substantially destroyed in the next half century. If present growth patterns continue, one-half to one million acres will be urbanized by the year 2000. For a century, forests have been recovering the New England landscape in the wake of farm abandonment. It is unfamiliar, and uncomfortable, to be talking of the forests disappearing again in a new cycle of land use change.

CHAPTER 2

New England's Forest Geography

ew England's forests are formed from the interweaving of the great boreal forest flora to the north and the temperate hardwood forest flora to the south.[1] From the north come the paper birch, fir, and spruces, and the bog flora that is of uniform appearance throughout the region. From the south come the oaks, white cedar, and tulip poplar of southern New England. White pine and hemlock are species characteristic of this transition belt and not of the far Canadian north or the southern United States. This broad zone of transition is what gives New England its distinctive vegetational contrasts, especially vivid in the fall color season (fig. 3; table 3).

The region's forests can be grouped in three distinctive ecological zones: forests of the mountains, of the northern New England lowlands, and of the southern New England lowlands. The distinctions are not so much in the presence or absence of groups of species as in their abundance and the way in which the species are associated.[2] Though for convenience I include the forest types described in table 3, which are useful for national data, I will use more locally familiar terms in the balance of this chapter.

Forests of the Mountains

Northern New England's mountains support the most dramatic forests in the region. Their special character derives from the rocky, cold, humid, windblown mountainsides where they grow. Their grandeur stems not from the size of the trees but from their setting, high on the peaks, overlooking the region's low hills and lakes.[3]

Walking up any of a dozen different peaks, from the Green Mountains to Katahdin in Maine, the observer sees a characteristic pattern of forest. First, at the roadhead in the valley, are lush mixed hardwood forests of maple, yellow birch, beech, and a scattering of oak, ash, paper birch, with a few small spruce and fir. In these stands grow scattered large pines and hemlocks. On sandy areas are stands of pine, and in the wettest spots of poor drainage will be spruce, fir, and tamarack. Farther up the trail, old burns may be seen supporting paper birch, aspen, and pin cherry. Higher on the rocky slope, the burns seem to come back to dense, even aged stands of white or red spruce, with little understory vegetation.

In steep ravines spared from cutting giant pines, hemlocks, yellow birches, and maples may be found. The ancient yellow birch are often flat-topped and have dark, deeply wrinkled bark that resembles yellow birch not at all.

Up the trail, spruce and fir increase. Occasional dense stands will be seen. If they have been undisturbed long enough, the overstory will be breaking up from wind-snapped tops or falling trees, opening the forest floor to sunlight and allowing a dense carpet of tiny seedlings to grow freely. As the trail steepens, there is an occasional glimpse at the broad gray peak, and the view opens outward over the valley. The trees are now all spruce and fir, densely packed. They stand in a soft mat of moss that covers rocks and gently oozes water after a rain. Tiny birches mix in with the fir and spruce. Soon the trees are head-high or shorter, and the hiker is free of the dark forest. The vegetation takes on a matted, dense, wind-formed aspect, called "krummholz" by botanists. Upward from the krumm-

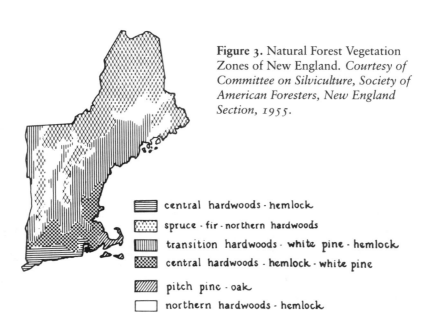

Figure 3. Natural Forest Vegetation Zones of New England. *Courtesy of Committee on Silviculture, Society of American Foresters, New England Section, 1955.*

central hardwoods · hemlock

spruce · fir · northern hardwoods

transition hardwoods · white pine · hemlock

central hardwoods · hemlock · white pine

pitch pine · oak

northern hardwoods · hemlock

Table 3. Major Types of Commercial Forest Land in
New England

Type	Acres (thousands)
White-jack-red pine	4,605.6
Spruce-fir	9,341.9
Pitch pine	142.6
Oak-pine	705.0
Oak-hickory	2,146.1
Elm-ash-cottonwood	4,212.0
Maple-beech-birch	7,577.9
Aspen-birch	1,973.6
Nonstocked	279.8
	30,984.5

SOURCE: USDA-FS, *Analysis*, app. 3, p. 26.

holz, the tiny trees fade into grass, sedge, and moss, rocks, and tiny alpine shrubs and flowers. The dwarf forest will penetrate to higher elevations on south slopes and in sheltered locations.

The forest takes shape in response to gradients in growing season, temperature, soil, aspect, and moisture. The shifts with elevation are similar to those found in traveling north to the treeline in the Arctic. The shrub and grassy vegetation above the treeline in both situations—arctic and alpine—share the name of tundra.

Forests of the Lowlands: Northern New England

A traveler through northern New England's lowlands passes diverse forests, shaped by soils, drainage, cutting history, insects, wind, and human rebuilding of the landscape.

A drive from Maine's coast to the interior of the "Big Woods" will pass through most of the forest types of this region. On the coastal points and islands are forests of spruce and fir, mostly on thin soils. Their growth is slow and the forest floor is made up of moss. Coastal windstorms occasionally flatten patches of these forests, allowing regeneration. Where deep soils occur in sheltered locations, mixtures of birch, ash, oak, and other hardwoods are found. Some distance inland, pines appear and large oaks occasionally dominate the stands.[4]

Roadside fields, recently grazed, will be dotted with ground juniper and an occasional wispy pine or birch. In wet pastures, tam-

Red spruce in a subalpine zone in the White Mountains, New Hampshire. *Courtesy of Bill Leak, USDA Forest Service.*

arack will invade from its haunts in wet spots and along streams. Giant maples and pines along the roads and old fences recall the former landscape of tree-lined fences amid fields. A hardwood forest of maple, beech, yellow birch, cedar, hemlock, pine, and occasional fir and spruce covers most of the landscape. Passing through a sandy region, the pines appear more prominently. A large roadside bog displays the pattern of pale green tamaracks slowly invading the margins, followed by spruce and pine, all tapering up in height to meet the surrounding hardwood forest.

To the north, the road crosses bouldery streams and large lakes, lined with pines. The terrain becomes gently rolling, and a distant mountain appears from time to time. Log trucks are encountered more frequently, and now and then a slash-littered landing appears, with a skidder and muddy pickup parked by a long woodpile. You pass through a milltown of old tenements clumped around a mill with a huge pulpwood pile. A giant Catholic church dominates the end of Main Street. As a line of motels disappears behind you, you move onto a broad hardwood ridge dominated by beech, maple, and paper birch, and notice that something has cleaned the leaves off the birch. You pass a large clearcut of recent vintage, with dark green spruce and fir trees poking through raspberries and pin cherry.

Coming down off the ridge, you enter a dark "fir thicket"—two miles of densely stocked trees, few larger than six inches in diameter. The dark overstory has shaded out all but the occasional understory plant, and few spruce or fir seedlings are seen. The trees have tiny spindly tops from being overcrowded. The stand is full of dead stems, standing and sprawled over the mossy ground. These fir flats are found on the low slopes of the ridges and the flat areas along streams. The old timber cruisers called these areas "black growth." The spruce-fir stands of Maine, New Hampshire, and Vermont are the prime source of pulpwood for the region's paper mills. These dense stands have often been created by spruce budworm outbreaks, which periodically kill most of the mature trees and start a new forest cycle. In the late 1970s, we saw evidence of the recent budworm outbreak in the thin foliage and occasional dead tops in these stands. In early June the foliage is covered with tiny green caterpillars; in early July, the damaged needles give the forest canopy a rust-brown appearance over millions of acres. In mid July, hordes of small brown budworm moths collect around lights at night.

Second-growth northern hardwoods, Bartlett Experiment Station, White Mountains, New Hampshire. *Courtesy of Bill Leak, USDA Forest Service.*

On many moist slopes, the spruce-fir and hardwoods mix in equal numbers to form mixedwood stands. In such situations, rapid wood growth is typical.

The northwoods landscape is sprinkled with tall pines that emerge above the general forest canopy. Early surveyors and timber cruisers used to climb these trees to view the surrounding area. Many of them were not cut in the logging days—they were too large to move, too far from water, and often rotten in the heart. The dense, extensive stands of pine found in southern Maine, New Hampshire, and Massachusetts are uncommon in northern Maine.

A gentle hillside now displays a stand of large spruce, mixed with small fir, spruce, paper birch, and maple. These large spruce display healthy deep crowns and show little damage from budworm feeding. They are old enough to have survived the massive budworm outbreak of 1912–20 and they now tower over younger trees. They will grow vigorously until age 200 or more. Because of their large size they are prized for lumber, and they formed the basis for the northern New England softwood lumber industry from the 1840s to World War I.

Forests of the Lowlands: Southern New England

New England's forests were shaped by the revegetation of a glaciated landscape over the past 12,000 years. The glacier left behind a wet, ill-drained landscape over much of northern New England. It left thin, "ledgy" soils and wide areas of sand plain in southeastern Massachusetts, Rhode Island, and Cape Cod. Walden Pond, surrounded by oaks and pines, is an example of the sandy landscapes.[5]

Oaks and chestnuts once dominated this landscape. Occasional hillsides of maples and yellow birches are found. The extensive stands of pines of this region contrast with the scattered pine of the far north, as does the prominence of oak. Fir is absent. Wet spots with poor drainage often are known as red maple swamps or may contain hemlock, ash, and elm. The bogs look as they do up north, with mosses, black spruce, and tamarack. A few bogs in coastal Connecticut contain Atlantic white cedar.

Abandoned farmlands make up half or more of the forest acreage of southern New England. A woodland of young oaks with mature and dead red cedar scattered through it is surely an old pasture, invaded by cedars, unappetizing to cattle, and later abandoned to the oaks. Most of the woodlots contain sprout growth, and old forest vegetation maps refer to this area as the sprout hardwood region. The sprouts come from heavy, repeated cutting. Many trees bear basal fire scars from light fires. The centuries of abusive cutting, fire, and neglect have left these woods burdened with cull trees of poor form or quality.

This is the region of old cellar holes by abandoned lanes, and forgotten graveyards; of villages that sent more men to the Civil War than inhabit them today; where the recession of agriculture turned over a previously settled landscape to the forest. Where the stone walls wind through the woods.

History of Disturbance

A useful perspective is to view New England's forest as one largely created, by intention or by chance, by human action. This is not to deny the basic influence of soils and climate, or the importance of wind, fire, and insects, but merely to assert that human efforts have broadly shaped today's New England forest. In the future, human action will be even more important.

The extent and nature of past disturbance of New England's forest can be estimated as follows (the figures are in millions of acres):

No disturbance	negligible
Light, infrequent cutting	15.0
Heavy past cutting followed by light cutting	8.0
Cleared for farming and naturally reforested	8.5
Cleared, planted to trees	less than .25
Cleared for agriculture, still in farms	2.5
Cleared and urbanized, now nonforest	4.0
Never forest	2.0
Total	40.0

A full 25 percent of the current forest area of the region has seeded in on abandoned fields (fig. 4). This secondary forest is in some places more than a century old but remains profoundly affected by its old-field origin. At the other extreme, the acreage of undisturbed ("virgin") forest is nominal—though it was estimated

Pitchpine on the sandy soils left by glaciers, Rhode Island. *Courtesy of Rhode Island Division of Forest Environment.*

Hardwoods on an abandoned field, Derry, New Hampshire. *Courtesy of American Forest Institute.*

as high as 2 million acres in 1920. In the early 1970s, the New England Natural Areas project identified 1.8 million acres, in 5,000 units, that were undisturbed enough to be considered natural areas. But the remaining acreage of truly virgin forest is probably less than the area planted by human hands to pines and spruces. Plantation forestry in New England has never attained the importance that it has in the Midwest and the South—and it probably never will.

Sometime in the 1950s or 1960s, the acreage of cleared land still in farms fell below the cumulative area converted to subdivisions, roads, and shopping centers.[6] This is a significant point in the land use history of New England, changing to a suburb from an agricultural region.

The lands remaining in forest throughout New England's history fall into two categories—those areas of southern New England that were once heavily cut but then ignored until recently, and a much larger area of the industrial forest that has been subject to periodic harvests at a relatively low level for more than a century and a half. In Connecticut, for example, about ten times as much timber was harvested in the 1860s as in the 1960s—and the earlier harvest was from a land area of half the extent.

The forest landscape of southern New England has been modified in ways more subtle than clearing and reseeding. According to J. J. Dowhan and R. J. Craig, 25 percent of Connecticut's flora, 30 percent of its fish, 7 percent of its mammals, and 4 percent of its birds were introduced from elsewhere.[7] Truly, even the creatures of Connecticut's landscape owe their presence there, many of them, to human action. The decline of farming has led to a noticeable decline in the birds of fields and openings, and an increase in forest dwellers. Beaver and turkeys are returning to areas where they had been long forgotten, while the wolf and several other species have vanished from the scene.

In sum, of today's New England forest, about one-fourth has regrown from farmland, one-half has a history of infrequent disturbance, and one-fourth is used less heavily now than a hundred years ago. Less than one-fourth of the original acreage has been converted to other uses. There is, of course, wide regional diversity in these patterns.

Man-made Forests

Throughout New England, trees have been planted for timber, erosion control, and aesthetics. Old fields and waste places have been planted to white pine, Norway and white spruces, red pine, and

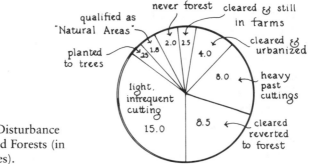

Figure 4. Past Disturbance of New England Forests (in millions of acres).

Pine stand in an old field, Waterboro, Maine. *Courtesy of Bill Leak, USDA Forest Service.*

Scotch pine. Occasionally, venturesome foresters or landowners have planted larches, domestic and exotic, and other less common species. The most popular in southern New England have been the pines, with white spruce being widely used in northern Maine.[8]

In many instances, white pine planted in old fields has disappointed foresters and landowners. The soils, degraded by farming and erosion, often seem low in productivity, and stands suffer heavy damage from blister rust, white pine weevil, and occasionally snow and ice. The New England traveler will drive past many overstocked plantations whose tending has been ignored. Overstocked, their trees do not develop deep full crowns and many will die from suppression. The forest floor in these plantations accumulates a fragrant brown mat of needles, littered with cones. Until the stand opens up by the death and blowdown of larger trees, little vegetation covers the forest floor.

Many of the red pine plantations in Connecticut have been cut, following insect and disease damage partly due to planting this species outside its natural range. Surprisingly, however, the region's Scotch pine plantations seem free of similar difficulties.

Replanting after harvest cuttings has been unusual in New En-

American chestnut, North Colebrook, Connecticut, 1912, before this species was virtually wiped out by the chestnut blight. This tree is two feet in diameter. This and the two following illustrations depict the few remaining virgin stands in New England. *G. E. Nichols Collection, Yale University, courtesy of Professor Thomas G. Siccama.*

Mature sugar maple, North Colebrook, Connecticut, 1912. *Courtesy of G. E. Nichols Collection, Yale University.*

Virgin white pine stand, Colebrook, Connecticut, 1911. *Courtesy of G. E. Nichols Collection, Yale University.*

gland until very recently. In the 1970s, several Maine paper companies began establishing nurseries and implementing extensive planting programs. They hope to overcome the frequent long lag in establishing new stands after clearcutting. An extensive research program, sponsored by the University of Maine and by the major landowners themselves, is working to develop improved tree varieties and management techniques for planted forests.

Plantations are costly to establish and yield their returns slowly. They will produce high-cost wood for their owners. On the other hand, they allow the use of selected strains of trees and their linear layout facilitates low-cost thinning and harvesting. All things considered, however, plantations cannot be expected to occupy a noticeable part of New England's forest landscape in the next twenty years.

CHAPTER 3

A Damp and Intricate Wilderness:
New England's Industrial Forest

ew England's industrial forest covers a vast extent of the region's wildland. The industrial forest includes the forests of northern New England that are managed primarily to produce industrial crops of wood. These forests of spruce, fir, pine, and hardwoods stretch from the Green Mountains of Vermont across northern New Hampshire and much of Maine. About 13 million acres of New England's forest is operated for industrial wood production. Industrial forests in southern New England are dwarfed in acreage by municipal watersheds and state forests. Across northern New England, more than half of the forest land is owned by forest industry or major woodgrowing landowners. Most of this region remains "a damp and intricate wilderness," as it was when Thoreau visited it in the 1850s.

Several key characteristics distinguish the industrial forest. First, it is the region where forest structure and composition have been least affected by past farming, planting, development, and other human action. Second, it is a forest largely owned by sizable corporations and wealthy individuals. Many of the owners are not living or headquartered in the states where the land lies. Thus, the industrial forest is the lead example of the absentee land ownership so prominent in New England. Third, the industrial forest is a region consciously managed for renewable wood crops to support wood-processing industries. These industries provide some local communities with 40 percent or more of their employment. A great deal of New England's wood industry employment lies outside the industrial forest, but—as in the Massachusetts paper industry—those jobs do not depend on locally harvested wood. Though primarily managed for timber, these forests supply wildlife, recreation, and water as well. Finally, the industrial forest consists of vast blocks of industrially owned land with few local settlements. People enter the industrial forest from outside to work there. Probably 10,000 people earn their livings in and near this forest, cutting and hauling the trees and servicing the logging industry. Because of the vast distances involved, logging camps persist in the remote Maine woods, though they have virtually vanished elsewhere in the United States.

These four principal features are responsible for many of the important trends, controversies, and public concerns over the industrial forest.[1]

History of the Industrial Forest

The industrial forest has been harvested at varying levels relative to its sustained yield growth capacity. Until the 1850s, the region was largely unexplored and harvested heavily only along its fringes. Until then, its margins were slowly receding in the face of expanding settlement and land clearing.

Between the 1850s and the turn of the century, New England's northwoods and highlands were heavily cut for merchantable spruce and pine. Much of that timber moved by water to distant mills—down the Penobscot, Kennebec, and Connecticut. The region's timber capital was being liquidated. Large, ancient trees, of sizes that will never be grown again, were felled. Despite heavy cutting, reseeding, sprout regeneration, or residual stands of small timber reestablished the forest quickly. The occasional depredations of spruce budworm and other pests (such as the larch sawfly) and birch dieback caused locally heavy mortality.

Maine, an early national leader among lumber producing states, was eclipsed before the Civil War by New York, Pennsylvania, and Michigan. The prime species was spruce, followed by pine and occasional hardwoods wherever logs could be shipped out by road. By the 1890s, the log drives were waning. On the Penobscot, the log drive at Bangor was not counted after 1905.

Much of the early lumbering in northern New England was done by New England capitalists and native men from Vermont, New Hampshire, and Maine. In northern Maine, New Brunswick lumbermen were active even into the mid nineteenth century. By the 1870s, absentee ownership of Bangor sawmills was common.

By World War I, the current pattern of ownership and use of the industrial forest had clearly emerged. This pattern underwent no significant change until the 1970s.

Between the 1890s and World War I, ownership of the industrial forest was radically reshuffled. The newly emerging paper industry arrived from its birthplaces in Massachusetts and New York. By 1900 the old Maine and New Hampshire lumber names were being nudged aside by new corporate giants familiar today from Fortune's 500: International Paper, Great Northern, St. Regis, and others. These firms, based in New England and New York, were augmented by smaller ones like St. Croix Pulpwood, Hollingsworth and Whitney, and Groveton. Several grew from old, established paper firms, like S. D. Warren of Westbrook, Maine, that predated wood pulp paper. Others were founded by aggressive businessmen, as was Great Northern—where an entire small town was built in the wilderness to house the mill workforce. In these times a pattern arose of pulpwood shipments to New York mills from Vermont, New Hampshire, and even northern Maine. This trade still exists on a more limited scale.

The newly arrived paper corporations eagerly bought land from the lumbermen, most of whom departed for Georgia or Michigan. The paper mills could use the smaller trees and the fir trees that were of little value for lumber. Even during the Great Depression they bought land. Again in the 1960s and 1970s, new corporations arrived on the scene, from the South and West. They bought established companies—land, mills, and all. These newcomers, which included Diamond International, Georgia-Pacific, and Scott, completed the transformation of the industrial forest into a region held by national corporations. They usually brought new ideas and invested capital in new mills. For example, Georgia-Pacific's local employment nearly doubled from 1963, when it acquired its land and mills, to 1980. They rebuilt the old mills, which had grown obsolete because of high pollution, low speed, narrow papermachine widths, and obsolete products.

Throughout this period, a small group of timber-owning families resolved to continue in the timbergrowing business and not sell out or industrialize. These names—Coe, Coburn, Pingree, Webber, Dunn, Carlisle, and others—remain prominent in the Maine woods and in local and state civic life.

From the turn of the century to the late 1970s, the industrial forest was again underutilized relative to its sustained yield capacity. The paper industry grew slowly after establishing itself in the region as the dominant landowner. After the 1912–20 budworm outbreak, the surviving trees were small and did not reach a salable size until the late 1950s. In some areas, the 1920s were years of hard scratching for wood to keep mills turning. Then came the Depression, when pulpwood requirements fell. Nationally, the paper industry grew rapidly from the late 1940s to the 1970s, but most of the growth passed New England by.

In the 1970s, growth returned to New England's paper industry, and large sawmills sprouted anew in the industrial forest. The forces behind this trend are discussed in Chapter 10.[2]

None of the major paper and lumber companies can supply all of their wood needs from their own land. They buy up to 50 percent of their wood requirements from the large nonindustrial or small owners. Most of the large industrial owners sell large volumes of wood, because of the location of the land, or because their mills do not use certain species of wood.

Imbedded in the industrial forest are many scattered units of public land. Except for the national forests, Baxter Park, and other state parks, these units are generally managed for multiple uses, including industrial wood production. These lands depend for their markets on the region's wood industry but contribute such a tiny flow of timber that the region has not seen the kind of battles over public-land timber policy that have resounded throughout the West in the past fifteen years.

Economic trends undermined the old river drives in the 1950s and 1960s. The drives tied up too much capital for too long, and the loss in breakage, scraped wood, and "sinkers" grew more worrisome to pulp-mill accountants. Also, the rivers would not float hardwoods, which grew on millions of acres and which the mills were beginning to use.

By the early seventies, bulldozers appeared and began pushing mainline haul roads into the backwoods. The silent fir flats of "black growth" and the peaceful lakeshores were invaded by massive diesel log-hauling trucks, carrying huge loads of tree-length wood. The roads are built entirely by the landowners, who share their cost and control their use. In remote corners of northern Maine, it will be another decade before the road network is fully completed, at which time it will be the largest privately owned road system in the country.

The region's rivers were once choked with wood for several months of the year. The demands of log driving led the lumbermen to modify the natural drainage of the entire region to improve water flows. Lakes were created or raised with dams. Some lakes were raised more than once, with powerful new dams submerging old ones. As the region passed into control of paper companies, log driving retained its importance but the rivers were highly prized for producing hydroelectric power. All major northern New England paper mills rely heavily on water power, so the waters of the region, as well as its forests, were firmly controlled for the needs of the paper industry.

River drives pushed aside recreational uses of rivers; sinkers and accumulations of bark damaged fish spawning grounds. Streams and lakesides were littered with abandoned logs. As the economic pressures against river driving rose, environmentalists worked to end the drives. Maine passed a law outlawing river drives by the end of 1976.

In the fall of 1976, the Kennebec Log Driving Company completed the last drive in New England, bringing pulpwood to Scott Paper Company's mill at Winslow. The company, and the log drives, then passed out of existence, ending an era in the region's history.[3]

Harvesting the Timber

In New England's industrial forest, methods of harvesting the crop remained unchanged from colonial times until the age of the motor truck. Some areas of the White and Green Mountains were entered with railroads for log hauling by the 1880s, but the other features of logging operations changed little.[4] Generation after generation of woodsmen followed the same seasonal cycle. Enter the woods in the autumn, often by canoe or boat. Build camps and prepare "tote" roads, skid trails, and log decks. Build or repair splash dams, bridges, booms, and other facilities. On the earliest snow, tote supplies into the camps by oxen and begin cutting. Axes were standard until the late nineteenth century, when they were replaced by one- or two-man saws. For large pines and spruce, long two-man "misery whips" were used. Oxen or horses skidded logs on sleds or directly over ice roads and snow to landings by streams or lakes. At ice-out, the drives began, ending many miles downriver at the mills. A low rainfall year might "hang" the drive upriver, leaving the mills without wood and in danger of bankruptcy.

Timber cruisers mapped wildland towns, seeking large spruce and pine. The markets required large logs, so small trees were left. Since logs were hauled away from the stump over snow, little soil

was disturbed. Young trees growing in the shade were often preserved. Large areas of fir or hardwood growth were generally
bypassed.

This was an ecologically benign system of exploiting the forest.
Experts debate whether the heavy cut of spruce reduced the repre-
sentation of that species in the forest, thus enhancing budworm
danger. But the forest's floor and its long-term productivity were
scarcely disturbed during this period of exploitation for lumber. It
was an age of careless land exploitation and little thought for the
future, but low-impact methods and a resilient forest meant that
loggers would often reenter heavily cut areas twenty or thirty years
later. Much of this cutting was highly wasteful, as noted by Austin
Cary: "Trees are killed that are not utilized. Stumps are cut high
and valuable lumber left in the shape of long tops to rot. . . . Much
is due to mere force of habit in our lumbermen. In the old days they
learnt wasteful habits." [5]

By World War I, the machine was entering the industrial forest.
Handsaws and horses still brought the logs to roadside, but steam-
driven log-haulers and trucks moved wood to the landing. In the
1920s woodsman "King Ed" Lacroix built a railroad between two
northern Maine lakes to move wood to the Great Northern Paper Company mill on the Penobscot. Lacroix's locomotives still lie
rusting in the woods, attracting the curious Allagash canoeist or
bush pilot flying by. By the early fifties, the chainsaw made its
appearance.

In the forest, however, the horse reigned supreme for skidding
logs well into the twentieth century. Horse operations on major industrial holdings were common until the 1960s in northern Maine.
The trails used in horse operations are still visible from the air in
millions of acres of the northwoods. Horse logging required a lot of
land to grow hay, and a lot of labor to cut it and handle the horses.
The increasing labor shortage in the woods during and after World
War II, the move away from river driving, and a desire for less seasonality in wood production led the companies to turn to machines
for skidding.

The skidder came into its own in the Maine woods only in the
1960s. Earliest models lacked the size, power, and toughness for
New England's rocky, steep, and often boggy woods. The skidder
made possible a tremendous boost in each woodsman's weekly output. A rising volume of wood could be cut with ever-fewer workers.

Skidders can operate in wet, boggy ground or in the snow, enabling cutting to proceed over much of the year. The cutting and hauling are suspended during New England's "mud season," since roads become quagmires, incapable of supporting huge trucks, and skidders bog down in the mire. In many areas, a late fall shutdown before "freeze-up" is also necessary.

Two men with chainsaw and skidder can cut and pile roadside 100 cords of wood (a pile the size of a modest house) per week in good timber and good weather, though the average for a year's work is much less. The skidder enabled loggers to increase their output and helped some earn a better living. But the high costs of financing and operating skidders left them more vulnerable to the frequent downswings in the pulpwood business. By the late 1970s, some foresters and loggers wondered whether the skidder system was in fact economically sound.

Changing mill technologies have had a major impact on the markets for timber and on the ability to manage the industrial forest. "Chip-n-saw" and other systems capable of making framing lumber from small trees have significantly increased the stumpage value of spruce and fir. New processes using hardwoods for pulp have allowed the increased use of hardwoods. Machines for chipping trees in the woods have made it possible to use low-grade hardwoods and small softwood trees. The arrival of these technologies in northern New England has transformed the opportunities for forestry.

Before the skidder, the woods were rarely clearcut, for reasons unrelated to silviculture but based on product requirements and logging costs. During the postwar decades, mills began using smaller trees and species of trees that had formerly been left behind. But the skidder, unless carefully handled, will rut the soil, sweep aside tiny young trees, and scrape bark off the trunks of trees to be left behind. As the need for wood grew in the 1970s, industry discovered that skidders make wonderful clearcutting machines. Clearcuts of up to one square mile began appearing. Environmentalists protested and some loggers argued that industry was liquidating the forest.

No sooner had skidders become well established in the industrial forest than the largest companies began testing giant mechanized harvesting machines. These machines are capable of still greater wood production per man-day. Though they are costly and demand skilled maintenance personnel to keep them running, they help companies keep a large volume of wood flowing. Some are capable of cutting a tree, clipping off its limbs, and laying it in a bunch with its neighbors. Some of these giant logging machines actually damage the soil less than skidders and cause fewer ruts. They are used primarily for block clearcutting, but are used also for strip clearcutting. Some operators are experimenting with them for partial cutting, and early results look promising. Since these machines have such high hourly operating costs, they must harvest a lot of wood each day to be worthwhile for their owners.

Clearcutting has attracted media attention and critical comment from ecologists, environmentalists, and some foresters. Legislation and zoning to ban clearcutting on public and private lands have been advocated. On the other side, foresters point to conditions common in New England where clearcutting is a sound means of regenerating the forest. Many hardwood stands are cluttered with overmature and deformed trees and lack advance regeneration. Many spruce-fir stands consist of overmature fir trees that have stopped growing. They may be starting to blow down and are often severely damaged by spruce budworm or balsam wooly aphid. Partial cuttings will not work in many such stands because there are no vigorous trees capable of surviving, or because the stand cannot be

The rubber-tired skidder revolutionized logging in the New England woods after the 1960s. *Courtesy of American Forest Institute.*

kept dense enough to resist windthrow. Often, desirable advance re-generation is absent. Clearcutting can remove these low-quality stands and start a new cycle of regeneration.

Some landowners practice site preparation and planting, trying to use genetically improved seedlings. When these plantations can be carefully managed, they may produce twice as much wood per year as the natural forest. Today only a small fraction of the indus-trial forest is managed in this way. In fact, planting, the only for-estry practiced in many regions, is not needed here in most cases.

The discussion of clearcutting has become so polarized that the issue has become a common test of ecological rectitude. If you op-pose it, you're an environmentalist. If not, you're an exploiter. This is why it is hard to find balanced information on the subject. For-esters and environmentalists opposed to clearcutting cite the soil erosion caused by skidders, soil compaction, the destruction of ad-vance regeneration, the loss through volatilization and erosion of nitrogen and mineral nutrients, the long period of raspberry compe-tition that can suppress desirable regeneration, and the impact on aesthetics and wildlife habitat.[5] Where a single management prac-tice becomes, by itself, the criterion for distinguishing good from bad forestry, the debate becomes irrelevant to reality. In fact, sloppy or thoughtless partial cutting has done more to degrade the timber productivity of New England forests than has clearcutting.

Professional foresters debate the merits of clearcutting at great length and have not formed a consensus on its role in New En-gland's industrial forest. In Maine, some of its strongest proponents and opponents are the woodlands managers of major paper com-panies. The debate over clearcutting will not be soon resolved. The widespread mortality from spruce budworm will intensify it.

Conflict on the Fringes

The margins of the industrial forest meet the suburban, rural, recre-ational, and even urban forests of northern New England. There is no clean line marking the boundary. Small private owners sell wood to the major industrial landowners, and the industrial owners hold scattered parcels in the midst of rural landscapes. For example, in the Bangor area, suburbs and rural strip developments intermingle with blocks of land owned by major paper companies. Two con-flicts that have been especially bitter in the industrial forest fringe have been recreational and industrial development, and taxes.

In the land market of the 1960s and early 1970s, several land-owners were briefly tempted into the resort development–land sales business. In Vermont, Weyerhaueser opened the Jay Peak ski resort. On the shores of Maine's Moosehead Lake, Scott Paper opened the Squaw Mountain ski area with a sizable lot-sales program. This venture lost money so badly that Scott donated it to the state, which has struggled with it ever since.

In 1969, the International Paper Company proposed a massive ski resort–land sales development in southern Vermont. The local public reaction was overwhelmingly negative. The governor personally talked the company out of pursuing it, and to prevent future developments of that kind the Vermont legislature passed a model land-use law, Act 250.[7] As the 1970s wore on, more and more major forest products companies took financial losses in recreational land developments. Several New England resort–land sales opera-

A Georgia-Pacific forest nursery produces seed-lings for replanting. *Courtesy of Georgia-Pacific Corporation.*

tions were in bankruptcy or serious financial straits, including Haystack and Mount Snow in Vermont, Evergreen Valley in Maine, and Bretton Woods in New Hampshire. The lure of easy money faded; no new major resort schemes appeared. The large landowners were spared further conflict with their neighbors over recreational land use.

Another classic confrontation occurred in Walpole, New Hampshire. The Parsons and Whittemore Company, a major papermill builder, proposed a 300-ton-per-day pulpmill there. It would use surplus hardwoods in the Connecticut Valley, expand the tax base, and create badly needed employment. The proposal became an environmental *cause célèbre*. The New Hampshire director of industrial development opposed the plan and was fired for publicly opposing the governor's supportive position. Local residents in the end refused to allow a zoning variance because of anticipated irritations and dangers from logging truck traffic and the conversion of a tiny rural hamlet into a paper company milltown. Area foresters and landowners, encouraged by the prospect of better markets for the area's low-grade hardwoods and pleased by the prospect of better business in forestry and logging, were angered by the outcome. No less a figure than economist John Kenneth Galbraith argued that the New England countryside was no place for industry anyway—the region's value was its scenery.

On its very fringes, then, the paper industry lost a contest over values with residents of a local community who were concerned over the impact of more timber cutting and did not want to live in a milltown. They valued their peaceful rural lifestyle more highly than improved forest utilization, more jobs, and more tax revenue. These concerns were not solely those of a tiny elite, but were widely shared by town residents. Perhaps the residents of Walpole were familiar with the grim milltowns nearby and did not like what they saw there. Perhaps the company was unable, or did not try, to deal directly with local concerns and fears. Whatever the case, the Walpole incident demonstrated that in many northern New England towns, industrial development is not always prized above other values. (Parsons and Whittemore later opened a larger pulpmill in Alabama, where the governor officiated at the ribbon-cutting ceremony.)

Within and on the fringes of the industrial forest are the milltowns. Many of them are cramped, grim, sad places. Three-story, smoke-stained, shingle-sided tenements line narrow streets in tight valleys. Drab main streets lie in the shadows of smokestacks and pulpwood piles. Such milltowns have been decaying all across New England. In these communities, industrial development means economic opportunity and is eagerly supported.

A second source of friction on the fringes of the industrial forest has been taxes. The forest tax problems experienced in Maine provide the classic example, for there the stakes are highest and the conflict is at its most intense.

In 1973, Maine adopted a new form of tax for its forest lands.[8] Called the Tree Growth Tax, it was based on the view that forest property taxes should be based on land productivity and not on current market value. The annual ad valorem property tax, proponents argued, discriminates against long-term investments like timbergrowing, which take a long time before harvest. Moreover, rising land prices due to speculation and residential development produce land values that cannot be supported by timbergrowing revenues. Further, periodic reassessments would escalate tax burdens to unpredictably high levels, rendering investment in timbergrowing unnecessarily risky.

The tax assessment for each property is based on U.S. Forest Service's forest survey annual growth rates for softwood, mixedwood, and hardwood for each county. Those growth rates are discounted for access and marketability, and then multiplied by current stumpage prices. The result is converted to a capital value representing the present worth of the land for growing wood. The rules have been changed several times, but today the assessments are multiplied by a millage rate that is based on the cost of state services to the unorganized territory (where local government does not exist).

In Maine's vast unorganized territory, no major problem arises. But where local governments exist in small towns and plantations on the fringes, the local taxes must be based on Tree Growth Tax assessments, which are determined by the state tax assessor. In the early 1970s, Tree Growth Tax assessments were at times higher than ad valorem assessments, since many rural tax assessors appraised woodland at nominal market values. But the rising land values of the 1970s changed all that, and revaluations shook the property tax structure of town after town. Many small towns, owned 50 to 90 percent by paper companies, found that residents paid taxes on $100 to $150 per acre assessments on their forty-acre woodlots, while absentee paper companies paid taxes on $40 per acre assessments. For small towns of forty to a hundred inhabitants, with low incomes and high unemployment, struggling to maintain municipal services, such a situation was intolerable. In every recent year, municipalities and rural legislators have campaigned hard to change or abolish the Tree Growth Tax, but they have been unable to overcome the resistance of the large landowners. More to the point, the opponents of the Tree Growth Tax have failed to convince the legislature and many state officials that they have an alternative that will not harm forestry in the long run. The Maine Department of Conservation has recognized the validity of concerns expressed about the Tree Growth Tax but has opposed its outright abolition.

The conflict, then, still festers. It is not easy to see how it will be solved. But it must be solved, for a stable, predictable tax regime is a crucial requirement if the owners of the industrial forest are to invest willingly in its maintenance and improvement. They must be convinced that their investments are secure from future confiscatory tax increases. At the same time, an equitable solution to local grievances about the tax must be found. The grievances are valid and cannot be allowed to fester indefinitely.

The conflict over taxation is one aspect of a complex and unfortunate love-hate relationship that exists between major forest landowners and their neighbors. Whether the owners are public or private is of no consequence. Just ask a Millinocket resident what he thinks of the Baxter Park Authority or a resident of Osborn Plantation about the state's Bureau of Public Lands. But for the industrial landowners, local feelings can run especially high. Most local communities depend heavily on the forest and the mills for their livelihood. Many families have worked in the woods and mills for generations. There are no other jobs. The dependence on the industry is clear. The industry's property tax breaks anger their neighbors. The practice of hiring Canadian workers angers others. In some areas, nearby residents oppose massive clearcuts by paper companies. Some have been the subject of paper company heavy-handedness in the past. Many families include workers whose pulpwood contracts were abruptly cut off by companies whose woodyards were full. Such cutoffs often meant financial hardship. In some places, landowners have driven off squatters, which always inflames local opinion.

So a list of grievances has accumulated in many towns. In part

Mechanical delimbing increases productivity in the industrial forest. *Courtesy of Georgia-Pacific Corporation.*

this reflects the normal human tendency to resent any large, absentee landowner. In part it flows from a history of paper company arrogance and abuse of power, and the desperate powerless feeling of the neighbors. We rarely love those on whom we depend for our livelihoods, when we have no choice of employers.

The local resentment undermines forestry. In its most visible form, it results in condoning of widespread timber thievery. Local residents do not think it a crime to steal paper company wood or butcher stands on firewood permits: "They've cheated us; they've got more than they can manage, haven't they?" Stories are told of loggers earning a living for years without ever paying for stolen timber. At its worst, the resentment flares in "Allagash lightning strikes" that keep landowners nervous and Maine Forest Service firefighters working overtime.

Working in the Woods

Woods work has never been very comfortable, pleasant, or financially secure and rewarding. The industrial forest in its earlier years was harvested by a temporary workforce consisting of farmers and nearby residents who regularly worked in the woods, supplemented by drifters. They would disappear into the woods in the fall and return in the spring on the log drive, after a winter of eating beans and hardtack, working ten-hour days in all weather, and sleeping in shabby, overcrowded shanties. The shiftless among them gave log-

A forester inspects an overstocked stand of spruce and fir in eastern
Maine. *Courtesy of Georgia-Pacific Corporation.*

gers their bad reputation by drinking, gambling, and whoring away
their winter's wages in the gin mills of Bangor's Commercial Street
and a dozen other lumber towns.

Today's loggers commute daily or weekly into the woods to
camps that are generally tidy and that serve immense meals of
meats, vegetables, and a prodigious variety of pastry. Wages are still
low for most independent crews, and work is not secure. A few far-
seeing organizations have put loggers on their own payrolls and
provide fringe benefits. A company logger on a mechanized opera-
tion earns fringe benefits and sits in a cabin on a huge logging machine, listening to the radio while working. His life is as far from
the nineteenth-century logger's as an astronaut's is from Orville
Wright's. But most loggers work in an illusory independent status
denounced by industry critics as "pulpwood peonage." Since the
loggers are legally contractors and not employees of the companies,
they have no collective bargaining rights.

Logging is inherently dangerous, and never more so than in today's age of chainsaws, skidders, and loaders. While the trees are

not large by western standards, they are quite capable of killing the unlucky or unwary. Logging has one of the highest accident rates of any industry. Though the Occupational Safety and Health Administration has made logging a target industry, singled out for special attention because of its poor safety record, it has in fact received little attention from the safety authorities in New England.[9]

The logger's high accident rate imposes severe burdens of injury, loss of life, and family hardship. It also exacts a financial toll through astronomical workmen's compensation insurance rates. A basic source of high accident rates is the piece-rate system of payment, which encourages loggers to push work too fast and take too many shortcuts. Officials of insurance companies have stated that the most positive safety step the industry could take would be to eliminate piecework.

Because it is arduous low-wage work, logging in the industrial forest has always been plagued by labor shortages. In the 1840s, Maine loggers were already bringing in workers from the Maritimes. In World War II, German prisoners-of-war were even put to work cutting pulpwood in the Maine woods.[10] Because of the dense settlements in Quebec on the edge of the isolated woods of northern New Hampshire and Maine, and because of the log trade to Quebec, more French Canadian workers have worked in the industrial forest since World War II. Near the border, foresters and other woods personnel require fluency in French to do their work.

The number of Canadian woodsworkers in the industrial forest has fallen but remains a source of conflict between the companies and American woodsmen. The Maine Woodsmen's Association has campaigned for the elimination of Canadian labor from the Maine woods to make jobs available for Americans. The companies claim that they cannot hire Americans for hard work deep in the woods. The workers have had little success to date in gaining assistance from the responsible government agencies. One union, the United Paper Workers International Union, has organized a number of logging camps.

The Spruce Budworm

The most dramatic problem facing the managers of the industrial forest today is the spruce budworm. This insect is a native of the spruce-fir forest of northeastern North America. Periodically, it erupts in regionwide outbreaks capable of killing up to 40 percent

Massive Koehring feller-forwarder carries whole trees to the landing on Great Northern Paper Company land. *Courtesy of Maine Department of Conservation.*

of the spruce-fir volume over large areas. In stands of mature fir of low vigor, mortality can reach 100 percent. Typically, these outbreaks are followed by regeneration and regrowth of spruce-fir forests. But there follows a long period of tight supplies of large timber. In the past, this was not a problem, since the industrial capacity using the wood was at a low level. Today, the wood industry supported by this resource is capable of using all of the forest's growth. Failure to control the outbreak, then, could mean costly dislocations, readjustments of mill production processes, and possible reductions in capacity in some areas. The entire wood-using industry from Quebec to northern New Hampshire, Maine, and the Maritimes is concerned with the current outbreak.[11]

Chemical spraying is the only available means of reducing tree mortality over large areas. Spraying is costly, is not completely effective, and cannot eliminate the outbreak. It is vigorously opposed by environmentalists and others opposed to the use of pesticides. The programs of spraying adopted in Quebec, Maine, and New Brunswick have therefore generated considerable public controversy. In Nova Scotia and Newfoundland, spraying programs were halted for several years by political opposition.

Experts who have studied this challenging problem believe that

Moving the wood. Scenes from
river drive on Vermont lands of International Paper Company, 1930s.
*Courtesy of International Paper
Company.*

in the spruce-fir forest, man cannot improve the forest silvicultur-
ally and have a steady wood supply without spraying. Long-term
efforts at harvesting to reduce stand vulnerability and salvaging
damaged trees can reduce the need for spraying. But these methods
can only be applied to 3 percent of the forest each year. Some stands
can be abandoned, but there seems to be no alternative to the spray
programs that is capable of sustaining a stable level of wood output. In recent years, forestry agencies have refined their procedures
for spray area planning and application but have not been prepared
to risk the consequences of a complete halt to spraying.

In Maine, the spray program costs $4 to $8 million per year. The
reduction of government subsidies for spraying since the mid 1970s
has raised the cost to landowners to levels that many feel they cannot afford. As a result, and because of spray program management
decisions, spraying has been withdrawn from much of the acreage
of the Maine spruce-fir forest. In some places never sprayed, mortality is rapidly approaching 100 percent, in contrast to 5 to 10 percent in sprayed areas. Landowners are moving as quickly as possible to salvage dead and dying trees, but the level of mortality now
in prospect cannot possibly be salvaged. Large volumes will blow
down and rot before they can be cut. The industry, therefore, faces
a period of readjustment to a changing timber supply. After a period of superabundant dead spruce and fir, it will need to adapt to a
wood supply of small and poorly stocked spruce and fir, and perhaps rely more heavily on hardwoods. This will be true in Maine
even with a continued successful spray program. In northern New
Hampshire, serious mortality is probable but the level of wood consumption there is relatively low so that no severe impact on industry is likely.

There will never be another spruce budworm outbreak in northern New England quite like the one now in progress. The reason the
outbreak of the 1970s and 1980s is so serious is that the forest
is not yet developed with logging roads, and it is seriously over-
balanced in mature age classes as a result of light harvesting pressure from 1920 to 1970. The result is a huge area of vulnerable forest, too large to spray, and so vast that it will take twenty to thirty
years to harvest all the vulnerable trees.

After the current outbreak subsides, another one will erupt in
thirty to fifty years. By then, however, the forest will be fully ac-
cessible. The high level of industrial capacity now in place will assure markets for the wood. This level of cutting pressure will allow

forest managers to remove more wood and bring the forest more closely into a regulated condition—one with a balance of young and old age classes. Much less of the forest area will be in overmature age classes, which will make the next outbreak easier to handle. With the early warning methods being developed by scientists, it may not be necessary to spray at all in that future outbreak.

The present outbreak will continue. Spray programs will help contain the damage and spread it out over a longer period. For most governments and landowners still involved, the stakes are too high to quit now. Forestry agencies have moved spraying activities farther from people, accelerated their assessments of human exposure and environmental impacts, and attempted to assure themselves and others that this use of pesticides is socially responsible. In most places, people ingest more pesticide from the food they eat than from the budworm programs. The newspapers they read recommend the same pesticides for garden use, which are sold in hardware and garden stores. Still, however, most people find the wide use of such materials in the forest highly distasteful, as do many forest managers. All concerned hope for an early end to the need for spraying.

A Paper Plantation?

Maine's industrial forest has been characterized in a highly critical book as a "paper plantation." [12] The image is meant to suggest the oppressive, irresponsible power of a plantation overseer over his tenants, together with the owner's absolute control over the state legislature.

The industrial forest has been a paper plantation in the sense that its principal product is paper, but the growth of sawmilling has changed that significantly. The major landowners receive considerable deference in state legislatures, as do large landowners in any state, be they farmers, house builders, railroads, or paper companies. But they no longer have everything their way. The companies occasionally find that state forestry agencies do not agree with them.

In the backwoods of Maine, local government does not exist: the territory is "unorganized." In 1969, Maine established the Land Use Regulation Commission to act as a zoning agency for the state's privately owned wildlands. [13] This triggered a ten-year battle over the issues of land use control and the minutiae of day-to-day zoning problems. The agency's planning and zoning functions are slowly achieving more acceptance, but forest landowners and the few families living in its jurisdiction never like to hear "no" to their development proposals. The commission is often forced to make planning, zoning, and regulatory decisions based on inadequate information, which does not enhance its popularity. It has never been given the staff or resources to do the necessary work. In early years it was plagued by a host of political and managerial problems.

In short, the paper plantation image is oversimplified and rapidly growing out of date. The view of the industrial forest as a paper plantation depicts a historical situation that is the basis for many current attitudes and grievances. But the image no longer squares very well (if it ever did) with a rapidly changing industrial forest.

Change in the industrial forest was at a slow pace for centuries. Logging, transportation, and marketing systems evolved gradually, absorbing trucks, saws, chainsaws, and skidders. Today, both horses and giant logging machines work in the woods. For a long period, Maine forest landowners faced limited markets and no real pressure for change. Since the 1960s, however, change has accelerated. The budworm outbreak, new machines, the burst of mill shutdowns and expansions, the growing log trade to Quebec, and public concern over management practices and taxation all contributed. Assertive loggers demanded attention for their grievances. And the legislature and bureaucracy were no longer uniformly sympathetic to the landowner's request. Political, economic, and technological change has been disorientingly rapid in the past two decades. There is no sign that the pace of change will slacken, so the future promises to be highly challenging to all concerned with the industrial forest.[14]

As later chapters argue, it will be impossible to meet the projected needs for wood from the industrial forest without a major increase in intensive management and upgraded utilization practices. The region's forest owners and managers have never before faced such a challenge.

CHAPTER 4

Rockwood's Pasture:
New England's Suburban Forest

n the Monday after Thanksgiving, 1979, carpenter Ralph Anderson and his crew began clearing a lot near the 1828 church at Rockwood Corner, Belgrade, Maine, for my new saltbox house. Anderson was participating in the latest cycle of land use changes in the forests of central Maine. It was wilderness in the 1790s, a farm in the 1800s, went back to a rural woodlot, and was cut several times up to the 1960s. This one and a quarter acres became an island of the suburban forest in the winter of 1979–80. Ralph Anderson repeated the labor of clearing and housebuilding first done, then abandoned, by farmer Rockwood and his descendants generations ago. Chunks of the birch, fir, and maple cut by Anderson's crew now burn noisily in my living room woodstove. Along this road, three other houses have appeared in two years.

Rockwood never lived to see his farm grow trees and later be sold by his descendants, who had moved away. He never imagined that one day his pasture would become part of the suburban forest, that it would grow tomatoes in a tiny plot by a house occupied by a bureaucrat, born in Illinois, who works by day in Augusta, twelve miles away.

The suburban forest displays the slow loss of economic, amenity, and wildlife values of New England's rural landscape. Since the 1940s, these losses have escalated as land use patterns became more wasteful of land. Still, a large forest remains in suburbia. Until the 1970s, the woods of suburbia were valued primarily as a green backdrop for housing. The resurgence of fuelwood for space heating, however, has changed this. Today, wood cutting is more and more widely accepted, setting off new tensions between local citizens. The increased acceptance of wood harvesting represents a major social change in suburban New England. Town and state governments will continue to mediate between shifting coalitions of landowners, conservationists, real estate groups, loggers, and wild-

life groups. Following a general review, this chapter will examine
how the suburban forest has developed in Connecticut, to illustrate
the forces at work in this region.[1]

Suburbanization

The story of Rockwood's pasture has been repeated on millions of
acres across New England and makes a suitable metaphor for the
suburbanization of New England's forest.

The forest most familiar to New Englanders is the suburban forest. Even in the fringe of large cities, trees set the tone of the landscape. The suburban forest is the result of a new cycle of land use
change—from farm to forest to tract development. A rigorous definition of the suburban forest would be based on studies of commuting patterns, settlement densities, and land use patterns. The suburban forest includes the undeveloped brush and forest overwhelmed
and bypassed by suburban-exurban sprawl. It consists of the fraction of an acre behind the house, the overlooked pasture and farm
woodlot, the water company forest, the Audubon Society preserve,
and perhaps the state park or forest. Its boundary fades gradually
into the rural landscape of the farm forest.[2]

Roughly 4 to 5 million acres of land lie in the suburban and urban regions of New England; nearly 3 million are open land and
forest. For purposes of this discussion, we need not fix the limits
with precision. The suburban forest is now the home of a major—
and increasing—portion of the region's population. As the central
cities lose population, settlement spreads. Ring highways sprout
electronics factories, and land prices in southern New Hampshire
catch up with the Boston suburbs.

The spread of suburbs, mostly into abandoned farms and regrown woods, has been a feature of New England urban geography
for generations. Spawned by the desires of middle-class families for
pleasant surroundings and promoted by trolley lines and freeways,
suburban settlement spread along the coasts and rivers, radiating
outward from the cities. In 1810, only the immediate Boston area
had a settlement density greater than ninety persons per square
mile. By 1850, this level of density had been reached in northern
Rhode Island; Cumberland County, Maine; Middlesex, Bristol, and
Norfolk counties, Massachusetts; and New Haven and Hartford
counties, Connecticut. By 1930, this level of density had been
reached in all but four counties in southern New England, plus

Hillsboro and Strafford counties in New Hampshire and Androscoggin County in Maine.

In ninety-six northeastern counties from 1950 to 1960, 0.22 acres
was removed from rural uses for each person added to the area's
population. In the Standard Metropolitan Statistical Area (SMSA)
counties in the region, the ratio was 0.20 acres per person. The
ratio was much higher in non-SMSA counties: 0.40 acres per person. In Eastern Massachusetts, population growth and suburbanization consumed one-half acre per person from 1960 to 1970, compared with one-eighth acre in the pre–World War I years.[3]

Population densities today exceed 10,000 persons per square
mile in the city of Boston. In the early 1960s, however, the greater
Boston region of 2500 square miles was only 25 percent developed,
and contained 110 square miles of dedicated open space. On the
developed land, population density was 5400 per square mile.[4]

Other New England metropolitan areas exhibit the same characteristics—moderate population densities on developed land while
the bulk of the land remains undeveloped, bypassed by expanding
sprawl. Most post–World War II suburbanites have found that
growth has removed suburbia's original attractions—green space
and low congestion. Today, persons seeking such amenities must
drive or ride buses and trains an hour or more one-way.

Changing Landscape

The bypassed lands will continue to be developed, often in multiunit apartments or office complexes. The remaining suburban forest will be under increasing pressure for development as land prices
rise and the energy costs of commuting translate into higher price
premiums for close-in land.

Strip-zoned and unplanned sprawl continue to erode the suburban forest's significant aesthetic and amenity values. The blight of
signs, plastic pizza parlors, and chain stores spreading along main
streets, and the splattering residential development along rural
highways and lanes have stranded the forest, cutting it off visually
for passersby. Even if only psychologically, the forest is cut off for
use by walkers and birders as well.

The suburban yard and street tree resource is one of enormous
economic value. Real estate brokers, landowners, and local tax ap-
praisers all agree that trees add value to suburban real estate. Recognizing these values, many cities employ foresters who specialize

Farmland, returned to woods, then cleared for house lots, shows land use change. *Courtesy of Rhode Island Division of Forest Environment.*

in the management, improvement, and protection of street and park trees. A lucrative business trade is carried on in trimming, removing, planting, fertilizing, and spraying suburban yard trees. Pests such as the gypsy moth and the Dutch elm disease require costly and often controversial management programs, and have given rise to the systematic study of urban pest management.

For many years, the forests of suburbia lay fallow. Many of the trees were small and of low quality. Builders found low-cost western lumber more suitable than native pine. The region's small sawmills found the suburban forest a high-cost and inhospitable business environment, and melted away. The giant lumber companies could deliver carefully graded lumber to tract housing builders by the trainload, which the tiny local mills could not do. The small size of the lots and the reluctance of owners to allow cutting made it harder for loggers to find timber and for mills to buy it. Since the wood consumption of the region is largely imported anyway, manufacturers needing lumber bought from outside, except for local specialty producers like lobster-pot makers and pallet plants. Because the southern New England paper industry became dependent exclusively on imported pulp, no market existed for low-grade softwood or hardwood.

These land use changes have converted the suburban forest into a patchwork of ever-smaller pieces. The progressive fragmentation of woods reduces habitat for songbirds and other wildlife species that require extensive areas of forest for breeding territories or feeding range.[5]

The amenities in suburbia, however, are all strictly for private consumption. Every vacant lot has a "No Trespassing" sign; town beaches are restricted to residents. High amenity areas use abundant "No Parking" signs to shoo curious outsiders on their way.

Suburbia is inherently oriented toward amenity, residential, and investment values, and not toward commodity production. Until recently, many suburbanites have opposed the use of forests for producing materials, seeing them only as a green backdrop. The fuelwood revolution is changing that. In the future, the suburban forest will be prized as it once was for producing fuelwood and other essential raw materials.

Policy Conflicts

The suburban forest is the scene of many policy conflicts. These range from how to tax tiny ten-acre woodlots that are worth $20,000 per acre for development, to how best to suppress the gypsy moth, to how to preserve green space by controlling development. In some towns, active programs of flood plain zoning, land use control, farm land preservation, and open space acquisition are under way. Private groups continue to do their part. State agencies are at work on parks, river corridors, and the like, but tend to concentrate their own efforts outside the suburban forest, where the land acquisition dollar goes further. The story of these policy conflicts could fill a book.[6]

Suburbanites have been legally mandating, through minimum lot sizes and restrictions on multiunit housing, the excessive consumption of open land for development. But they have also become increasingly conscious of the value of open space. State and federal governments encourage localities to acquire open space with bond issues and liberal subsidies. Originally the province of small Audubon groups, land trusts, and academics and bureaucrats, the open space movement seems to have made its point. In a few communities, such as Wilton, Connecticut, and Lincoln, Massachusetts,

The wild turkey, once eradicated from the New England woods, has been restored through the diligent efforts of state wildlife agencies. *Courtesy of Massachusetts Division of Fish and Wildlife.*

they have been so successful as to be accused of using open space land acquisition to defend elite prestige communities, to raise real estate values, and to prevent outsiders from moving in. Whatever the justice of such criticisms, it is clear that many New England communities, both through government and nonprofit group action, have worked vigorously for open space preservation.

The most difficult obstacles to open space preservation have been lost tax revenue and the perception that there is really no general public benefit from conserving open space. But the unbalanced tax bases of most suburban towns produce a striking result. Often, new development increases municipal costs more than it increases revenues. Residents in some towns have been persuaded that new development should be resisted and that open land is a good buy to prevent development. No one ever mentions that most *existing* residents *also* contribute less to revenues than to costs.

With the revival of local sawlog markets and the tremendous increase in fuelwood cutting, a major social change in attitudes toward the forest is being expressed. The increased cutting, however, has raised fears of extensive overcutting, aesthetic and wildlife habitat losses, and erosion. These fears have been joined to the remaining concerns that the green backdrop be the prevailing forest use in suburbia. An increasing number of towns are considering zoning restrictions or actual bans on commercial timber harvesting. This spreading regulatory mood poses a severe challenge to the region's foresters and wood-using industries. How can they address the concerns that motivate these restrictions? They will have to convince suburbanites that harvesting wood is consistent with other forest values, and that wood production plays an important, albeit limited, role in the local economy. In addition, loggers, foresters, and the industry will have to police themselves.

A useful way to study the dynamics of the suburban forest is to study its development in Connecticut.

Suburbs and Forests in Connecticut

The history of forest, land, suburbanization, and forest industry in Connecticut illustrates the dynamics of land use change in the suburban forest (table 4). Despite its location in the Boston-Washington megalopolis, and an average 1970 population density

Small machines are needed to log most woodlots in the suburban forest. This machine is being tested at the School of Forest Resources, University of Maine at Orono. *Courtesy of American Forest Institute.*

of 605 persons per square mile, Connecticut's forest land area increased 22 percent from 1,483,000 acres in 1913 to 1,806,000
acres in 1972. Most of the increase was due to the forest invading
abandoned farm land, which was also absorbing postwar development pressures. During this period, the state's population grew dramatically, by 1.9 million people. The Connecticut State Planning
Office has estimated that 172,200 acres were developed for residential, commercial, industrial, and transportation uses between
1960 and 1970. Development drew heavily on farms and forest
plantations—for 105,000 acres. The remaining acreage came from
brushland and forest.[7]

Forest area in Connecticut increased from 1913 to 1952, then declined slightly, with a small net gain from the entire period to 1970.
Surprisingly, the forested area increased by 43 percent in rapidly developing Fairfield County while that county's population rose by
about half a million persons.

Population growth has been only one of several influences on the
remaining acreage of farm and forest land. Changes in landownership have been dominated by the marginal character of agriculture

Table 4. Forest and Farmland Area of
Connecticut, 1600–1977

Year	Acreage (thousands)			
	Forest	(%)	Land in Farms	(%)
1600	3,010	(96)	–	
1700	2,130	(68)	–	
1800	1,644	(52)	–	
1860	923	(29)	2,504	(81)
1900	1,276	(41)	2,312	(75)
1920	1,489	(48)	1,899	(61)
1945	1,907	(61)	–	
1969	–		540	(17)
1972	1,806	(60)	–	
1977	1,860	(60)	470	(15)

SOURCES: E. V. Zumwalt, *Taxation and other factors affecting private forestry in
Connecticut*. New Haven: Yale School of Forestry, Bull. 58, 1953; N. Kingsley, *The
Forest-landowners of southern New England*. USDA-FS NEFES Res. Bull. NE-41,
1976; USDA-FS, *Analysis*, Appendix 3; R. Sherman, et al., *Open-land policy in Connecticut*. New Haven: Yale School of Forestry and Environmental Studies, Bull. 87,
1974; USDA, *Agricultural statistics*, Washington, D.C.: GPO, 1978.
    NOTE: Usage may not total 100 percent because of urban and other land uses
and the inclusion of woodland in farm acreage.

in most upland towns. Land use change has been dominated, state-wide, by the reappearance of forest on abandoned pasture and crop lands not needed for intensive development. Most counties contain more forest land now than they did in 1913. Even at the extremes the past coexistence of suburbanization and the forest is striking. Most of the twentieth-century population growth in Connecticut occurred in New Haven, Fairfield, and Hartford counties, yet each experienced an increase in forest acreage.

Connecticut, a state long settled and farmed, has only 147,000 acres (8 percent) of its commercial forest land in public ownership. The bulk of this is in state forests and parks, mostly acquired between 1900 and 1940. Farmers own about 7 percent of the state's forests, a great change from their dominance in the 1880s, while private owners other than farmers control 85 percent. N. Kingsley's survey showed that 58 percent of the 61,200 individual private owners in the state were white collar, executive, professional or retired. A relatively high proportion of the acreage—25 percent—was owned by individuals who reported their occupations as skilled labor.[8]

The water utilities, including both public and private organizations, own a total of roughly 150,000 acres. These tracts include the largest forest properties in the state. The Hartford Metropolitan District Commission owns about 32,000 acres, while the New Haven Water Company owns some 26,000. These lands produce regular timber harvests.

From 1946 to 1973, the number of holdings less than 10 acres increased almost tenfold (table 5). The amount of land affected, however, was only 9 percent of the state's privately held acreage in 1973. The tracts between 10 and 100 acres in size show remarkable stability. Ownerships between 100 and 499 acres declined somewhat, while the 500 and larger class actually increased in importance. This means that much of Connecticut's forest remains in parcels that can be effectively managed for timber, wildlife, and recreation.

The subdividing process was accompanied by accelerated ownership turnover. In Fairfield County, 82 percent of a sample of thirty-eight parcels were sold at least once between 1940 and 1959. In the three southern New England states, 43 percent of the owners, with 35 percent of the acreage, had owned their tracts less than ten years. One-fourth of the owners, with 29 percent of the land, had

Table 5. Connecticut Private Forest Ownerships by Size Class

Size (acres)	1946				1973			
	Owners	(%)	1000 Acres	(%)	Owners	(%)	1000 Acres	(%)
1–9	3,925	(11)	22.3	(1)	36,100	(55)	152.4	(9)
10–49	19,729	(56)	440.8	(26)	20,800	(31)	460.4	(28)
50–99	7,429	(21)	529.9	(31)	5,800	(9)	397.5	(24)
100–499	3,889	(11)	646.5	(38)	3,200	(5)	522.0	(31)
500+	70	(–)	75.5	(4)	100	(–)	126.7	(8)

SOURCES: E. V. Zumwalt, *Taxation and other factors affecting private forestry in Connecticut*, New Haven: Yale School of Forestry, Bull. No. 58. 1957; N. Kingsley, *The forest-landowners of southern New England*. USDA-FS NEFES, Res. Bull. NE-41, 1976.

owned their properties longer than twenty-five years. A 1975 survey of Connecticut forest landowners found that the average tenure was only seven years. Seventeen towns sampled in that study displayed averages ranging from as low as four years to eleven years.[9] Ownership as brief as seven years is not long enough to develop an interest in forest management, much less to perceive the benefit of long-term forest husbandry. Since suburban land markets are blind to timber values, the market provides no incentives, except to the extent that rutted, slash-piled woodlots may be harder to sell. Strikingly, nonresident ownership of forest land is quite high in Connecticut suburbia.

Because of small parcels and past owner attitudes unfavorable to logging, a significant part of the total forest of Connecticut has been unavailable for industrial wood production, although the small parcels are now producing an increasing amount of firewood. Even in this suburbanized state, however, fully 63 percent of the woodland is in parcels larger than fifty acres and therefore still economically manageable for timber. These lands belong to only 14 percent of the owners, or about 10,000 people. Thus, only 10,000 people need to be contacted and encouraged to promote private forestry in this state.

Growth and Cut of Connecticut Forests

By the mid nineteenth century, Connecticut's original forests had been greatly reduced in area. The remaining stands were being heavily cut. The cut for fuelwood alone was far greater than today's harvest for all uses. The woodlands were a sprout forest, where trees rarely grew beyond thirty years before being cut. In 1909, 95 percent of the hardwood acreage in Litchfield County was less than forty-one years old.[10] In the first decades of the twentieth century, Connecticut's forests lost the valuable, fast-growing chestnut to the chestnut blight. Chestnut then accounted for one-half of the state's hardwood timber inventory, and three-fourths of the state's 1909 hardwood lumber cut.

After the boxboard boom peaked around 1909, and after coal and oil replaced fuelwood, the drain on Connecticut's forests lessened. In the same period, forest area was increasing dramatically. In contrast to northern New England, no pulpwood market emerged.

Forest land in Connecticut decreased from the early 1950s to the mid seventies. Much timber was harvested in the course of land clearing, but it was poorly utilized. For southern New England as a whole, in the early 1970s, land clearing and other nontimber product removals accounted for 85 percent of the drain upon forest growing stock. Fully 56 percent of all timber removed from inventory was unused.[11]

The low removals in relation to growth permitted Connecticut hardwood inventories to rise by 74 percent between 1952 and 1972. Softwood inventories increased over the same interval by 127 percent. In the early 1970s, growth/removal ratios were still highly favorable for both hardwoods and softwoods. If these relationships had persisted, the resulting buildups in growing stock would have made many areas overstocked and overloaded with mature and disease-prone trees. Increased cutting in the 1970s has substantially altered the balance, but the forest surveys of the early 1980s will have to tell us how much.

Forest Industries since World War II

After World War II, Connecticut's primary forest products industry settled into a condition of stability based on harvesting a suburban forest. The period from 1952 to 1971 saw an increase in the production of sawlogs, pulpwood, miscellaneous products, and piling, but wooden post output declined. Total industrial roundwood consumption probably rose. At the same time, forest land clearing increased greatly.

Wood-using firms in Connecticut are small. Only 30 lumber and

Table 6. Connecticut Forest Industries, 1947–77

	Lumber and Wood Products				Paper and Allied Products			
	1947	1958	1972	1977	1947	1958	1972	1977
Employment (thousands)	1.4	1.5	1.9	2.1	7.5	8.3	6.9	7.2
Establishments	113	153	152	197	91	107	99	111

SOURCES: Federal Reserve Bank of Boston, *Economic Almanac*, 1971; U.S. Dept. of Commerce, Bureau of the Census, *1972 Census of Manufacturers*, 1974, and 1977 Census of Manufacturers MC77-A-3(p), Sept. 1979, preliminary data.

wood products establishments (out of 152) employed more than 20 persons in 1972. The primary forest products industry of Connecticut today consists of about sixty sawmills, one mill buying pulpwood, several hundred persons employed in logging, and a collection of specialty operations such as turnery plants, post and piling plants, and pallet mills. The converting branch of Connecticut's forest industry is substantial, accounting for the bulk of the state's 9,000 or so individuals working in forest industries. The largest single converting activity is paperboard containers and boxes. The converting plants depend on raw materials from other states: paper and board for envelopes and boxes, lumber and cut stock for millwork and furniture.

Overall, employment in the forest products industry has risen slightly since 1947 (table 6). These groups account for just over 2 percent of the state's manufacturing employment, though the percentage is higher in the rural counties. The stability of forest products employment in a suburbanizing state is striking.

The Future of the Suburban Forest

New England's population will grow in coming decades. The importance of different settlement densities can easily be illustrated. While each town has its own reasons for setting minimum densities, no government seems able to take account of the unplanned cumulative impact of small decisions that affect total land consumption.

To accommodate an additional population of 2 million by the year 2000—a guess from recent projections—New England's suburban forest and rural landscape would have to give up the following amounts of land:

	Acres (thousands)
Urban density	
(28 persons/acre)	71
Density of 1950s–60s suburbanization	
(4 persons/acre)	500
Density of large lot suburbanization	
(2 persons/acre)	1,000

Probably little future development will be at urban densities. The main question is what level of suburban densities will prevail. The low-density scenario would see much of the current suburban forest developed by 2020 except for that owned by governments, non-profit groups, and wealthy golf clubs. The low density would allow a substantial resource of open land to persist inside the current suburban frontier and in the newly developed zone beyond.

Whether there will even *be* a suburban forest forty years from now depends on real estate markets and on public policy. Those market and policy decisions will not consider their regional consequences. They will accumulate from literally millions of subdividing, public acquisition, zoning variance, and tax policy decisions.[12]

There is a distinct possibility, then, that despite its high value for open space, amenity, watershed protection, wildlife, and wood production, the suburban forest will vanish in two generations. Some might argue that little would be lost, since many of that forest's values are already severely compromised. To the extent that those values survive, they have been held tightly in private hands by the suburban "No Trespassing" mentality.

The values of the suburban forest are substantial enough, however, to motivate a drastically expanded effort for their conservation. The aesthetic, wildlife, watershed protection, and wood-producing values of these woods will increase in every future decade. The last chance to conserve these values, however, is in the hands of the current generation of landowners, conservationists, and public officials.

To illustrate just one area of impact, consider the wood production value of 100,000 acres of forest—less than a decade's recent land consumption in Connecticut. These acres, even under extensive management, could produce enough wood to heat 6,000 homes for the winter, or to employ about a hundred people year round in logging and sawmilling. One hundred jobs seems like nothing until you consider how starved most suburban areas are for manufacturing jobs and tax base.

Similar exercises could be performed for all of the other values of the suburban forest.

Past and Future

The land use changes now engulfing metropolitan New England's forests are best seen in historical perspective. The first wave of land use change in the region was the farm clearing, which persisted until 1840–80. The peak years of cleared land were estimated to be 1850 in Rhode Island, 1860 in Connecticut, and 1870 in Massachusetts. Before these peak years, however, birch, red cedar, and pines were already appearing in old fields in the older settlements where rural populations dwindled in response to urban opportunity and the opening of the West.

In tens of thousands of pastures like Rockwood's, the decline of farming returned millions of acres to woods from 1850 to the late 1960s. Even after the suburban boom began, farmland supplied most of the land required for housing. Many growing suburbs retained their wooded character. Even the major metropolitan regions are only 25 to 50 percent developed.

Strikingly, in the rapidly suburbanizing state of Connecticut, forest industry maintained its employment level over thirty years after 1947. This was largely due to the state's use of imported pulp and substantial imports of lumber. Still, a small lumber industry using local timber survived in an economic setting not favorable to such enterprise.

Communities in the suburban region have forgotten the seventeenth century. Then, town and colony governments built public policies on the essential character of fuelwood, sawtimber, shingles, barrel staves, and bark. As the forest regrew on abandoned farms, it continued to be heavily cut for fuel and boxboards. After World War I, however, the woods lay fallow, growing in size, stocking, age, and value for multiple forest uses.

Suburbanites saw the forest as a green backdrop, a place to stroll, and little more. Many were hostile to wood-producing uses of the forest. For a period, public policy treated the suburban forest as open space or greenbelt—simply the absence of anything else. To violate such greenspace with the axe seemed unthinkable.

Today, the fuelwood boom has returned the commodity use of the forest to respectability. Suburbanites have lugged 10,000 cords per year from the state forests of Connecticut. The state forester recently closed a three-year waiting list. A new willingness to accept timber harvesting and, I hope, an awareness of the need to conserve sawlogs for higher uses will emerge. At the same time, local and export markets for southern New England sawtimber have improved, and prices have risen dramatically. There are many exceptions, and all too many examples of woodlot butchery. An overreaction back to the greenspace mode of thinking is still possible, and may be occurring in towns that are considering zoning restrictions on logging.

The suburban forest is a fortuitous clutter of bypassed real estate that happens to grow trees. In the face of the development pressures of the next few decades, its very survival as a component of the region's land use pattern is in doubt. By firm public and private action, much of it could be saved.

Economists say that one of New England's last major economic advantages is its high quality of life. The suburban forest is without doubt one of the key amenities contributing to this quality of life. If the suburban forest is lost, it will harm not only our present quality of life but our region's economic future.

One thing is clear. The survival of the suburban forest is a land use issue. Survival cannot be assured by the traditional tools of forest policy alone—use-value taxation, fire control, landowner assistance. If foresters want to save the suburban forest, they will have to work closely with all the other agencies and groups concerned with land use policy.

The suburban forest can be saved—to become an amenity and quality-of-life asset unique in the nation. It should be saved not just to grow fuelwood, as in the colonial era, or as a leafy backdrop for bungalows, as in the 1950s, or to keep people out, as in the 70s. It should be saved for its broad conservation, amenity, production, and cultural values.

If Walden Pond and the other public parks are all that remains of New England's suburban forest by the 2020s, it will be because of a failure of public and private vision and will. The losses to the region's future quality of life will be beyond calculation.

CHAPTER 5

Stone Walls in the Woods:
New England's Rural Forest

isitors to New England often remark on the oddity of stone walls rambling through the roadside woodlands. Many are surprised to hear that large areas have been out of farm production so long that they have grown several successive crops of trees.

Farmers have by themselves wrought the greatest visible changes in New England's landscape. They cleared up to 16 million acres of forest, of which about half has since naturally returned to woodland and brush. A sizable fraction of today's rural forest, then, is former cropland or pasture. Reflecting their history, these woods are interlaced with crumbling stone walls. Farmland now occupies less land than houses and factories (fig. 5).

The acreage of New England's rocky hills cleared by grueling labor and later abandoned far exceeds the current acreage of crop and pasture. These vanished farmers leave reminders of their passing in the stone walls, the forlorn and forgotten cemeteries by remote lanes, and the leaf-filled cellarholes stumbled on by hunters.

In most rural towns, longtime residents can recall the distant, open view once seen from the hilltops. Today the views are blocked by dense woods. As one writer put it, the region's hills were engulfed by "a rising sea of woodlands." [1]

New England's rural forests remain the home of its farming, logging, and rural population, and the surviving bastion of New England town goverment. Most of these towns have lost population since the Civil War.

These towns are beyond the megalopolitan fringe now swamped by suburbia, and distant from the mountainsides and lakes of the recreational forest. On the fringes of the industrial forest, tiny villages linger after most of the land has been absorbed by giant paper companies and timbergrowing landowners. Farmers and rural resi-

Huge maple grows beside rock wall of abandoned field in New Hampshire. *Courtesy of American Forest Institute.*

dents are the principal landowners here, but much is owned by summer people, nonresidents, and investors. Still this is the region where farms set the characteristic tone of the landscape. Of the 11 million acres of forest in the rural forest, farmers now own roughly one-quarter. The rural forest gains its character from *past* farm ownership, not from present farm ownership.

The history of the rural forest is one of overextension and contraction of agriculture, and neglect of the woods because of poor wood markets. That story is told in histories of the region's agriculture, and reports of the state foresters and the U.S. Forest Service.[2] The classic rural forestry problems are public access to the land for hunting, fishing, and walking, and the problem of promoting better forest management. These stories are the work of this chapter.

Farm Expansion and Retreat

Agricultural decline in New England has occurred from the earliest years, as a result of competition from other regions, soil exhaustion, overpopulation, and greener grass elsewhere. At maximum ex-

Figure 5. Crop and Pasture Cover. *From U.S. Army Corps of Engineers,* North Atlantic regional water resources study, *1972, Appendix G: Land use and management, Figure G-7.*

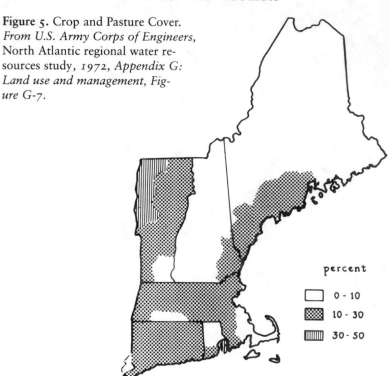

percent

☐ 0 - 10
▨ 10 - 30
▥ 30 - 50

tent, farmers owned about 20 million acres, or half of New England's total land area. Today, they hold less than 5 million acres. The farmers still own more than 2 million acres of woodland. Their neighbors who do not live by farming or rural industry own perhaps half of the total land area in the rural forest region.

Since 1880, farmers have sold three-eighths of New England to others—they still own one-eighth. Almost 90 percent of the farms in use in 1880 have been abandoned. The story of agricultural retreat is best told by examples from different regions and time periods.

Concord, Massachusetts, was settled in 1635 by hardy immigrants. The town was slowly developed into farms. By the Revolution, the soil was declining in fertility under poor management. Landlessness increased, and land values fell. Dividing farms could no longer provide for farmers' sons. R. A. Gross chronicled the impact of overpopulation on family life, politics, and economic opportunity in Concord: "on the eve of the Revolution, Concord was a declining town facing a grim future of increasing poverty, economic stagnation, and even depopulation."[3]

By the 1790s, the effects of this overpopulation were clearly evident. More than half of the young Concord men who had fought in the Revolution had already left town forever.[4] Many went to farmsteads in northern New England or New York.

Pressure on the land, emerging with striking speed, was clearly documented by C. S. Grant in his study of Kent, Connecticut, a charming town on the Housatonic River settled in 1739. Kent was one of the auction towns sold by the General Court in the last major land sales in the colony. Within three generations, pressure on the land was excessive, reflected in declining farm sizes, emigration, and rising poverty. Birthrates were extremely high:

There was insufficient land for the third generation. Some stayed and remained in a poorer status than that of their fathers and much poorer than that of their grandfathers. Others left at the rate of about 50 a year.[5]

By 1796, 42 percent of the men in Kent were poor by Grant's standard, and "for the first time there emerged a significant number of men destined to remain poor."[6]

In 1845, Thoreau noted the evidence of declining settlement near Walden Pond. Thoreau wrote as well of old cellarholes as has anyone since:

Now only a dent in the earth marks the site of these dwellings, with buried cellar stones . . . some pitch pine or oak occupies what was the chimney nook.

. . . These cellar dents, like deserted fox burrows, old holes, are all that is left where once were the stir and bustle of human life. . . .

. . . Still grows the vivacious lilac a generation after the door and lintel and sill are gone.[7]

Despite the decline in old regions, farmers continued to open land in parts of New England into the 1880s. The competition from midwestern grain took the attraction from New England farming after the 1840s. But shifts to sheep and dairying and to specialty crops like apples, potatoes in Maine's Aroostook County, and tobacco in the Connecticut Valley helped maintain farming. In many areas, much of the land was never cleared. As farming waned, forests began invading old pastures. Thoreau wrote of the pines growing in old fields, and how they are replaced by hardwoods.[8]

By the 1890s, visible decline in farming was underway across New England. Decline was hastened by difficulty in competing with farmers elsewhere, the disappearance—due to the railroads—of small rural industries that had supplied employment to off-season farmers, and the lure of high wages in the mills. The story is well told and fully documented by Harold Wilson, in *The Hill Country of Northern New England*.[9]

In 1890, the State of Maine became concerned about farm abandonment and conducted a statewide survey to determine its extent and causes. Nearly 3300 abandoned farms, totaling 254,000 acres, were noted. The survey found that many abandoned farms were incorporated into neighboring farms.

Town officials reported divergent trends, and some astute remarks. One noted,

I have reported thirty abandoned farms, a large portion of which are used for grazing, and will ultimately return to scrub forest. They should never have been cleared.

In another town:

Say 40 years ago, the inhabitants numbered about 1,000, and now we think our census enumerator cannot give us 400. . . . Very many of the abandoned farms are well fenced with good stone walls dividing fields, where trees are thickly growing, fast making timber of all kinds for another generation.[10]

Regionwide, land cleared for farming reached its greatest extent by 1880. Farm numbers peaked later than acreage, but declined faster. Acreage in farms slid slowly to about World War I, then plunged rapidly. From 1880 to 1940, land in farms fell by 7 million acres—to 13.9 million. Woodland remained constant while harvested cropland fell to 3.7 million.[11]

Fast as was the decline of New England farming up to 1940, the events since World War II have been dazzling. The cost pressures led to the disappearance of most of the small part-time farms. The spread of suburbia, consuming land at new, higher rates per family, engulfed entire counties that had been sleepy farming communities in 1940. Wartime service showed many rural young men a new world; they never returned to their farm homes (fig. 6).

Figure 6. Percent Decline in Acreage of Agricultural Land from Peak Development to 1950. *From U.S. Senate,* Land and water resources of the New England–New York region, *Sen. Doc. No. 14, 85th Congress, 1st Session, Jan. 17, 1957, plate 56.*

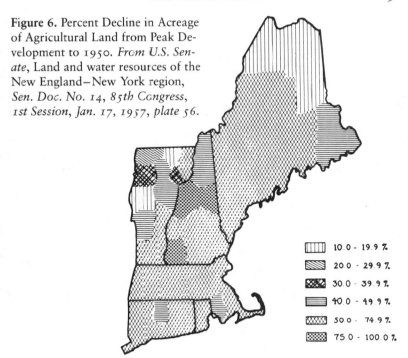

▦	10.0 - 19.9 %
▨	20.0 - 29.9 %
▩	30.0 - 39.9 %
▤	40.0 - 49.9 %
▥	50.0 - 74.9 %
▦	75.0 - 100.0 %

In Connecticut, for example, change was slow until about World War I. In 1910, more than two-thirds of Connecticut was in the cropland, pasture, wetland, and woodland of about 27,000 farms. By 1950, over 11,000 farms, containing 1.3 million acres, had disappeared. Suburban growth consumed only a small fraction of these farms, few of which were providing full-time livelihoods for their owners. In 1950, fully 45 percent of the state's farms were part-time, residential, retirement, or low-income operations. Farmland disappearance after 1950 was still more dramatic: nearly 800,000 acres in only twenty years. The number of farms fell to about 3,600 by 1979. Losses were especially rapid in the suburbanizing counties of Fairfield and Hartford (table 7).

Examples of postwar decline elsewhere are common. From 1940 to 1974, in Maine coastal counties, farms fell from 19,000 to 3,000, from 33 percent to 9 percent of the area of those counties.[12] In Stowe, Vermont, from 1940 to the early 70s, about 70 farms vanished, containing almost 11,000 acres.

In much of northern New England, as in this New Hampshire site, old fields are colonized by red or white spruce. *Courtesy of Bill Leak, USDA Forest Service.*

Table 7. Percent Changes in Land in Farms, Connecticut, 1910–70

County	1910–50	1950–70
Fairfield	−64	−74
Hartford	−39	−56
Litchfield	−40	−50
Middlesex	−49	−68
New Haven	−51	−62
New London	−31	−56
Tolland	−28	−63
Windham	−35	−48
Total	−42	−57

SOURCE: U.S. Department of Agriculture, Censuses of Agriculture, for years shown.

Horse loggers still operate on rural woodlots throughout New England. *Courtesy of Maine Department of Conservation.*

In the 1930s, H. I. Baldwin estimated that farm forests still provided a large portion of New England's timber harvest.[13]

Product	Percentage	Product	Percentage
Sawlogs	56	Fuelwood	80
Pulpwood	26	All products	56
Fenceposts	100		

From the 1950s to the present, a rising wood harvest per acre has balanced the drastic drop in farm ownership, leaving the harvest of wood from farm woodlands constant at about 350 million cubic feet per year.

Two major forestry issues in today's rural forest are public access for recreation and the improved practice of forestry on these lands.

Public Access to the Rural Forest

The posting of private land against public use has disturbed those concerned with outdoor recreation, especially hunting and fishing, for decades. Considerable private land remains open to public use. The U.S. Department of the Interior estimates that 32 percent of the noncorporate land acreage is open to the public (217 million acres) and 54 percent of the corporate land is open (40 million acres).

Most of the land owned by forest products companies is open to the public.[14]

Land posting results from social change and social conflict. In the past, rural landowners in many regions accepted the right of others to cross their property for hunting, fishing, and travel. In the past, the hunters were neighbors, and the owner himself expected to hunt on neighbors' lands, so a supportive social consensus favoring public access to private land could exist. Today, the users are increasingly strangers from a distance. They at times damage roads with four-wheel drive vehicles, hot-rod snowmobiles, or hunt birds in the backyards of persons who disapprove of hunting. The consensus supporting public use wrinkles. When fences are broken and buildings vandalized, it collapses. The increasing population of rural regions means that residents are closer together, but even neighbors are often strangers.

Several U.S. Forest Service studies display considerable variation in landowner reactions to different public uses of their land (table 8). The importance of these landowner preferences cannot be overemphasized. A change of 10 percentage points in the proportion of owners allowing a given activity can nullify the effect of millions of dollars spent on land acquisition, leaving the general public no better off than before.[15]

Posting is likely to continue to increase, based on the social trends now visible in rural America. To preserve access to land and water in the face of changing landowner attitudes will require that

Table 8. Activities Permitted on Private Lands, Selected Northeastern States 1970s

	Hunting	Fishing	Hiking	Snow-mobiling	All Use	Total
Southern New England 1972–73						
Owners (% permitting)	25	17	42	N/A	–	18,400 owners
Land (%)	37	30	48	N/A	2/3	4.4 million acres
New Hampshire & Vermont 1973						
Owners (% permitting)	51	37	51	50	51%	164,000 owners
Land (%)	50	59	73	59	–	8 million acres

SOURCES: For southern New England, Kingsley, *The forest-landowners of southern New England*; for New Hampshire and Vermont, Neal P. Kingsley and Thomas W. Birch, *The forest-land owners of New Hampshire and Vermont*, USDA-FS NEFES, Res. Bull. NE-51, 1977.

the major conflicts be addressed. User groups and public agencies will have to assure landowners that vandalism, littering, and noise will be controlled. Owners may have to be paid for allowing recreational uses. Users will have to accept "corridoring" along designated paths and corridors that avoid gardens, tree plantations, and homes. Snowmobile groups have successfully used this approach in many states.

In states where citizens have enjoyed common law rights of access to seashore, to great ponds, and to undeveloped wildland, the basis in custom exists to rebuild support of public use. A possible model is the program of public footpaths in England, in which the public is secured the right of transit over private lands for recreation. The footpaths are well marked and provided with occasional parking places off small rural lanes. Thus, a medieval system of public rights necessitated by the three-field system of farming and the lack of public roads has been turned into a basis for recreational walking by visitors from afar. The rights are supported by a public consensus.

In efforts to prevent the loss of public access through posting, most states have provided laws limiting landowner liability and otherwise promoting public access.[16] These laws are probably of greater importance in reducing the anxiety level of large owners than they are in promoting public use on small ownerships.

Forestry in the Rural Forest

One might assume that farmers would have the time and inclination to manage their woodlots carefully. Forestry surveys, however, show that the level of timber management on these lands is often inadequate. The causes of poor timber management on New England's rural forest have been limited landowner interest and poor markets for wood. These woodlots still yield aesthetic and speculative benefits to their owners, and provide wildlife habitat.

Forests have always presented a key portion of the economy of every New England farm. Farmers burned trees in clearing and sold the ash as potash. The woodlot supplied fifteen to thirty cords each year of fuelwood for cooking and heating all winter. Merely harvesting and working up such a woodpile was a massive, year-round effort. Some farmers tapped maple syrup. Many worked as loggers in winter to bring in extra cash. As the principal source of fuel and building material, the farm woodlot has truly been an important adjunct to New England agriculture. In the oak regions, open range grazing of hogs and cattle was important in colonial times, leading to endless quarrels over stray animals damaging crops and constant employment for the town animal wardens and fence viewers.

State forestry agencies have adopted programs to assist rural landowners in managing their woodlots. Most offer free forestry assistance, help in tree planting, and marketing advice. Where state foresters actually work on the land and supervise timber sales, they are limited to a maximum acreage or number of days of service per landowner. As a result, the average size of treatments accomplished by state programs is extremely small. In the Northeast, timber sales and marketing assists average:

area	28 acres
volume	128 cords
tree planting assists	8 acres [17]

These are averages for the Northeast, but they ring true for New England.

The state forestry agencies helping rural landowners are too understaffed to handle all of the region's forestry needs. Few forest owners are even aware of the assistance available to them. Perhaps this is fortunate, or the service forester's waiting lists would be much longer than they are now.

These programs have promoted better forestry and have helped educate landowners about their woodlots. They are so thinly staffed, however, that they have touched only a tiny fraction of the land needing attention. Most estimates are that it would take a century or more for the state foresters to handle every woodlot needing attention now. As the report of the 1979 New England Private Non-Industrial Forestry Conference noted, most of the forestry advice in New England is actually dispensed by loggers.

These state programs, however, are not without their critics. Points of concern include:

1. Competition with private consultants, removing business that could sustain private consultants (though the rules minimize this).

2. Small scale effort and poor education programs, hindering the spread of forestry information.

3. A tendency to spend time heavily on "repeaters" who are already interested in forestry rather than trying to convert new own-

ers to better forestry. Many of these repeaters would probably do the work without subsidy.

4. A tendency to be ruled by the in-box, serving all inquiries rather than setting priorities based on regional needs and real economic payoffs.

The free gift of forestry practices has had serious effects. It has made it harder to convince owners that forestry is really worth paying for. As a result there is little follow-through on many management practices. Further, lack of emphasis on follow-through encourages a shallow idea of forestry as the application of isolated practices rather than as sustained long-term planning.

Examples of poor follow-through abound. Plantations have been paved for housing, or forgotten to be overtaken by aspen—a costly way to grow aspen. Blister rust or budworm control is applied to stands that are not being managed anyway. Plantations are not thinned when they should be. Landowner turnover or changes in objectives frustrate state foresters by upending their plans regularly. These constant changes, however, are the basic weak point in any forest management program on a small woodlot, whether managed with public or private assistance.

Changes Needed in Forestry Assistance Programs

What are the biggest needs, then, in delivering forestry services to the rural forest? They can be briefly listed:

1. Better information for owners of woodlots. Improved extension, education, and general information programs about forestry are needed. Ultimately, education is the key to better management because there will never be enough foresters and conscientious loggers to do the job.

The university-run cooperative extension services are important, though understaffed. An important contribution, in the New England tradition, is being made by private groups. One example is the American Tree Farm System, which recognizes and publicizes well-managed woodlots.

2. More private consultants. The improving markets for wood are helping to make it possible for consulting foresters to earn a living. The region has hundreds of consulting foresters, but most of

Service forester checks regeneration on small Maine woodlot. *Courtesy of Maine Department of Conservation.*

them earn their living on surveying and real estate work and not primarily on forest management. There is little doubt that public programs may have created a more favorable climate for consultants, especially in New Hampshire, where the state foresters emphasize education rather than performing free services. Massachusetts has several sizable firms, while Maine seems to have few independent full-time consultants. One remarkable organization, the nonprofit New England Forestry Foundation, manages and owns land all over New England. The favorable forest-tax laws recently passed in Vermont and Massachusetts require that owners have forest management plans to qualify. These laws have triggered a massive increase in business for consultants.

3. Improved sense of landowner responsibility. For serious forestry to occur, landowners must accept their own responsibility for sound forest stewardship. They must recognize that if a logger butchers their lot, it is because they allowed it. It is not the logger's fault. Public programs, handing out free trees, free stand improvement, free fire and insect control, all encourage the view that forestry is really the government's responsibility.

This improved sense of landowner responsibility for multiple use management must be vigorously fostered by all private and public agencies concerned with forestry.

4. Improved logging equipment and systems for light partial cuttings on small areas.[18] New small machines are becoming available to cut small volumes of small trees economically. In some areas, loggers are buying and using them. These machines avoid the ruts and damage to residual trees caused by large skidders. They are less costly to own and operate. Their improved availability will help sell forest management to owners who do not want large skidders on their land.

Recently, horse loggers, who have survived all along in New England, have received increased attention. Horse logging is a hard way to earn a living but an extremely attractive way for small owners to harvest timber. I do not expect to see a real increase in horse logging, because it is such a strenuous occupation, but horses will continue to be part of New England's logging industry.

Improved education and training for loggers will help. There are many conscientious and careful loggers working in New England's woods, whose work is a pleasure to see. Foresters would like to see such operators receive more recognition.

5. A sound and stable approach to forest taxation. Forest landowners and foresters understandably spend a lot of time arguing about taxes and advocating that they be kept low. They argue that high annual property taxes and estate taxes eliminate the incentive to hold capital in the form of trees. The recent regional and national conferences on nonindustrial private forestry exemplify this concern with taxes.

Many of the most contentious issues of taxation involve equity aspects of property or capital gains taxation, and really do not hinge on the incentive effects of the taxes. And it is certainly understandable that owners of capital—as trees—would like to see low taxes on capital. The typical spokesman for small woodland owners is a retired, middle-class person who has managed a forest property for years. Rising land values have raised the annual property taxes. Because of his age, he is concerned with estate taxes and fears the breakup of the property so diligently assembled.

Yet no evidence has ever been offered that reducing such a landowner's tax problems would induce others to start practicing forestry. Until such evidence is produced, it will be difficult to design forest tax policies that will truly promote forestry. In all too many instances in the past, programs of special tax assessment have subsidized owners who plan no timber management and have helped reduce carrying costs for speculators. And they have reduced cash outflows of those who would have managed their lots anyway.[19]

Still, certain basic desirable features of forest taxes can be identified:

a. Eligibility should hinge on the preparation of an acceptable management plan and its careful implementation, as is done in Vermont and Massachusetts.

b. Tax payments should be timed to coincide with harvesting so that revenue is available to pay them.

c. To the extent that lowered taxes on forests are below *ad valorem* values, two problems must be solved:

   — The transfer of tax burden to other taxpayers owning nonforest real estate. This transfer is severe in some Maine towns and is a chronic political irritant.

   — Means to "recapture," with interest, the value of the tax subsidy when the land is sold for development.

d. Landowners should be able to count on predictable levels of taxation that are stable relative to prices of stumpage. The greatest threat to forestry is not high current taxation but the threat of future confiscatory tax levels.

Many forest landowners have been caught in a serious tax bind by annual tax bills that have increased faster than timber prices. Annual charges against future crops devour profits quickly. Recent years have seen dramatic increases in assessments and annual tax bills, making owners fearful of still more tax escalation.

Forests in New England were once valued at zero for local property taxes. They have been, until recent decades, undertaxed in relation to their true economic value. The future holds the fear, for many owners, of dramatic overtaxation as speculative land values reach unheard-of levels.

At the same time, however, the owners of rural real estate are the holders of large, unrealized capital gains from high land prices. The tax problems of rural forestry stem from the fact that these owners are land-poor.

6. Improved emphasis on multiple-use forest values. Our past programs have been too timber-oriented. Most New England foresters recognize this and are skilled in harmonizing timber management wth wildlife, aesthetic, and other landowner concerns. But the message has still not reached many rural landowners. Until the

revival of interest in fuelwood, I despaired of ever getting across the message that timber management does not eliminate other forest values.

We need to improve our ability to manage sensitively for wood, wildlife, and water, with one eye out for how it looks from the road or the back porch. We need to inform rural landowners. Properly educated, most owners will be willing to forgo some timber returns to benefit nontimber forest values.

7. Cooperation among forest landowners must be fostered. Recent years have seen the emergence across New England of organizations representing wood users, landowners, loggers, and consultants. These groups work at educating members and promoting their interests.

It has been customary for foresters to urge the formation of forestry cooperatives. New England is not especially favorable ground for cooperatives, because of the stoutly independent landowners, poor wood markets and low prices, and the small size of most of its ownerships. Few owners hold lots large enough to produce substantial annual income, which means that their interest in investing time in a co-op is limited.[20]

Still, where enough medium-sized parcels (100–1000 acres) exist, and where local leadership is present, forestry cooperatives should be tried. One notable recent experiment is the Forest Products Marketing and Management Association of Dover-Foxcroft, Maine, which is getting started with assistance from the Maine Forest Service and the U.S. Department of Agriculture.

Other institutions, such as farm co-ops, soil conservation and resource conservation and development districts, and regional planning agencies, provide excellent parent groups for local landowner cooperatives. The importance of landowner interest and cooperation cannot be overemphasized. Without landowner commitment to long-term management, the efforts of foresters are wasted. Plantations are lost to brush, are not thinned properly, or succumb to disease. Thinned and improved hardwood stands degenerate through neglect. Soil conservation improvements deteriorate from poor maintenance.

No program of favorable taxation, free forestry services, or forestry television shows will mean a thing for the long-run productivity of the rural forest without landowner commitment to management.[21] Developing such commitment is the true challenge facing

New England's forestry community. The most promising approach is both to demonstrate the financial advantages and to promote the acceptance of a conservation ethic. Such an ethic argues that sound land stewardship is an obligation of ownership and not just one of a number of options. Good citizens do not strip their woodlots.

CHAPTER 6

A Place in the Country:
The Recreational Forest

or generations, New Englanders have built remote camps along lakeshores as retreats for fishing and hunting expeditions. In the twentieth century, families began buying entire farms for rural vacation homes. The overall effects of this activity on the region's rural economy and land use pattern were benign. In the 1960s and 1970s, however, the region was hit by an explosion in land speculation that resembled such previous bursts as the short-lived nineteenth-century sheep boom. The distinctive feature of this new boom was the sale of land as subdivided lots, usually to distant nonresidents. Many of the sales were made by high-pressure campaigns using television and magazine advertising, touting the beauties of cabin life in the New England woods. Many played on greed, hawking the high profits to be made from investing now. Projects registered for interstate advertising, only a tiny fraction of the total subdividing activity, totaled 49,000 acres regionwide between 1968 and 1977 (table 9).

The recreational forest includes those areas in which the forest land is principally a green backdrop for resorts and second homes. The ownership pattern has become so altered by subdivision, nonresident ownership, and scattered development as to make future use of the land for commercial timber, recreation, or other purposes difficult or impossible. Probably some 3 million acres of forest land lie in the recreational forest.

The distinctive impact of the recent land boom is best seen in Vermont, a state that took vigorous public action to control its worst effects.

Outdoor recreation has become a major Vermont industry, accounting for 15 percent of the gross state product in 1972. The future of this industry is of great economic, social, and environmental importance. In the late 1960s, however, the state's recreation economy began to change in ways that destroyed important social val-

Table 9. Projects, Acres, and Lots Registered with
the Federal Office of Interstate Land Sales
Registration, 1968–77

State	Projects	Acres	Lots
Connecticut	5	2,747	2,079
Rhode Island	0	0	0
Massachusetts	30	8,249	11,363
Vermont	26	12,250	8,319
New Hampshire	53	14,756	10,784
Maine	27	10,827	10,814
Region	141	48,829	43,359

SOURCE: R. C. Ragatz, Trends in the market for privately owned seasonal recreational housing, in W. LaPage, ed., *Proceedings, 1980 national outdoor recreation
trends symposium*, USDA-FS NEFES, Gen. Tech. Rept. NE-57, 1980. New England
vacation homes totaled 221,806 in the 1970 census.

ues. In many towns, rural occupations were displaced; land was
sold to nonresidents. The future productivity of farm and forest
land was seriously impaired by parcel fragmentation and absentee
ownership.

The recreation boom repeats a historical pattern of boom and
bust in rural land use. But the current expansion has created farm
and forest land use patterns much less capable of adjustment to
meet changing future needs than were previous land use systems.
The following sections review Vermont's changing rural economy,
examine the recent recreation boom, and discuss major social and
economic effects of the boom.

Changing Land Uses

Agriculture has, until recently, dominated Vermont's rural landscape.[1] Farm numbers and acreage began to decline in Vermont in
the late nineteenth century, with abandonments concentrated at
first on the poorer soils and higher elevations. The typical Vermont
farm during this period included twenty to sixty acres of tillage and
pasture, with the remainder in forest.

In 1949, 3.5 million acres, 60 percent of Vermont's area, was in
farm ownership. By 1969, farm acreage had fallen to 1.9 million
acres, or 32.6 percent of the state land area. In 1949, Vermont had
19,000 farms. More than 12,000 disappeared by 1969.[2] These

trends reflect the general retreat of marginal farming in northern New England as well as the new demand for recreational land.

In 1973, Vermont was 76 percent forested. In contrast, cropland covered only 13 percent of the state's area. The forest has risen in total area—by 20 percent since 1948—but its ownership composition has changed. Public forest agencies and forest industry have increased their landholdings. Farmers have reduced their woodland ownership by nearly half since 1948. Other private owners, many nonresidents, increased their acreage by 100 percent in less than two decades. The average parcel size is declining, and turnover in forest land ownership is high.[3]

Tourism and recreation are familiar features of the Vermont rural economy. Towns as far north as Stowe developed into important resorts as early as the 1860s. With the advent of the automobile, a significant trade developed based on farmers taking in summer boarders. Improved roads accelerated this process. Recreation brought seasonal jobs, extra income, and improved markets for farm products and property all across northern New England. This process continued slowly through the 1950s; some areas became concentrations of rural miniestates owned by the "summer people" from the city.

The town of Stowe, for example, had eighty-eight farms, including 15,000 acres of woodland, pasture, marsh, and tillage in 1940. This number fell to about thirty farm units by 1960, with 7,300 acres of land. During this period, farmland prices roughly tripled, and the brisk market for their land enabled many farmers to leave agriculture. Out-migration, a normal part of Vermont farm life for a century, continued.

After 1960, the pace of change accelerated. Only eight farms survived by 1975, covering less than 3,000 acres. Stowe was no longer an agricultural community. Farmland prices rose to nearly $2,000 per acre by the mid seventies. Woodland prices, which remained stable from 1940 to 1960, thereafter rose dramatically.[4]

From 1940 to 1975, farming declined because of poor land fertility, distance from markets, and low farm incomes. Up to the late 1960s, the recreational land market provided for an orderly succession of land uses that minimized social disruptions. As the 1970s land boom got underway, however, the effect became active displacement of rural land uses by a new speculative land market. Tillable land, pasture, and forest were all affected.

Recreational forest serves as a green backdrop at Saltwater Farm, Merry Meeting Bay, Maine coast. *Photo by Chris Ayres.*

The Recreation Boom: Trends, Impact, and Community Response

Up to the 1960s, recreation land uses grew slowly, primarily through the sale of farms and their conversion to second homes or full-time residences. But recent land use changes were based on entirely new markets and institutions. The three dominant themes were the growth of ski recreation, the expansion in second homes specifically constructed as leisure units, and the conversion of the land into a commodity, subdivided and sold by experienced marketing firms.[5] These developments increased the economic, social, and environmental impact of recreation on the state.

Tourism and recreation are important to New England's economy. In 1972, four New England states ranked in the top ten states in the ratio of travel expenditures to gross state product:[6]

Maine	27%	New Hampshire	13%
Vermont	15%	Massachusetts	10%

In Vermont, for 1971, it was estimated that recreation accounted for $220 million in spending in the state and about 13,000 jobs.[7]

Skiing is one of Vermont's major industries. There are more than

The recreational forest: ski area, Vermont. *Courtesy of Greg Gurdel, Vermont Agency of Develop. and Comm. Affairs, Vt. Travel Division.*

14 million skiers in the country; their numbers have been growing rapidly each year.[8] This growth is expected to continue. In Vermont, the industry has grown steadily. In the 1973–74 season, out-of-state skiers accounted for 75 percent of the skier visits and 90 percent of skier expenditures.[9] The ski boom brought a shift in the location of the state's recreation industry, away from established lakefront locations and into previously declining mountain villages, although some established resorts such as Stowe shared in the growth.

Based on state surveys, second home numbers in Vermont increased as follows: [10]

	1968	1973	Percentage Change
Number of vacation homes	22,600	29,600	31
Vacation home taxes raised (millions)	$ 4.3	$ 9.5	121
Average tax per vacation unit	$191	$322	68

Second homes are an important part of the tax base in many towns. In 1973, fifty towns derived more than 25 percent of their tax revenues from second homes. A number of towns receive half of their tax revenue from second home property. Many Vermont second homes are owned by nonresidents—62 percent of them in 1973 (up from 58 percent in 1968). Connecticut and New York residents together owned 32 percent. Second homes owned by out-of-staters, in fact, contributed nearly 7 percent of the total town taxes raised in the state.

The Land Boom in Dover and Wilmington, Vermont

Dover and Wilmington are southern Vermont towns that illustrate the changes prompted by the new recreation boom. By the mid seventies, only eighteen farms remained in these towns. The recreation expansion based on skiing and the automobile accelerated the removal of land from farming, replacing agriculture with an economy dependent on supplying lodging, recreation, and other services to out-of-state residents. In addition, the region has been living off its capital. Local and out-of-state real estate and development firms have been selling land. Many of the customers are nonresidents. In

Wardsboro, the town immediately north of Dover, 62 percent of the private land is owned by nonresidents.[11]

According to a survey taken in 1975–77, after the peak of the land boom, 202,000 acres of forest land in tracts larger than 10 acres were transferred in Vermont, of which 87,000 acres were purchased by nonresidents. This included more than 4,000 acres purchased by owners of record with Canadian or foreign addresses.[12]

Commercial development has been largely oriented toward tourism. Dover and Wilmington in 1973 contained 83 ski lodges and motels, 24 restaurants, and 12 real estate firms. In 1968, the towns contained 609 second home   1973, the number had grown to 1,054. In 1973, second homes accounted for about one-third of total land taxes raised. There are more than 60 subdivisions in the area. Several planned subdivisions have never been offered for sale. Others have been offered and have made negligible sales. In contrast, the large subdivisions, which hired experienced land-marketing firms, have sold relatively well.

The state's stiff capital gains tax on short-term land turnover has been cited as a major reason for a standstill in new subdivisions since 1971.[13] Additional factors are gasoline prices, the effects of environmental legislation, and the prior purchase and preparation for development of most of the area's large available tracts by that time. The slow demand for lots since 1972 would have slowed subdivision activity in any case. Since the 1972 peak in land sales, statewide sales of forest tracts larger than 10 acres fell significantly, and the acreage involved fell by nearly two-thirds—from 153,410 acres in 1972 to 57,130 acres in 1977.[14]

Economic and Social Impact

The rapid pace of development, and the state's increasing dependence on tourism have prompted heated discussion of the economic and social impact of the new recreation economy. Based on current research, a few tentative generalizations can be made.[15]

Since many ill effects of resort and second home growth are claimed, it is well to note some of the positive effects. Growth in rural towns has enabled some areas to improve the supply of public services, through an increased tax base and growing revenues from nonresidents. In some areas, the amenities associated with skiing and rural life have stimulated settlement by professionals whose services are made available to residents and who often are active in civic life as well. These immigrants are often leaders in movements for zoning and planning in their towns. In existing summer resorts, the growth of winter recreation has eliminated winter lulls in activity, leading to less seasonality of employment and more efficient use of social overhead facilities and private capital. Finally, the growing demand for land has helped many a farmer make a comfortable exit from agriculture by selling to a nonresident or developer. The land market has thereby eased the social strains resulting from the steady retreat of agriculture.

Concern has been evident over the effects of the recreation boom on local government costs and revenues. A number of studies suggest that this concern is not warranted. The large direct and indirect additions to the tax base and revenue from nonresident landowners and visitors generally outweigh the costs. Resorts do not place heavy demands on public services. Many ski areas are largely self-sufficient for services. Second homes do not contribute children to the local school system. There is some basis for the view, however, that cost-revenue impacts will be unfavorable if a large proportion of second homes become primary residences for families with children. This seems unlikely in most of Vermont because of the shortage of employment opportunities.

The recreation boom, however, has had some serious undesirable effects. Most important are its effects on seasonality of employment, the creation of an uneconomic settlement pattern, the removal of land from productive use, and the creation of an unbalanced economy.

Although some communities have reduced employment seasonality through winter recreation, many towns have simply shifted from summer peaks to winter peaks. In Stowe, for example, employment in the first quarter of 1970 averaged 1,097; in the second quarter, the "mud season," employment averaged 622. But employment in many rural occupations was traditionally slack during mud season.[16] Seasonality is a basic characteristic of a resort economy, as are low wages and high employment turnover.

The conversion of farm and forest land to recreational uses proceeded slowly in the first half of the twentieth century. Since it was based on the transfer of farms and large tracts, its impact on settlement patterns and land use was small. But the land boom of recent decades has followed entirely different principles.[17] Land is cut up into one-acre lots and sold. Roads are cut through wooded hillsides and condominiums or detached dwellings appear. This process, occurring in a totally unplanned fashion, has created uneconomic sprawl over large areas, resulting in excessive land consumption and high service costs.

Development has been uneconomic in another, perhaps more durable and important way. The land-marketing industry proceeded with little regard for economically important natural values. As a result, there are countless examples of flood-plain encroachment, water pollution, aesthetic blight, and other lost environmental values. These values are intrinsically important, but they are also the basis of the region's attractiveness to tourists.

The land boom has removed large areas of land from commodity-producing and job-producing uses. This reduction has come about temporarily through speculation, in which developers hold land for future sale or development. Frequently, existing productive uses cease for this period.

The land boom has emphasized trading in small land parcels. From 1968 to 1977, the price of Vermont forested tracts larger than 500 acres rose little, while prices rose significantly for smaller tracts. The average size of parcels sold fell by half in that period—from 80 to 41 acres.[18] The price differentials between land in small and large parcels create irresistible incentives for owners to subdivide. In 1973, 54 percent of Vermont's forest landowners owned less than 20 acres of woodland.[19] Although this is only 3 percent of the state's commercial forest land, it is still more than 150,000 acres of land that will be difficult to manage for tree crops, wildlife, or public recreational uses.

The wood-processing industry in Vermont has been suffering from declining timber quality, obsolescence, and distance from markets for decades. From 1952 to 1972, almost three hundred wood-using plants closed in Vermont.[20] Most employed only a few people. Continued parcel fragmentation, increased absentee ownership, and more rapid ownership turnover make forest harvesting and management less likely on larger areas of land each year. If these trends continue, Vermont's forest resources, which now are growing timber at twice the rate of harvest, will not contribute their full potential toward employment and economic health for rural communities. Especially where there is overdependence on recreation, wood products jobs will be important.

The invisible processes of subdivision and parcel fragmentation, which may not change surface features at all, can permanently remove land from forest or farm uses because of the prohibitive cost of reassembling economically operable units from one-acre lots owned by residents of a dozen distant cities. Another effect of speculative land sales has been the creation of land parcels that could never, by reason of their shape or size, be economically useful for any other purpose. Subdivision regulations and environmental restrictions have encouraged this perverse process. Oddly shaped properties created with long, narrow sections to allow minimal road or water access are common in the Vermont landscape.

The removal of land from productive uses for farming and forestry has been widely blamed on the rising taxes per acre that accompany rural recreation developments. This view seems clearly erroneous for most Vermont recreation areas. The land boom does destroy existing productive land uses, but it does so by paying high prices for land and by subdivision. The "push" effect of rising taxes is much less important than the pull of high demand for land.

Finally, the recreation land boom has created a new and unbalanced economy for many Vermont towns, and, indeed, for the whole state. New England's history of dependence on one-industry towns seems destined to be repeated in the recreation-oriented villages of Vermont. In Vermont, poor snow years or gasoline shortages can create serious hardship. For example, state surveys estimate that skier outlays in Vermont fell from a peak of $54 million in 1971−72 to $35 million in 1973−74.

A study of Appalachia's economic development seems relevant for Vermont. The study concluded that because of its seasonality and low-wage workforce, "recreation alone can almost never provide a base for a viable economy."[21] The recreation boom in Vermont has been overextended. Instead of providing a valuable addition to a diversified economy, it has replaced one kind of imbalance with a new imbalance, which may prove much more difficult to correct.

Response: Social Innovation in Planning

The development brought on by the state's recreational expansion prompted state legislation to establish a planning program. Vermont now possesses a land use control program that incorporates statewide performance standards while assuring a degree of local autonomy and flexibility.[22] This program consists of a water pollu-

In some towns, skiing, land sales, and the land have coexisted relatively well. Stowe, Vermont. *Courtesy of Greg Gurdel, Vt. Agency of Develop. and Comm. Affairs, Vt. Travel Division.*

tion control program (Act 252), a land use regulation system (Act 250), and local and regional planning.

Act 250 created the State Environmental Board and a series of regional environmental commissions.[23] It also established a detailed system of performance standards that must be met by all large developments. Each district commission holds hearings on proposed developments, following examination of the site by the county forester. The commission has the power to reject an application or to authorize the project with modifications. Decisions may be appealed to the State Environmental Board. Among other provisions, the act provides strong protection for all lands above 2500 feet in elevation. Finally, the Vermont statutes authorize the creation of local planning commissions, boards of adjustment, and regional planning commissions.[24]

The program of state-level controls has been supplemented by vigorous local activity in many Vermont towns. At a minimum, towns struggled to remain independent of state rules and district environmental commissions. Some went beyond this, however, to install planning and zoning boards, to draft land use plans, and to establish subdivision ordinances and building and plumbing inspection programs. The debates over these innovations often divided residents along factional lines of "old-timers" versus "newcomers," or farmers versus tourists. However, it is now widely accepted that local government cannot ignore land use control and regulation. The state-mandated program of environmental controls is seen by many as a shift of power to Montpelier, but the new programs in fact allow, for the first time, a measure of local public influence on developments affecting a town's future.

Conclusion

That recreation was potentially destructive of values important to New Englanders was shrewdly forecast by John Wright, editor of a major survey volume on New England, in a 1933 essay:

A surging tide of humanity sweeps out of the cities. . . . If allowed to take their own course without control these floods are a menace. There is a real danger that they may submerge in a welter of ugliness the little that remains, at least in the environs of the larger centers, of the Old New England of quiet villages and tranquil vistas.[25]

This prophecy is amply fulfilled along countless miles of roadside near New England's seacoasts and mountains.

Tourism, of course, has been important in New England for more than a century. Until the 1960s, tourism and recreation in northern New England played an important role in easing the social transition away from an overextended agriculture. Change was gradual and had minimal affects on land use, social structure, or roads and schools. The demand for land and employment opportunities created by tourism assisted individual and community adjustment to a declining farm economy, as the Stowe example shows. The new recreation industry of the 1960s, based on capital-intensive resort development, rapid sale of land as an investment commodity, and construction of second homes, has created a new form of overextension. Many Vermont communities are now heavily reliant on an economy whose disadvantages in seasonality, vulnerability to economic instability, and nonresident ownership are only now becoming apparent. The recreation boom has created an economy of new one-industry towns, based on an industry that economists agree to be a poor community economic base. Much research to date has addressed narrow issues of fiscal cost-revenue analysis; little attention has been paid to these broader issues.[26]

There is a full research agenda here for social scientists and planners. Long-term studies are needed to assess the effects of the land boom on local communities. Where have second homes been built? Have recreation-oriented businesses reduced their seasonality and recruited a more stable labor force? Have the newcomers been effectively assimilated into existing communities? What has been the fate of forest and farmland withdrawn from active use by subdivision and speculation? How have surviving farms and wood-using enterprises fared? How effective have new environmental controls been in reducing stresses in the rural environment?

Vermont's economy has adjusted to change as past booms subsided. Adjustments have been facilitated by an industrious population, by a flexible system of land use, by a resilient ecosystem, and by the opportunity for out-migration. The current boom, with its overextended recreation industry, has created a land use system far less flexible. Large acreages are in unsold or partially sold subdivisions, which will probably never be fully "built out" because of the current slow pace of sales and the new environmental restrictions on construction. The resulting patchwork of numerous ownerships, consisting of parcels too small for economical farm or forest management, will preclude their use for producing wood for building products or energy, and food and fodder for humans and livestock.

Since the mid 1970s, the recreational land boom in Vermont and elsewhere in New England has subsided. Several spectacular bankruptcies of speculative resort and land sales operations gave evidence that the tide was receding. The current energy and financial outlook suggests that remote corners of New England will not see a resurgence of these activities. The economic slowdown has not affected the principal fact, however, which is that the speculative land sales boom of the past two decades has left behind some serious, widespread, and durable land use problems that will hinder the economic future of rural New England communities.

The future of the recreational forest is uncertain, but the desire of suburban families for a place in the country assures it a continuing significance in New England life.

CHAPTER 7

New England's Wild Forest

ince the days of Thoreau, New Englanders have appreciated wild forest landscapes. New Englanders were leaders in the move to protect the nation's forests. They pushed for state forests and parks early in this century.[1] Local citizens pressed for federal acquisition of land in the White Mountain National Forest. New England contains a splendid example of a privately created wilderness—Baxter State Park. But much of the acreage in New England's wild forest dates to the 1960s and 70s.

Though little virgin forest remains in New England, the forest has regrown so completely that few hikers realize that a trailside vista was once abusively cut and often burned. The few remaining scraps of virgin forest are mostly outside the region's large, formally designated wilderness areas.

New England's wild forest is difficult to define. Large acreages are devoted to such specialized uses as watershed protection. These areas may be lightly cut for timber, but recreation is prohibited. Perhaps a quarter of a million acres of such lands are found in New England. Since they are available for timber cutting, they fit no rigid definition of wilderness, but since they form large green blocks in the midst of cities and suburbs, they fill most of the functions of the wild forest.[2] They are protected from development and lightly used by people. Likewise, the tiny parcels owned as greenspace or preserves by towns and nonprofit groups are so small that they could not accommodate backpacking trips, yet they also are part of the wild forest, protected from development, logging, and often from hunting as well.

All told, the wild forest of New England comes to more than a million acres of land, mostly forested, plus an additional quarter million acres now in dispute on the national forests. This is about 2.5 percent of the region's land area. The wild forest is a product of the aspirations of the region's citizens for greenspace, for a place to stroll in quiet woods, and for conserving natural processes. The wild forest is a hallmark of New England's land use pattern and quality of life.

Mount Katahdin, centerpiece of Maine's Baxter State Park, part of New England's wild forest. *Photo by Chris Ayres.*

Since it appears in such tiny units, the wild forest is not easily mapped. Except for Maine's Baxter Park and Allagash Wilderness Waterway, few of the designated units would make more than a hefty dot on a small map of the region (fig. 7).

Services of the Wild Forest

There is a common view that wildlands "locked up" in reserved areas provide nothing of benefit to society, only quiet preserves for a few hikers. New Englanders have long known better. When state government action seemed inadequate, private organizations took to the land acquisition business themselves with a vengeance. In fact, much of New England's wild forest is a direct result of private effort, not just of interest groups lobbying government agencies. In this, New England is distinctive.

The citizens who promoted the creation of New England's wild forest did so—and still do so—from a variety of motives, from crass to idealistic. In some instances, people sought to create preserves and parks to conserve peace, quiet, and undeveloped views at no cost to themselves. The most conspicuous example is Acadia

Figure 7. New England's Wild Forest Examples.

National Park, donated to the federal government by wealthy
Mount Desert vacationers led by the Rockefeller family. Though in
a family tradition of magnificent conservation gifts (Smoky Mountains, Virgin Islands, and Grand Tetons national parks), the gift certainly helped real estate values and kept out development.

Large portions of the wild forest were created for utilitarian conservation purposes—to preserve game, fish, and clean water supplies or to conserve channel storage and prevent flood plain encroachment. Recreation, birdwalking, and open space values have
been high on the list of objectives in virtually every instance. Finally, the pure "preservation" motive, best expressed by Baxter
State Park, is seen in dozens of the tiny parcels of woods and marsh
held by the private nonprofit groups. Whatever the motives of the

private or governmental groups involved, preserved wildlands serve a broad range of social values, which may be outlined as follows:

1. Scientific
   a. Preserving key ecosystems to ensure biotic diversity.
   b. Conserving gene pools and potentially useful organisms.
   c. Providing natural areas for research and monitoring ecosystems.

2. Economic
   a. Backcountry recreation.
   b. Enhancement of nearby real estate values.
   c. Conserving wildlife and fish.
   d. Protecting watersheds and water quality.
   e. Conserving scenic resources to benefit tourism.
   f. Avoiding costs of development (services, pollution, congestion).
   g. Promoting a balanced land use pattern.

3. Cultural
   a. Conserving a cultural heritage.
   b. Preserving aesthetic values.
   c. Providing educational opportunities.

4. Ethical
   a. Providing for "rights of rocks."
   b. Providing scope for individual freedom.
   c. Social value of exercising restraint.

Most of the values benefit individuals who never visit the areas involved. It is also true that parcels of well-managed forest can provide most of these services—it is a matter of degree and of which services hold priority.

One value of wild forests not often discussed is the promotion of a balanced land use pattern. It is not easy to define a balanced land use pattern, but it is easy to cite examples of imbalance. Every reader probably has a favorite example, but I think long stretches of U.S. Highway 1 will do well—uninterrupted stretches of shabby commercial strip development. Furthermore, I assert that the large acreages devoted to development each year should be balanced by proper commitments of land for open space, recreation, water supply protection, and aesthetic relief from visual blight.

If we can afford to pave and develop hundreds of thousands (millions?) of acres in the next few decades, can we not afford to preserve for the future a corresponding undeveloped acreage? This could be in working farms and forests and not necessarily in classic wilderness. I believe that failure to make such a major conservation commitment now, while there is still time, would be serious folly.

Recreation in the Wild Forest

The best publicized use of New England's wild forests is recreation: backpacking, mountain climbing, cross-country skiing, snowshoeing, and fishing. In the scattered patches of wild forest in southern New England, day walks, picnics, and nature walks are popular.

The organized hiking community in New England takes national leadership in the efforts of the various trail and outing clubs, organized under the Appalachian Trail Conference, to maintain hiking trails. The volunteer efforts of these groups give the trails their distinctive character and display a special New England self-sufficiency and enterprise.[3]

Nationally, use of wilderness areas has been rising rapidly, at a rate of 7 percent per year since 1960.[4] National surveys estimate that 5 to 10 percent of the adult population participate in backpacking and a higher percentage in "dispersed camping."[5] The U.S.D.A. Forest Service expects the use of wilderness areas to grow at 2 percent per year.

Data for New England wild areas do not seem to reflect these trends.[6] Figures collected by the Appalachian Mountain Club and the U.S.D.A. Forest Service show that use levels have peaked in major public wild areas in northern New England. In a few instances, this may reflect crowding and the imposition of rationing or reservation systems at some areas. Or it may represent a market saturation for backcountry recreation, together with the aging of the baby boom generation. These recent trends may, on the other hand, be merely a plateau before continued growth. Walking and related activities popular in the wild patches in southern New England are enjoyed by 50 to 60 percent of the population and fill a major role in the supply of recreation there.

The heavy use pressures on these lands create overcrowding and reduce the enjoyment of users. Trails are beaten down, fuelwood disappears, and litter proliferates. Tenting sites are increasingly threadbare. Forest and park managers have resorted to limits on party sizes, first-come/first-serve reservation systems, carry-in/

Great Gulf Wilderness, White Mountain National Forest, New Hampshire, protected from development by the Wilderness Act of 1964. *Courtesy of USDA Forest Service.*

carry-out programs, and intensified maintenance, management, and patrolling.[7]

The cost of these management programs is becoming an important issue for recreation managers. Costs directly attributable to backcountry recreation management on major public areas in northern New England approach $2 million per year. The users, who benefit the most and whose activities occasion these outlays, contribute little. Costs per user-day of $3 to $6 are common. The total costs of wilderness allocation and management are larger than generally realized.[8] Since recreation budgets in public agencies are facing cuts in purchasing funds, the issue of higher user contributions to management cost will surely concern managers and recreationists in the 1980s.

Baxter Park

New England's wild forest owes much to private initiative. The most splendid example is Baxter Park, which protects Mount Katahdin, the northern terminus of the Appalachian Trail. The park was purchased over a period of years by the late Gov. Percival P. Baxter and donated to the state. In making his donations, the governor asked the legislature to accept the deeds by resolves, to give them the effect of law. He donated a substantial endowment to fund the management expenses and specified that the park be administered by the Baxter Park Authority, which consists of the commissioner of Inland Fisheries and Wildlife, the director of the Bureau of Forestry, and the attorney general. These officials provide broad policy guidance to the staff. Strictly speaking, the 200,000 acres of the park are not state land, but are held in trust by the state for the people of Maine.

The authority has recently engaged in complex management planning for the park. It has been embroiled in litigation over proposals to salvage blown-down spruce trees and to spray for budworm control, and over fire control procedures. The fire controversy erupted after an intense 3500-acre fire in August 1977, which was contained by conventional bulldozed firelines. That fire started in blown-down timber and damaged a sizable acreage of nearby paper company land, destroying a nice crop of postcut regeneration. Critics questioned whether the fire should have been controlled, and if so, whether heavy equipment was appropriate. In addition, the park authority has fought with users and neighbors over the use of snowmobiles on park roads.

Governor Baxter specified that the park be managed in its natural state, as a "sanctuary for birds and beasts." He modified this mandate in one corner, where hunting was permitted, and in another, where "scientific forestry" was to be practiced.

The park's managers have learned from experience that managing a large wilderness in the midst of New England's industrial forest is a complex and contentious matter. Citizens and lawyers have haggled endlessly over the deeds of trust establishing the park. But a management program is getting underway to address the park's long-term needs.[9]

Baxter Park remains the region's largest dedicated wilderness, and it may always be. Its size dwarfs the entire acreage of federal wilderness in New England. It sprang from the conviction of one man, and not from a loud controversy, as did other New England wild areas. There was no "save Mount Katahdin" lobby.

Federal Wilderness

The best-known elements of the wild forest are the federal wilderness units, which totaled about 54,000 acres in 1980. These units owe their origin to the establishment during this century of major federal reservations—national forests and wildlife refuges. These were intended to protect watersheds and timber supply or to shelter wildlife.

In 1964, following a seven-year battle, Congress passed the Wilderness Act, which stated that land preservation was to stand on an equal footing as a potential use of federal lands. Congressional designation as a wilderness was to protect an area strictly from development. In New England the two areas in wildlife refuges proposed by the U.S. Fish and Wildlife Service were not controversial because their designation threatened no locally important resource uses. Similarly, the Great Gulf Primitive Area was soon formally designated a national wilderness, but since it was already managed as wilderness there was little dispute over its official dedication. The other national forests were a different matter.

For several years after passage of the Wilderness Act, matters were quiet, reflecting a general lack of regional interest. In the early 1970s, hikers and wilderness advocates in the region gained in numbers and organizational strength. Sierra Club groups were formed in New England and began serious studies of national forest wilderness potential. They finally concluded that about two-thirds of the White Mountain National Forest qualified as wilderness.[10] They were enraged when an extensive Forest Service wilderness review, released in 1972, gave no attention to New England wilderness, and when ongoing national forest land use plans allocated insufficient land to wilderness.[11] To get around the agency's unwillingness, wilderness groups went to Congress with an eastern wilderness bill. They shrewdly lined up Sen. Henry Jackson of Washington, chairman of the Senate Interior Committee, as sponsor.

After a complex legislative fight, the Eastern Wilderness Areas Act of 1974 emerged, designating the Presidential–Dry River Wilderness in New Hampshire and the Bristol Cliffs and Lye Brook Wildernesses in Vermont.[12] The Bristol Cliffs area was ill-planned and drew intense local opposition. Its provisions for including privately owned land were later deleted by an irritated Congress. All of these areas were tiny by western standards; all were second growth on previously logged areas. And they did not satisfy the wilderness advocates, who worked still harder for more.

The next opportunity came in 1977–78, when the Forest Service conducted a new wilderness review (RARE-II). This time, the review included substantial emphasis on eastern areas. Its recommendations emerged from complex deliberations and were transmitted by Pres. Jimmy Carter to the Congress in spring 1979.[13]

The RARE-II evaluation identified six areas in the Green Mountain National Forest, totaling 55,720 acres, as roadless. In its conclusions, however, no areas were recommended as wilderness. In the White Mountains, thirteen areas totaling 262,257 acres were studied—less than half of what the wilderness advocates sought. Of these, three units of about 160,000 acres were recommended for wilderness (table 10). This would represent a sixfold increase in wil-

Table 10. RARE-II Areas, 1979

	Gross Acreages (including private)	Final Recommendation
Vermont		
Breadloaf	19,850	NW
Wilder Mountain	8,590	NW
Devils Den	8,830	NW
Griffith Lake	9,671	NW
Lye Brook Addition	2,660	NW
Woodford	6,120	NW
	55,721	
New Hampshire		
Carr Mountain	17,200	NW
Wild River	46,262	W
Pemigewassett	74,610	W
Sandwich Range	34,084	W
Great Gulf Extension	15,383	FP
Presidential–Dry River Extension	21,011	FP
Waterville	4,200	NW
Kinsman Mountain	8,420	W
Cherry Mountain	9,272	FP
Dartmouth Range	10,142	FP
Mount Wolf–Gordon Pond	12,379	FP
Jobildunk	4,920	FP
Kersarge	4,374	NW
	262,257	

KEY: NW = nonwilderness
FP = further planning
W = wilderness
SOURCE: USDA Forest Service, RARE-II, Final Environmental Statement, 1979.

derness in the White Mountains. Congress has not yet acted on the proposals emerging from RARE-II in New England. Years will pass before the outcome of this struggle over national forest wilderness allocation is settled.

State and Local Wild Areas

State and local governments manage thousands of acres of forest that would qualify for inclusion in the wild forest. These range from the 14,000 acres of natural areas managed by Vermont's Department of Forests and Parks to the municipal watersheds of southern New England. It would include Maine's Bigelow Preserve, although timber will be harvested there. Much of the acreage in state parks would be considered wild forest. Improved land use planning on state and municipal lands may result in more areas being so designated.

Wild and Scenic Rivers

Rivers have formed the central axis of New England's economic history. They have floated logs, powered mills, and carried cargoes, which led to the location of much of the region's manufacturing and settlement along their banks. Most New England rivers work hard—they are everywhere dammed for power and navigation. They carry huge waste outflows from cities and factories. A vigorous tradition of canoe travel in the northwoods has attracted a rapidly growing following and has spawned imitators in calmer southern New England waters.

Surprisingly, however, an active interest in stream fishing and canoeing did not translate itself into a strong citizen movement for river conservation. Perhaps people had written off the poisoned and dammed streams and did not perceive threats to the great northwoods streams—the Allagash, St. Croix, Machias, Penobscot. So, while citizen conservationists labored for the southern New England parks, for the national forests and community preserves, they ignored the rivers.

In the early 1960s, this changed. A new assertiveness for conservation was felt nationally, expressed by Rachel Carson's *Silent Spring*, Stuart Udall's *The Quiet Crisis*, and the spectacular sales of Aldo Leopold's reissued *Sand County Almanac*. The catalog of na-

The controversial Bristol Cliffs Wilderness, Green Mountain National
Forest, Vermont. *Courtesy of USDA Forest Service.*

tional conservation legislation of the decade is notable. This new
movement was also expressed at state levels.

In particular, a movement, led by the Maine Natural Resources
Council, emerged to seek protection of Maine's historic Allagash,
a major nineteenth-century logging river.[14] Its peace and beauty
seemed threatened by a rise in timber harvests and new truck logging roads that were supplanting the river log drives. Unlike many
controversial wild rivers, the Allagash was not subject to any immediate threat from a dam. In 1964, following a massive public controversy and threats of federal designation, the Maine legislature
created the Allagash Wilderness Waterway, from Telos Lake to
below Allagash Falls. A state bond issue was used to buy a narrow protective corridor, and private logging was to be regulated
in a one-half-mile corridor to allow logging consistent with preserving the scenery.

The Allagash was, and remains, the essence of the mystique of
northwoods wilderness canoeing. It is not pristine—it is dammed
in several places and crossed by logging roads. But it retains its wild
atmosphere. Some canoeists complain that, since its designation,

the use level has risen and destroyed the wilderness experience. The Allagash is managed by the Bureau of Parks and Recreation, an agency of the Maine Department of Conservation.

In 1968, the U.S. Congress passed the Wild and Scenic Rivers Act,[15] which designated a series of instant wild rivers on federal lands. It included Maine's Allagash and Wisconsin's Wolf by state request and set a ten-year schedule for federal studies of twenty-seven streams, among them Maine's Penobscot. After publication of the U.S. Bureau of Outdoor Recreation's wild river recommendation in 1976, the state engaged in lengthy negotiations with Great Northern Paper Company, the principal landowner, to develop a protection program. Preferring to manage the river by its own guidelines, the state does not favor federal designation.[16] As of fall 1981, complex legal documents and management plans had been adopted by the Maine Land Use Regulation Commission, which incorporate the plans into its zoning rules for the riverway.

Since passage of the 1968 act, other New England streams have been designated for federal studies.[17] The Housatonic in southwestern Massachusetts and northeastern Connecticut, which flows through a charming green valley filled with estate farms and tidy villages, and under a covered bridge, is one. Its tributary, the Shepaug, is another. Each spring, wet-suited kayakers dare its foaming freshets. In 1980, the St. Croix, along Maine's border with New Brunswick, was being considered as a study river.

New England has spawned innovative efforts to conserve river corridors. One is the Saco River Corridor Association, which administers a zoning program protecting the Saco, a well-used canoe route. This program has been highly successful because of intense local interest and involvement. The Saco, Allagash, and Penobscot efforts all involve private lands, as do the other study streams. Purely private initiative has also been at work. Examples are the Mianus River Gorge Association's work on a tiny creek in New York and Connecticut, and the Coe-Pingree-Brown Company ownership in the Thirteen Mile Woods along the Androscoggin River.[18]

Federal agencies have made their contributions as well. In the Boston area, the U.S. Army Corps of Engineers proposed the purchase of marshlands and easements along the Charles River to preserve channel storage for flood control. The New England River Basins Commission backed a plan, after years of debate, for reducing flood damages in Massachusetts and Connecticut along the

Connecticut River by floodplain management. It recommended against constructing upstream dams, proposed since the 1930s, in Vermont.[19]

Spiraling energy costs have raised interest in small hydroelectric dams, many of them to be rebuilds or expansions of existing dams. Restoring such dams has already generated conflict among power developers, fish and game interests, and lakefront cottagers. The trend could pose concerns for wild river interests as well.

More serious, however, is the booming market for rural real estate and the dramatic cleanup of many badly polluted streams. These include remote streams like the Androscoggin in New Hampshire and the Penobscot below Millinocket. While choked with logs and stinking from pulpmill effluent, these streams offered few attractions. Now being cleaned up, and with fishing improving, they display miles and miles of high-value, developable real estate.

The gains in water and fishery quality on thousands of miles of New England streams are a source of great satisfaction to all concerned with the outdoors. But those gains are likely to be funneled into private pockets unless vigorous public and private effort is exerted to protect riverside corridors and maintain and expand public access points. In many more instances, the taxpayers whose dollars paid for pollution cleanup will go to these streams and find "No Trespassing" signs.

Because much of New England is privately owned, these programs will be difficult and costly. Only one state—Massachusetts—has pursued the issue vigorously. Its wild rivers program reviewed 180 streams and considered 663 miles for a statewide system. The system will include five categories of streams, including recreational urban rivers.[20]

Under a 1971 legislative resolution, the New Hampshire Office of Comprehensive Planning, through a consultant, identified sixty-seven streams of wild, recreational, or scenic importance and outlined a protection program. In Maine, a comprehensive wild rivers data bank project is underway.[21]

The Heritage Conservation and Recreation Service has completed a new national survey of potential wild and scenic rivers. That survey identified about fifty river segments that met the criteria of the 1968 act.[22] This study is to be supplemented by an additional survey of rivers of cultural or recreational significance. When that inventory is completed, New England river conservationists will have a challenging agenda of work before them.

Conclusion

New England has no wilderness, if by wilderness we mean large tracts of untouched virgin forest. Aldo Leopold once wrote that a wilderness ought to be large enough to absorb a two-week pack trip. By that definition, none remains.

But few New Englanders would guess that the region harbors more than a million acres of land in its wild forest, where active land management is banned or restricted in favor of natural processes. Little of this wilderness is in the well-known federal areas—most is privately owned or was conveyed to public agencies by active private groups.

New England expresses a particular pragmatic branch of wilderness politics. In the RARE-II debate, California sued the federal government to compel it to designate more wilderness. In New England, local political leaders threaten dire consequences if the Forest Service designates *any*. The region's largest wilderness, Baxter Park, is owed to the vision and generosity of a single man, not to a popular movement with signs, brochures, petitions, and lobbyists. Maine's 1976 referendum creating the 35,000-acre Bigelow Preserve is the exception, not the rule—and timber cutting is allowed there. Such a wilderness could not pass muster in California.[23]

New Englanders support wildland preservation, but only to a limited degree compared with other regions of the country. They are prepared to allow the logger and builder a place in the landscapes where they hike and camp on weekends. Local groups of snowmobilers in particular oppose wilderness everywhere since it bars use of vehicles.

The region is developing its own approach to the wilderness question, and it is doing it quietly and slowly. Major scenic jewels of New England's landscape have been preserved for nature's slow work. More acres will be devoted to such uses in the future, but only slowly and mostly by strictly private initiatives. As an example, in the 1970s, the private, nonprofit Nature Conservancy acquired more land in Maine than did the Maine Departments of Conservation and Inland Fisheries and Wildlife put together. As in the Appalachian Trail tradition of volunteerism, this arrangement is consistent with New England values and ways of doing things.[24]

I believe that a sensible program of land acquisition and planning for New England would attempt to double the acreage in the wild forest by the year 2000—to 2 million acres. This would still be only

Municipal Watershed, Scituate Reservoir, Providence Water Supply Board, Rhode Island. Such lands are an important part of southern New England's wild forest. *Courtesy of Rhode Island Division of Forest Environment.*

5 percent of the region's land, and the effort should rely heavily on private groups acquiring small, key parcels. A 2-million-acre wild forest would be a prize bequest for this generation to pass to future New Englanders. Since the bulldozers and skidders will be busy, time is not on our side.

If the land could be acquired for $1,000 per acre, the outlay would equal $4 per year for every New England resident. Many acres would be donated and acquired by bargain sale, while others would fetch high prices.

If the forecasters are right, about 2 million more people will live in New England by the year 2000. Providing houses, streets, and shopping centers for these people and for urban emigrants will easily consume another million acres of land and possibly more. It is time to plan for preserving an acre for each acre that will be developed. The price will be cheap, compared with the benefits that will be enjoyed by our grandchildren.

Virgin hemlock stand, Colebrook, Connecticut, 1912. *Courtesy of G. E. Nichols Collection, Yale University.*

CHAPTER 8

Forest Landownership

n important perspective on New England's forest land is achieved by simply asking, "Who owns it?" The ownership of the land will largely determine its uses and its future contribution to New England's economy and landscape.

New England's history of forest landownership is a rich and colorful one, reaching back to original Indian occupancy and royal claims based on discovery and conquest. Some Indian claims are being reasserted, but that story will not occupy us here. In the original distribution of the land from royal ownership to private hands, New England exhibited official corruption, timber stealing, and speculation leading to fortunes and bankruptcy. Because of chaotic, overlapping royal land grants and poor surveying, land titles were uncertain in northern frontier areas for generations, where many titles were obtained by squatting.

At times, big speculators and royal governors amassed large holdings, as in the 2-million-acre Maine Purchase of William Bingham, and the New Hampshire holdings of Benning Wentworth and his family. These empires collapsed under inadequate markets for wilderness land or dissolved in periodic financial panics. Their names remain on maps of Maine and New Hampshire, but their original owners are long forgotten.

In early days of the colonies, English monarchs made extensive land grants to favored royal associates. The Great Proprietors (like John Mason and Sir Ferdinando Gorges), the Lincoln proprietors, and the Kennebec proprietors controlled vast unsurveyed frontier domains, hoping to convert them into thriving communities, enriching their owners through trade and land sales.[1] Gorges was the earliest great landholder in Maine. He is said to have dreamed of establishing a full-blown medieval society in Maine, where he would be the absentee lord, gathering wealth through rents and duties paid by local barons and tenants owing him fealty. Of course, these efforts all quickly failed, and New England led the new nation in the wide distribution of landownership. This pattern prevailed until the end of large-scale land disposal in northern New England, between 1780 and 1878.

New England land passed into private ownership over the period 1620–1878. This is an astoundingly long period, spanning the entire history of the nation until the very peak of agricultural growth in southern New England. During this time, New England remained a major factor in national manufacturing, shipbuilding, finance, and trade. By contrast, most of the land held by the federal government was disposed of in less than a century after the Louisiana Purchase.

Land distribution in southern New England was virtually complete by the Revolution. The bulk of the land there was owned by farmers; little was retained for public purposes. These colonies did not go through a long stage of massive private landholdings because, by and large, towns were sold or granted one by one for settlement, not in large blocks. They were not held for long periods in speculative hands, but for the most part were quickly settled.

Patterns of Forest Landownership

The best statistics on forest ownership in New England are U.S. Forest Service estimates, based on the best available surveys and data sources. At times, the figures reflect differing definitions or administrative choices about land use (wilderness) rather than actual forested area. Since the most convenient figures are for commercial forest land area, they will be used here. Assessing the forest this way emphasizes economic values, not ecological ones. Commercial forest is land that is available for timber harvesting and is also capable of growing more than twenty cubic feet of wood per acre per year. This is about one-fourth of a cord, or a pile of four-foot sticks two feet high and four feet long. Commercial forest land does not include about half a million acres of forested land not available for timber cutting because of wilderness designations, and almost a million acres that is forested but of extremely low timber productivity, such as spruce and tamarack bogs. About half of the noncommercial forest land in New England is in Maine.

New England's forests are 94 percent private, with equal acreages in the nonfarm holdings less than 500 acres in size, and in industrial and large holdings (table 11). Nonprofit groups hold about 1 percent of the region's forest. The public forest estate is about 7 percent of the total, comprising roughly equal amounts of federal and state land, and a county and municipal share roughly equivalent to the nonprofit sector.

Few large land holdings have persisted. In Connecticut, the largest parcels held by private individuals are roughly 5,000 acres. The larger state forests and the 20,000- to 30,000-acre ownerships of several major water companies were laboriously assembled by buying up one farm after another. Because of this history, the basic unit of trading in land in southern New England has traditionally been the individual farm or "lot," usually surveyed but often laid out by metes and bounds. The typical sizes of these farms varied in different parts of New England, but a 100-acre size was common in northern New England. Many of these lots acquired the names of their early owners and are so indicated even on tax records.

From dominating landownership in southern New England, farmers have vanished rapidly. The decline of farming after the mid nineteenth century still left land in the hands of farmers. But from the mid twentieth century, farmers sold land rapidly—first to "summer people," then to tract developers, investors, and recreational subdividers. Improved roads and widespread automobile ownership have promoted rural subdivision and recreational land pur-

Table 11. Ownership of Commercial Forest Land, 1970s

Owner	Acres (millions)	Percentage
Private		
Nonfarm, less than 50,000 acres	13.1	42
Industrial	9.8	32
Large nonindustrial timbergrowing (50,000 acres or more)	3.4	11
Farm	2.4	8
Nonprofit	0.3	1
Total private	29.0	94
Public		
Federal	0.8	2
State	1.0	3
Local	0.3	1
Total public	2.1	6
Total	31.1	100

SOURCE: USDA-FS, *Analysis*, and author's estimates.

Many small woodlots participate in the American Tree Farm program, which recognizes more than 40,000 landowners for sound forest management. *Courtesy of American Forest Institute.*

chases. On the fringes of the industrial forest, paper companies have been active buyers of farms.

Regionwide, from 1952 to 1977, much of the forest land remaining in farmers' hands was sold—a total of 5.4 million acres (table 12), or one out of every six forested acres in New England. Farmers sold three-fourths of the land they owned in 1880 in the succeeding century. The land sold, however, retains a profound imprint in its parcel size, land use, and forest condition from its period in farm ownership. Farmers owned most of Connecticut's forest in the nineteenth century, but only 7 percent in 1977—though this was out of a forest area double what it had been in the nineteenth century.

Land Booms

From colonial times to recent decades, the boom-and-bust cycles of New England have left behind growing forests. The booms up to the 1840s were speculative. They rearranged ownership of the land but not its timber stands. The mast trade and shipbuilding booms resulted from technical and market trends. They were not halted by timber exhaustion but by changes in shipping that made the products obsolete. With that bust went the employment base of many coastal towns, especially in Maine.

Table 12. Forest Landownership Trends and Patterns, 1952 and 1977

State and Year	All Owners	Thousand Acres (Percent of Total)						
		Public				Private		
		All	Federal	State	County & Municipal	Total	Forest Industry	Farm
Connecticut								
1977	1,805.6	146.6 (8)	2.4 (–)	119.8 (7)	24.4 (1)	1,659.0 (92)	0.0 (0)	128.3 (7)
1952	1,973.0	159.0 (8)	1.0 (–)	122.0 (7)	32.0 (1)	1,818.0 (92)	3.0 (–)	670.0 (34)
Percent Change 52–77	–8	–5	+240	–2	–25	–9	–100	–80
Maine								
1977	16,864.0	541.0 (3)	73.3 (–)	393.7 (2)	114.0 (1)	16,323.0 (97)	8,082.8 (48)	1,093.3 (6)
1952	16,609.4	182.0 (1)	90.0 (–)	41.0 (–)	51.0 (–)	16,427.4 (99)	6,617.0 (40)	2,923.0 (18)
Percent Change 52–77	+2	+197	–19	+760	+120	–	+22	–63
Massachusetts								
1977	2,797.7	365.4 (13)	9.6 (–)	240.1 (8)	115.7 (4)	2,432.3 (87)	30.1 (1)	253.6 (9)
1952	3,259.0	399.0 (12)	29.0 (1)	280.0 (8)	90.0 (3)	2,860.0 (88)	259.0 (8)	887.0 (27)
Percent Change 52–77	–14	–8	–69	–14	+28	–15	–88	–71
New Hampshire								
1977	4,692.0	579.7 (12)	471.6 (10)	79.2 (2)	28.9 (1)	4,112.3 (88)	946.9 (20)	215.4 (4)
1952	4,818.6	682.0 (14)	585.0 (12)	45.0 (1)	52.0 (1)	4,136.6 (86)	771.0 (18)	1,333.0 (28)
Percent change 52–77	–3	–15	–19	+75	–44	–	+23	–84

Rhode Island								
1977	393.5	32.1 (8)	0 (0)	20.1 (5)	12.0 (3)	363.2 (92)	0 (0)	24.6 (6)
1952	430.0	26.0 (6)	0 (0)	13.0 (3)	13.0 (3)	404.0 (94)	0 (0)	104.0 (24)
Percent change 52–77	−8	+23	—	+54	−8	−10	—	−77
Vermont								
1977	4,429.9	422.0 (10)	212.8 (5)	168.2 (4)	41.0 (1)	4,007.9 (90)	668.3 (15)	646.9 (15)
1952	3,845.9	297.0 (8)	199.0 (5)	79.0 (2)	19.0 (–)	3,548.9 (92)	528.0 (14)	1,925.0 (50)
Percent change 52–77	+15	+42	+6	+112	+115	+13	+26	−66
Region total								
1977	30,984.5	2,086.8 (7)	769.7 (2)	981.1 (3)	336.0 (1)	28,897.7 (93)	9,726.1 (31)	2,362.1 (8)
1952	30,935.9	1,741.0 (6)	904.0 (3)	580.0 (2)	257.0 (1)	29,194.9 (94)	8,178.0 (26)	7,842.0 (25)
Acreage change	+48.6	+345.8	−134.3	+401.1	+79	−297.2	1,548.1	5,479.9
Percent change	—	+20	−15	+69	+30	−1	+19	−70

SOURCE: USDA-FS, *Analysis*, app. 3.

It has been written that if the country had been settled from West to East, much of New England would remain a wilderness. This may be so. But in fact, millions of acres of forest were cleared, mostly in a brief period of growth from 1790 to 1880. The farms scratched out of the forest simply could not provide reasonable livelihoods and could not compete with midwestern farms. In the vast contraction of settlement and farming after 1880, forests reclaimed millions of acres, as Torbert put it, in "a rising sea of woodlands." Though soils may have been degraded during this interlude, it was the impersonal market for crops and labor that released these lands to forests, not any decline in the land itself. Poorer lands are now farmed productively in Europe, after centuries of utilization. A brief sheep boom from the 1840s to the 1880s was but an episode in this longer expansion and retreat of farming.

The northwoods saw rapid lumber expansion in the 1840s through the 1890s. The log drives on the Penobscot peaked in 1872. This boom was ended by the exhaustion of large pine and spruce, and by competition from cheap West Coast lumber, which was opened to the midwestern market by rail in the 1880s and to the East Coast by the Panama Canal in 1919. Again, exhaustion of the forest itself was not the cause.

From the 1890s to the 1920s, southern New England was swept by the "boxboard boom." Hundreds of tiny mills cut low-grade boards and box shook from old field pines, pushing the region's lumber output to its all-time peak of about 3 billion feet in 1909. The current lumber cut is only about 1 billion.

In the north, a pulpmill boom followed the wane of the sawmill business, making New England the source of one-third of the nation's pulp and paper by World War I. Because of more favorable profit opportunities elsewhere, New England papermaking grew only slowly for the next half-century. By the mid seventies, a new competitive vigor swept the northwoods and created a broad increase in paper, sawmilling, and waferboard capacity.

These lumber and paper booms again reflect outside market forces, relative costs, and corporate investment calculations. They also reflect changing perceptions of timber supply conditions as well. But they have all left behind a producing, growing forest.

The expansion now underway is of a different character. The speculative land boom of the sixties and seventies, described in chapter 6, significantly reduced the productive potential of a large area of forests. This was not a biological change but simply the result of parcel fragmentation and absentee ownership, together with scattered residential and commercial development creating local vested interests opposed to forest disturbance.

Suburban development after World War II was much more wasteful of land than previous development. Farms and woodlands vanished before the bulldozers with alarming speed. In Connecticut, by the early 1970s, land clearing was the principal cause of timber removals.

The consumption and fragmentation of land and spiraling land prices have threatened much of the region's agriculture with extinction, but have left behind a substantial suburban forest. Continued wasteful sprawl, however, could eliminate that forest in a few decades.

The commitments of forest to houses, pavements, and tiny isolated parcels are largely permanent in terms of forest values of wood, wildlife, and amenity. The suburban sprawl of the post-1950 era will not be a transitory feature of the region's landscape.

The energy crisis of the 1970s spurred a dramatic fuelwood boom that has brought the use of wood for energy back up to a par with the paper industry's consumption. If the use of wood for fuel continues to rise and is sustained, overcutting of the forest is possible in some areas.

As the above discussion shows, stability in land use and ownership is not characteristic of New England's history. Instead, waves of land use change sweep the region over long periods. This will continue to occur, modifying the region's forests and their uses.

Industrial Forest Owners

Wood-using companies, especially those in the capital-intensive pulp and paper industry, have found it desirable to supply a certain proportion of their wood needs from their own land. Over the years, they have built an impressive empire in northern New England, where valuable trees grow well and where large acreage blocks were available. Today, no major firm acquires all of its wood needs from its own land. They buy wood from the large nonindustrial owners and individual truckloads from farmers and weekend woodcutters. They also sell large volumes to others who process species that their own mills do not use, whose mills are more favorably located, or who can offer a better price.

The forest industries now own 32 percent of the region's commercial forest. Most of the industry ownership is in Maine, where fully 49 percent of the forest is owned by large pulp, paper, and lumber companies. An additional 20 percent of Maine's forest is owned by large landholders who do not own mills but are in the business of selling pulpwood and sawlogs to Maine and Canadian mills. Several of these massive holdings, of 150,000 acres and more (equal to all the public forest in Connecticut), are owned by direct descendants of the men who bought the towns in the 1840s.

In Maine, forest industries have added 1.6 million acres to their holdings since 1952. In the three northern New England states, perhaps three dozen firms control 10 million acres of forest—an empire *twice* the size of southern New England's entire forest area. In these vast domains, local government is often absent, and population is low—only a few thousand people live year-round in the entire ownership. Several owners dominate the scene. The three largest industrial owners control 4 million acres. The largest is the Great Northern Paper Company, which owns just over 2 million acres.

In Maine and northern New Hampshire, a special form of land ownership persists. This is "common and undivided" ownership, a survival from two colonial practices. The colonies sold or granted towns to groups of buyers, each of whom exercised one "right" in the town. Many southern New England towns were sold to groups of thirty to fifty owners. Some promptly sold their rights, seeking greener pastures. Some accumulated rights in groups of towns. Many settled the lands they acquired. The Massachusetts lottery towns of eastern Maine were sold in this way after the Revolution. Where districts were later settled, the rights were located on the ground by various methods, usually in such a way as to assure equitable distribution of a village lot, and some marsh, woods, and good tillable land to each right-holder. In some instances, the holding of rights in common and undivided form ("unlocated") persisted.[2] In Maine, the state itself held—and still does to this day—some of its reserved lands in undivided ownership.

The second root of this ownership pattern was the leading role of shipowners and merchants in early Maine land investment and speculation. These men, like David Pingree of Salem, Massachusetts; were accustomed to owning undivided shares in individual ships. They naturally applied the same concept to joint ventures in land. This helped amass capital and spread risk, and allowed owners to take in partners readily by selling undivided interests. Common tenancy also minimized the cost of subdividing distant and poorly surveyed parcels. Division of estates among heirs was also simplified. As a result of such repeated divisions, some towns are now owned in minute fractional interests (table 13). Their interests are looked after by large land management firms, like Maine's Seven Islands Land Company, Prentiss and Carlisle, or James W. Sewall Company. Common and undivided ownership has worked well for forest owners in northern New England wildlands, and towns are rarely partitioned among owners. The majority owners or their representatives normally make management decisions and send cotenants their share of net revenues.

The recent drive toward intensive management has led some owners to work for 100 percent ownership by trading out cotenants. These rearrangements at times involve large acreages. For various other reasons, owners from time to time trade land with one another, to straighten boundaries or render their holdings more convenient to their mills, but the basic pattern appears durable.

In Maine, the state is a common and undivided owner with private companies and individuals in many towns. The state holds many unlocated "public lots" reserved from sale in the nineteenth century but never laid out on the ground. The state receives its income share from the manager of the majority interests. In a few large parcels, the state is a majority owner and shares its revenues with the minority owners. These public-private cotenancies have

Table 13. Common and Undivided Interests in
the Northwest Quarter, Township 11, Range 4,
WELS, Aroostook County, Maine

Owner	Interest
Irving Pulp and Paper Co., Ltd.	66/180
Prentiss and Carlisle Co., Inc.	4/180
McCrillis Timberlands, Inc.*	1/180
State of Maine, Bureau of Public Lands	23/180
E.G. Dunn Heirs	33/180
Fernald Group, E.G. Dunn Heirs	23/180
Marjorie D. Fernald	20/180
Peter Dunn Heirs	10/180

SOURCE: Maine Bureau of Public Lands.
   NOTE: This table includes common and undivided interests in the quarter town, and in the timber and grass on the public lot. T11R4 lies southwest of Presque Isle, Maine. The northwest quarter is northwest of Squapan Lake.
* Managed by Prentiss and Carlisle. This 1/180 interest is equivalent to about 30 acres.

over the years worked to the satisfaction of all parties and there is no immediate urge to sort them out, except as a by-product of land trades pursued for other objectives.

New England's Public Forest Estate

New England has a rich and diverse public forest estate. Most of this estate was acquired by purchase or tax default in the twentieth century—after the public values of forests for recreation, watershed protection, wildlife habitat, and timbergrowing became appreciated.[3] Citizen interest in protecting especially scenic areas and important watersheds like the White Mountains was high.

A minor portion of the public estate traces back to reservations from land sales made to provide for local schools and churches. The "public lots" in Maine's unorganized towns and Vermont's "glebe lands" are the notable examples.[4] Sizable portions of the public estate were acquired by donations made by wealthy individuals—the grandest examples being Baxter State Park (Gov. Percival Baxter) and Acadia National Park (John D. Rockefeller and others). In southern New England, public parks, forests, and water supply lands were pieced together from abandoned farms, brushlands, and cutover. Eager foresters planted pines on every bare acre they could, and many such plantations have already yielded one or more harvest of wood.

The White Mountain and Green Mountain National Forests were acquired under the 1911 Weeks Act, which authorized federal purchases of land for national forests in the East. Much of the land so acquired had only been in private hands for several decades and had been skinned by lumber companies; it was often tax delinquent.

Despite its pioneering role in forestry, conservation, and parks, and its longstanding conservation traditions, New England remains a region of private forest ownership. Only 6 percent of the region's commercial forest is publicly owned. In many cases, these lands are of poor or degraded productivity for commercial timber. In the past most public units have been plagued by inadequate wood markets. The need to acquire the lands by purchase has been a decided hindrance in a region of small local governments jealous of their local tax base and opposed to landholding by distant senior governments. Until recently—and even today in parts of northern New England—overabundant timber, general public access to privately owned land, and the absence of immediate threats to green spaces have minimized the perception of a need for public land acquisition, except for wildlife and hunting, and the occasional park, extraordinary scenic point, or boat ramp. Much of the dispersed recreation activity in northern New England occurs on private land.

Slight additions to federal ownership have been offset by significant allocations of land to wilderness and limited use, so that federal commercial forest acreage fell by 15 percent from 1952 to 1977. The federal agencies—especially the U.S. Forest Service, which administers the Green and White Mountain National Forests—owned about 2.4 percent of New England's commercial forest in the late 1970s. As further wilderness allocations are made in these forests, federal commercial forest will decline somewhat further, though the timbergrowing potential will not fall significantly because the wilderness lands tend to have low productivity.

States and counties have aggressively added to their landholdings, through bond issues, federal grants for parks and wildlife habitat, donations, and other measures.[5] The net increase in commercial forest owned by states and counties was 250,000 acres from 1952 to 1977. At times in the past, especially during the Great Depression, states and counties acquired land through tax delinquency, but never on the scale that occurred in the Lake States, where millions of acres fell into the hands of states and counties through tax forfeiture.

Nonindustrial Private Owners

About 13 million acres of New England forest is owned by individuals like you and me—who hold small parcels as parts of a residence or recreation property, as a farm bought for a vacation retreat, or as an investment. While these owners are highly varied and may live in other states and regions, they have been of considerable interest to foresters. The owners of many small tracts seem uninterested in investing in woodgrowing, in selling timber, in allowing public recreation, in managing for wildlife, or even tolerating hunters. In some areas, however, owner preferences are changing.

Because these owners hold such a vast acreage, they control the key to industrial and fuelwood production in most of New England, outside the industrial forest.

Because of busy real estate markets, a predominance of speculative motives, and our national mobility, ownership of land is highly unstable. Compared with the Dunn or Pingree heirs of Maine, who still hold lands acquired soon after 1840, the average period of tenure in most of New England is short. In southern New England, lands held twenty years or longer by the same individual amount to 25 percent of the owners but 29 percent of the land. Fourteen percent of the land was owned less than five years. In New Hampshire and Vermont, the figures are similar, with fully 37 percent of the landholders owning less than five years.[6] This figure undoubtedly reflects rapid population growth in southern New Hampshire and the speculative land sales boom in these states of the 1960s and 1970s. This pace of ownership turnover may be of little consequence in itself for aesthetic, investment, and some wildlife values of forest land. Such high turnover, however, does not help in establishing long-term plans for timber management and reduces the chance that owners will apply management treatments with deferred returns.

The size distribution of forest land ownership in New England is highly skewed—between Great Northern's 2 million acres, and the suburbanite's one-fourth acre. Of an estimated 455,000 forest landowners in the region, only 8 percent own more than 100 acres. These 8 percent, however, account for 76 percent of the private land (table 14). In southern New England, 1.9 million acres of forest remain in nonindustrial holdings larger than 100 acres (though they may consist of more than one parcel). The number of forest

Table 14. Forest Acreage by Ownership Size Class, New England, 1970s

Size Class	Vermont	New Hampshire	Southern New England	Maine[a]
1–19 acres	164,100	262,500	708,500	319,200
20–99	840,100	740,200	1,825,000	896,800
100–199	772,500	604,700	911,300	733,400
200–499	946,300	596,800	624,000	722,000
500+	1,265,300	1,877,900	385,700	14,222,600
Total commercial forest land[b]	3,988,300	4,082,100	4,454,500	16,894,000
In ownerships 100 acres or more	2,085,100	3,079,400	1,921,000	15,678,000

[a] Maine: estimated data for illustrative purposes only.
[b] The total forest land areas shown here do not match those shown in Table 12 because different time periods were used.
SOURCES: Kingsley, *The forest-landowners of southern New England*; Kingsley and Birch, *The forest-landowners of New Hampshire and Vermont*; author estimates for Maine. Maine estimated based on 3.8 million acres of land owned by small owners outside of the spruce-fir region, distributed by size class in the same way as New Hampshire nonindustrial owners, using data from R. H. Ferguson and N. P. Kingsley, *The timber resources of Maine*, USDA-FS NEFES, Res. Bull. NE-26, 1972.

Table 15. Number of Forest Landowners by Parcel Size Class, 1970s

	99 Acres or Less	100 Acres or More	Total
New Hampshire	80,200	7,300	87,500
Vermont	65,800	11,500	77,300
Southern New England	174,300	9,800	184,100
Maine	98,100	8,900	107,000
Total	418,400	37,500	455,900

SOURCES: Same as table 14, plus author estimate.

landowners in New England has been rising. In Connecticut from 1946 to 1973, the overall number of owners almost doubled, with the largest increase occurring in the 1- to 9-acre size class. In that category the number of owners multiplied tenfold but only increased its ownership from 22,000 to 152,000 acres. In northern New England, the number of nonindustrial forest owners increased from 155,000 in the late 1940s to 272,000 in the 1970s, so the median size of holding declined. The median size of forest holding is now below 10 acres in New Hampshire, Massachusetts, and Connecticut, and only slightly larger in Vermont and Rhode Island. This is dramatically down from medians clustering around 40 acres in 1945.[7]

We could consider a size of 100 acres to indicate potential for serious future timber management, though some foresters would use 50 acres. At 100 acres, there are only 37,500 nonindustrial owners, plus a few dozen industrial and land management concerns, who really count in New England's industrial wood supply (table 15; fig. 8). This is not to say that timber cutting and some management will not occur on the smaller tracts, only to emphasize how few owners control the best management opportunities. Parcels in this size class present the most attractive opportunities for wildlife management and are most likely to remain available for public recreation.

Ninety-two percent of the owners control a small total acreage of land, hold their properties for brief periods, and own too little land to be interested in planned timber management for financial gain. These tiny tracts are hard to harvest because they usually cannot supply enough wood to make a job economically attractive. Traditionally, logging jobs on ten to twenty acres have received few bids unless the wood was standing next to a mill or was all veneer logs.

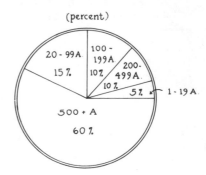

Figure 8. New England Private
Forest Acreage by Ownership
Size Class.

Better timber markets and the fuelwood market are making small
sales more common.

Nongovernmental, Nonprofit Organizations

New England has fostered a vigorous and diverse community of
nonprofit groups that own land for education, research, conservation, and preservation. I would estimate that 300,000 acres of land,
mostly forest, are owned by these groups. The region's long history
of scientific research and its strong private universities have provided some of the largest and the best-known properties, such as
the Harvard Forest. The region was an early home of the conservation movement: the Audubon societies, the Nature Conservancy,
and hiking groups play strong roles as major landholders.

New Englanders have always been energetic founders of local organizations. The state-level conservation groups, like the Massachusetts Trustees of Reservations and the Society for the Protection
of New Hampshire Forests, operate major preserve systems. The
trustees, with a total ownership of nearly 20,000 acres, have a seasonal staff of more than seventy people, a permanent staff, and hold
very special places like Bartholomew's Cobble in southwestern
Massachusetts.

Land ownership is pursued by a bewildering variety of local Audubon chapters, hunting clubs, and community recreation groups,
such as the Boy Scouts, churches, and YMCAs. In the aggregate
these groups must be important landholders though no detailed figures are available. In the region's pattern of forest use, they are important because they preserve shorelines and other significant lands

Nonprofit forest: Bartholomew's Cobble, Massachusetts, owned by the Trustees of Reservations. *Courtesy of Trustees of Reservations.*

from development. In some cases, the lands may be available for timber harvesting.[8]

A special institution that apparently developed in New England is the land conservation trust, which is especially common in southern New England. These trusts are usually based in a single town. They acquire small but sensitive habitats like bogs, salt marshes, and woodlands for preservation and recreation. They use intensive fund-raising methods but rely heavily on outright land donations.

They have been able to acquire and manage a multitude of tiny properties. Being community-based, they are able to identify and acquire small tracts without the resentment that often accompanies state and federal land purchases. The lack of county-level governments in New England has made government an especially blunt instrument for identifying and meeting local land conservation needs. New England communities have faced intense suburban growth, farmland conversion, and loss of natural amenity. The established farmers and wealthy suburban families have contributed extensively, in land gifts and in dollars, to making land trusts and state groups important features of the New England conservation scene.

In southern New England, the nonprofit sector rivals state government as a landowner, measured by acreage. In general, the private groups have devoted more energy to expanding ownership and developing effective public use and interpretation programs than have state agencies.

Though traditionally tax-exempt as charitable and educational institutions, New England's nonprofit landholders are under increasing pressure as taxes rise, especially in suburban and coastal areas. Revenue-strapped towns refuse to accept tax exemptions readily. Some groups must pay property taxes on some of their lands, which dilutes their fund-raising efforts. An increasingly skeptical public attitude toward tax exemptions must be countered by aggressive efforts to demonstrate the public benefits of conserving open space.

Overview

Forest landownership in New England has gone through major waves of change. The land passed almost entirely into private hands over two and a half centuries. But in the late nineteenth century, public and nonprofit groups began a land acquisition drive that has returned at least 2 million acres to public or nonprofit ownership. Since 1880, farmers have sold land, retreating from ownership of fully half of the land. The most stable ownership has been the large nonfamily holdings of northern Maine and New Hampshire. Since the 1890s, industry has acquired, and sold and resold among different companies, almost a third of the region's landscape.

Recent trends in rural landownership have radically increased the number of owners—to almost half a million. The median size of a forest parcel is now about ten acres outside of the industrial forest.

George Washington State Management Area, Rhode Island. Killing the overtopping hardwoods has released these pines. *Courtesy of Rhode Island Division of Forest Environment.*

Despite the trend toward parcelization, fully three-fourths of New England's forest is owned by only 37,500 individuals and companies. These are the ownerships of 100 acres and larger. Though a good deal of wood will be produced on tracts below 100 acres, the opportunities for serious long-term management are greatest above this size. The good news for timber and wildlife management, and public access, is that this category accounts for most of the region's forest, and involves a fairly small number of landowners.[9]

CHAPTER 9

New England's Timber Budget

 perspective on New England's forest that is perhaps unique to foresters is that of the timber budget. Using statistical samples, foresters try to estimate tree growth, the harvest, and losses to mortality. From such estimates, they can determine if the current cut is sustainable, assess management measures, and make recommendations about industrial developments. As for a woodlot, also for a region. This chapter reviews the history of New England's timber budget and the current condition of the forest.

Colonial Times to 1920

Until the mid twentieth century, statisticians, foresters, and industrialists were unable to calculate the balance of New England's timber budget with precision. Data on timber inventories did not exist. Instead, people faced direct and dramatic evidence of the local timber situation. In the earliest Massachusetts Bay settlements, fuelwood and building material scarcity made some locations less desirable for settlement, as William Wood commented in his *New England's Prospect*, published in the 1630s. In Boston as early as 1637–38, fuelwood was seriously short. Later in the century, Boston was regularly importing fuelwood, and the shipbuilding towns of Cape Cod were importing ship timber. By 1690, Rhode Island colonists were relying heavily on construction and ship timber brought in from elsewhere.[1] Winter fuelwood shortages were commonly felt by the urban poor. Town officials took steps to supply fuelwood for the indigent as early as 1635.

So even before the Revolution, the timber budgets of local regions were clearly evident to all, if not in quantitative terms of acres, cords, growth, and cut, at least in practical everyday business terms. In these years, local overseers of the poor distributed fuelwood to the needy, a tradition that survives in parts of rural New England. Schoolteachers and ministers were paid partly in fuelwood, and widows were provided with fuelwood in the wills of deceased husbands—customs that may yet reemerge.

By the 1690s, His Majesty was being squeezed by the Baltic timber merchants. The lords of the admiralty were nervous about the
ease with which an opponent could cut off shipments from that region by blocking the Danish straits. This situation stimulated their
interest in North American sources of masts and tar. The Broad Arrow Acts, passed beginning in 1691, implemented a policy of re-
serving large pine, twenty-four inches in diameter and up, for the
king, on all unappropriated lands in New England. This policy produced a colorful history of pine-rustling, sporadic arrests by timber
agents, stealing by the agents themselves, and general irritation
among rural colonials against the distant monarch's policies. It also
produced large amounts of twenty-three-inch paneling in colonial
houses.[2]

The mast trade revealed the changing geography of a specialized
resource—large straight pine and spruce trees—under a primitive
transportation system. The mast traders moved slowly north from
the Merrimack and its tributaries to the Piscataqua and the Maine
coastal streams. By the mid eighteenth century, Falmouth, Maine,
became the major masting port. From stream after stream, the best
mast pines close to water were cut, skidded to water by oxen, and
floated out.

During the nineteenth century, farmland clearing reached its
zenith, railroad and industrial use of fuelwood achieved enormous
proportions, the wooden shipbuilding industry peaked and declined, and the center of the nation's lumber industry moved westward. The region's timber budget was visible in the long distances
fuelwood was shipped—from the Maine coast to Boston; down the
Connecticut River to Long Island and New York. It was also evident in the import of timber for ships. By 1850, local wood no
longer met the needs of the Essex and Gloucester yards.[3] Because of
its rising population and industry, the region ceased to be self-sufficient in lumber after 1880–90.[4] In the mid nineteenth century,
Connecticut probably consumed five to ten times as much wood as
it did a century later—and this volume was harvested from half as
much forest land.

The statistics of lumber production told the story clearly:

	New England (billion board feet)	United States (billion board feet)	New England as % of United States
1869	1.4	12.8	11
1879	1.5	18.1	8

1889	1.7	27.0	6
1899	2.2	35.1	6
1909	3.0	44.5	7

After the Civil War, lumber industry growth was in the Midwest, South, and West.[5]

The regional statistics concealed local declines, mirrored in falling employment in major lumber towns like Bangor, the coastal Maine lumber ports, and large milltowns along the Connecticut River. From the 1890s to the 1920s, a brief boxboard boom throughout southern New England boosted production there, so that all the region's states experienced production peaks about 1907–09, at a level of roughly 3 billion feet.[6]

Even by the 1840s, New Englanders were cutting pines from stands grown on farmlands that were abandoned before the Revolution. They were still clearing land, but at a diminishing pace. Sizable areas, as on coastal islands and Cape Cod, had been denuded of forest cover by generations of fuelwood cutting and sheep grazing.

Even before the Revolution, several indicators of changes in the region's timber budget were clear. These indicators reflected specialized product requirements (as for masts) or high transport costs (as for fuelwood). They mirrored the changing geography of national lumber production as the vast pineries were opened up in New York, Pennsylvania, and the Midwest. The New England forest was never literally "cut out." Its utilization simply shifted in response to changing economic needs.

In 1846, George B. Emerson wrote his "Report on the Trees and Shrubs Growing Naturally in the Forests of Massachusetts." He urged that a comprehensive forest survey be conducted and listed the familiar values lost by forest devastation—their aesthetic value, shade, healthfulness, and usefulness for building materials. He noted that in the coastal towns, most wood was already imported. He estimated the fuelwood consumption of the average family at thirteen to fourteen cords per year, at a price of four dollars per cord.[7]

Even in the nineteenth century, merchants accepted fuelwood in payment for debts. During the Civil War, urban fuelwood prices rose, and cordwood was sent by water to New York from Maine. A search of New England state boards of agriculture reports from the Civil War to the turn of the century will yield a large harvest of essays and speeches decrying forest destruction and urging planting, research, and fire control.

In the late nineteenth century, New Englanders became more concerned about the region's timber budget. They noted the decline of lumber output in its traditional regions, the expanding acreages of unproductive abandoned pasture, the losses to fire, and the continually increasing demand.

In 1864, George Perkins Marsh decried the destruction of forests in North America and the damage to rivers from log driving. He argued, "I doubt whether any one of the American States, except perhaps Oregon, has, at this moment, more woodland than it ought permanently to preserve."[8] In the same paragraph, he admitted that the scant market value of forest land gave slight incentive for owning it. He attributed the general waste and plunder of forests to this cause and noted that "the diffusion of general intelligence" on forest values would be the only source of improvement in this situation, as legislation could not be expected to correct private mismanagement.

In his 1874 national report on forest policy, F. B. Hough noted New England's situation but only in passing—an indication that the region's economic prominence in the timber industry had already faded.[9]

A few hardy workers began to examine their local timber budgets in a more rigorous and quantitative way. In 1875, the New Hampshire Forest Commission reported on the loss of timber volume in wasteful cutting, and the prospect of imminent exhaustion of the forests around the White Mountains.[10] In the late 1890s, pioneer forester Austin Cary conducted a detailed personal field survey of the timber in Maine woods.[11] Since river log driving was the only transportation, he reckoned the timber situation by river drainages—the Androscoggin, Kennebec, Penobscot. He showed the trend in log drives and assessed remaining timber stands. In many areas he found that previous cuttings, taking only large trees, had left behind well-stocked stands for new harvests. By 1919, the forest commissioner of Maine was able to estimate the remaining stand of timber in Maine. He estimated that the timber cut exceeded the growth by tenfold.[12]

In Connecticut, foresters conducted a rough survey of the state's forests in 1913, yielding the first statistical picture of forest area and condition in that state. The first survey of Massachusetts, re-

Sawmill, North Colebrook, Connecticut, 1912, just after lumber output in New England passed its historic peak. *Courtesy of G. E. Nichols Collection, Yale University.*

ported in 1929, took state foresters fourteen years to complete![13]

A report on Rhode Island, issued by the state's Agricultural Experiment Station in 1902, listed a significant increase in forest area from 1887 (24 percent of the state) to 1900 (40 percent); the forests were mostly overcut coppice. Only thirty-three tiny sawmills cut a meagre 18 million board feet per year of mostly pine lumber.[14]

Regional Surveys, 1920–76

The first statistical overview of New England's timber budget was prepared in 1920 by the U.S. Forest Service. The foresters painted a lurid picture of the evils then occurring and to be expected from timber depletion, rising prices of lumber, and concentrated ownership of timberland.[15] The national picture at that time was grim: 326 million acres of cutover forest; 8 to 10 million acres of forest fires per year; rising lumber prices; companies overcutting because of overextended financing; burdensome taxation. Comprehensive forest policy and agencies to implement it were lacking.

The foresters made their best estimate of New England's forest conditions. In using these statistics, and in comparing them with later surveys, it must be remembered that they are based on limited data, a good deal of judgment, and on prices and marketing standards of the times. They cannot be compared with more recent estimates prepared using statistical sampling, field plot measurements, aerial photos, and broader standards of commercial usefulness. For example, different species are now cut, and smaller trees are now used. But each forest survey shows the best knowledge at the time, which informed people's understanding of events. Since it was on those understandings that legislators, governors, administrators, and industrialists made policy, the view of the time is significant even if statistically weak by current standards.

The federal foresters estimated that New England still had 2 million acres of "virgin" forest left in 1920—this must have been largely hardwood in northern Maine, New Hampshire, and Vermont, on rough terrain far from drivable water. The remaining productive sawtimber covered 8.8 million acres, cordwood covered 8.4 million, and nonstocked lands reached the shocking total of 5.4 million.

The timber budget in 1920 was not reassuring. Annual growth of 475 million cubic feet was far exceeded by total drain (products removed plus mortality) of 670 million. About one-third of the drain was for fuelwood and posts. For sawtimber-sized trees, the drain was three and a half times the growth, raising the prospect of severe future problems for lumber supply. Regional lumber output had already fallen dramatically from its prewar peak. Just after World War I, the region that had led the nation a century earlier (and that now has 6 percent of the nation's commercial forest) supplied only 2 percent of national lumber output, and relied heavily on imported lumber and pulpwood.

At this time, wood was still a major raw material. Fuelwood still outweighed lumber in national wood consumption, but pulpwood was only about 5 percent of the timber cut, taking an amount less than the national mortality. Per capita lumber use was higher in 1920 than today.

The timber supply outlook for the region's paper industry, said the analysts, "holds no particular promise." [16] Some mills were estimated to have only ten years' supply of pulpwood. It appeared that without better forestry and major pulpwood imports, the north-eastern pulp industry would be "a thing of the past within 30 years." Interestingly, though a massive spruce budworm outbreak had just severely damaged Maine's forests, the U.S. Forest Service's 1920 Capper report did not mention it.

The 1940s saw further reviews of New England's timber budget. The first was prepared by Henry Baldwin for the National Resources Planning Board in 1942.[17] This report, the first specifically directed to New England, summarized statistics and reviewed major forest policy issues. The report gave considerable attention to the effects of the 1938 hurricane that blew down trees across large areas. Its timber data were based on judgment and limited data, since detailed field surveys of New England's forests had yet to be conducted. Of an estimated annual drain from 1932 to 1942 of 570 million cubic feet, fuelwood comprised 42 percent—a high level due largely to the collapse of other markets for wood in those years. In the early 1940s, the drain still exceeded the growth of sawtimber. The pulpwood harvest now eclipsed the lumber harvest, and losses to mortality were on about the same scale as lumber drain. The forests at that time were young, recovering from budworm and heavy cutting, and regrowing rapidly in old pastures. Baldwin called for detailed field surveys of forest conditions, such as were under way elsewhere.

After World War II, the U.S. Forest Service conducted its reappraisal, a major review of the nation's timber budget.[18] The estimates for New England showed continued overcutting of sawtimber trees—a projection for the next twenty years showed a 16 percent decline in sawtimber volume. The growth/cut ratio for sawtimber was 0.81. For all timber, however, the balance was marginally favorable—at 1.13. By 1944, fuelwood drain was only 25 percent of the total drain, nearly as great as lumber but in excess of that for pulp. Mortality, a major component of drain, continued to take an amount of timber roughly equivalent to the harvest for lumber. The reappraisal set a long-term growth goal for New England of 1.14 billion cubic feet. Growth at that time stood at 0.90 billion cubic feet.

In 1947, Dr. V. L. Harper, director of the U.S. Forest Service, Northeastern Forest Experiment Station, depicted a grim timber supply situation for a paper industry audience.[19] He noted the heavy dependence on imported pulpwood, the looming budworm epidemic, the high mortality, and the waste in cutting. There was a rough balance in growth and cut, he said, but timber quality was poor and going steadily downward. He urged his listeners to support more use of hardwoods, better harvesting practices, and protection from fire and insects.

It was not until the 1950s that the first detailed field forest inventories were taken of each New England state. Fortunately, these detailed surveys coincided with an era in which the region's timber situation turned around.

Turnaround at Midcentury

In the quarter century after World War II, the New England timber budget changed markedly. Growth of sawtimber doubled while removals increased by 60 percent. Growth of growing stock increased by 70 percent, to 1.35 billion cubic feet—18 percent above the reappraisal growth goal (table 16). Growth was up even more sharply—by 104 percent—on forest industry lands, partly because of industry's increased acreage. Total timber removals were up by

Table 16. Net Annual Growth and Removals of Growing Stock on Commercial Forest Land, New England States, 1952 and 1976

	1952	1976	Percentage Increase
Growth (million cubic feet)			
Softwood	490.5	838.2	71
Hardwood	302.8	506.4	17
All species	793.3	1344.6	69
All species by owner:			
National forest	24.5	34.2	40
Other public	24.2	62.8	160
Forest industry	233.7	475.1	103
Farm and other	510.8	772.5	51
Removals (million cubic feet)			
Softwood	339.0	395.6	17
Hardwood	148.5	243.6	64
All species	487.5	639.2	31
All species, by owner:			
National forest	5.2	12.0	13
Other public	8.5	21.3	150
Forest industry	123.2	249.7	103
Farm and other	350.6	356.2	2

SOURCE: USDA-FS, *Analysis*, app. 3.

NOTE: These numbers are affected by changing acreages owned by each owner class, most significantly so for farmers. See table 12.

31 percent, with hardwood removals increasing faster and soft-woods slower. Forest industry roughly doubled its softwood removals. The region's timber budget showed a growth/cut ratio in 1976 of 2.1—the best since foresters began compiling such budgets in 1920 and a healthy physical surplus by any standard. These figures are the first to have been based on two detailed field surveys of each state and hence are more reliable than earlier data.

The trends projected over the years, and in particular in 1948, were wrong. Why? The forest land area of the region did not change significantly—it remained at about 31 million acres over the entire period. Industrial use of wood actually grew substantially.

The major reason was that the growth potential of the forest and the significance of its young age were not appreciated in the late 1940s. At that time, stands were still young. Baldwin estimated that fully 38 percent of the region's forests were under twenty years old in the early 1940s. The highest proportions of stands younger than twenty years were in Massachusetts, with 58 percent, and Rhode Island, with 79 percent. Though about 2 million acres were tallied in 1941 as cutover, nonrestocked, those lands have regrown better than expected—nonstocked acreage in the 1976 estimates was nominal. In the 1950s through 1970s these young stands were entering the stage of their lives when they would gain merchantable volume rapidly. They will now mature and their growth will slow unless they are carefully tended.

The 1976 growth/cut ratio is not cause for complacency. Harvesting has risen since 1976, and growth has decreased (estimated wood consumption in 1980 is shown in table 30). In parts of southern New England, the cut is now rapidly approaching the growth. Also, the physical budget is not the whole story.

Limitations of the Physical Timber Budget

With an immense physical surplus of timber, timber prices remained relatively low in New England until the late 1970s. This undermined the incentive for management, as did the limited competition for wood among major mill owners who owned large areas of land. The southern New England paper industry gave up pulpmaking and subsisted on imported pulp, recycled stock, and rags. Lumber production limped along.

In fact, the poor marketability of forest land persisted until the 1970s in some remote areas—land could be bought for less than

A new factor in the timber budget—the firewood pile. *Photo by Chris Ayres.*

the value of the timber standing on it. Shrewd operators can still do this today in northern New England.

The data from 1976 show an impressive timber balance in physical terms. But there are reasons to doubt that this situation will continue for very long. First, the regional timber land base continues to erode slowly through land conversion to other uses. Second, timber harvests are rising with increased mill capacity and the rising demand for fuelwood. More seriously, the vast spruce-fir resource is in the late stages of a spruce budworm outbreak that has reduced growth dramatically and is beginning to kill trees. This resource could lose 25 percent or more of its volume by 1995. Finally, all across New England, unmanaged stands are growing older and are often overstocked. They are, over widespread areas, at an age and in a condition in which growth will naturally decelerate.

For most of this century, forest owners faced their most difficult problems in marketing wood, not in growing it. High-grade logs could always find buyers, but many stands could not be managed without markets for lower-grade wood, and those markets were skimpy and erratic.

The principal reason for the resurgence of New England forests was that local mills could not compete, from World War I to the 1970s, with paperboard and construction lumber cut from the forests of the South and the Pacific coast. During this period, New Englanders brought much of their wood from other regions.

As would be expected in a maturing, largely unmanaged forest, mortality is high relative to product use. In Vermont and southern New England, where pulpwood markets are limited, pulpwood harvests have been less than the average annual mortality. Even in Maine, by the early 1970s, pulpwood harvests were only slightly greater than mortality. Markets were so poor that much of the wood harvested in land clearing—a volume that in the early 1970s exceeded harvests for industrial uses in Connecticut—was simply piled and burned or buried. During much of this century, the White Mountain and Green Mountain National Forests have at times been unable to sell the wood volumes that need to be harvested to maintain forest productivity.

New England foresters and landowners, especially in southern New England, where growth exceeded cut fourfold, faced at midcentury the problems of timber abundance for the first time. The public and professional sense of urgency about timber shortage faded. State forests acquired to assure a timber supply were slowly turned into forest preserves for walking and birdwatching. State foresters had trouble finding time to manage them properly, even in Maine. The demands of a healthy wood market were not present. Public support for timber husbandry seemed as distant in time as the Broad Arrow Acts.

But the impressive quantities displayed in the timber budget concealed some serious problems of economic supply and wood quality. These problems have meant wood supply troubles for small mills in some areas. In view of recent and expected increases in consumption, a massive forestry job is needed for New England even in the face of the statistics of abundance.

Economic supply refers to the willingness of landowners to sell trees for harvest. With the increase in absentee ownership, ownership of farm woodlots as green backdrops for second homes, and fragmentation of parcels, the difficulty of buying wood has increased. Many owners are unwilling to let loggers on their land, having seen a neighbor's lot rutted by sloppy skidding, a few spindly survivors tottering over a field of slash.

I expect that the growing use of fuelwood will enhance landowner willingness to cut trees. Higher wood demand and prices in southern New England have already stimulated higher harvests. If so, the economic supply problems of New England wood users may be less serious in the coming decades. At present, however, the economic supply of wood is considerably less than the measured growth of wood. How rapidly this is changing, nobody knows.

Timber quality is a serious problem. Much of the spruce-fir forest grows on wet, shallow soils that make trees prone to butt-rot and windthrow. The white pine resource is badly damaged by repeated weeviling, which reduces lumber value; many trees are crippled by blister rust. Hardwood stands everywhere suffer from centuries of abuse and neglect. Past cutting has removed high-quality trees. Sprout regrowth, grazing, and fire have promoted butt scars and rot. Diseases and insects, like the beech scale, reduce quality. As early as 1920, the Forest Service estimated that fully 60 percent of the volume in New England's forest was "fit only for firewood," though utilization standards have changed since then. Still, skillful loggers can find high-quality trees if they take the trouble.

The forest surveys of the 1970s show that the tree quality problem remains serious. In southern New England, the 1972 surveys found that an average acre carried 605 trees.[20] Of these 205 were rough and rotten trees. Fully 34 percent of all stands there are understocked with commercially valuable trees by reason of their burden of cull trees. Estimating the log grade in hardwood trees, the federal foresters found that only 29 percent of the sawtimber volume was in the top two grades—suitable for quality lumber and veneer.

In Maine, the quality of the sawlog inventory declined significantly from 1959 to 1972. The average grade of hardwood sawtimber fell, and the sawtimber volume in the top log grade fell by a striking 35 percent.[21] Hardwood sawlog quality in Vermont and New Hampshire likewise declined. In Vermont, the forest is seriously burdened by low-quality trees. As forester Neal Kingsley wrote, "Almost 30 percent of all the live trees in the State over 5 inches dbh [diameter at breast height, 4.5 feet above the ground] are considered rough and/or rotten. In comparison, in the other 5 New England states only 15 percent are rough and/or rotten."[22]

Poor tree quality exacts heavy economic costs. Low-grade trees, though useful for fuel, are poor material to support industry. Their presence reduces stumpage values and fills growing space that could be occupied by high-quality trees or by young regeneration. Many New England woodlots could be improved dramatically if one-third or more of their poorest quality trees could be made to vanish, or be sold for fuel or pulp.

Of course, rough and rotten trees are valuable as den and nesting trees for birds and wildlife, and may provide a mast crop for deer, squirrels, and bear. For these reasons, no forester would strip all the low-grade trees from a woodlot. Many large public organizations have guidelines for retaining den trees in harvesting operations.

Poor tree quality is a major reason why foresters, landowners, and citizens concerned with wood supply cannot be complacent about the future of New England's forest.

Changing Harvest Level

The course of timber harvests in New England during this century can be traced, though the earlier estimates are rough. Prior to about 1920, the data available do not allow useful estimates (table 17).

Still, from what is known of trends in major products, it can be estimated that the all-time high in New England timber harvest occurred about 1907, when the boxboard boom in southern New England peaked. This was after the peak of spruce lumbering in northern New England, and before pulpwood amounted to even as much as firewood. From 1907 the industrial and fuelwood cut slowly fell until the 1960s, with a temporary trough during the Depression. The principal causes of the decline were the steady dwindling in fuelwood use and the decline in lumber output.

Since 1962, increases in pulpwood use, in sawmilling, and in log exports to Quebec have almost doubled the total harvest of New

Table 17. Annual Removals of Growing Stock, 1907–77 (million cubic feet)

Year	Softwood	Hardwood	Total
1907 (est.)	n/a	n/a	1,000
1920	n/a	n/a	650
1941	n/a	n/a	506
1944	n/a	n/a	631
1952	339.0	148.5	487.5
1962	274.0	153.7	427.7
1976	395.6	243.6	639.2
1980	n/a	n/a	810

SOURCES: USDA-FS, *Timber depletion, lumber prices, lumber exports, and concentration of timber ownership*. Report on S. Res. 311. Washington, D.C.: GPO, 1920; H. I. Baldwin, *Forestry in New England*. Boston: National Resources Planning Board, Region I, Bulletin No. 70, 1942; USDA-FS, Forests and national prosperity: A reappraisal of the forest situation in the U.S. Washington, D.C.: USDA Misc. publ. 668, 1948; USDA-FS, *Analysis*, app. 3, and author estimate for 1980.

Table 18. Products from New England's Forest, 1976

	Product Units	Cords[a] (thousands)
Sawlogs	1,407 million board feet	2,800
Veneer Logs	54 million board feet	110
Pulpwood	3.2 million cords	3,200
Cooperage	2.3 million board feet	5
Piling	367,000 linear feet	2
Poles	6,000 pieces	–
Posts	1 million pieces	11
Other	15 million cubic feet	–
Fuelwood	445,000 cords	445
Total		6,706

SOURCE: USDA-FS, *Analysis*, app. 3, table 47.
[a] At 85 cubic feet per cord

England timber. In the 1970s, the decline in fuelwood cutting was reversed. Since 1976, a boost in pulpwood and fuelwood harvesting has occurred, which brings the total timber cut in New England to roughly 800 million cubic feet. By these estimates, then, timber harvest in the region has only now exceeded its 1920 level. Whether it will return to the level of 1907 before the close of the century is uncertain. In southern New England, cutting may be balancing growth already.

The products harvested from New England forests in 1976 were equivalent to 6.7 million cords of wood (table 18). They were worth, delivered at roadside and local mills, about $150 million to those selling, cutting, and hauling them. This sum does not count the value of services applied in converting the raw logs to products. Since 1976, major increases in fuelwood and pulpwood cut have occurred.

Fuelwood

Fuelwood has long been an essential New England commodity. In 1880, it was estimated that New England fuelwood cut for residential use alone totaled 4.1 million cords.[23] In rural areas, woodpiles never completely vanished from farm and village dooryards. Hikers in remote areas of abandoned farms and villages find rusting cookstoves left in cellarholes and dumps. These relics symbolize a change in energy technology and way of life that many of us took to be permanent. In the mid 1970s, New Englanders stopped taking kitchen woodstoves to the dump, and their makers expanded capacity and sales. Thrifty Yankees hauled cookstoves and heating stoves out of barns or from the hardware store and restored chimneys to service. They wired copper tubing through wood furnaces to heat water and fostered a booming business in renting woodsplitters.

Until the late nineteenth century, wood and water were New England's premier energy sources. The aggregate economic cost of woodfuel, counting the labor time spent in its production, must have been enormous—a hidden item in the region's gross product. Even into the twentieth century, fuelwood was important in major New England industries. Fully one-third of the region's 1920 timber cut was for fuelwood, or about 2.5 million cords. Estimates of varying quality have been made since, but they all reflect a steady level of use until the 1940s. Consumption then probably fell steadily until the mid 1970s, when the U.S. Forest Service estimated about 0.5 million cords. A regional survey for the winter of 1978–79 showed that about 3 million cords were used. These are highly imprecise figures, but they show the large regional expansion in woodfuel.[24]

In the days before World War I, woodstoves and industrial furnaces consumed more wood than did the region's paper industry, and an amount comparable to that of the lumber mills. Today, after a long decline because of the temporary switch to oil and coal, fuelwood use is again roughly equal to timber consumption for lumber. If fuelwood use continues to grow at recent rates, by 1985 it will overtake the paper industry again. The region will have come full circle in its wood use patterns, returning to its colonial preoccupation with the forest as a source of energy.

Residential use of wood for fuel has been most visible and is a standard topic of coffee break and cocktail party discussion today. But a sizable amount of industrial and commercial energy is being generated from wood. Churches, schools, and public buildings are being converted. One well-known example is the Vermont State Hospital at Waterbury, which uses 2800 cords of chips per year. In Concord, New Hampshire, a district heating utility providing steam is converting to wood. The forest products industries have always used woodwastes and bark for energy. Papermills obtain a sizable part of their process energy by burning waste liquor, which contains wood sugars and nonfiber materials. Recently, papermills have begun installing bark burners to generate electricity. At Great Northern Paper Company's Millinocket mill, a bark burner is nearing completion. At a cost of $35 million, it will generate power for the mill, displacing 400,000 barrels of oil per year. Most of the large and medium-size sawmills of the region use woodwaste for steam power, and some are considering installing turbines for cogeneration. Surplus power would be sold back to the area electric utilities.

In Vermont, considerable attention has focused on electricity generation. The Green Mountain Power Company and Burlington Electric Company have explored wood electricity seriously, and the Burlington Electric Company, after converting one furnace to wood, is now proposing to construct a wood-fired system.[25] Conservationists and foresters are concerned that the large wood volumes required by such systems be harvested in a sound silvicultural manner, with minimal impact on soil, aesthetics, wildlife, and forest productivity. But most experts agree that burning wood for electricity or heat will not provide as many local jobs and as much value added to the local economy as would more traditional uses of the same wood.

Equipment designed for supplying chips to pulpmills can chip

Whole-tree chipping permits increased yield from each acre harvested. *Courtesy of Georgia-Pacific Corporation.*

trees in the woods, including bark, branches, and leaves. Few New England papermills use such whole-tree chips today. When the whole tree is chipped, along with all small trees, the biomass removed per acre substantially exceeds the wood volume removed for traditional products. In some situations, it is economical to use such total forest chips for energy to produce steam or electricity. This practice remains in its infancy today, supplying only 4 percent of the region's pulpwood output in 1978.[26] If wood-fired electric generating plants and wood pelletizing plants appear, however, whole-tree chipping can be expected to increase. This has caused scientists and conservationists to be concerned over possible nutrient depletion of the soils by nutrient removal. In cutting for traditional products, a residual stand is often left, which protects the site and retains nutrients. As branches and tops decay, they restore the nutrients to the ecological cycle of the site. Many New England forest soils are shallow and infertile. Because of high moisture content and acidity, some nutrients are not readily available to plants. Clearcutting accelerates organic matter decomposition and the loss of nutrients to volatilization and erosion. Under New England conditions, it is likely that repeated removal of all forest biomass—for whatever use—would lead to reduced soil productivity. Such management practices would damage most other forest values as well. The conditions under which this is a problem are under intense study now. As knowledge increases, it will be possible to design forest harvesting practices to avoid depleting soil nutrients.[27]

Losses to Mortality

The New England forest, when Europeans first arrived, was in a dynamic equilibrium. Wood growth roughly balanced mortality over the landscape as a whole. A patchwork of stands, many of which were extremely old, held high standing volumes and were gaining little or no net growth. Periodic fires, major storms, and insect outbreaks flattened large areas, restoring young, vigorous stands.

In northern New England, mortality has always been high, because of occasional insect outbreaks, fires, extensive areas of mature trees, and frequent windthrow of individual mature trees. Spruce budworm outbreaks, every forty to eighty years, are most dramatic. The 1912–20 outbreak killed enough spruce and fir to keep Maine's current paper industry going for ten years.

In the nineteenth century, mortality was low in the rural forests outside of the wildlands. Because of heavy cutting, the trees simply never lived long enough to suffer old age decline, insect and disease damage, and windthrow. In the early twentieth century, the chestnut blight eliminated within fifteen years the most important timber tree of southern New England. The introduced white pine blister rust inflicted serious damage. After its introduction in the 1890s, the gypsy moth killed large volumes of oak on dry sites. It has been less important as a mortality factor recently, as it has acquired more natural enemies. And most people know that Dutch elm disease has ravaged the region's streets and country roads—some of which are still littered with silvery elm skeletons. New Haven, Connecticut, the Elm City, now holds that title in name only.

Dramatic losses in white birch were caused by the birch dieback, a syndrome of unknown cause, in the late 1940s. This epidemic swiftly killed mature birch over most of northern New England. Later, a massive plague of beech scale moved westward from New Brunswick and Maine, killing and stunting beech. Since beech, because of poor markets, was seen as a weed tree at the time, the damage was of little concern to foresters and landowners, concerned with timber values. Newly killed beech makes good firewood.

Trees in New England are subject to massive hurricane damage, an average of once per century on exposed sites. The famous 1938 hurricane blew down 2½ billion board feet of timber, much of it pine. At the lumber production rates of that time, that volume represented perhaps a decade's cut of timber. Large fires have in the past consumed much timber. They often started in budworm-killed or blown-down stands, or in logging slash. Intensive fire control programs have made fire risks low today despite the high hazard presented by extensive recreational uses.[28]

The periodic forest surveys have attempted aggregate estimates of mortality losses. For 1976, the U.S. Forest Service estimated that mortality came to 226 million cubic feet, an amount comparable to the total harvest of pulpwood. The impact of damaging agents on the forest remains huge, despite a growing level of cut and improved methods of forest protection.

Future Production Potential

The current wood production in New England's forests is well below what could be grown if most of the forest were carefully managed. Net growth is reduced by high mortality, by cull increment

Table 19. Average Annual Growth of All Commercial
Forest Land, 1970s

State	Net Annual Growth (cubic feet per acre)
Vermont	24
New Hampshire	44
Southern New England	44
Maine	45

SOURCES: N. P. Kingsley, *The timber resources of southern New England*. USDA-FS NEFES Res. Bull. NE-36, 1974. R. H. Ferguson and N. P. Kingsley, *The timber resources of Maine*. USDA-FS NEFES Res. Bull. NE-26, 1972. N. P. Kingsley, *The forest resources of Vermont*, USDA-FS. NEFES Res. Bull. NE-46, 1977; and N. P. Kingsley, *The forest resources of New Hampshire*. USDA-FS NEFES, Res. Bull. NE-43, 1976.

(growing wood on valueless trees), by poor stocking of desirable trees, or by overstocking or overmaturity. Current annual growth is just about half a cord per acre (table 19).

In the near term, large, nonsustainable increases in timber harvests can come from two sources: the harvest of massive spruce-fir mortality caused by spruce budworm[29] and the consumption of surplus hardwood trees that are of low quality or represent excessive stocking for optimum value growth. D. J. Brooks and D. B. Field estimated that surplus hardwood in Maine alone amounts to 5 billion cubic feet—or 62 million cords. This is a truly staggering quantity, but it would not all be economically available at today's logging costs and wood prices.[30]

Henry Baldwin in 1942 estimated that New England forests

Table 20. Commercial Forest Land in New England
by Productivity Class, 1977

Cords per Acre per Year	Million Acres
1.4 or more	3.5
1 to 1.4	8.0
0.58 to 1.0	10.8
0.25 to 0.58	8.7
	31.0

SOURCE: USDA-FS, *Analysis*, app. 3, p. 26.

Veneer plant produces high value product and pays high prices for logs, Vermont. *Photo by Bill Gove.*

could grow 39 million cords per year under management. This is about *five times* the current level of cut for industrial and fuelwood, and four times the current total drain.

More recently, Owen Herrick of the U.S. Forest Service estimated that a high level of softwood timber consumption in the year 2000 could be met by placing less than 25 percent of the forest land under intensive management.[31] The outlook for hardwoods was not as bright, but under intensive management, projected hardwood needs for year 2000 could be met with less than 75 percent of the land. The most recent Forest Service summary indicates that if fully stocked and well-managed, 37 percent of the forest land in New England could grow more than one cord per acre each year (table 20).

Summary

New England's timber budget has reflected the region's changing needs for wood, its success in subduing the native forest, and the retreat of farming. In this century, wood products from the South and from the West have been so cheap that New Englanders let the woods grow. The recent resurgence of industry and the boom in fuelwood use has rapidly eaten up the surpluses measured in the early 1970s. Growth can be significantly increased by better management. A major challenge will be to upgrade timber quality. The 1960s were a decade of concern for nontimber values of forests during which inadequate markets hampered timber management. The 1980s will be a decade of new concerns—controlling overcutting in local areas, harmonizing conflicting forest uses, and adjusting industry to a changing timber supply.[32]

CHAPTER 10

Wood Products and
New England's Economy

apermaking and converting, sawmilling, logging, and wood product fabrication employ more than 100,000 New Englanders. Of these, perhaps 60,000 depend directly on the region's forests. The output of these industries totals almost $6 billion, or almost 9 percent of the region's manufacturing production. If federal projections for the 1980–2030 period come true, the region could double its timber harvest and substantially increase its industrial capacity using wood. This chapter describes the changing economic importance of these industries and explores their future for the next half century.[1]

Sawmilling and Logging

Sawmilling is one of New England's oldest industries, second only to fishing. South Berwick, Maine, is said to have been the home of the nation's first sawmill, in the early 1630s. For generations sawmills were extremely important to New England's rural communities, and towns offered millmen water rights, free timber, and local monopolies as inducements to build. Pit-sawn lumber was produced for a time in the colonies, but watermills, often built with gristmills, dominated the region. Water-powered mills still were numerous as late as 1870. Of the 3,577 sawmills counted in New England in the census of that year, only 269 had steam power. These would have been the market-oriented mills on major rivers.[2]

New England has always had two distinct sawmill industries. One has been the large market-oriented mills, which prepared large volumes for distant markets—the staves and headings, pine boards, and spruce lumber of previous centuries. Or the pine clapboards, spruce 2 × 4's, and high-grade hardwoods produced in the mills of the 1970s. The other sawmill industry, comprising most of the mills, operates tiny mills, often roofless, cutting several million feet or less per year, usually on a part-time basis. From the 1900s to the 1950s, portable mills were common. These were small rigs that were moved from woodlot to woodlot with the loggers, leaving piles of sawdust and slabs and edgings. Even today, these rotting piles of waste can still be found in the woods.

At the time of the Civil War, before the Great Lakes and southern forests were exploited, New England produced about one-sixth of the nation's lumber. At the time of the national peak of production in 1909, the region's contribution had fallen to 7 percent. Today, producing a bit more than a billion board feet, New England supplies only 2.6 percent of national softwood lumber output, and 3.5 percent of the hardwood. This is less than proportionate to the region's forest area, though it must be recalled that the forests of the Pacific Northwest provide far larger volumes of logs per acre.

Because of the small size and part-time nature of many mills, census workers still have difficulty counting sawmills. For this reason, counts of mills, employment, and production must be handled with care, even today. Despite this, some broad generalizations are possi-

Georgia-Pacific waferboard plant, Woodland, Maine. This technology, new to New England, will promote forestry by improving markets for wood. A plant like this employs about one hundred people. *Courtesy of Georgia-Pacific Corporation.*

Table 21. Lumber Production, New England States, 1978
(million board feet)

	Total	Softwood	Hardwood
Maine	522	482	40
New Hampshire	211	177	34
Massachusetts	107	48	59
Connecticut	44	13	31
Vermont and Rhode Island	162	84	78
Total	1,046	804	242

SOURCE: U.S. Dept. of Commerce, Bureau of the Census, Current Industrial Reports, *Lumber production and mill stocks, 1978*, MA-24T(78)-1, March 1980.

NOTE: Most of the numbers below 200 have sampling errors above 15 percent. Because of the high sampling errors for Vermont and Rhode Island, they are listed together by the Census Bureau.

ble. Regional employment in sawmilling grew slowly to a peak in 1900–10 of about 20,000 jobs, not counting logging. Since that time, lumber production has fallen by nearly two-thirds, and major classes of products—boxboards, staves, lath—have vanished. Employment in sawmilling today is probably no greater, and may be less, than at the industry's historic 1909 peak.

Employment in logging is the most difficult to count of all sectors of the forest products business. Included in the lumber and wood industry, the census figures definitely understate logging employment. The New England region must employ about 10,000 people each year on a full- or part-time basis.[3]

Currently, the region produces about one billion feet of lumber per year (table 21). In addition, several hundred million feet per year are produced in Quebec and New Brunswick from Maine and New Hampshire timber.

Pulp and Paper

New England's pulp and paper industry is a diverse one. It includes mills relying solely on purchased pulp, and mills that ship only pulp but do not make paper (table 22). The mills specialize in higher-grade papers and in converting (tables 23, 24). New England can no longer compete with the South in commodity items like newsprint, kraft bag paper, and paperboard used for cardboard boxes. Further, the large paper industry of southern New England now relies almost exclusively on purchased pulp. Those mills make print-

Great Northern Paper Company mill at Millinocket, Maine. *Courtesy of Great Northern Paper Company.*

ing, writing, and art papers, which demand extremely high standards of manufacturing technology and quality control.[4]

New England produces only 5 percent of the nation's pulpwood but accounts for 14 percent of the nation's paper output. Maine leads the nation in paper capacity. The region's paperboard output is nominal though paperboard makes up half the output of the national pulp and paper industry.

The New England paper industry emerged in colonial times, using rags, straw, and other raw materials. Papermakers were so highly valued that they were exempted from the draft during the Revolution. Papermills in the colonial period were small (employing as few as 6 persons) and numerous. Mills grew larger in the nineteenth century. The 1890 census counted 180 mills (85 in Massachusetts), employing 12,304 persons, or 68 per mill. At this time, most of the region's paper was being made from nonwood materials. The development of woodpulp paper in the 1880s produced a spectacular boom in the region's paper industry, and the industry

Table 22. Number of New England Papermills, 1977

State	Pulpmills	Papermills integrated with a pulpmill	Papermills not integrated with a pulpmill	Paperboard mills
Connecticut	–	–	4	7
Rhode Island	–	–	–	–
Massachusetts	–	7	33	7
Vermont	–	–	10	1
New Hampshire	–	3	12	5
Maine	4	10	4	–
Total	4	20	63	20

SOURCE: U.S. Dept. of Commerce, Bureau of the Census, 1977 Census of Manufacturers, *Pulp, paper and board mills*, MC77-1-26A, Sept. 1980.

Table 23. Inputs and Products of New England's
Paper Industry, 1978

Pulp produced (thousand tons)	2,597
Pulp consumed (thousand tons)	3,583
Pulpwood consumed (thousand cords)	4,124
Employment, 1977 (number)	64,900
Total Paper Produced (thousand tons)	4,096
book, uncoated	1,091
bleached bristols	65
cotton fiber, writing, thin paper	168
packaging, industrial and converting	345
sanitary	417
other	2,010

SOURCE: U.S. Dept. of Commerce, Bureau of the Census, Current Industrial Reports, *Pulp, paper and board, 1978*, M26A (78)-13, March 1980.

moved north to find the wood. By 1919, when the boom was leveling off, the industry employed 34,849 people in 243 mills, or 143 per mill. Maine mills employed 300 people each on average. Massachusetts, which led the region with 63 percent of the paper industry jobs in 1890, fell behind Maine in 1919 but still increased its employment by 5,000 jobs in the period. In 1919, New England contained 30 percent of all the paper industry jobs in the nation.

Enduring a Depression crash and slow growth from the 1940s to the 1960s, regional paper employment has still doubled again since 1919—to about 65,000 jobs in 1977. But the region has fallen behind national growth—it now contains only 9 percent of the nation's pulp paper and board industry employment.

This substantial sustained employment growth over an entire

Table 24. New England Pulpwood, Woodpulp, Paper and
Board Output, 1978

	Pulpwood (thousand cords)[a]	Woodpulp Produced (thousand tons)	Paper (thousand tons)	Paperboard (thousand tons)
Maine	3,955.0	2,149	2,883.6	(D)
New Hampshire	508.1	(D)	310.4	(D)
Vermont	287.8	(D)	(D)	(D)
Massachusetts	28.1	–	617.6	249.4
Rhode Island	1.0	(D)	–	–
Connecticut	11.1	(D)	(D)	295.9
Total	4,791.1	2,597	4,096.4	800.1

[a] Includes residues, which amount to 22 percent of the regional total pulpwood output. In Connecticut and Massachusetts, residues exceed roundwood output.
SOURCES: R. L. Nevel, Jr., and J. T. Bones, Northeastern pulpwood, 1978, USDA-FS NEFES, Res. Bull. NE-62, 1980; U.S. Dept. of Commerce, Bureau of the Census, Current Industrial Reports, *Pulp, paper and board, 1978*, M26A(78)-13, March 1980.
NOTE: (D) means not released because of disclosure rules. Undisclosed figures account for totals larger than the sums of the disclosed figures.
– means negligible.

century has been of critical importance in the region's economy. It has sustained employment in milltowns buffeted by declining leather, textile, and food-processing industries. It has helped support economic opportunity in rural northern New England. As the Maine commissioner of Industrial and Labor Statistics wrote in 1906, the paper industry

is constantly adding wealth to our state. . . . It is adding prosperity to our old settled towns and building up new towns in the wilderness. It is giving employment to thousands of our young men who otherwise might be obliged to seek a livelihood in distant parts of the country.[5]

Importance to New England's Economy

The total output of New England's wood-based industry was almost $6 billion in 1977. Industries based on wood account for about 2 percent of total regional employment and personal income. They are a significant part of the region's manufacturing sector, especially in the three northern New England states (tables 25, 26, and 27). While wood-based employment is approximately equal in Massachusetts and Maine, the wood industries are 30 percent of all manufacturing employment in Maine, compared with 5.5 percent in Massachusetts.

Total employment based on wood in New England exceeds

100,000 persons (table 28). This contribution to employment and output has steadily increased over this century, making the lumber and paper industries a stable, slowly growing sector of New England's economy.

Dependence on wood products for employment varies within New England (fig. 9). It remains high in the old papermaking regions of central Massachusetts and is extremely high in northern New England.

Economic development was a policy concern for monarchs, governors, selectmen, and farmers from 1620 to the early nineteenth century. Sawmills and gristmills were encouraged with monopolies

Table 25. Employment in Lumber and Paper Industries,
New England, 1977

(thousand workers)

State	Lumber and Wood Products	Paper and Allied Products	Total
Connecticut	2.1	7.2	9.3
Rhode Island[a]	0.4	2.6	3.0
Massachusetts	5.7	28.8	34.5
Vermont	3.5	2.6	6.1
New Hampshire	4.4	6.5	10.9
Maine	12.9	17.2	30.1
Total	29.0	64.9	93.9

SOURCE: U.S. Dept. of Commerce, Bureau of the Census. *1977 Census of Manufacturers, Area Series*, reports for New England states, preliminary data.
[a] For Rhode Island, no figure for sawmills was published. This tabulation uses the 1972 figure instead, from the same source for 1972.

Table 26. Value of Shipments, Lumber, Paper, and All
Manufacturing, 1977

State	Million Dollars				Percentage of All Manufacturing in Lumber and Paper
	Lumber and Wood	Paper and Allied	Total Lumber and Paper	All Manufacturing	
Connecticut	75	548	623	19,984	3.1
Rhode Island	17	131	148	5,410	2.7
Massachusetts	234	1,667	1,901	30,663	6.2
Vermont	138	195	333	2,204	15.1
New Hampshire	208	467	675	4,029	16.8
Maine	571	1,666	2,237	5,146	43.5
Total	1,226	4,674	5,917	67,436	8.7

SOURCE: Same as table 25.

Table 27. Lumber and Paper Employment in Relation to All
Manufacturing, 1977

(thousand workers)

State	Lumber and Paper	All Manufacturing	Percentage in Lumber and Paper
Connecticut	9.3	413.1	2.2
Rhode Island	3.0	125.7	2.4
Massachusetts	34.5	627.1	5.5
Vermont	8.4	42.8	19.6
New Hampshire	10.9	94.9	11.5
Maine	30.9	103.1	30.0
Total	97.0	1,406.7	6.9

SOURCE: Same as table 25.

Table 28. Estimated Employment, New England
Wood-Based Manufacturing Industries, 1977

Lumber and wood, including logging	34,000[a]
Paper and allied	65,000
Other industries using wood raw material	10,000[b]
	109,000
Deduct other secondary	−10,000
Deduct southern New England paper	−38,600
Add jobs in Quebec lumber using Maine timber	+2,000[c]
Jobs dependent on New England forests	62,400

[a] Census estimate (Table 25) plus estimated 5,000 undercount in logging.
[b] Principally wood household furniture, wood partitions, and wood prefabricated buildings. Wood furniture data are not fully published in census publications.
[c] Author estimate.

and free timber and water rights. Public lands were granted for support of schools, churches, and other public purposes, and roads were built to promote settlement. Towns regulated the removal of roadside trees, trespass, export of wood, and measurement of wood.

The reasons why an age of complete *laissez faire* followed this period would be a social and economic history of nineteenth-century New England. The climate of the age was one of public promotion of private economic objectives, of reducing public land-

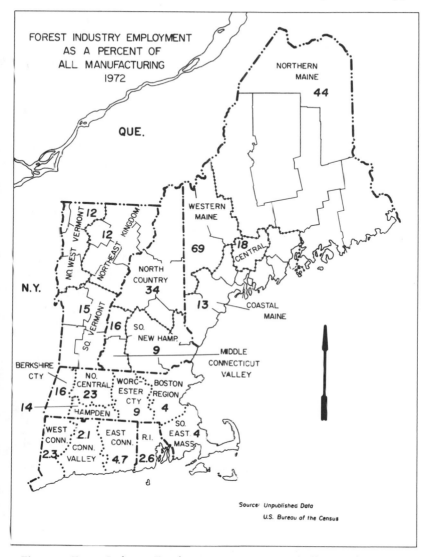

FOREST INDUSTRY EMPLOYMENT
AS A PERCENT OF
ALL MANUFACTURING
1972

NORTHERN
MAINE
44

QUE.

WESTERN
MAINE

NO. WEST VERMONT 12

12

NORTHEAST KINGDOM

69

18
CENTRAL

NORTH
COUNTRY
34

13

COASTAL
MAINE

N.Y.

15

SO. VERMONT

16 SO.
NEW HAMP.
9

MIDDLE
CONNECTICUT
VALLEY

BERKSHIRE
CTY

NO.
CENTRAL 23

WORC-
ESTER
CTY 9

BOSTON
REGION
4

16

14

HAMPDEN

WEST
CONN. 2.1

EAST
CONN.

R.I.

SO.
EAST
MASS.
4

2.3

CONN.
VALLEY 4.7

2.6

Source: Unpublished Data

U.S. Bureau of the Census

Figure 9. Forest Industry Employment as a Percent of All Manufacturing, 1972. *From Joseph, Irland, and Howard, 1980.*

ownership, and minimal government supervision or concern with land use. An attitude that natural resources were endless was certainly in part responsible for these views.

By the 1950s, everyone realized that New England's decaying farm economy and collapsing milltown industries left behind serious poverty and economic loss.[6] New efforts to promote state and regional economic development were made, mostly using federal funds. A new emphasis on economic development seized state policy. Governors began to run for office on issues of jobs and favorable business climates. Strangely, though, the green backdrop concept of the forest and the poor regional competitive setting for forest products meant little emphasis in public policy on wood as a source of products and jobs. Partly because of poor wages and working conditions in some branches of the wood-using industry, the sector did not seem an attractive economic development prospect.

By the late seventies, however, this had changed. New Englanders were relearning what their forefathers knew about the utility of forests for products and appreciated the jobs that wood processing can bring. A few communities suffered when obsolete mills were closed.

Today, then, a new awareness of the income-producing potential of the forest is emerging, bringing the region back to its colonial interest in the commodity values of the forest.

Outlook for Output and Employment

In the late 1970s, about 100,000 New Englanders were directly employed in the region's wood-processing plants. Most of those in the southern New England paper and converting industry, plus a substantial fraction of those in secondary wood employment, are not dependent on the region's own forests for raw material, though in principle they could be. Probably only 60,000 jobs are really based on New England timber, though several thousand jobs in Quebec sawmills depend on Maine timber. Whether the other industries would use more local timber in the future is hard to guess.

The region has not been a high-growth forest products region in the last few decades. More attractive growth opportunities were available in Canada, in the Pacific Northwest's large timber, and in the South's abundant and low-cost timber. Markets, especially in the Sunbelt, grew rapidly. New England's industry remained stagnant until a revival of investment in the 1970s. This revival was sparked by spiraling timber prices and vigorous competition for

Small sawmill, Vermont. Small mills like this one are critical to the life of rural New England towns. *Photo by Bill Gove.*

wood in the South and Northwest, and the reduced competitiveness of Canada as a supplier of paper and lumber. A new cycle of investment in forest products in New England is underway. It is occurring in the large corporations of the industrial forest as well as in the smaller family lumber companies of the rural and suburban forest. Mills are being rebuilt, modernized, or started from scratch. Improvements in pollution control equipment are being made.

Several New England papermills closed in the 1970s because of high costs and the inability to justify the expense of modernizing and installing up-to-date pollution control equipment. In a few instances, companies were faced with the practical requirement to shut down old mills or rebuild them to meet modern environmental standards. For example, in the late 1970s, Scott Paper closed the pulp end of an old mill at Winslow, Maine, on the Kennebec. The papermaking part of the mill stayed in use, supplied with pulp by a new state-of-the-art pulpmill upriver at Hinkley. Numerous other major modernizations and expansions were accomplished in the 1970s, notably the upgrading of International Paper Company's mill complex at Jay, on the Androscoggin, making it the largest white-paper mill in the United States.

Experts argue that the competitive balance for the forest products industry in the Northeast has improved and looks favorable for future growth, based in part on continued market growth and on higher production costs and shipping costs for other producing regions.[7]

Recent U.S. Forest Service projections for the northeastern states, which contain about 86 million acres of forest, illustrate the expected trends (table 29). The percentage increases in output over the next fifty years are less than the national rate for pulp, but greater than the national rate for lumber.[8]

An additional product not reflected in these projections is waferboard, a product glued up in large presses from chipped or "wafered" wood. At this writing, new plants are being operated by Elemendorf Board at Claremont, New Hampshire, and by Georgia-Pacific at Woodland, Maine. Louisiana Pacific is building one at Houlton, Maine, and others are known to be on the drawing boards. This new industry will supply a needed market for aspen, fir, and low-grade hardwoods. Its boosters expect the product to eliminate shipments of southern and western softwood sheathing and particleboard to the Northeast in a decade.

Table 29. Wood Products Output Levels, United States and Northeastern States,[a] 1952–2030 (Projections based on future equilibrium price levels.)

Item	1952	1976	2000	2030	Percentage Increase 1976– 2030
Paper and Board					
U.S. total production (million tons)	24.4	59.9	116.1	182.0	203
Northeast					
Pulp production (million tons)	2,700	3,720[b]	7,005	10,460	181
Roundwood consumption (million cubic feet)	–	374[b]	634	899	140
Chip consumption (million cubic feet)	–	94[b]	156	228	142
Lumber (billion board feet)					
U.S. consumption	39.2	42.8	52.1	55.9	31
U.S. production	37.5	36.3	39.9	47.0	29
Northeast production					
Softwood	1.3	0.8	1.0	1.2	50
Hardwood	8.9	1.5	1.9	2.7	80

SOURCE: USDA-FS, *Analysis*, pp. 442, 444, 450, 451.
[a] Northeastern states: New England plus New York, Pennsylvania, New Jersey, West Virginia, Maryland, and Delaware.
[b] Data for 1975.

Table 30. New England Timber Production Outlook,
Stylized Data

| | Million Cubic Feet | |
	1980	2030
Lumber and Veneer	250	410
Pulpwood	300	720
Miscellaneous products	20	30
Fuelwood	240	480
	810	1,640

SOURCE: Author estimate based on USDA-FS data. It also assumes increases in pulp
and lumber since 1976 and incorporates an estimated 3-mi lion-cord fuelwood cut.
This is far larger than the fuelwood cut estimated for 1976 It anticipates a 50 percent increase in miscellaneous products and a doubling of fuelwood to 2030.

NOTE: This table is based on the assumption that New England output will grow
at same rate as the entire northeastern region as projected by the U.S. Forest Service.

Allowing for increases in New England wood consumption since
1976, estimated 1980 timber consumption by industry is roughly
810 million cubic feet (table 30; fig. 10). This is about 9.5 million
cords, which represents a significant increase over the 639 million
cubic feet estimated by the U.S. Forest Service for 1976. If the output projections for the Northeast are fulfilled, we can expect a
rough doubling of total wood consumption in New England by the
year 2030. This is only a half century off and is certainly not to be
ruled out on economic grounds alone. The assumptions used in this
projection may turn out to be in error, but I think that it gives us a
simple way to assess the region's timbergrowing opportunities and
constraints for the future. Anyone preferring other assumptions can
adjust these figures accordingly.

If the New England wood products production comes anywhere
near what the U.S. Forest Service projects for the Northeast as
a whole, a rough doubling of timber cut and product output is
in prospect for the next half century. What does this mean for
employment?

In recent decades, employment per unit of wood cut has fallen
significantly. In the late 1970s, however, a national slowdown in labor productivity occurred.[9] It is impossible to predict the future
trend of productivity and hence of jobs per unit of wood cut. We
can say that, if productivity trends of 1950–74 continue, there will
be fewer jobs in New England forest industries by the year 2030. If
continued development of new products is seen, and labor produc-

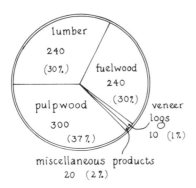

Figure 10. New England Round-wood Consumption, 1980 (million cubic feet). *From author estimates.*

tivity growth slows, employment will rise somewhat. If the timber cut and output levels fall short of these projections, however, there will be fewer New Englanders employed in wood products businesses in the year 2030 than today. Of course, the large number of forest products jobs in New England that depend on imported pulp and solid wood will be governed by interregional competition in those particular industries, which is extremely difficult to assess.

Outlook for Wood Energy

A continuing rise in residential use of fuelwood seems likely for the next few years. By the mid 1980s, fuelwood use should stabilize as the potential market is saturated. Many households will find the advantages of coal appealing and will tire of splitting wood and of continually restoking fires. Oil dealers, losing business rapidly, will convert to coal and promote it aggressively to keep themselves in business. These considerations suggest to me that we may never reach a level of residential fuelwood use above 4 or 5 million cords per year. It is certainly possible that residential use by 1990 could be below the current level. What the future may hold for industrial and commercial uses of wood, however, is uncertain.

In industrial and commercial uses, increased use of wood residues and roundwood can be expected, especially if more pelletizing plants appear. The technology for efficient, nonpolluting combustion of wood is available in units of sizes that fit these end uses well, for process heat, space heating, steam, and even electricity generation and cogeneration. At least in northern New England, additional use of wood for commercial energy can be expected, and it is likely to be a stable future wood market. These users may be prepared to pay a premium in current energy costs in return for the stable supply that wood can provide, in contrast to oil.

The future of central electricity generation from wood is uncertain. Though the Burlington Electric plant is proceeding, electricity does not seem to be the most attractive way to use the energy in wood. In highly specialized situations, it may be serviceable, but cogeneration at industrial plants seems a more promising opportunity.

The rapid changes in costs, technology, and energy regulatory policies make it dangerous to forecast fuelwood use, but for all markets together, the outlook favors an increase in the 1980s. Whether further increases will occur cannot be foreseen. But fuelwood will remain an important factor in New England's timber budget in coming decades.

Spurred by rising oil prices, investigators have studied the feasibility of short-rotation biomass forests for energy. These are plantations of fast-growing genetically improved trees like poplar, sycamore, and cottonwood. They are carefully planted and tended, and mowed every three to five years, regenerating immediately from the rootstocks. High yields of biomass can be obtained in this way. Although New England energy costs are high, I do not see short-rotation biomass forests being planted on a noticeable scale. The promise of wood energy for this region can be amply fulfilled without biomass plantations.[10]

Will the Wood Be There?

These projections are based on detailed economic analyses by the U.S. Forest Service. They assume that New England will grow at a pace equal to that projected for the rest of the Northeast. These estimates probably are optimistic for New England.

The Forest Service expects that net growth will fall significantly in the Northeast to 2030—by 25 percent for softwoods and 39 percent for hardwoods—as a result of stand maturity and overstocking. Because of the large growth/cut surpluses projected, however, a rising wood products output can be produced while inventories (in cubic feet) increase by 67 percent for softwoods and 55 percent for hardwoods.

Can we expect the situation in New England to be consistent with the whole Northeast in this respect as well? There are several barriers to such a large increase in cut.

First, the region's spruce-fir resource is under heavy stress from spruce budworm, and the inventory in those species, at least in Maine and New Hampshire, will decline in the next two decades. In the pine-hardwood regions of New England, timber quality is poor. Large diameter classes of pine and some hardwood species are being overcut in some areas.

Second, forest parcels in much of New England are small and getting smaller. Loggers and mills there will find expanding log supply and output costly and difficult.

Finally, at the current level of effort, I do not believe that intensive management practices are being implemented at a pace that could significantly boost overall timber growth on the region's forest lands in the next half century. The most intensively managed properties will undoubtedly increase their growth significantly, but I doubt that this will have a significant effect on regionwide growth.

Let us conduct a short arithmetic exercise. I will estimate the region's real commercial forest land base at about 23 million acres. This figure assumes that one-half of the recreational and suburban forests and two-thirds of the rural forest are available for sustained timber production. If the region harvested 810 million cubic feet from this resource in 1980, it achieved a rate of 35 cubic feet per acre, or about four-tenths of a cord. This rate is roughly equal to the region's average rate of wood growth over its entire forest. A rate of cut higher than this can be sustained for a decade or more by using low-quality and non-growing-stock timber. But a harvest level of double the current level would mean a rate of 70 cubic feet or about nine-tenths of a cord per acre per year.

To put the matter somewhat differently, the average growth on 31 million acres of commercial forest land in 1976 was about half a cord per acre, or 15 million cords. On the estimated 23 million acres available for commercial harvesting, this translates into 11.5 million cords. The current (1980) harvest level is about 9.5 million cords. This is 63 percent of the growth on the entire forest, but 82 percent of the growth on the commercially available forest. Any significant future decreases in forest land available for cutting will reduce the margin of safety. But these figures clearly show that a doubling of the cut by the year 2030, at today's level of management, is a dubious proposition.

To produce a sustainable timber harvest at that level, there are three fundamental requirements:

1. The current growth rate needs to be doubled, on the average, over the entire commercial forest area.

2. The acreage of forest land available for harvesting must be maintained to the maximum extent possible, though I would still urge a doubling of the region's preserved wilderness.

3. Utilization of new species and of trees cut must be improved.

It is not, therefore, a question of biological potential. It is a question of landowner motivation to harvest timber, and to cut in a way that increases rather than decreases future growth. It is also a matter of size and quality. Average log sizes in several major species will continue to decline, and I cannot see log quality improving in the next few decades. Lastly, it is a matter of land use planning.

Several changes must be made in order for New England to be able to double its timber cut in the next half-century. Better technology for making solid wood products from small and low-quality logs will be needed. Better management of all forest lands will be required. Industries like particleboard that can use low-quality trees and species that are now undercut will have to grow. And minimizing the shrinkage of the commercial forest land base through parcel fragmentation, speculation, and land use conversion would help. Finally, if the bulk of the fuelwood cut comes from lands in suburbia not now available for harvesting sawlogs and pulp, conflicts between these wood uses will be minimized.

All of these trends, except the last one, are now visible in their early stages. I think that serious efforts in technological improvement, industrial development, and improved forestry can allow New England to double its product yield, even from a declining forest land area. The region could then take full advantage of its recently improved competitive position in forest products manufacturing, and maintain or even increase the forest's contribution to regional employment and economic well-being.

Impacts of Higher Harvest Level

Would a doubling of New England's timber cut be an ecological disaster? Some fear it. Personally, I do not think it will be. The abusive cutting practices of the past will not be allowed. A higher timber cut will definitely change the forest, but not in ways that most travelers and recreationists would notice. A higher harvest level will benefit some species of wildlife, and den trees and buffer areas can be preserved wherever needed. The intensive management will not produce long-term degradation of site potential. Horror-show scenarios can be imagined, but I believe they can be easily prevented.

In sum, I think a doubled product yield from New England's forests can be entirely consistent with the high value New Englanders place on amenity, recreation, and wildlife, but only if determined owners and foresters make it so.

What remains to be seen, however, is whether the wood-using capacity needed to double the region's industrial wood consumption will actually be built. That will depend on competitive forces, national and international markets, and the investment decisions of large corporations. It also remains uncertain whether the investments in silviculture required to double growth are economical, and whether the funds and the determination to make them will materialize. In view of all of the uncertainties, it will be essential to monitor closely forest inventories, wood use, and trends in forest management.

It is essential to recall that the projections to 2030 are statements of what *might* be, not what *will* be. If the general standard of forest management does not improve, if companies do not expand their wood-using capacity, or if more and more owners refuse to supply timber, these projected increases will not materialize. Fifty years ahead is a long time, and wood markets, processing technologies, and values placed on different forest uses will probably be unrecognizable at that time.

Equally, even a continuation of the *present* level of regional timber harvest could be seriously damaging in its impact on streams, wildlife, and the scenery, if conducted abusively and thoughtlessly. Likewise, if landowners, loggers, foresters, and wood users care enough to do the job properly, a doubled timber harvest can be consistent with a high-quality multiple-use forest. Even if the harvest level hardly grows at all, better regard for nontimber forest values will pay high benefits.

Whether future wood harvests degrade or improve New England's landscape will depend on thousands of decisions made daily by loggers, landowners, foresters, wood users, and local and state governments. As I argue in the next chapter, we cannot secure favorable performance by passing laws or subsidizing forest practices. It can only be done by developing the ecological conscience of all people concerned with the forest.

CHAPTER 11

Forest Policy:
Themes, Challenges, and New
Directions

he history of forest policy in New England presents a series of major themes, changing slowly as economic conditions and public attitudes changed over the decades.
Though forests and wood products have been critically important
to New Englanders, there was no institutional focus for forestry
programs until the 1890s, nearly three centuries after settlement. It
followed the liquidation of many of the forest's most valuable products, and the clearing of 40 percent of the original forest. There is
no evidence that early New Englanders seriously considered maintaining significant acreages of land in public ownership for timber,
water supply, and multiple use values. A detailed analysis of the region's forest policies has never been attempted, so the story can
only be sketched here. I will also outline the challenges of the future
and my own ideas on how to meet them.[1]

Because of the limits of time and space, federal forest policies as
they affect this region are not discussed; this is not to suggest that
these policies have been unimportant.[2]

Changing Forest Policies

Changing themes in forest policy have been based on public attitudes about the role of government, and on perceptions about the
serious forest problems of the day (table 31).

In the colonial period, forest products were critical to individual
welfare, to trade, and to the promotion of economic activity. Colonists were accustomed to mercantilist regulation of the economy.
For example, laws requiring fire control measures were common,

Table 31. Outline History of New England Forest Policy

Period	Themes
Colonial	Land disposal by governments to promote settlement
	Promotion manufacturing
	Supervision of utilization and trade
	Laws against fire
	Minimal reservations for public use
Revolution to 1890	Complete land disposal to raise revenue and place land in private hands
	Low rates of forest taxation
	Occasional tax preferences for tree planting
1890–1917	Establishment of state forest agencies
	Establishment of forestry research and educational institutions
	Beginning of extensive state land acquisition programs (excluding Maine)
	Institution of pest control programs: blister rust, gypsy moth
1917–50	Increased federal cooperation
	Tree planting, nurseries
	Continued land acquisition
1950–70	Establishment of small-landowner programs
	Open space programs
	Parks land acquisition
	Land and Water Conservation Fund and SCORP process

though we know little of how they were enforced.[3] In this age, there was a veritable "compulsion to control."[4]

Through their policies on land distribution, the colonies tried to promote farming and settlement, and to prevent widespread absentee ownership, land speculation, and large consolidated ownerships. But when the need for revenue pressed hard, they offered towns for sale faster than they could be settled. The buyers had to keep returning to the legislators to have their obligations "to plant so many settlers" deferred. Some grants or sales defaulted for noncompliance with their terms. In most of southern New England, the objectives were achieved, if only temporarily. Towns were also granted in support of canals, seminaries, and colleges.[5]

In legislating about the forest itself, the towns and colonies took a meticulous interest in enforcing the quality of products, controlling prices, controlling trade, promoting mills by grants of monopolies, timber, and water rights, and assuring close utilization of timber. In places, timberlands were reserved from sale to be used to support local government, schools, and the ministry.[6] Colonists regulated forest use as open range for livestock, and even in one case granted bounties for the removal of barberry, an alternate host for a wheat rust.

Efforts to conserve long-term timber supply were nonexistent, except where towns and colonies controlled the export of various wood products. Even the famous Broad Arrow Acts only viewed pines as a stockpile of material for short-term use and made no effort to assure a long-term supply. Even these limited efforts, however, were a complete failure.

In the nineteenth century, the colonial concepts of control withered. Though the forest remained economically important, it was virtually ignored by public policy. Except for Maine, which retained sizable forest ownership until 1878, there was little legislative concern with forests until the 1880s and 90s.

The period may be characterized as one of indifference. During this period of laissez-faire, public opinion and legislative inclinations favored private landownership. Public opinion supported the free use of private capital unhindered by larger social concerns. But, as J. W. Hurst argues in his magnificent book, "a crude laissez faire was never the guiding doctrine."[7] Legislatures and courts supported the speedy disposal of public lands. States subsidized railroads and established patterns of law supportive of industry objectives, in allocating water rights, adjudicating conflicts over navigation, and a thousand other ways.

The 1880s to the 1920s saw rapid change. In traditional lumbering areas production waned, as large trees diminished and cheap western lumber began to reach midwestern markets. Public and legislative interest in conservation rose, and state forest agencies, nurseries, forestry schools, and research stations were created. In this period, the decline of New England's farm economy was painfully apparent. Trees seemed a fine way to use abandoned pastures. A new consciousness of timber supply and the environmental values of forests emerged. It was this period that gave New England its fine national forests and park systems, and saw the creation of specific administrative units for forests and parks. It also spawned the private organizations that have contributed so much to forestry and land conservation in New England.

The 1930s saw a brief increase in rural populations, extensive concern with "land use adjustment," and a dramatic collapse in consumption of lumber and paper. The federal government led in conservation and economic recovery programs. The Civilian Conservation Corps built trails and parks and planted trees. The hurricane of 1938 stimulated a cooperative venture, the federally funded New England Timber Salvage Administration, to help salvage blown-down pine timber. World War II produced labor shortages in the northwoods and stimulated a new exodus of population from the hill farms and logging towns of northern New England. Many of the soldiers who grew up in these areas never went back. What many of them wanted was a house in the suburbs.

The late forties, then, sparked the new development pattern that created, and now threatens to destroy, the suburban forest. Though the hard times of the thirties were a clear memory in northern New England, forests continued to play a key economic role. But in southern New England, they came to be seen by many merely as potential houselots and green backdrops for suburbia. There, the public and policy makers almost forgot about the products of the forest. To the extent that public policy troubled itself at all with the forests, the concern was only casual. The forestry agencies were active in setting up service forestry programs, modernizing fire control, and planting soil bank plantations.

The new conservation movement of the 1960s brought a new emphasis on open space policy. The Land and Water Conservation Fund and the natural beauty programs of Lyndon Johnson's administration helped spark a new interest in land acquisition for recreation and conservation. Funds went to towns and cities for open space uses. The Cape Cod National Seashore dates from this period.[8]

By the 1970s, the political interest in amenity values reached a peak.[9] A new interest in management of public lands arose. Federal and state agencies revived land management programs with new emphasis on land use planning and multiple use. The preservation wing of environmentalists asked that two-thirds of the White Mountain National Forest be considered for wilderness. The surging real estate market brought forest taxation again to the fore, and Maine, Vermont, and Massachusetts adopted new ways of taxing woodlands.

By the end of the seventies, new and different attitudes toward the forest were emerging. More people took axe in hand to heat their homes and found themselves interested in the productive potential of the forest. A revived competitive position of the forest in-

Fire control has been one of the more successful forest policies in New England. Buck Hill Tower, Rhode Island. *Courtesy of Rhode Island Division of Forest Environment.*

dustry brought investment and jobs to rural areas that badly needed economic balance but that were not close enough to U.S. Route 128 to benefit from the electronics boom.

How have these policies actually affected events? Were they successful in terms of their original objectives? We hardly know. The kings saved a few pines with their Broad Arrow policy. Many of the soil bank plantations are forgotten and overgrown with brush. The forest tax programs are now highly controversial and it is difficult to tell whether they have promoted forestry.

Beyond doubt, the most successful policy was the fundamental one of avoiding public ownership of land. New England today contains less public land than any other forested region. Most of what is now a magnificent system of state and federal forests, parks, and wildlife refuges was purchased or donated. Despite the tiny ownership held by government, however, these lands offer the possibility for regional and national leadership in multiple use management under growing pressure for wood products, intense recreational use, and other social values.

Perhaps the next most visible success of New England forest policies has been in fire control. Damage due to fire has been reduced to its practical minimum—in fact, dangerously so, because there is no longer serious legislative and public concern with maintaining fire control funding. Only after rare major fires do the fire control units receive funds for equipment and maintenance backlogs. As the early foresters believed, effective fire control is an essential precondition for private investment in forest management.

The programs of help for small landowners have been a mixed success. Many acres of land have been thinned, planted, and cut successfully with the help of the service foresters. Probably these foresters help bring a better appreciation of conservation to thousands of New Englanders each year. Yet the programs are criticized by some observers for an excessive timber orientation, lack of provision for long-term follow-through, and subsidy of management practices that make little economic sense. Most of the practices applied have been on such tiny areas that they cannot affect future timber production very much. Finally, most forest landowners, after thirty years of these programs, remain unaware of the services available.[10]

The really troubling fact about all of these forestry programs, however, is that we cannot evaluate them fairly. We do not have the data. There is only a clash of opinion that leaves everyone baffled and results in little real change. The promoters of expanded programs, critics say, cannot justify the expansions. The critics have no evidence, say the promoters.

So the record is mixed, controversial, and the facts are not all in. Can we, though, ask if these policies seem to fit the needs of the *next* few decades?

The answer, I believe, is that they don't.

Challenges of the Next Half-Century

My review of the trends in New England's forest tells me that the forest of the future will face the following challenges:

1. Suburban sprawl, poorly controlled and lacking provision for forests as a positive landscape feature, will continue.

2. There will be rapid change in public values about forests, with greater acceptance of logging by most people, but still intense opposition by groups committed to the green backdrop philosophy.

3. Timber prices and demands will rise, which will increase harvesting pressure throughout New England.

Wildlife are an important resource of New England's forest. Efforts to maintain public access to private land for hunting and other wildlife-related activities will be a key policy issue in New England. *Courtesy of Massachusetts Division of Fish and Wildlife.*

4. Recurring speculative booms in rural land are likely. Even without them, parcel size and length of ownership tenure will fall.

5. Private forest land will be less available for hunting, fishing, walking, and winter sports.

6. Mechanization will reduce the number of jobs per cord of wood processed.

7. New England's current national status as a prime location for making imported pulp into high-grade papers will slowly diminish.

Thes trends, if they materialize, will pose several practical problems. Current policies are not capable of addressing them.

Today, shoddy harvesting and inappropriate clearcutting are more serious threats to future productivity than are failure to plant, thin, or improve timber stands. The rapid turnover in ownership, land use conversion, and parcel fragmentation will continue to erode the forest landbase. Too many subsidized plantations are forgotten, to be overwhelmed by aspen or stripped for subdivisions. Too many are losing value growth to overstocking because timely thinnings are ignored by owners who never invested much in the stands anyway. Too many publicly funded pruning, thinning, or stand improvement projects on private land have been wasted because no incentive exists to follow through on them.

To overcome these difficulties, forest management assistance must develop in landowners a sense of their own responsibility for their forests. the poorest cutting today is found on small holdings and in a few places where giant owners practice extensive clearcutting. Today's assistance programs encourage the idea among landowners and the public that good forestry is government's responsibility, not theirs. New England foresters can lead us out of this dead end, if they want to. Some of them are trying hard right now.

Today's forest tax, land use planning, and land acquisition programs are grossly inadequate to deal with the effects of suburbanization and future rural land subdivision booms. We cannot keep lands in forest, assume that they will be managed, and maintain them in a developed landscape simply with low taxes. More is required.

The short time horizons of landowners will be an increasing problem outside the industrial forest. Today's programs, which do not effectively tie tax breaks and subsidized management practices into future follow-through, simply will not meet the needs of the future.

What Can Be Done?

The first need is to develop a shared professional recognition among resource managers, planners, and political leaders of their seriousness, and to convey the resulting ideas to the public. The vigorous public leadership displayed by foresters in the turn-of-the-century conservation movement and in the 1930s must be restored.

Some ingredients of a forest policy for coming decades are:

Reform taxation and small-owner assistance programs to require management follow-through. Contracts, refund clauses, or other devices should be used to bind recipients of public funds to deliver the follow-through to final harvest and regeneration. No more forgotten soil bank plantations.

This is the first step in the larger process of landowner education. Educate landowners, through all available channels, to take responsibility for their land, without holding their hands out for government funds or tax breaks.

Reeducate professional foresters. Our dogmas of low taxes and handouts for forest landowners demean our trade. Since many of us are also landowners, these dogmas smack of unhealthy conflict of interest. We should believe that forestry is worth paying for, and that good forestry is responsible land stewardship—not a favor to the public that owners must be bribed to bestow. Foresters who cannot accept these ideas are one of our greatest impediments to progress.

Abandon subsidies that undermine responsibility, particularly federal funds for fire control, for spraying gypsy moths in suburbia and state parks, and for spraying budworm (the latter has almost been completed).

Increase the emphasis on job creation based on wood. The economic development offices of each New England state should have forest industry specialists.

Promote a vigorous sector of private forestry consultants.

Promote a return to the old New England ethic that allows free public recreational use of undeveloped land. Seek ways to persuade owners to take down the "No Trespassing" signs.

Vigorously acquire land and less-than-fee interests such as easements and development rights. Emphasize acquisition by towns and local districts. The objective should be to double state and local land ownership and control by the year 2000, to 2.2 million acres, or 6 percent of the region. This means acquiring 55,000 acres per year, surely an attainable proposition. One-half of the program should be devoted to the suburban forest and one-half to scenic and other significant natural areas and river corridors across the landscape, outside the industrial forest.

Support a comparable tripling of ownership or control by the nonprofit sector.

Upgrade forest research and information. Conduct detailed surveys of timber cut no less than every three years. Apply increased funds to evaluating economical means of boosting forest yields of timber, wildlife, and recreation with minimal environmental impact. Design and test more effective programs of landowner assistance and taxation.

Reform forestry education. We train many foresters in New England, but too few of them are well prepared to meet the region's future needs. The turn-of-the-century foresters spent most of their energy convincing landowners that forestry was worthwhile. The foresters of the future should be equipped to do the same. Today, all too often, forestry students are told that forestry on small wood-

Research is a key government contribution to progress in forestry. USDA Forest Service scientists tally trees, Bartlett Experimental Forest, New Hampshire. *Courtesy of USDA Forest Service.*

lands is not worthwhile without government subsidy. My own experience suggests that careful silvicultural analysis does not receive adequate emphasis in New England forestry education. Educators should correct this situation at once.

Start thinking now about how states will respond if the developing market forces lead to overcutting. Will they stand aside and watch? What limits can be applied to prevent sustained episodes of overcutting?

Strongly support the region's nonprofit sector in its education efforts.

Attend to the information, training, and other needs of logging contractors, who dispense much of the practical forestry advice in the region. Develop ways to recognize professionalism and good craftsmanship among loggers. In particular, roadbuilding practices and skidding, which cause much of the aesthetic and environmental damage in logging, are under the logger's control.

These programs will have to be attempted by redirecting a declining staff and budget. In Maine and New Hampshire, 1981 saw substantial cuts in forestry staffs and funding. To meet the needs outlined above, persons concerned with forest conservation will have to work more effectively and find help and allies wherever they can.

A Case for Laissez-Faire?

I have colleagues who believe that I am simply imagining a lot of problems. They say that when wood gets costly enough, people will manage the forests. Don't worry about the suburban forest—that land is worth more for houses anyway. If folks can cut up rural woodlots and hustle them to distant buyers for $5,000 per acre, why not? Landscape values are just a matter of taste, in which government should not interfere.

Why not, indeed? A productive and attractive forest landscape is an essential part of New England's quality of life—for the scenery, fuelwood, jobs, and walking it provides. I cannot imagine that these values will be conserved by the unrestrained forces of private speculation, public agency indifference, and a landowner and professional attitude that places responsibility for conservation on the government.

A Case for Subsidies?

The received wisdom of government forestry agencies today is that in the future we will want a lot more wood. This is probably true. According to this doctrine, to have that wood we must subsidize woodgrowers. Why not? We subsidize suburban homeowners, farmers, fishermen, and nearly everyone else.

Great programs have been planned to subsidize forestry on private lands, and administrators continue to hope for new infusions of funds. Their continued appeals for tax breaks and subsidies seem to keep this major client group happy. Indications are that the national mood following Ronald Reagan's election will not support such outlays.

These programs will never work. They undermine responsibility. They have no built-in assurance that the land benefiting will ever produce a timber crop or be available for public use. They encourage the lazy view that conservation is the government's job. And finally, programs like these are simply not going to get enough funding today to make any difference.

In the past, even the U.S. Forest Service, the current leading advocate for subsidies, did not believe in their effectiveness: "after careful study it was concluded that incentive payments do not form a sound major approach to forest conservation." [11] This statement was no doubt made to scotch the major competing alternative to the favored program of land acquisition and regulation, but I think time will prove it correct nonetheless. Aldo Leopold, decrying the bureaucratizing of conservation, characterized the attitude behind this trend: "whatever ails the land, the government will fix it." [12]

A Case for Government Regulation of Forest Practice?

In the past, American forestry leaders believed that private owners would not voluntarily manage forests properly. The profits were too limited; most landowners held land simply for liquidation and not for long-term management. They concluded that the states and the federal government must apply detailed regulation to private forest management. Leaders of the U.S. Forest Service publicly advocated government regulation until the late 1940s.

I do not believe that government regulation of forest practice can meet the challenges of the next half-century. Tempting as the idea may be to some, it is administratively impossible to implement. Giving this task to already understaffed agencies would produce little but frustration. The tremendous adversary debate that would ensue would serve nothing. In short, programs of general regulation of forest practice would be a huge misallocation of resources. They would not succeed in building a sense of landowner responsibility, but would undermine it further. They would not address the largest problems, which are landowner indifference and conversion of forest to speculative lots and other uses. If New Englanders are concerned enough about the forest's future to consider regulation, then they should support the program ideas outlined above as being more likely to produce results.

A case can be made, however, for regulating forest practice in particular areas of environmental or scenic importance, like roadsides, streamsides, lakeshores, wetlands, and sensitive wildlife habitats. This is being done now in a variety of ways, most thoroughly under the jurisdiction of the Maine Land Use Regulation Commission. Such a pattern of regulation does not seek to control forest practices generally, but only seeks to assure that nontimber values are properly protected in limited areas of true environmental importance. Setting minimum standards for building, maintaining, and "putting to bed" skid trails and logging roads is a fruitful role for regulatory agencies. Of course, the use of chemical insecticides and herbicides should continue to be subject to strict public regulation.

The English monarchs and their governors were unable to impose the Broad Arrow policy on enterprising and ornery colonial woodcutters—and those pines were the king's own legal property. We would experience much more serious difficulty in imposing general forest practice regulation on the decendants of those unruly colonials. George Perkins Marsh, the nineteenth-century conservationist, had little faith in regulating forest practice:

For prevention of the evils upon which I have so long dwelt, the American people must look to the diffusion of general intelligence on this subject, and to the enlightened self interest, for which they are remarkable, and not to the action of their local or general legislatures.[13]

The Program in Brief

Since the days of the Broad Arrow policy, New England's forest policies have frequently been inadequate to meet the region's changing needs. Today, the New England states possess effective fire control organizations, some form of open space or use-value taxation for rural land, and a corps of trained foresters available to assist small landowners. They are upgrading management of their own public land. The upsurge in wood demand presents opportunities for serious forestry and helps more consultants earn a living. Yet it also threatens overcutting. Dramatic land use change seems likely in the future.

The successes of the past cannot carry us through the next half-century. Today's programs and policies were not designed to meet the challenges we now face. They should not be scrapped, but intelligently overhauled. I propose the following guidelines for policy:

1. Implement a major public and private program to acquire land and easements, especially in the suburban forest. The objective should be a tripling of land controlled by the nonprofit sector (to

0.9 million acres), and a doubling of state and local government ownership (to 2.2 million acres) by the year 2000. This increase should be at the state and local level and should emphasize nonfee control wherever feasible. This would place about 4 million acres, or 10 percent of the region's land in public and nonprofit control. As part of this program, the wild forest should be doubled in acreage, to 2 million acres. Financing this program will be a challenge. Given the low priority conservation enjoys in an age of fiscal constraint, new funding sources will have to be developed. Support of the political leadership at the highest levels will be required. But such a public land system will be the most magnificent heritage that this generation could pass on to the future.

2. Accelerate efforts to develop in forest landowners an ethic supportive of responsible long-term forest management, to convince them that good forestry can pay its way, and that it is the right thing to do. All available public and private channels, including the schools, should be enlisted. It is possible, with current staff, to make personal contact with every owner of more than 100 acres in the next ten years.

3. Abandon subsidies to individual forest practices that do not include rigid requirements for landowner follow-through.

4. Work with rural landowners to restore New England's traditional ethic of public use of private land. This will require the recreationist and government to assume some obligations in return.

5. Upgrade our base of information of land use change, timber consumption, wildlife resources, and the ecological characteristics of New England's forests, particularly as they respond to management.

This program provides a good start toward the effective assertion of forestry leadership in New England. Not all foresters, citizens, and legislators will accept each part of it, but I hope these ideas may stimulate a constructive debate and critique of policy. These proposals are consistent with the best of New England's forestry and land use traditions.

What I am urging is the complete reform of landowner attitudes toward their forests. In the future, the only guarantee of good forest stewardship will be the widespread acceptance of what forester Aldo Leopold called the land ethic, "an ethical relation to the land." [14]

CHAPTER 12

The Forest:
Past and Future

he future forests of New England will be shaped by the same forces that have shaped them in the past: external forces and internal forces. Also, several basic abiding conditions will continue to influence the role of the forest in New England life.

External Forces

The forces from outside New England affecting the forest include, first and foremost, those of the market. Market forces were best expressed in the early export trade, which called into being large industries for shipping lumber, masts, and other forest products overseas and to other coastal towns. Later, cheaper midwestern farm products and the demand for labor in the industrializing cities triggered a massive decline in farming that returned 8 million acres of cleared land to forest. In the twentieth century, the markets for recreational lots and suburban homesites have again modified the forest, redirecting its principal uses over millions of acres. Other market influences have brought about a high degree of absentee, corporate ownership and a limited degree of foreign ownership of land. In the 1970s, the dramatic increase in oil prices brought an ancient wood use—energy—to the fore again in the consciousness of thrifty New Englanders. The national forest products market, with rising demand, escalating costs in other regions, and new technology, contributed to a reconstruction and resurgence of the region's wood-using industries in the 1970s. While this was principally visible in northern New England, in southern New England sawmills were modernized, fuelwood demand grew, and a boom in oak export markets boosted the sawlog market.

Imported insects and disease have had major effects on the forest. New England's forests are home to many native forest pests, such as the spruce budworm, beech scale, and birch dieback, which occasionally inflict spectacular widespread damage. As a result of colossal ecological bungling, the region's forests have been afflicted and reworked by imported pests as well. The imported blister rust has killed young white pines and reduced tree quality regionwide. The European strain of scleroderris canker threatens similar damage to several pine species. The gypsy moth has killed susceptible hardwoods across southern New England and periodically makes itself a major suburban nuisance.

The most serious losses, however, have been the chestnut, a dominant hardwood tree of the southern New England forest, highly valued for its timber and nuts, and the American elm, a major shade and street tree. With these trees went two species important to the region's way of life, though in different ways. Thus has human folly remodeled the region's forest, much to everyone's loss. These losses, it will be recalled, occurred only within this century. No one can be certain that similar disasters will not befall other important New England trees.

Internal Forces

From within New England have emerged other forces affecting the forest. The colonial policies governing land ownership and settlement left half of the forest dominated by 100-acre blocks, relics of past farming and land sales. The wildlands of the north result from mass land sales to speculators, for revenue rather than settlement. This change anticipated the later retreat of farming from the fringes of the wildlands.

Also from within have emerged major waves of conservation leadership. The early conservation movement resulted in the establishment of forestry schools and state forestry agencies. To the same period, we owe the rich diversity of private nonprofit groups who have recreated a public forest estate in this century. They acted by pressuring governments into action, by acquiring land themselves, and by inspiring philanthropists to donate land.

Unique to New England is its system of town government with limited county government. This arrangement means that there are few government agencies capable of taking action on natural resource issues, such as park acquisition, on a regional basis. It means that towns ignore needs of wider areas, while the state is excessively distant and distrusted by most citizens.

New England has generated considerable literary and scientific interest in forests, expressed in the writings of Thoreau and Marsh, and in a series of scientific research stations, the best known perhaps being the Harvard Forest and the Hubbard Brook Experimental Forest. At Hubbard Brook, scientists have worked out with meticulous care the inner ecological cycles about which Marsh wrote a century earlier. The literary and scientific works originating in New England forests have continuously inspired people across the nation who care about forests.

New England's Future Forests

While projections of the future are not my concern here, a few speculative scenarios may help suggest what the region's forests might be like in fifty years.

The year 2030 will be four centuries after white men settled at Massachusetts Bay and began clearing the forest. During that time, their descendants have recycled roughly 8 million acres of land back into forest from farming. In fifty years New England's landscape will still be dominated by its forest. There will probably still be more forest than there was in 1880. The principal differences between optimistic and pessimistic scenarios will be the kinds of values these forests will be able to serve (table 32).

My optimistic scenario projects no revival of investment boom subdivision of rural forests, a modest erosion of the industrial forest, and a doubling of the wild forest. It assumes that a more land-conserving pattern of suburban development will prevail. If this is so, erosion of the current suburban forest will be slight, and areas that become suburban forest by being embraced by expanding sprawl will be planned for and conserved.

The pessimistic scenario envisions a significant erosion of the industrial forest by conversion to recreational subdivisions and reserves for small groups. The suburban forest nearly vanishes in the face of inefficient, land-consuming, unplanned sprawl. There is no expansion of the wild forest, and the parcel size distribution of the rural forest flip-flops, to one-third of the acreage above 100 acres in size, from the present two-thirds.

These are entirely plausible outcomes. They will mostly be determined by land markets and the values placed on land by people. They are thus beyond the reach of traditional forest policy tools like favorable taxation, financial aid to landowners, or information pro-

Table 32. Two Speculative Scenarios for New England's Forests: 2030
(million acres)

| | 1980 | 2030 | |
		Optimistic	Pessimistic
Industrial	13	12	10
Recreational	3	3	6
Suburban	3	3	1
Wild	1	2	1
Rural	11	9	9
Total	31	29	27
Estimated acreage available for timber production	23	21	15
Developed	4	5	8
Farmland	3	2	1
Fraction of acreage outside of industrial forest in holdings 100 acres or more	⅔	½	⅓

SOURCE: Author estimates.

grams. They can only be affected by planning and zoning, by public
and nonprofit landownership, and by developing in landowners an
ethical relationship to the land. Sound tax policies for rural land
can help but are insufficient by themselves.

The Fate of the Forest Matters

What difference does the fate of the forest make? We can briefly
compare one aspect, the commercial forest land base available for
serious investments in long-term timber production. The 31 million
acres shown for 1980 are now only partially available. Perhaps one-
half of the suburban and recreational forests might be used for occasional timber crops, and two-thirds of the rural forest (the amount
exceeding 100 acres in size). This places the wood production land
base at 23 million acres. This is not to say that smaller lots will produce no wood at all, only that they offer limited opportunities for
intensive forestry. Other analysts might use other assumptions, but
these will serve our purpose here.

Under the pessimistic 2030 scenario, expanding use of land for
speculative subdivisions plus highly space-consumptive patterns of
sprawl would reduce forest acreage to 27 million acres. Of this, only
15 million acres might be available for serious timber management.

Suburbanization. How this cycle of land use proceeds will determine the fate of a large area of New England's forest. Courtesy of U.S. Dept. of Agriculture.

The implications of these trends for commercial timber supply are serious. The optimistic scenario implies an available timber supply to the commercial market, at 1976 growth rates, of 11.5 million cords per year. The pessimistic scenario would produce 7.5 million, or 35 percent less. This reduction in supply is equal to two-thirds of the entire 1980 timber harvest in the state of Maine. Again, these figures are meant to illustrate the magnitude of the long-term consequences of land use changes. They are not intended as predictions.

For hunters, fishermen, and cross-country skiers, the implications of the high land consumption of the pessimistic scenario are serious. Sportsmen will find their ability to use the landscape seriously impaired. The aesthetic values of New England's countryside would fall markedly.

So the fate of the forest does make a difference—a big difference. Which scenario becomes reality will affect wood supply and wood-based employment, and all the aesthetic and other nontimber benefits of the forest. If the pessimistic outcome occurs, the quality of life in the region, and its attractiveness for tourism, will decline. Scenic values consumed by scattered development will account for most of the decline.

In the coming half-century, significant changes will occur in the composition of New England's forests as a result of natural ecological succession and timber harvesting. In the industrial forest, stands will be much younger, on average, than today, especially for the intensively used softwoods. The combined effects of the current spruce budworm outbreak and rising timber harvests will mean that much of the spruce-fir forest will be managed on a thirty- to forty-year rotation for pulp and small sawlogs. Its average age may be less than half what it is today. The industrial forest will present a mosaic of young and middle-aged stands, and increasingly plantations will be evident. By the year 2030, the extensive hardwood resource of that region will be displaying the effects of increased management. The aesthetic appeal of this "damp and intricate wilderness" will decline somewhat.

The birch-aspen stands of the north will be replaced by more tolerant softwoods and maple and beech, unless heavy cutting and soil disturbance or fires regenerate these short-lived early successional species. The outlook for birch log supply is thus not very good. How the spruce-fir stands now being harvested will develop is still being debated by scientists and foresters.

Large areas of old-field brushland will return to hardwood and mixed forests. Many oak stands will become oak-pine as pine enters the overstory. Many pine stands, especially on old fields, will be converted to hardwoods and fir, as their understories are released by cutting or windthrow.

Many of the heavily cut stands and old-field stands are complex transitional mixtures. How they will develop in the future is hard to predict—our knowledge of long-term forest development after severe disturbance is weak.

Abiding Conditions

Most of this book has concentrated on change, its sources, and its effects on New England's forest. But besides constant change, there are several abiding conditions that will influence the forest. These conditions will constrain and undergird policies attempting to improve the forest.

The basic conditions are ecological. These are expressed in the region's forest geography, in its abundance of early successional forests, and the resilience of those forests. The ecological potential for sustained production of wood and other forest services will remain high, and may even increase. To what extent the cumulative effects of acid precipitation will alter this basic ecological productivity remains to be seen.

The other abiding conditions are social. They begin with the historic landownership pattern and the system of town government. These conditions include widespread private ownership of forest land and diverse centers of policy decisionmaking. They assure that change will be slow, but they offer some useful resistance to the rapid diffusion of bad ideas. The town system of government allows flexible innovation by local groups but hinders consideration of regional concerns.

An abiding condition of great importance is the basic attitude of New Englanders about the forest. Individual attitudes vary, of course, from approval of exploitation to rabid preservationism. Especially in suburbia, tension between advocates of green backdrop policies and proponents of commercial interests will continue. But in rural areas, New Englanders are suspicious of public landownership and support the commodity uses of the forest. Few New Englanders favor widespread use of forests for wilderness. The region's basic belief in the free right of private landowners to do as they please conflicts with another widely held value, that recrea-

Private effort and generosity will contribute to conserving future scenes across New England. Notchview Preserve, Massachusetts. *Courtesy of Trustees of Reservations.*

tional use of private land is a public right. While this value has been forgotten by suburbanites regarding their own land, they vigorously advocate it for the owners of the industrial and rural forests.

New England citizens are willing to recognize legislatively that farms and forests should be taxed differently from house lots. But the economic pressures of today mean that the current ferment over forest taxation will not subside. We can expect wrangling over farm and forest taxation to be a permanent item on the agenda of harassed legislators and tax assessors, as well as a perennial concern of the owners themselves.

The corollary of extensive private ownership is limited public ownership. This will not change. Even if the most ambitious goals for expanded public ownership are met, the region would still only have a small public forest estate. This seems to be what people want and is no problem in itself.

Sprawling, uncontrolled suburban growth and future rural land speculation booms will destroy forest values and community amenities on an unprecedented scale. The addition of 2 million people to our region's population in the next twenty years could cause as much environmental and visual damage as was caused by the entire previous population growth of this century. This is partly due to the excessive, often legally mandated, appetite for space of our modern development patterns and to the public subsidies that promote sprawl. It is made worse by the ugliness of modern construction and the mindlessness of its development patterns. Accompanying this massive demand for land for development will be a continuing decline in farming. The expected loss of open space, forest production, and wildlife habitat should motivate vigorous action by those concerned with the natural values of farm and forest.

The ability of government to deal with these problems will decline. Tighter budgets will erode the effectiveness of existing programs. Federal funding cuts will hinder further progress in land acquisition. Conservation and forestry will slide lower on the priority lists of legislators and governors, who will face massive and baffling fiscal and policy problems.

The region's active and vigorous nonprofit sector will have to take up the challenge. The conservation commissions, land trusts, and statewide groups will have to fight legislative budget cuts every year. They will have to strive even harder to raise funds and snatch tidbits of open land from the path of bulldozers. They will have to provide most of the leadership in convincing their neighbors of the value of forest conservation, rational development, multiple use forestry, and sensible preservation of outstanding areas.

Another abiding condition will be an escalating world, national, and regional demand for wood products. This growth may stimulate continued industrial development based on wood. Unless the secondary processing of wood expands markedly, however, employment in wood-based industry could fall considerably. This would constrain community prosperity and individual economic opportunity across all of rural New England.

As they respond to increased demand, the region's landowners, led by the large industrial concerns, will have to raise the quality and sophistication of management practice. Careful management of the hardwood forests of the North may become possible for the first time. The region's battered pine stands will be upgraded, and neglected farm woodlots will be more carefully tended. The spruce-fir forest will experience a significant inventory decline because of budworm and harvesting, but its long-term productivity need not suffer. I expect an improvement in the general level of forest practice by the year 2000 more radical than in any previous twenty-year period in New England's history. All of these changes will affect the region's wildlife populations, each species in different ways. Aesthetic values need not suffer markedly, but limited areas will display a noticeably managed look.

This is a mixed picture, a subtle one. On the one hand, major forest values will be lost to shoddy development, land posting, and unproductive land speculation. On the other, expanded wood markets, greater knowledge, and better landowner attitudes will permit major improvements in the region's standards of forest practice. As New Englanders begin to see what has been lost, they will appreciate more what has been saved. The Allagash, national forest wilderness, and the local land trust sanctuaries will be ever more highly prized as part of the region's natural heritage. Never before has New England's forest promised to mean so much to so many people.

For foresters, legislators, landowners, and citizens, the coming decades promise abundant challenge. We must convince owners of their responsibility to upgrade management of the rural and industrial forests. The acreage of wild forest should be doubled. Vigorous steps are necessary to save what we can of the rapidly eroding suburban forest. The recreational forest should be better managed and its expansion stopped. A principal means of meeting these challenges should be a major public-private land conservation program, aimed at doubling the acreage in state and local ownership, and tripling the acreage in nonprofit hands by the year 2000. Access to private forests for fishing, birding, hunting, and wasting time in the woods must be assured.

The policies of the past are not equal to these challenges. New leaders and new policies will be needed. In New England's best traditions, they will emerge.

And through all of this change and tension, one reality will abide: New England will remain, as it was in 1620, a region of forests.

NOTES

Chapter 1

1. The story of New England's forest as it was discovered by the settlers is a rich and fascinating one but cannot be recounted here. A few useful sources are S. W. Bromley, The original forest types of southern New England, *Ecol. Monographs* 5(1) (1935): 61–89 and references therein; T. G. Siccama, Presettlement and present forest vegetation in Northern Vermont with special reference to Chittenden County, *Amer. Midland Naturalist* 85(1) (1971): 153–72; G. M. Day, The Indian as an ecological factor in the New England forest, *Ecology* 32(2) (1973): 329–46; and C. G. Lorimer, Presettlement forest of northeastern Maine, *Ecology* 58(2) (1977): 139–48. Maine's coastal forests are discussed in P. W. Conkling, *Islands in time: A natural and human history of the coastal islands of Maine* (Camden: Downeast Books, 1981). The postglacial history of New England forests is reviewed by T. E. Bradstreet and R. B. Davis, Mid-postglacial environments in New England with emphasis on Maine, *Arctic Anthropology* 12(2) (1975): 7–22, with full references.
2. A useful article expressing concern for the future of New England's forest is John G. Mitchell, Whither the Yankee Forest?, *Audubon* 83(2)(1981): 78–99.

Chapter 2

1. Readers interested in pursuing New England's forest as naturalists will enjoy N. Jorgensen, *Sierra Club naturalist's guide to southern New England* (San Francisco: Sierra Club Books, 1978) and J. Burk and M. Holland, *Stone walls and sugar maples: An ecology for northeasterners* (Boston: Appalachian Mountain Club, 1979); the classic is B. F. Thompson, *The changing face of New England* (Boston: Houghton Mifflin, 1977), a highly readable overview. A superb and readable technical treatment of the ecology of the northern hardwood forest is G. E. Likens and H. F. Bormann, *Pattern and process in a forested ecosystem* (New York: Springer Verlag, 1979). For a geographic perspective on the suburban forest, see J.-P. Gottman, *Megalopolis: The urbanized northeastern seaboard of the United States* (Cambridge: MIT Press, 1964), esp. chs. 4–8. A brief overview is found in J. W. Barrett, *Regional silviculture* (2d ed., New York: John Wiley, 1980). A recent, more technical treatment covering northern New England forests is *Proceedings, Symposium on intensive culture of northern forest types*, USDA-FS NEFES, Gen. Tech. Rept. NE-29, 1977. Anyone interested in this subject has probably read and reread Henry David Thoreau's *Walden* but may not have encountered his *Excursions* (New York: Corinth Books, 1962), especially the essays entitled "The natural history of Massachusetts" and "The succession of forest trees." More technical treatments are J. L. Vankat, *Natural vegetation of North America* (New York: John Wiley, 1979), and R. Daubenmire, *Plant geography* (New York: Academic Press, 1978). The all-time classic is E. L. Braun, *Deciduous forest of eastern North America* (Philadelphia: Blakiston, 1950).

Publications of the U.S. Department of Agriculture, Forest Service, Northeastern Forest Experiment Station are cited frequently, abbreviated as USDA-FS NEFES.

2. The forests of New England are so complex and so extensively disturbed that vegetation zones are difficult to define. A standard approach used by foresters is found in M. Westveld et al., Natural forest zones of New England, *J. Forestry* 54(5) (1957): 332–38, on which figure 3 is based.
3. Valuable sources for the mountain forest include L. C. Bliss, Alpine plant communities of the Presidential Range, N.H., *Ecology* 44(11) (1963): 678–91; D. E. May and R. B. Davis, *Alpine tundra vegetation on Maine mountains*, Augusta: State Planning Office, Critical Areas Program, Planning Report No. 36, Jan. 1978; and T. G. Siccama, Vegetation, soil, and climate on the Green Mountains of Vermont. *Ecol. Monographs* 44(3) (1974): 325–49.
4. Useful descriptions of these forests are found in the Forest Survey reports, cited in ch. 4, below, and in R. M. Frank and J. C. Bjorkbom, *A silvicultural guide for spruce-fir in the Northeast*, USDA-FS NEFES, Gen. Tech. Rept. NE-6, 1973; W. B. Leak and S. M. Filip, *Uneven-aged management of northern hardwoods in New England*, USDA-FS NEFES, Res. Pap. NE-332, 1975; W. B. Leak, D. S. Solomon, and S. M. Filip, *A silvicultural guide for northern hardwoods in the northeast*, USDA-FS NEFES, Res. Pap. NE-143, 1969; D. A. Marquis, D. S. Solomon, and J. C. Bjorkbom, *A silvicultural guide for paper birch in the northeast*, USDA-FS NEFES, Res. Pap. NE-130, 1969; R. W. Nash and E. J. Duda, *Studies on extensive dying, regeneration, and management of birch*, Augusta: Maine Forest Service, Bull. No. 15, 1951; K. F. Lancaster and W. B. Leak, *A silvicultural guide for white pine in the northeast*, USDA-FS NEFES, Gen. Tech. Rept. NE-41, 1978; and P. W. Conkling, *Old growth white pine stands in Maine*, Augusta: State Planning Office, Critical Areas Program, Planning Rept. No. 61, Aug. 1978.
5. A large literature exists on the forests of this region. A few items I have found useful are D. M. Smith, Changes in eastern forests since 1600 and possible effects, and G. Stephens, Forests of Connecticut, both in J. F. Anderson and H. K. Kaya, eds., *Perspectives in forest entomology* (New York: Academic Press, 1976); and M. Pochan, Forest succession in Connecticut: A case history, the forest and trees of Westwoods, *Connecticut Woodlands* 29(4) (1974–75): 17, 18. A classic on old field successions in southern New England is H. J. Lutz, *Trends and silvicultural significance of upland forest succession in central New England*, New Haven: Yale School of Forestry, Bull. No. 22, 1928.
6. This statement is based on my own judgment estimate that, by 1979, about 5 million acres of land had been suburbanized and developed. The USDA data for 1979 in table 1 show less than 3 million acres of open land left in farms.
7. J. J. Dowhan and R. J. Craig, *Rare and endangered species of Connecticut and their habitats*, Hartford: State Geol. and Nat. Hist. Survey, Rept. of Investigations, No. 6, 1976, p. 8.
8. See H. Abbott, Artificial regeneration, and G. Weetman, Present methods and technology available for intensive management, in *Proceedings, Symposium on intensive culture*.

Chapter 3

1. General sources on the management of New England's industrial forest include Austin Cary, Maine forests, their preservation, taxation, and value, in Maine Bureau of Industrial and Labor Statistics, *Twentieth Annual Report*, Augusta, 1906, pp. 181–93; D. C. Smith, *A history of lumbering in Maine, 1861–1960* (Orono: Univ. of Maine Press, 1972); and R. S. Wood, *A history of lumbering in Maine, 1820–1861* (Orono: Univ. of Maine, 1935). Both deal almost exclusively with the region that I call the industrial forest. See also H. L. Shirley, Large private holdings in the North, in *Trees—the 1949 Yearbook of Agricul-*

ture (Washington, D.C.: GPO, 1949), pp. 255–75; and E. G. Kelso, Forestry on large holdings in the northeast, *Jour. Forestry* 48(12) (1950): 866–70. A little-known report summarizes cost and returns data for the 1950s: Forest land as an investment in New England, *New England Business Review* (publ. by Federal Reserve Bank of Boston, Oct. 1956). A highly critical report, biased and journalistic, is W. C. Osborn, *The paper plantation* (New York: Grossman, 1974); one-sided as it is, the book is informative and documents, if in an exaggerated manner, the political power of Maine's leading landowners. Current management problems are thoroughly reviewed in *Proceedings, Symposium on intensive culture of northern forest types*, USDA-FS NEFES, Gen. Tech. Rept. NE-29, 1977. On recreation management, see J. L. Hengsback, *A recreational study of the upper St. John River watershed*, Maine Agr. Exp. Sta. Bull. 682, 1970; and B. E. Steward, *Recreational use of private land in a portion of eastern Maine*, Maine Agr. Exp. Sta. Misc. Publ. 658, 1963.

2. For more detail on Maine, see J. Joseph, L. Irland, and T. Howard, *Maine's forests and economic development*, Augusta: Maine Forest Service Planning Program, Tech. Doc. No. 2, 1980; and D. B. Field, *The economic importance of Maine's spruce-fir resource*, Orono: Univ. of Maine, School of Forest Resources, Coop. For. Res. Unit Res. Bull. 2, 1980. On the Canadian log trade, see Jack Aley, *The export of Maine sawlogs to Quebec*, Augusta: Maine Forest Service, April 1981.

3. The story of Maine log driving is found in A. G. Hempstead, *The Penobscot boom* (privately printed, 1975); E. D. Ives, The Argyle boom, *Northeast Folklore* 17, 1976; and Smith, *Lumbering in Maine*, chs. 3 and 4, which cite full references. An excellent view of how Maine lumbermen carried these methods to the Midwest is in *Michigan log marks*, WPA and Mich. Agr. Exp. Sta., Memoir Bull. No. 4, 1941. On Maine's last log drive, see James Nachtwey, The last log drive, what price progress? *New England Business* (Aug. 1976), and S. D. McBride, America's last log drive, *Christian Science Monitor*, Oct. 29, 1976.

4. Frances Belcher, *Logging railroads of the White Mountains* (Boston: Appalachian Mountain Club, 1980).

5. Austin Cary, in *Report of the Forest Commissioner, 1896*, Augusta, p. 179.

6. Environmentalists have been highly critical of large clearcuts and incidents of poor care for erosion control. See Maine Natural Resources Council, *The fourth forest*, Augusta, 1974. A later study by the Land Use Regulation Commission argued that these incidents were rare and did not justify detailed additional regulation. See Land Use Regulation Commission, *Survey of erosion and sedimentation problems associated with logging in Maine*, Augusta, May 1979.

7. See R. G. Healy and J. G. Rosenberg, *Land use and the states* (2d ed., Baltimore: Johns Hopkins Univ. Press, 1979), ch. 3.

8. The tax law is at 36 MRSA 571–584, amended by Ch. 308, Sec. 1–18, P.L. 1973. No thorough, balanced discussion of this tax is readily available. An excellent review of the general issues is J. K. Wood, *Timber taxation in the states*, Lexington, Ky., Council of State Governments, 1978.

9. A valuable review from the woodsworker's perspective is in J. Falk, *The organization of pulpwood harvesting in Maine*, New Haven: Yale School of Forestry and Environmental Studies, Working Paper No. 4. General background on woodsworker problems is found in L. C. Irland, ed., *Manpower—forest industry's key resource*, New Haven: Yale School of Forestry and Environmental Studies, Bull. No. 86, 1975.

10. The story is well told in A. Wilkins, *Ten million acres of timber* (Woolwich, Me.: TBW Books, 1978), ch. 10.

11. To summarize the budworm situation briefly is difficult. Readers seeking more

information might consult L. C. Irland, Pulpwood, pesticides and people, *Environmental Management* 4(5) (1980): 381–89; and USDA Forest Service, State and Private Forestry, Proposed cooperative five year spruce budworm management program for Maine, *Draft programmatic environmental statement*, Broomall, Pa., 1980. The classic policy analysis of the budworm problem is *Report of the task force for evaluation of budworm control alternatives* (the "Baskerville Report"), Fredericton, N. B., Dept. of Natural Resources, 1976; an application of similar methods to the Maine case is R. Seymour, S. Kleinschmidt, and D. G. Mott, *Future impacts of spruce budworm management: A dynamic simulation of the Maine forest 1980–2020*, Univ. of Maine at Orono, School of Forest Resources, Greenwoods Project. Processed. A review of the economic issues is L. C. Irland, *Notes on the economics of spruce budworm control*, Univ. of Maine, School of Forest Resources, Tech. Note 67, 1977. See also the *Maine Forest Review* (Fall 1980), a periodical published by the Maine Chapter, Society of American Foresters; and Maine Forest Service, *Spruce budworm research in Maine: A users guide*, Augusta: Dept. of Conservation, 1979, with supplement for 1980.

12. Osborn, *The paper plantation*.
13. See Land Use Regulation Commission, *Comprehensive land use plan*, Augusta: Dept. of Conservation, 1976.
14. A good sense of the current issues in Maine's industrial forest can be obtained by perusing *Proceedings, Blaine House conference on forestry*, Augusta: Dept. of Conservation, 1981.

Chapter 4

1. The Connecticut case study in this chapter is based on research supported by funds provided by the Northeastern Forest Experiment Station of the USDA Forest Service through the Pinchot Institute of Environmental Forestry, Research Consortium for Environmental Forestry Studies, Grant No. 23-820, by the Yale School of Forestry and Environmental Studies, and by the University of Maine Cooperative Forestry Research Unit. This project was conducted while coinvestigator David B. Field and I were assistant professors at the Yale School of Forestry and Environmental Studies. Dr. Field is now Demeritt professor of Forest Policy, School of Forest Resources, University of Maine at Orono. An abridged version of the report appears in *Connecticut Woodlands* (Summer 1980).
2. Commutersheds are used to define suburban areas in B. Pushkarev, *The Atlantic urban seaboard*, Regional Plan News, No. 90, Sept. 1969, pp. 14, 15. A detailed analysis of suburbanization is found in J.-P. Gottman, *Megalopolis: The urbanized northeastern seaboard of the United States* (Cambridge: MIT Press, 1964), esp. chs. 4 and 5, and p. 223.
3. R. W. Dill and R. G. Otte, *Urbanization of land in the northeastern United States*, USDA, Econ. Research Service Publ. 485, 1971; L. Susskind and C. Perry, The dynamics of growth policy formulation in implementation: A Massachusetts case study, *Law and Contemporary Problems* 43(2) (1979): 147–48. For other more detailed analyses of land consumption, see Pushkarev, *Atlantic urban seaboard*, and North Atlantic Regional Water Resources Study Coordinating Committee, *North Atlantic regional water resources study*, Appendix G. Land Use and Management (New York: U.S. Army Corps of Engineers, 1972), esp. p. 6ff.
4. Gottman, *Megalopolis*, pp. 181, 223; Pushkarev, *Atlantic urban seaboard*, p. 14.
5. See C. S. Robbins, Effect of forest fragmentation on bird populations, in R. M. DeGraaf and K. E. Evans, *Management of north central and northeastern for-*

ests for nongame birds, USDA-FS, North Central Forest Experiment Station, Gen. Tech. Rept. NE-51, 1979, pp. 198–213; and M. A. Gratzer, *Land use inventory for open space planning in eastern Connecticut*, Storrs Agr. Exp. Sta., Univ. of Conn., Res. Rept. No. 38, July 1972, n.p.

6. A nice short summary has already been written: R. C. Sherman, N. C. Shropshire, P. S. Wilson, and A. C. Worrell, *Open-land policy in Connecticut*, New Haven: Yale School of Forestry and Environmental Studies, Bull. No. 87, 1974. A review like this for each New England state would be very useful.

7. Connecticut Dept. of Finance and Control, Office of State Planning, *Proposed: A plan of conservation and development for Connecticut*, Hartford, 1973. For more detailed data, see R. M. Field and Assoc., *Land use: Planning report for the Long Island Sound Study* (Boston: New England River Basins Commission, 1975). An early and valuable series of reports is by N. C. Whetten et al., *Studies of suburbanization in Connecticut*, issued in three parts by the Storrs Agr. Exp. Sta., Bull. 212 (Oct. 1936), 226 (May 1938), and 230 (Feb. 1939).

8. N. Kingsley, *The forest-landowners of southern New England*, USDA-FS NEFES, Res. Bull. NE-41, 1976.

9. USDA, Econ. Res. Serv., *Potential new sites for outdoor recreation in the Northeast*, Outdoor Recreation Resources Review Commission Study Report No. 8 (Washington, D.C.: GPO, 1962), Kingsley, *Forest landowners*, and Field and Irland, note 1 above.

10. A. F. Hawes and R. C. Hawley, *Forest survey of Litchfield and New Haven counties, Connecticut*, Conn. Agr. Exp. Sta. Bull. 162 (Forestry Pub. 5), 1909.

11. N. Kingsley, *The forest resources of southern New England*, USDA-FS NEFES, Res. Bull. NE-36, 1974. On forest landowner attitudes, see T. Holmes and J. Diamond, *An analysis of non-industrial private woodland owners' attitudes towards timber harvesting and forest land use in Windham County, Connecticut, 1979*, Storrs Agr. Exp. Sta., Univ. of Conn., Res. Rept. 63, 1980.

12. P. M. Raup, Urban threats to rural lands, *AIP Journal* 41(6) (1975): 371–78, nicely summarizes the problem. See also A. A. Schmid, *Converting land from rural to urban uses* (Baltimore: Johns Hopkins Univ. Press, 1968).

Chapter 5

1. E. N. Torbert, Evolution of land utilization in Lebanon, N.H., *Geographic Review* 25 (1935): 209–30. Studies of farm and forest land use change in New England history are beyond counting, and extensive research can only unearth a sample. I include here no town histories; the few that I have perused are very weak in land use and economic matters.

In no particular order, items that I have found helpful include H. I. Winer, *History of the Great Mountain forest* (Ph.D. diss., Yale School of Forestry), which contains a splendid case history of the largest forest area held by a private individual in Connecticut. Winer provides a useful summary of the confusing and inaccurate botanical nomenclature used by early explorers and writers (p. 64ff). W. Meyer and B. Plusnin, *The Yale forest in Tolland and Windham Counties, Ct.*, New Haven: Yale School of Forestry, Bull. 55, 1945, and J. W. Brown, Forest history of Mt. Moosilauke, New Hampshire (master's thesis, Yale School of Forestry, 1941). Studies of specific towns include D. B. Wight, *The wild river wilderness* (Littleton, N.H.: Courier Printing Co., 1971), about the area now incorporated in the Evans Notch District, White Mountain National Forest, Maine; H. C. Woodworth and J. C. Holmes, *The influence of forest management on the local economy of Dorchester*, Durham: New Hampshire Agr. Exp. Sta., Circ. 66, June 1943; N. L. Leroy, *Nonindustrial resident forest landowners in northern New Hampshire*, Durham: Univ. of New Hampshire and USDA, Econ. Res. Serv., Res. Rept. 10, 1970; H. C. Woodworth, M. F. Abell, and J. C. Holmes, *Land utilization in New Hampshire. I. Problems in the back highland areas of southern Grafton County*, Durham: New Hampshire Agr. Exp. Sta. Bull. 298, 1937 (an excellent review of land use change involving farms, forest, and recreation); R. M. Carter, *The people and their use of land in 9 Vermont towns*, Burlington: Vermont Agr. Exp. Sta. Bull. 536, 1947 (a detailed view of conditions in poor rural hill towns in the 1930s); H. L. Wilson, The roads of Windsor [Vermont], *Geographic Review* 21(3) (1931): 379–97; J. W. Goldthwait, A town that has gone downhill, *Geographic Review* 17(4) (1927): 527–52; and H. M. Raup and E. C. Reynolds, *History of land use in the Harvard Forest*, Petersham, Harvard Forest Bull. No. 20, 1941.

2. A standard history is John D. Black, *The rural economy of New England* (Cambridge: Harvard Univ. Press, 1950). This work is especially valuable for its critical analysis of census data on farm numbers and acreage, which are unreliable before the 1930s. Also, Howard S. Russell, *A long deep furrow* (Hanover: Univ. Press of New England, 1976). On the colonial and early national period, P. W. Bidwell, Rural economy in New England at the beginning of the 18th century, *Trans. Conn. Acad. Arts and Sciences* 20 (1918): 241–399 is widely cited. For a useful overview of northeastern farming in the 1970s, see L. P. Schertz, The Northeast, in L. P. Schertz et al., *Another revolution in U.S. farming?*, USDA, ESCS, Agr. Econ. Rept. No. 441, Dec. 1979, and the other excellent papers in this volume. On the disappearance of farmland, see *Perspectives on prime lands*, USDA, 1975; U.S. Council on Environmental Quality and USDA, *National agricultural lands study* (Washington, D.C.: GPO, 1981); and L. U. Wilson, *State agricultural land issues*, Lexington, Ky.: Council of State Governments, 1979. On trends and programs for Connecticut agriculture, see P. H. Cody and I. F. Fellows, *Trends in Connecticut farmland acreage*, Univ. of Conn., Coop. Ext. Serv., May 1979; Fellows and Cody, *A food production plan for Connecticut, 1980–2000: A guide to the purchase of development rights on farmland*, Storrs Agr. Exp. Sta., Univ. of Conn., Bull. 454, March 1980; C. James Gibbons, *Land use issues related to Connecticut's agricultural resources*, Univ. of Conn., Coop. Ext. Serv., 1980.

3. R. A. Gross, *The minutemen and their world* (New York: Hill and Wang, 1976), p. 74.

4. Ibid., p. 177.

5. C. S. Grant, *Democracy in the Connecticut frontier town of Kent* (New York: W. W. Norton, 1972), p. 100.

6. Ibid., p. 97.

7. H. D. Thoreau, *Walden* (illus. ed., Princeton: Princeton Univ. Press, 1973), p. 263.

8. H. D. Thoreau, The succession of forest trees, in *Excursions* (New York: Corinth Books, 1962).

9. Harold F. Wilson, *The hill country of northern New England* (New York: Columbia Univ. Press, 1936).

10. Maine Bureau of Industrial and Labor Statistics, *Fourth Annual Report*, Augusta, 1891, pp. 130–31. The reader of this document will be rewarded by an eloquent speech by William Freeman extolling the virtues and promise of Maine agriculture. The reader is moved to hope that Mr. Freeman never knew that he spoke when the state's agriculture stood at the threshold of its epic decline in the twentieth century.

11. J. D. Black, *Rural economy of New England*.

12. Maine State Planning Office, *The Maine coast: A statistical source*, Augusta: Maine Coastal Program, 1978, p. 77.

13. H. I. Baldwin, *Forestry in New England*, Boston: Natural Resources Planning

Board, Bull. #70, processed, 1942, p. 12. See, for a detailed survey, J. C. Pettie, Wayne G. Banks, and G. E. Doverspoke, *Preliminary survey of the marketing of farm woodland products in the northern New England states*, USDA-FS NEFES, Sta. Paper No. 25, 1949.

14. U.S. Department of the Interior, *Third nationwide outdoor recreation plan*, Draft (Washington, D.C.: GPO, 1979).

15. L. Irland and T. Rumpf, Trends in land and water available for outdoor recreation, in W. F. LaPage, ed., *Proceedings, 1980 national symposium on outdoor recreation trends*, USDA-FS NEFES, Gen. Tech. Rept. NE-57, vol. I, pp. 77–88. Data on trends in posting over time are sparse: I have been able to locate none in New England. A Michigan study showed threefold to sixfold increases in land posting from 1929 to 1960 (U.S. Outdoor Recreation Resources Review Commission, *Hunting in the U.S.*, Special Report No. 6. [Washington, D.C.: GPO, 1962]). In New York, posting increased 63 percent from 1963 to 1972 (T. C. Brown and D. Q. Thompson, Changes in posting and landowner attitudes in New York State, 1963–73, *New York Fish and Game Journal* 23[2] [1976]: 101–37).

16. These problems have been thoroughly reviewed in W. L. Church, *Private lands and public recreation*, National Association of Conservation Districts, 1979; R. T. Quarterman, *Incentives to the use of land for outdoor recreation: Insulation from tort liability, tax relief*, Office of Special Projects, Univ. of Georgia School of Law, 1975; and G. L. Strodtz and C. W. Dane, Trespassers, guests and recreationists on industrial forest land, *Jour. Forestry* 66(12) (1968): 898–901.

17. D. A. Gansner and O. Herrick, *Cooperative forestry assistance in the Northeast*, USDA-FS NEFES, Res. Paper NE-464, 1980.

18. Useful papers on this subject include Owen W. Herrick, Profile of logging in the Northeast, *Northern Logger* 24(4 and 5) (1975): 14, 15, 20, 21; W. J. Gabriel et al., *Machines and systems suitable for logging small woodlots in the Northeast*, State Univ. of New York, Applied Forestry Res. Inst. Rept. No. 26, April 1975; and J. Falk, *Harvesting systems for silvicultural control of spruce budworm*, Univ. of Maine at Orono, Life Sci. and Agr. Exp. Sta., Misc. Rept. 221, Dec. 1979, which provides extensive references.

19. Forest taxation is a complex topic. A short review of New England forest taxation is in D. B. Field, Influences of property tax and land price levels on timber management, in L. Irland and H. Gatslick, eds., *The future of forest industry in New England and eastern Canada*, Papers from 42d Yale Industrial Forestry Seminar, Jan. 1976, New Haven, Yale School of Forestry, processed, pp. 85–95.

20. The standard references on forestry co-ops are G. F. Dempsey and C. B. Markeson, *Guidelines for establishing forestry cooperatives*, USDA-FS NEFES, Res. Paper NE-133, 1969; and G. F. Dempsey, *Forest cooperatives: A bibliography*, USDA-FS NEFES, Res. Paper NE-82, 1967.

21. The problems of the small forest owner have received extensive professional attention, so the reading list is long. USDA, *The federal role in the conservation and management of private nonindustrial forest lands*, Washington, D.C., Jan. 1978 is the report of an interagency committee. It provides a useful summary of current programs, but is more interested in justifying higher budgets than in really evaluating how well the programs are working. It is most useful as documentation of the smugness and lack of imagination of the Washington forestry community when it comes to the problems of rural forestry. Of more intellectual interest is R. A. Sedjo and D. Ostermeier, *Policy alternatives for nonindustrial private forests* (Washington, D.C.: Society of American Foresters, 1978).

In 1979, the National Association of State Foresters conducted a series of regional conferences on nonindustrial private forestry (NIPF) under the leadership of William Towell, former executive vice president, American Forestry Association. The New York–New England conference gathered fifty-five persons from the region and produced the informative little *Report, Conference on NIPF, Waterville Valley, N.H.* (Washington, D.C.: National Association of State Foresters, 1979). The effort produced a national report, *Proceedings, NIPF Conference,* USDA-FS, Gen. Tech. Rept. WO-22, 1980. Though it contains some highly self-serving recommendations from the small landowners, and the usual self-congratulatory bureaucratic rhetoric, it is a useful summary of the state of thought—and nonthought—on the subject. The chapter by Theodore Natti, state forester of New Hampshire, is a useful summary.

The literature of forest economics is becoming clogged with reports purporting to evaluate federal and state programs helping small forest owners. Most of them, on close reading, are simply attempts to cook up "stronger justification" for perennially threatened program budgets. I am aware of no recent studies of this sort in New England. A valuable summary is D. A. Gansner and O. Herrick, *Cooperative forestry assistance in the Northeast,* USDA-FS NEFES, Res. Paper NE-464, 1980. This summary documents the small acreages treated by individual management practices in these programs. John A. Zivnuska, forestry professor at the University of California at Berkeley, summarizes the economist's critique of service forestry in his paper in M. Clawson, ed., *Forestry policy for the future,* Washington, D.C.: Resources for the Future, Working Paper LW-1, 1974, pp. 240–42.

Valuable for background are R. O. McMahon, *Private nonindustrial ownership of forest land,* New Haven: Yale School of Forestry Bull. 68, 1964, which is a thoughtful review and analysis; and M. Clawson, *The economics of U.S. private nonindustrial forests,* Washington, D.C.: Resources for the Future, Research Paper, 1979. See also, with particular emphasis on taxation, Comptroller General of the U.S., *New means of analysis required for policy decisions affecting private forestry sector,* Washington, D.C.: GAO, EMD-81-18, Jan. 1981; for a more analytical treatment, see C. Binkley, Timber supply from private nonindustrial forests (New Haven: Yale School of Forestry and Environmental Studies, Bulletin 92, 1981); a classic statement of the "problem" can be found in W. A. Duerr, *The economic problems of forestry in the Appalachian region* (Cambridge: Harvard Univ. Press, 1949), esp. chs. 3–6.

For a view of budgeteers, USDA Forest Service professionals, and others, see the papers by S. Satterfield, J. Fedkiw, F. Kaiser and G. Dutrow, and others, in J. Royer and F. Convery, eds., *Nonindustrial private forests: Data and information needs,* Conference Proceedings, Duke Univ. Center for Resource and Environmental Policy Research, 1981.

Chapter 6

1. See H. F. Wilson, *The hill country of northern New England* (New York: Columbia Univ. Press, 1936); J. D. Black, *The rural economy of New England* (Cambridge: Harvard Univ. Press, 1950); *Vermont land capability,* Montpelier: State Planning Office, 1974.
2. B. Huffman, *The Vermont farm, and a land reform program,* Montpelier: State Planning Office, 1973, vol. 2, app. D. These land *ownership* trends are not equivalent to land *use* changes. While total farmland ownership has declined, agricultural land uses have shown varying trends. For the state as a whole, harvested cropland fell from 858,000 acres in 1949 to 511,000 acres in 1969. From 1949 and 1969, land used for pasture actually *increased* in Vermont: from 219,000 acres to 279,000.
3. N. P. Kingsley, *The forest resources of Vermont,* USDA-FS NEFES, Res. Bull. NE-46, 1977; R. O. Sinclair and S. B. Meyer, *Nonresident ownership of prop-*

erty in Vermont, Univ. of Vermont Agr. Exp. Sta. Bull. 670. 1972; F. H. Armstrong, *Valuation of Vermont forests, 1968–1974*, Univ. of Vermont, Dept. of Forestry, 1975. Armstrong estimated that 31 percent of the potentially marketable Vermont forest land was sold in the years 1968–74. Considering parcels ten acres or larger, the average parcel sold fell from eighty acres in 1968 to forty-five acres in 1974. See also F. H. Armstrong and R. D. Briggs, Valuation of Vermont forests 1968–1977, Univ. of Vermont, Dept. of Forestry, 1978 (draft). For an analysis of factors in land values in a similar area, see D. H. Vrooman, An empirical analysis of determinants of land values in the Adirondack Park, *Amer. J. Econ. and Sociol.* 37(2) (1978): 165–77.

4. Brian Payne and Lloyd C. Irland, unpublished data on file at USDA Forest Service, Northeastern Forest Experiment Station, Amherst, Mass. See also note 3, above.

5. U.S. Council on Environmental Quality, *Subdividing rural America, executive summary* (Washington, D.C.: GPO, 1976).

6. Booz, Allen and Hamilton, *Sensitivity of the leisure-recreational industry to the energy crisis*, Report to the Federal Energy Office, Washington, D.C., 1974. For a survey of summer recreation, see Chilton Research Services, *Economic impact of recreation-tourism in the Connecticut River basin*, prepared for New England Division, U.S. Army Corps of Engineers, 1968.

7. Vermont Agency for Environmental Conservation, *Vermont State comprehensive outdoor recreation plan—1973*, Montpelier, 1973, p. 69. The economic impact of tourism has been closely studied in neighboring New Hampshire: B. Foster and V. Dahlfred, *New Hampshire's outdoor recreation activities and their role in the state's economy*, Durham: New Hampshire Agr. Exp. Sta., Res. Rept. No. 29, 1973; and Paul S. Hendrick and Assoc., *Impact of recreation, vacation and travel on New Hampshire*, Concord: Office of State Planning, 1971. See also P. E. Polzin and Dennis L. Schweitzer, *Economic importance of tourism in Montana*, USDA-FS Intermountain Forest and Range Experiment Station, Res. Paper INT-171, 1975.

8. C. R. Goeldner and S. Standley, Skiing trends, in W. F. LaPage, ed., *Proceedings, 1980 national symposium on outdoor recreation trends*, USDA-FS NEFES, Gen. Tech. Rept. NE-57, vol. I, p. 105ff. See also USDA-FS, Growth potential of the skier market in the national forests, Washington, D.C., Res. Paper WO-36.

9. George Donovan, Vermont skiing industry, 1973–74, Montpelier: Agency for Development and Comm. Affairs, Econ. Res. Rept. 7304.

10. Vermont Agency of Environmental Conservation, *Vermont second home inventory, 1973*, Montpelier, 1974.

11. This section based on L. C. Irland and T. G. Siccama, National forest on 3 sides . . . , Report to the Conservation Foundation, 1975. USDA-FS, 1977. *Final environmental statement, Deerfield River land use plan*, Rutland, Vt., 1977. Green Mountain National Forest.

12. Armstrong and Briggs, Valuation of Vermont forests.

13. R. L. Baker, Controlling land use and prices by using special gain taxation: The Vermont experiment, *Environmental Affairs* 4, (summer 1975), provides a full analysis of this tax. See also R. G. Healy and J. S. Rosenberg, *Land use and the states* (2d ed., Baltimore: Johns Hopkins Univ. Press, 1979), p. 69ff.

14. Armstrong and Briggs, Valuation of Vermont forests.

15. See, e.g., M. I. Bevins, Seasonal home impact on taxes, *Farm and Home Science* (winter, 1973); R. Frazer and T. Donovan, *Vacation home survey of 8 Vermont towns*, Montpelier: Agency for Devel. and Comm. Affairs, 1972; *Downhill in Warren*, Montpelier: Vermont Public Interest Research Group, 1972; E. L. Johnson, The effect of second home development of Ludlow, Vt., Springfield: South Windsor County Regional Planning Comm., 1973; and Brian Payne, R. Gan-

non, and L. C. Irland, *The second home recreation market in the Northeast*, Washington, D.C.: USDI, Bureau of Recreation, 1975; A. Klein and D. Phelan, *Second homes and vacation homes: Potential impact and issues*, Springfield, Ill.: Council of Planning Librarians Exchange Bibliography No. 839, 1975.

16. Unpublished data, Vermont Dept. of Employment Security.
17. R. L. Ragatz Assoc., *Recreational properties: The market for privately owned recreational lots and leisure homes*, Report to the U.S. Council on Environmental Quality, 1974; and R. L. Ragatz, Trends in the market for privately owned seasonal recreational housing, in LaPage, *Proceedings*, vol. I, pp. 179–94.
18. Armstrong and Briggs, Valuation of Vermont forests.
19. N. P. Kingsley and T. W. Birch, *The forest-landowners of New Hampshire and Vermont*, USDA-FS NEFES, Res. Bull. NE-51, 1977.
20. James T. Boros, Nicholas Engalichev, and William G. Gove, *The timber industry of New Hampshire and Vermont*, USDA-FS NEFES, Res. Bull. NE-35, 1974.
21. R. R. Nathan Assoc. and Resources Planning Assoc., *Recreation as an industry*, Appalachian Regional Commission, Appalachian Res. Rept. No. 2, 1966, p. 3. For a stronger statement regarding the same issues, see R. R. Gottfried, Observations on recreation-led growth in Appalachia, *American Economist* 20 (1976): 54–60.
22. See Healy and Rosenberg, *Land use*, ch. 3; and F. O. Sargent, Vermont's Act 250 enabling legislation for environmental planning, *Proceedings, conference on rural land use policy in the Northeast*, Northeastern Center for Rural Development, Publ. No. 5, 1975. For a critical review see John McClaughry, The new feudalism, *Environmental Law* 5 (spring 1975); also R. G. Healy, *Land use and the states* (Baltimore: Johns Hopkins Univ. Press, 1979), ch. 5.
23. 10 Vermont Statutes Annotated ch. 151.
24. 24 Vermont Statutes Annotated pt. 2, ch. 91.
25. John K. Wright, The Changing Geography of New England, in J. K. Wright, ed., *New England's Prospect* (New York: American Geographic Society, 1933), p. 464.
26. A more thorough version of the Vermont case study is published as L. C. Irland, Recreation, land use change, and the economy: Vermont's recreation boom, in W. R. Burch, Jr., and D. B. Field, eds., forthcoming book. A useful early survey of recreational land use in Connecticut is N. L. Whetten and V. A. Rapport, *The recreational uses of land in Connecticut*, Storrs Agr. Exp. Sta., Bull. 194, March 1934. This survey contains detailed data and estimates that 416,000 acres were in recreational use at that time, one-eighth of the state.

Chapter 7

1. The history is ably told in R. Nash, *Wilderness and the American mind* (New Haven: Yale University Press, 1967); also highly readable is Frank Graham, *The Adirondack Park* (New York: Knopf, 1978). The full history of the conservation movement in New England has yet to be written.
2. The story is briefly told in L. C. Irland and S. M. Levy, Southern New England Water Supply Lands, *J. New England Water Works Assn.* 91 (March 1977), pp. 12–39.
3. For detail on the trail, see J. Sperling, Securing the trail: Maine A. T. project nears completion, *Appalachia* (Jan.–Feb. 1981), pp. 20–22; U.S. Department of the Interior, National Park Service, *Comprehensive plan for protection, management, development, and use of the Appalachian National Scenic Trail*, Harpers Ferry, W. Va., Sept. 1981.
4. USDA-FS, Assessment (draft), 1980, pp. 141–42.

5. M. I. Bevins and D. P. Wilcox, *Outdoor recreation participation—an analysis of national surveys, 1959–78*. Vermont Agr. Exp. Sta. Bull. 686, 1980.

6. E. L. Spencer, H. E. Echelberger, R. E. Leonard, and C. Evans, Trends in hiking and backcountry use, in W. LaPage, ed., *Proceedings, 1980 national symposium on outdoor recreation trends*, USDA-FS NEFES, Gen. Tech. Rept. NE-57, 1: 195–98; T. Cieslinski, Jr., Trends in Allagash Wilderness waterway uses in the 1970's, ibid., 2: 147–50; B. Wagner and E. Spencer, Historical trends in backcountry use, *Appalachia* 42(4) (1979): 129–42.

7. For background, see the overview in L. Irland, *Wilderness economics and policy* (Lexington, Mass.: Heath-Lexington, 1979), ch. 9, and the comprehensive treatise by J. C. Hendee, G. H. Stankey, and R. C. Lucas, *Wilderness management*, USDA-FS, Misc. Publ. 1365, Washington, D.C.: GPO, 1978. Valuable local details may be found in D. P. Teschner, G. M. Dewitt, and J. J. Lindsay, Hiking impact on boreal forest vegetation and soils in Vermont's Green Mountains, Burlington: School of Natural Resources, Res. Note SNR-RM6, June 1979; and W. R. Burch, Jr., ed., *Long distance trails*, New Haven: Yale School of Forestry and Environmental Studies, 1979.

8. R. W. Guldin, Wilderness costs in New England, *Jour. Forestry* 78(9) (1980): 548–52; and L. C. Irland, *Costs of managing backcountry recreation areas in Maine, 1978*, Augusta: Bureau of Parks and Recreation, Tech. Note No. 5, 1980.

9. Baxter Park Authority, *Management Plan*, Millinocket, Me., 1978.

10. New England Sierran, Nov. 1977; and New England Chapter, Sierra Club, submission to U.S. Forest Service Regional Office, Sept. 28, 1979.

11. USDA-FS, *Roadless areas review and evaluation*, Final Environmental Statement, Washington, D.C., 1973.

12. Eastern Wilderness Areas Act, PL 93-622.

13. USDA-FS, *RARE-II. Supplement to Draft EIS, Northern Appalachian and New England States*, June 1978, and *Summary—Final Environmental Statement*, Jan. 1979.

14. Lew Dietz, *The Allagash*. Thorndike, Me.: Thorndike Press, 1968.

15. National Wild and Scenic Rivers Act, PL 90-542.

16. USDI, Bureau of Outdoor Recreation, *Penobscot River wild and scenic proposal*, Final Environmental Statement, 1976.

17. For more information, see USDA-FS, *Assessment* (draft), pp. 116–18; E. C. Leatherberry, D. W. Lime, and J. L. Thompson, Trends in river recreation, in LaPage, *Proceedings*, vol. I, pp. 179–94.

18. J. Heinrichs, Thirteen Mile Woods, *American Forests* (Sept. 1980): 50–52.

19. NERBC, *The river's reach*, Boston, 1976.

20. Massachusetts Dept. of Env. Mgt., Scenic Rivers Programs, *Massachusetts Scenic and Recreational Rivers*, Draft, June 1979.

21. Office of Comprehensive Planning, *Wild, scenic, and recreational rivers for New Hampshire*, Concord, 1977; and Maine Bureau of Parks and Recreation, Maine Rivers study proposal, Draft, Augusta: Dec. 1979. See also, J. E. Hickey, Proposed rivers preservation program for Connecticut, *Connecticut Woodlands* 45(3) (1980): 3–7.

22. Memo from Regional Director, HCRS, Final list of potential wild and scenic rivers, Philadelphia: USDI, HCRS, Northeast Region, Mar. 8, 1979.

23. For example, see W. G. Scheller, Stalking the red herring: Sportsmen's rights and wilderness preservation, *Appalachia* No. 171 (1980): pp. 63–71.

24. The literature on the subject of wilderness is immense. A fine place to start is Aldo Leopold, *A Sand County almanac* (New York: Oxford University Press, 1966). I have summarized the arguments in L. Irland, *Wilderness economics and policy*. For the technically minded, J. Krutilla and A. Fisher, *The economics of*

natural environments (Baltimore: Johns Hopkins Univ. Press, 1975), is still the classic statement. See also J. Sax, *Parks without handrails* (Ann Arbor: Univ. of Michigan Press, 1980).

Chapter 8

1. C. E. Clark, *The eastern frontier* (New York: Knopf, 1970), is an excellent source for the early history of landownership in southern New England. Land use studies summarized in ch. 5, note 1, illustrate the local picture.
    On the Great Proprietors, see Clark, *The eastern frontier*; Roy H. Akagi, *The New England town proprietors* (Philadelphia: Blakiston, 1924); G. E. Kershaw, *The Kennebec proprietors, 1749–1775* (Portland: Maine Historical Society, 1975); and F. S. Allis, Jr., ed., *William Bingham's Maine lands, 1790–1820* (Boston: Colonial Society of Mass., v. 36–37, 1954). For a vivid summary of colonial land policy and its social implications, see R. Hofstadter, *America at 1750: A social portrait* (New York: Vintage, 1973), pp. 142–51.
2. A useful summary of the landownership history of Maine and discussion of common and undivided ownership are in A. H. Wilkins, *Ten million acres of timber* (Woolwich, Me.: TBW Books, 1978), pp. 5–23.
3. For a valuable early survey, see H. A. Reynolds, Inventory of New England's public forests and parks, *Jour. Forestry* 29 (1929): 923–26, who estimates 1.2 million acres in 1929.
4. See Lee M. Schepps, Maine's public lots: the emergence of a public trust, *Maine Law Review* 26(2) (1974): 217–72; State Forestry Department, *Report on public reserved lots*, Augusta, 1963.
5. Older reports on state and local landownership contain much useful data. P. L. Buttrick, *Connecticut public lands*, Connecticut Geological and Natural History Survey, 1936; D. Dozman and R. E. Sherburne, *Public landownership in rural areas of Massachusetts*, Amherst: Univ. of Mass. Agr. Exp. Sta. Bull. No. 489, 1955.
6. N. Kingsley, *The forest-landowners of southern New England*, USDA-FS NEFES, Res. Bull. NE-41, 1976, p. 16; N. Kingsley and T. W. Birch, *The forest-landowners of New Hampshire and Vermont*, USDA-FS NEFES, Res. Bull. NE-51, 1977, p. 36.
    For earlier estimates, see J. C. Rettie, W. G. Banks, and G. E. Doverspoke, *Preliminary survey of the marketing of farm woodland products in the northern New England states*, USDA-FS NEFES, Sta. Paper No. 25, 1949, and land-ownership section of Northern Region Technical Committee, *Marketing forest products from small woodland areas in the Northeast*, Burlington: Vermont Agr. Exp. Sta. Bull. 595, 1956, v. 1, esp. pp. 16, 18.
7. For Connecticut, see table 5. For northern New England, see Rettie, Banks, and Doverspoke, *Preliminary survey*, and table 15. The median ownership sizes are from C. Binkley, Modeling timber supply from private nonindustrial forests, paper presented at forestry workshop, International Institute for Applied Systems Analysis, Laxenburg, Austria, Jan. 8–11, 1980, mimeographed.
8. See, for details on natural areas owned by private groups, New England Natural Resources Center, *Protecting New England's natural heritage* (Boston, 1973). Estimating land owned by the nongovernment nonprofit sector is difficult. I quickly abandoned hope of accomplishing a comprehensive inventory. U.S. Forest Service publications provide some clues (Res. Bull. NE-51, 1977, p. 33, table 3). Publications of the owning groups often fail to distinguish between fee and leased land and to give useful acreage summaries. For colleges and land trusts, it is difficult to arrive at a listing of organizations involved. Some of the major groups transfer land to public owners, so that their cumulative acquisitions over

time may inadvertently be double-counted with public holdings. Though I was unable to complete a full inventory, I am indebted to representatives of many groups who contributed information in response to my informal queries.

9. For more on New England forest landownership, see E. V. Zumwalt, *Taxation and other factors affecting private forestry in Connecticut*, New Haven: Yale School of Forestry, Bull. No. 58, 1953; S. C. Barraclough, Forest landownership in New England (Ph.D. diss., Harvard University, 1949), and C. Binkley, *Timber supply from private nonindustrial forests*, New Haven: Yale School of Forestry, Bulletin 92, 1981.

The serious student will have to pay close attention to discrepancies and weaknesses in the data sources. Past surveys use various definitions and study populations and so may lack comparability over time. Local sample surveys frequently do not match the overall U.S. Forest Service data. For some states, because of differing samples and definitions, the forest land in farms figures differ markedly among sources.

Chapter 9

1. Peter N. Carroll, *Puritanism and the wilderness* (New York: Columbia Univ. Press, 1969), p. 183ff; and Carl Bridenbaugh, *Fat, mutton, and liberty of conscience: Society in Rhode Island, 1639–1690* (Providence: Brown Univ. Press, 1974), p. 75.

2. Robert G. Albion, *Forests and sea power* (Cambridge: Harvard Univ. Press, 1926), and J. J. Malone, *Pine trees and politics* (Seattle: Univ. of Washington Press, 1964) are standard works on the mast trade. Samuel F. Manning, *New England masts and the king's Broad Arrow* (Kennebunk: Thomas Murphy, 1979) is brief and contains charming illustrations. See also Charles E. Clark, *The eastern frontier* (New York: Knopf, 1970), p. 98ff. Valuable background on the colonial economy and the role played by forest products is found in C. E. Carroll, *The timber economy of Puritan New England* (Providence: Brown Univ. Press, 1973); E. J. Perkins, *The economy of colonial America* (New York: Columbia Univ. Press, 1980); and D. R. McManis, *Colonial New England: A historical geography* (New York: Oxford Univ. Press, 1975). On the timber trade in Britain, see also B. Latham, *Timber: A historical survey* (London: George G. Harrap, 1957).

3. Howard I. Chapelle, *The American fishing schooner 1825–1935* (New York: W. W. Norton, 1973), p. 76.

4. USDA-FS, *Timber depletion, lumber prices, lumber exports, and concentration of timber ownership*, Report on S. Res. 311 (Washington, D.C.: GPO, 1920). Hereafter, "Capper report," so called after Senator Capper, whose Senate Resolution called for the report.

5. Data from H. B. Steer, *Lumber production in the U.S.: 1799–1946*, USDA Misc. Publ. 669, Oct. 1948.

6. Sources differ—Steer gives 2.8 billion feet of reported production in 1904; Capper cites a peak of 3.2 billion.

7. George B. Emerson, *A report on the trees and shrubs growing naturally in the forests of Massachusetts* (Boston: Little-Brown, 1887).

8. George Perkins Marsh, *Man and nature* (1864; reprint, Cambridge: Harvard Univ. Press, 1964), p. 258.

9. F. B. Hough, *Cultivation of timber and the preservation of forests*, House Rept. 259, 43d Congress, 1st Session, March 18, 1874.

10. Report of the Forestry Commission of New Hampshire, Concord, 1885.

11. Austin Cary, in *Report of the forest commissioner, 1896*, Augusta.

12. *Report of the Forest Commissioner*, Augusta, 1919, p. xxviii.

13. A. E. Moss, *Annual report*, Conn. Agr. Exp. Sta., Storrs, 1915, p. 197ff.; and H. O. Cook, A forest survey of Massachusetts, *Jour. Forestry* 27 (1929): 518–22. Other forest surveys and analyses of this period are R. C. Averill, W. B. Averill, and W. I. Stevens, *A statistical forest survey of seven towns in central Massachusetts*, Petersham, Mass.: Harvard Forest Bull. No. 6, 1923; A. F. Hanes and R. C. Hawley, *Forest survey of Litchfield and New Haven counties, Conn.*, Conn. Agr. Exp. Sta. Bull. 162, Forestry Publ. No. 5, 1909; R. C. Bryant, Report of the Committee on the Timber Supply of Connecticut, in *A forest policy for Connecticut*, Report of the Connecticut Forestry Assoc., Nov. 24, 1920. A useful summary is A. Wilkins, *The forests of Maine*, Augusta: Maine Forest Service, Bull. No. 8, 1932.

14. Fred W. Card, *Forests of Rhode Island*, Rhode Island Agr. Exp. Sta. Bull. No. 88, Oct. 1902.

15. Capper report.

16. Capper report, p. 28.

17. Henry I. Baldwin, *Forestry in New England*, Boston: National Resources Planning Board, Region I, Bull. No. 70, 1942.

18. USDA-FS, *Forests and national prosperity: A reappraisal of the forest situation in the U.S.*, Washington, D.C.: USDA Misc. Publ. 668, 1948.

19. Vernon L. Harper, *Timber resources of New England and New York with special reference to pulpwood supplies*, USDA-FS NEFES, Sta. Paper No. 5, 1947.

20. N. P. Kingsley, *The timber resources of southern New England*, USDA-FS NEFES, Res. Bull. NE-36, 1974.

21. R. H. Ferguson and N. P. Kingsley, *The timber resources of Maine*, USDA-FS NEFES, Res. Bull. NE-26, 1972.

22. N. P. Kingsley, *The forest resources of Vermont*, USDA-FS NEFES, Res. Bull. NE-46, 1977; and N. P. Kingsley, *The forest resources of New Hampshire*, USDA-FS NEFES, Res. Bull. NE-43, 1976.

23. C. S. Sargent, *Report on the forests of North America*, Tenth Census of the U.S. (Washington, D.C.: GPO, 1884), p. 489.

24. USDA-FS, *Analysis of the timber situation in the U.S., 1952–2030.* Review Draft. Appendix 3, p. 112, Washington, D.C., 1980. See also fuelwood use surveys in New England including G. S. Nagle and R. S. Manthy, *The market for fireplace wood in an urban area of Connecticut*, USDA-FS NEFES, Res. Paper NE-51, 1966; L. Palmer, R. McKusick, and M. Bailey, *Wood and energy in New England*, USDA, Econ. Stat. and Coop. Serv., Bibliogr. and Lit. of Agr., No. 7, 1980.

25. R. W. Bryan, Getting serious about wood fuel: Public utility begins conversion, *Forest Industries* (May 1979): 31–33; J. P. R. Assoc., *Feasibility of generating electricity in Vermont using wood as fuel*, Montpelier: Vermont Agency of Environmental Conservation, 1975.

26. R. L. Nevel, Jr., and J. T. Bones, *Northeastern pulpwood, 1978*, USDA-FS NEFES, Res. Bull. NE-62, 1980, p. 4.

27. The classic analysis of this problem is based on the work of G. E. Likens, F. H. Bormann, and others at the Hubbard Brook Experimental Watershed in the White Mountains. The most useful general report on their work is Bormann and Likens, *Pattern and process in a forested ecosystem* (New York: Springer Verlag, 1979). For detailed studies, see *Proceedings, Impact of intensive harvesting on forest nutrient cycling*, State Univ. College of Environmental Science and Forestry, Syracuse, 1979.

28. On forest pests, see J. F. Anderson and Harry K. Kaya, *Perspectives in forest entomology* (New York: Academic Press, 1976), and R. W. Campbell, *Gypsy moth: Forest influence*, USDA-FS Agr. Info. Bull. 432, 1979. See also W. A. Sinclair and R. J. Campana, Dutch Elm disease—perspectives after 10 years,

Search-Agriculture 8(5) [1978), Cornell Univ. Agr. Exp. Sta. On spruce bud-worm, see ch. 3. On fires, see Austin Wilkins, *Ten million acres of timber* (Wool-wich, Me.: TBW Books, 1978).

29. M. Houseweart, *Impact of the spruce budworm in the Maine spruce-fir region 1975–1979*, Orono: Univ. of Maine, Co-op. For. Res. Unit, Res. Bull. 3, 1981.

30. D. J. Brooks and D. B. Field, *Potentials of charcoal production for forest stand improvement and domestic space heating in Maine*, Orono: Univ. of Maine, Co-op. For. Res. Unit, Res. Bull. 1, 1980.

31. Owen Herrick, *Impact of alternative timber management policies on availability of forest land in the Northeast*, USDA-FS NEFES, Res. Paper NE-390, 1977. For more on current and potential timber productivity, see *Proceedings, Symposium on intensive culture of northern forest types*, USDA-FS NEFES, Gen. Tech. Rept. NE-29, 1977, especially papers by Morris Wing of International Paper Company (on long-run output from a northern Maine township), by H. M. Klaiber of Scott Paper Company (on amazing yields of recently cut plantations), and by W. Carmean (on assessing site productivity). A brief report on Maine's timber-growing potential was prepared by the Forestry Industry Council-National Forest Products Association Forest Productivity Committee, *Maine Forest Productivity Report*, Washington, D.C.: Forest Industries Council, 1979.

32. Useful perspectives on forests and wood use over time are found in M. Clawson, Forests in the long sweep of American history, *Science* 204 (1979): 1–7; and R. V. Reynolds, How much timber has America cut? *Jour. Forestry* 33(1) (1935): 34–41. On the difficulties of comparing early timber volume estimates, see M. Dietz, Review of the estimates of the sawtimber stand on the U.S., 1880–1946, *Jour. Forestry* 45(12) (1947): 865–74.

I have not discussed here the findings of the 1958 *Timber Resources Review* (data for 1952), the *Timber Trends* report of 1965 (data for 1963), the *Outlook* (1973), or the U.S. Forest Service *National Assessment of 1975*. These documents can fill out the statistical picture for the serious student—but they would add little to this story. Other reports, less well known, are cited in these sources. Another useful compendium is H. I. Baldwin, *Wooden dollars* (Boston: Federal Reserve Bank, 1949).

The most recent forest surveys for New England are cited in notes 20, 21, and 22 above. For additional information on Maine, see J. Joseph, L. Irland, and T. Howard, *Maine's forests and economic development*, Augusta: Maine Forest Service, Department of Conservation, Eval. Doc. No. 1, 1980; and D. B. Field, *Economic importance of Maine's spruce-fir resource*, Onoro: Univ. of Maine, Co-op. For. Res. Unit, Res. Bull. 2, March 1980.

Chapter 10

1. Numerous detailed surveys of New England's wood-using industries provide information on the products, raw materials, and markets of the time. Examples include James T. Bones, *Primary wood products industries of southern New England*, USDA-FS, Res. Bull. NE-30, 1971; and J. Dickson, *The veneer industry in the Northeast*, USDA-FS, Res. Bull. NE-33, 1972; Nicholas Engalichev and William G. Gove, *The timber industries of New Hampshire and Vermont*, USDA-FS, Res. Bull. NE-35, 1974; C. P. Cronk, *The forest industries of New Hampshire*, Concord: N.H. Forestry and Recreation Commission, 1936; H. Maxwell, *A study of the Massachusetts wood using industries*, USDA-FS (Washington, D.C.: GPO, 1910); H. Maxwell, *The wood using industries of Vermont*, USDA-FS (Washington, D.C.: GPO, 1913); Jesse C. Nellis, *The wood using industries of Maine*, USDA-FS (Washington, D.C.: GPO, 1912; also reprinted in the Report of the Forest Commissioner, Maine, 1912); Albert H. Pierson, *The wood*

using industries of Connecticut, USDA-FS (Washington, D.C.: GPO, 1913); Roger E. Simmons, *The wood using industries of New Hampshire*, USDA-FS (Washington, D.C.: GPO, 1912); A. Cline, *Marketing of lumber in New Hampshire*, Harvard Forest Bull. No. 10, 1926; J. B. Downs, *Wood-using industry of Massachusetts*, Harvard Forest Bull. No. 12, 1928; O. P. Wallace, *Lumber use in New Hampshire wood-using industries*, Durham: N.H. Agr. Exp. Sta. Bull. No. 474, 1962; A. H. Wilkins, *The forests of Maine, their extent, character, and products*, Augusta: Maine Forest Service, Bull. No. 8, 1932; G. Baker, *The primary wood-using industries of Maine*, Orono: Maine Agr. Exp. Sta. Bull. 448, 1947; T. S. Foster and R. S. Bond, *Use of lumber by selected wood product manufacturing industries of Massachusetts*, Amherst: Univ. of Mass. Agr. Exp. Sta. Bull. 547, Nov. 1964; R. S. Bond and P. E. Sendak, *Structure of the wood-platform industry of the northeast*, Amherst: Univ. of Mass. Agr. Exp. Sta. Bull. 586, Sept. 1970.

2. For more, see D. C. Smith, *History of lumbering in Maine, 1861–1960* (Orono: Univ. of Maine Press, 1972), relevant sections of J. E. Defebaugh, *History of the American lumber industry* (Chicago: American Lumberman, 1906), and L. C. Irland, *Is timber scarce?*, New Haven: Yale School of Forestry and Environmental Studies, Bull. 83, 1974, ch. 4, and notes therein.

3. For details on the problems of counting employment in logging and sawmills, see L. C. Irland, Importance of forest industries to New England's economy, *Northern Logger* (March 1975): 16ff.

4. See, e.g., D. C. Smith, *History of lumbering*, chs. 9–16; D. C. Smith, *History of the paper industry of the United States 1690–1970* (New York: Lockwood's, 1971); and J. A. Guthrie, *An economic analysis of the pulp and paper industry* (Pullman: Washington State Univ. Press, 1972), which includes a good summary of papermaking technology and products. H. Hunter, Innovation, competition, and locational change in the pulp and paper industry: 1880–1950, *Land Economics* 31 (1955): 314–27 is a valuable summary. L. C. Irland, Maine timber supply: Historical notes and speculation on the future, *Proceedings, Blaine House conference on forestry*, Augusta: Dept. of Conservation, 1981.

5. Bureau of Industrial and Labor Statistics, *Twentieth Annual Report*, Augusta, 1906, p. 140.

6. A useful overview on the region's economy can be found in J. K. Wright et al., *New England's Prospect: 1933* (New York: American Geographic Society, Spec. Publ. No. 16, 1933). The standard source is R. W. Eisenmenger, *Dynamics of growth in New England's economy, 1870–1964* (Middletown: Wesleyan Univ. Press, 1967). See also J. R. Meyer and R. A. Leave, The New England states and their economic future, *American Economic Review* (May 1978): 58, 110–15.

7. See relevant sections of Guthrie, *Economic analysis*; *Proceedings, Symposium on structural flakeboard from forest residues*, USDA-FS, Gen. Tech. Rept. WO-5, Sept. 1978; O. W. Herrick, Structure and change in northern U.S. forest products industry: A shift-share analysis, *Forest Products Journal* 26 (Aug. 1976): 29–34, and R. W. Haynes and D. M. Adams, Possible changes in regional forest products output and consumption during the next 50 years, *Forest Products Journal* 29 (Oct. 1979): 75–80. The careful reader will note that Haynes and Adams are basing their production forecasts on a production level for the Northeast that is notably lower than that estimated for New England alone in table 17 of this chapter. The difference is due to the growth in New England sawmill and pulp capacity since 1976 (their base data) and the unforeseeable and dramatic increase in fuelwood use.

8. The projected doubling from 1976 to 2030 is based on projections with equilibrium prices in the *Analysis* review draft, pp. 424 and 435, which yield a 67

percent increase for softwoods in the Northeast and a 2.7-fold increase for hardwoods, or a 203 percent increase for the total.

9. For an analysis of Maine, see J. Joseph, L. C. Irland, and T. Howard, *Maine's
    forests and economic development*, Augusta: Maine Forest Service, Planning
    Program, Tech. Doc. No. 2, 1979. On the Canadian log trade, see Jack Aley, *The
    export of Maine sawlogs to Quebec*, Augusta: Maine Forest Service, April 1981.

10. C. C. Burwell, Solar biomass energy: An overview of U.S. potential, *Science*
    (199) (1978): 1044. See also J. Grantham and T. H. Ellis, Potentials of wood for
    producing energy, *Jour. Forestry* 72 (Sept. 1974): 552–56; J. T. Bones and T. N.
    Bowers, Wood residues, how much are we recovering?, *Northern Logger* (Sept.
    1971): 22–24; C. L. Brown, Forests as energy sources in the year 2000, *Jour.
    Forestry* 74 (Jan. 1976): 7–12; D. W. Rose, Fuel forest vs. strip-mining: Fuel
    production alternatives, *Jour. Forestry* 73 (Aug. 1975): 489–93; J. P. R. Assoc.,
    Feasibility of generating electricity (Montpelier, 1975). Excellent general reviews
    are Society of American Foresters, Forest biomass as an energy source, Washing-
    ton, D.C., 1979; E. L. Ellis, *Energy from forest biomass*, Madison, Wis.: Forest
    Products Research Society, 1979; *Governor's task force on wood as a source of
    energy*, Montpelier: State of Vermont, 1975; *Four papers on biomass*, Research
    program on technology and public policy, Thayer School of Engineering,
    Dartmouth College, Hanover, N.H., Jan. 1978; L. Palmer, R. McKusick, and M.
    Bailey, *Wood and energy in New England*, USDA, Econ. Stat. and Coop. Serv.,
    Bibliogr. and Lit. of Agr. No. 7, 1980. For a world perspective, see E. Eckholm,
    The other energy crisis: Fuelwood (Washington: World Watch Paper 1, 1975).
    Wood energy is a major theme of John G. Mitchell, Whither the Yankee Forest?,
    Audubon 83(2) (1981): 78–99.

Chapter 11

1. For an entry into state forest policies, see R. R. Widner, ed., *Forests and forestry
    in the American states* (Washington: National Association of State Foresters, [c.
    1968]), and the annual reports of the state forestry agencies. The serious student
    will find that the superagency boom of the 1970s and legislative restraints on
    published reports make finding reports difficult for the post-1970 period. There
    is little in the literature dealing specifically with the policy problems of New En-
    gland. Worthwhile still are *Toward a New England forest land use policy: Pro-
    ceedings of a symposium* (Boston: New England Natural Resource Center,
    1972), and Carl Reidel, *The Yankee forest: A prospectus*, New Haven: Yale
    School of Forestry and Environmental Studies, 1978.
        During the 1970s, the New England states, with the financial assistance of
    the USDA Forest Service in most cases, undertook reviews of their forest pol-
    icies, and set out on major resource planning efforts. A few of the resulting re-
    ports are: E. M. Gould, *Report, Massachusetts forestry program review board*,
    Petersham, Mass.: Harvard Forest, 1977, processed; Division of Forests and
    Lands, *Forests and forestry in New Hampshire—action program for the
    eighties*, vol. I. Durham, 1980; Vermont Forest Resource Advisory Council, *Op-
    portunities and choices: The future of Vermont's forests*, Montpelier: Vermont
    Natural Resources Council, 1981; Joint Select Committee on Forest Resources,
    Report on the forest resources of Maine, legislative staff, Augusta, 1977.
        In nearby New York, a major forest policy review was undertaken by the
    Adirondack Park Agency, motivated by similar considerations: T. M. Ruzon,
    Why is the APA sponsoring a major study of clearcutting?, Ray Brook, N.Y.:
    Adirondack Park Authority, 1980.

2. For an introduction to federal policies, see S. T. Dana and S. Fairfax, *Forest and*

range policy (New York: McGraw-Hill, 1980), and H. K. Steen, *The Forest Service* (Seattle: Univ. of Washington Press, 1976), and references cited in both works. On the eastern national forests, W. E. Shands and R. G. Healy, *The lands nobody wanted* (Washington, D.C.: The Conservation Foundation, 1977), is valuable.

3. J. P. Kinney, *Forest legislation in America prior to Mar. 4, 1789,* Ithaca: Cornell Univ. Agr. Exp. Sta., New York State College of Agr., Bull. 370, Jan. 1916.

4. R. L. Bushman, *From Puritan to Yankee: Character and social order in Connecticut, 1690–1765* (Cambridge: Harvard Univ. Press, 1967), p. 4. See also the comprehensive work by O. Handlin and M. F. Handlin, *Commonwealth: A study of the role of government in the American economy: Massachusetts, 1774–1861* (New York: Columbia Univ. Press, 1947), and J. R. T. Hughes, What difference did the beginning make?, *Amer. Econ. Rev.* 67(1) (1974): 15–20.

5. Recently, scholarly interest in the origins of New England's land system, land disposal policies, and their effects seems to have withered. I regret that space prevents extensive discussion here, but refer the student to the major secondary sources. Sections of C. E. Clark, *The eastern frontier* (New York: Knopf, 1970), are highly relevant, as is D. R. McManis's brief *Colonial New England: A historical geography* (New York: Oxford Univ. Press, 1975). Classic histories of New England land tenure and land disposal policies include Roy Akagi, *The town proprietors of the New England colonies* (Philadelphia: Univ. of Pennsylvania Press, 1924), and M. Harris, *Origins of the land tenure system in the United States* (Ames: Iowa State College Press, 1953). See also A. C. Ford, *Colonial precedents of our national land system as it existed in 1800,* Madison: Bull. Univ. of Wisconsin History Series, 2(2) (1910): 321–478; and M. Eggleston, *The land system of the New England colonies,* Baltimore: Johns Hopkins Univ. Studies in History and Political Science, 4 ser., 1886. For a detailed study of implementing Massachusetts land disposal policy, see L. D. Bridgham, Maine public lands, 1781–1795: Claims, trespassers, and sales (Ph.D. diss., Boston University, 1959).

6. L. M. Schepps, Maine's public lots: The emergence of a public trust, *Maine Law Review* 26(2) (1974): 217–72.

7. This is a simple caricature made necessary by brevity. For a penetrating and full account, see J. Willard Hurst's *Law and economic growth: The legal history of the lumber industry in Wisconsin, 1830–1915* (Cambridge: Harvard Univ. Press, 1964). The quote is at p. 601. Also, for Maine, see D. C. Smith, *A history of lumbering in Maine, 1861–1960* (Orono: Univ. of Maine, 1972), chs. 7, 11, 12.

8. The history of this period has yet to be written. See reports of the U.S. Outdoor Recreation Resources Review Commission and the Public Land Law Review Commission, and Dana and Fairfax, *Forest and range policy,* chs. 7–12. Key works setting the tone for the era were Stuart Udall's *Quiet crisis* and Rachel Carson's *Silent spring.*

9. Works embodying the green backdrop philosophy are W. H. Whyte, *The last landscape* (New York: Doubleday-Anchor Books, 1970), and Ian McHarg's influential work, *Design with nature.*

10. Rising criticism of these programs and sustained opposition to their funding by the Office of Management and Budget and the White House have stimulated among U.S. Forest Service officials and academics high interest in producing the data to "justify" these programs. Most of the evaluations I have read from other regions seem to be motivated more by a desire to justify higher program outlays than to evaluate program effectiveness and suggest serious improvements. See ch. 5, n. 21.

11. USDA-FS, *Forests and national prosperity* (Washington, D.C.: GPO, 1948), USDA Misc. Publ. 668, p. 6.
12. Aldo Leopold, *A Sand County almanac* (New York: Oxford Univ. Press, 1966), p. 187.
13. G. P. Marsh, *Man and nature* (1864; reprint, Cambridge: Harvard Univ. Press, 1964), p. 259. For more on this important episode, see Dana and Fairfax, *Forest and range policy*, p. 16cff., and Steen, *The Forest Service*, ch. 13, pp. 222–37, and pp. 259–71.
14. Leopold, *Sand County*, p. 217ff. Anyone interested in conservation should read the entire book of which this famous essay is a part.

Index

LIBRARY OF CONGRESS CATALOGING IN PUBLICATION DATA

Irland, Lloyd C.
  Wildlands and woodlots.

  (A Futures of New England book)
  Includes bibliographical references and index.
    1. Forests and forestry—New England. I. Title.
II. Series.
SD144.A12174   333.75'0974   81-69943
ISBN 0-87451-227-1   AACR2

Life
AFTER THE
STORM

JAN HARRISON

Cover by Harvest House Publishers Inc., Eugene, Oregon

Cover photos © pixhook, kaisphoto / iStock; Szasz-Fabian Jozsef / Shutterstock

Back cover author photo © Stacey Van Berkel

LIFE AFTER THE STORM
Copyright © 2015 by Jan Harrison
Published by Harvest House Publishers
Eugene, Oregon 97402
www.harvesthousepublishers.com

Library of Congress Cataloging-in-Publication Data
Harrison, Jan (Bible study teacher)
Life after the storm / Jan Harrison.
    pages cm
    ISBN 978-0-7369-6177-6 (pbk.)
    ISBN 978-0-7369-6179-0 (eBook)
    1. Consolation. 2. Loss (Psychology)—Religious aspects—Christianity. 3. T
tianity. I. Title.
    BV4905.3.H375 2015
    248.8'6—dc23

To my husband, Frank

Sharing life with you has
doubled the joys and halved the sorrow.

* * *

"A cord of three strands is not quickly torn apart."
Ecclesiastes 4:12

Contents

PART 1

The Storm Clouds Gather

1

My Storm Strikes

*I*t was a glorious early October afternoon in North Carolina, the kind of day that makes you feel glad to be alive. A cloudless blue sky, brilliant shining sun, and rich amber leaves on the trees signaled the approach of fall. All of the signs were present. Change was in the air.

I was home working in my office when I heard the sound of hard-sole dress shoes on the hallway floor. I turned to see my husband standing in the doorway. I wondered what he was doing home in the middle of the afternoon. I was surprised because I knew his plans for that very hour were to be in an important meeting. Without a word, he quietly motioned for me to come with him to our bedroom. When he turned around, the pain on his face told me something was horribly wrong. He whispered, "Jan, we lost James today."

In an instant, with no warning, the day turned very dark and everything in our lives changed. My heart split in two while my mind tried to process the news that our only son was dead. He was in Africa, thousands of miles away from us, and we had no idea how he had died. A thick fog enveloped me, and I started to tremble. Shock and sickening fear welled up from depths I didn't know existed, and guttural cries escaped my mouth from some foreign origin. It was as if a line in the sand were drawn. Time would now be marked by before or after James

9

died. We were thrust on a dark and perilous journey called grief and sorrow, and there was no turning back.

Willing to Walk with You

How do you walk a path you've never been on before? How do you withstand a storm that threatens to wipe out your family and ruin your dreams? How do you keep from becoming wrecked by the uncertainties and disruptions in life? My dramatic disruption was the sudden death of my beautiful 27-year-old son. Yours may be a diagnosis, an addiction, an accident, or a disability. It could be abandonment, rejection, divorce, infertility, or the loss of a job creating both physical and emotional insecurity. Because of these situations, many of us feel as though we are adrift at sea with no compass or purpose other than survival.

I want you to know my heart joins with yours in care and compassion. Although none of us can fully understand the circumstances and unique experiences of another person's life, it's comforting to know others are willing to walk with us through pain, grief, and despair. I want you to know I consider it a privilege and a blessing to come alongside to encourage you and be a companion as you walk your personal trail of tears. My purpose isn't to try to give you answers. It's to help you find the Answer.

It may be that you are the one sorrowing, or it could be you are sharing in the struggle of a child, family member, or friend. All of our lives touch others, so it's inevitable that we take on the load of the people we love. As my children have all become young adults with their own families, I am beginning to understand the obvious but somehow surprising truth that "you are a mother as long as you live." Their cares and concerns are mine. We find our roles reverse as our parents age, and it's straining and unsettling for all. Sorting through the many decisions with patience and a gentle spirit can be exhausting. Trying to carefully balance the roles and demands of several generations often becomes more than we can take.

Some of us become entangled in a swirl of unwelcome and unsolicited activity based on the actions of others. Maybe you've been raped or violated, falsely accused and lied against, misled and manipulated by people you thought you knew and could trust.

Even when we're surrounded by people we can end up feeling all alone. We're convinced we're unwanted and unaccepted because of what has happened to us. Feelings of despair and depression are common and understandable when shame or guilt is our constant companion. When we realize we have made bad choices and many of the problems we are experiencing are really our own fault, it can cause a deep sense of hopelessness and even the desire to die.

We could be trying to weather a storm alone, or we may be surrounded by a strong group of supporters. Either way, there's a point where the resolution to our pain depends on how we choose to deal with it. At the end of the day, it's individual attitude and action that will determine how this disruption or disappointment will be used in our lives. Will we allow this to ruin us or refine us?

Because I've been through my own storms, may I offer you a word of hope and encouragement? There is life after the storm. There is a journey that will always lead you to the other side. I am praying you will allow me to take your hand and place it in the outstretched hand of Jesus. He will walk you through your storm and take you to the other side of the crisis.

Defining Your Storm

Any disruption of your "normal" defines a life storm. Disruptions come in many shapes and sizes. They vary in magnitude and destructiveness. Sometimes they are predictable and sometimes they are sudden. Cameras in outer space studying the atmosphere on planet Earth record that there are as many as 2000 storms taking place at once. It seems that everywhere you turn and everyone you talk to is either going into, in the midst of, or coming out of a storm.

While teaching a women's Bible study for 16 years, I have had numerous opportunities to share in the many varying and deep challenges women face. We have bared our heavy and anguished hearts in prayer for all sorts of people and circumstances. The searing pain of my own loss and my deep need for care serve to make me more sensitive to the painful trials others are going through.

- A wife becomes a widow when there was so much left to share with her husband.
- A single friend falls into despair after another relationship fails.
- A young mother grapples with the diagnosis of bone cancer in her toddler.
- A parent comes to terms with the meaning of raising a child with autism.
- A rebellious teenage son/daughter disrupts and divides a whole family.
- A wife discovers her husband is deeply involved in pornography.
- A grown daughter struggles to satisfy or please her mother.
- A woman struggles with infertility and deeply desires a baby of her own.

These situations represent a few of the many examples in our lives of the variety of dashed dreams and hopes.

You may be wondering if answers really exist. I know they do because I have had my life abruptly disrupted and dramatically changed. Yet I live with tremendous hope and absolute assurance that God has a plan. I want to share it with you because your circumstances and your storm are not exceptions. You are not excluded from the offer to have that same hope and assurance.

Some Storms Seem to Surge Forever

There are many layers to the losses our life storms cause. They are rarely confined to one specific set of circumstances or have nice, neat start and stop dates. In fact, many of them will have repercussions and aftereffects that last forever. Take for example the woman who discovers her husband is unfaithful. The storm dumps pain in bucket loads when she initially uncovers the email that reveals another woman. The truth slowly and surely begins to surface as she finds more evidence of compromise and betrayal. The storm begins to change her and her children. It affects their security and stability. Deep wounds are inflicted that cause major disruption and undermine the whole foundation on which her family has been established. It often continues to the next generation as those who were innocent are dragged into the web of sin and chaos. What can we do to keep from being pulled under by the riptide or tossed like refuse on a deserted beach?

Maybe you see storm clouds far off in the distance, and you're listening carefully to see if that was thunder you heard. Is there a hint somewhere on the horizon of your conscience that a storm is brewing? It may be growing dark and the winds starting to rise, causing a scurry to find protection and cover. For some, the storm is raging. Lightning is ripping through the backdrop of a black sky, and the waves are beginning to crash with deafening volume. The wind is furious, and everything in its path is turned over and uprooted. Brokenness and destruction are shattered all around your feet. Or maybe the storm of your life is in a momentary lull. The eye is hovering over now, but you know the back side has yet to come.

I Will Go Before You to Galilee

The Bible is full of stories where men and women encountered awful circumstances they never imagined would happen. They felt the same confusion and despair we experience today. What if you were about to face a storm of unparalleled pain, disillusion, and fear?

Consider when Jesus' 12 disciples sat down with Him for what became known as the Last Supper. For the previous three years, they had been eyewitnesses to and participators in many amazing meetings and miracles. Yet they are unaware they have just eaten their last supper with Him. Although they have been told many things concerning the future, they don't understand what it all means. Some things are not intellectually understood because they have to be spiritually revealed.

The disciples were much like us. They were focused on the things they could see with their eyes and the things they thought they understood. They were wrapped up in the present circumstances and even concerned with their place and position in the future.

A crisis of epic proportion is ahead for all of them. Jesus is about to be betrayed, apprehended, convicted, and crucified. They have no idea how dark and difficult the next three days are going to be. Jesus even says to them, "You will all fall away because of Me this night" (Matthew 26:31).

What's ahead for the disciples? Denial, betrayal, disappointment, fear, false accusation, threats, abuse, lies, jealousy, anger, suicide, desertion, rumors, cruelty, loss of hope, pain, sorrow, aimlessness, hopelessness, directionless days, and the death of future dreams, plans, and position.

However, before these storms hit, Jesus makes the disciples a promise tucked within a passage of Scripture that is often overlooked. In Matthew 26:32, He says, "But after I have been raised, *I will go before you to Galilee*" (NKJV, emphasis added).

Look at those last words carefully: "I will go before you to Galilee." Jesus didn't just vaguely tell the disciples He would rise again from the dead. Instead, He specifically told them where they would meet again after the crisis was over—in Galilee. He explicitly stated they would survive the upcoming crisis and experience life after the storm.

Jesus knows the difficulties our personal storm may bring. Our situation has not taken Him by surprise. He knows what is ahead. He knows where we will struggle and fail. He knows the pain and the sorrow we will endure. He knows the depth of our fear and the power of our doubts to send us to the edge of existence. But in these final hours, He leaves His friends with a promise that declares hope and a future are ahead of them.

Before your crisis hits, Jesus has already given you a promise concerning your future. There will be days when it will seem as if all is lost. After all, Jesus was crucified and bled to death on a cross. He was laid in a tomb with a stone rolled across the entrance and Roman soldiers standing guard. Jerusalem turned against all who followed Him, and the disciples hid in fear for their lives. Rest in Jesus' words: "After I have been raised…I will go before you…to Galilee." We have an appointed place where we will all gather together again.

Right now, you may be in a very dark and lonely place, but you are not abandoned. You are not left without the same promise. Jesus will meet you after the storm.

Oh My God, What Are We Going to Do?

As I tried to comprehend the news of my son's death, I needed to get outside because I felt as if I would suffocate. All I knew was scant information from the US Embassy in Nairobi, Kenya. "I'm sorry to inform you that your son, James Franklin Harrison IV, is dead." James had been overseas assisting a local pastor in ministry in a small town on the Kenya–Tanzania border.

My first thought was, "Oh my God, what are we going to do?" The gut-wrenching task of notifying James' three sisters and our family members had to start. Plans and arrangements to go to Nairobi to get his body had to be made. Questions and thoughts churning in my mind tumbled out of my mouth.

The adverse winds of life were raging against me with powerful force. The cold breath of death was trying to suffocate me and rob my spirit. The physical sensations of desperation and violent motion sickness assaulted me with fevered sweats overruled by cold chills. Gasps of air tried to force back the waves of nausea.

If you've ever been very seasick, you know the best place to look is out to the horizon. Everything around you is rocking and rolling, the waves on the surface are steadily pounding, and the boat is tossing you around. The captain says, "Find a fixed point and don't take your eyes off it."

When my life storm hit, I had to find a place to focus because I was reeling with doubts, fears, and questions. I had to look at something that could not shift or shake. I had to train my eyes on Jesus. He never changes. He remains the same—always. And when I did, His still, quiet voice whispered to my heart many words of hope and assurance. *I am with you always…I will never leave you nor forsake you…Fear not…Peace I give you.* I began to have a sensation of balance, and my emotional equilibrium became calmer and steadier. I had a deep assurance of the presence of God as the storm slammed against me. I knew we were not alone, and I knew Jesus was in the very midst of this crisis. At that moment I couldn't imagine life after this storm, but He had a plan.

Many difficult decisions and days were ahead. I knew our lives would never be the same again. I knew I was living in the midst of every parent's worst nightmare—the loss of a child. It seemed surreal for my three daughters and me to sit down and write James' obituary. It was devastating to open the paper, see his picture, and read it. The casual question, "How many children do you have?" became a dagger in my heart and a painful question to answer. Two months later, I opened a box of Christmas decorations and pulled out his stocking. Suddenly I had to decide, do I hang it or stuff it back in the box as if he never existed? Over that first year, unanticipated reminders of loss were everywhere. Sorting through James' belongings and searching for personal pictures, letters, cards, and emails were both comforting and tormenting. In the midst of it all I knew the One who would take us through and promised hope on the other side of this deep loss.

He didn't do one thing for me He has not promised to do for all who call on His name and believe in His Word. I am not different or special. There I stood, a mother with a shredded heart and a scorching pain in the pit of my stomach. When I thought to myself, *Oh my God, what are we going to do?* I heard the Spirit whisper back, *Trust Me.* He would tenderly whisper it many times through those first few years—and He still does today.

Are you being tossed and tormented by a storm in your life? Do you feel as if you will never again have a steady path under your feet and a sense of calm in your spirit? Do you feel hopeless and helpless to find balance and peace? Allow me to walk with you through this storm. I want to share my personal experiences in the hope they can encourage you and point you toward healing. I understand that may sound unrealistic and impossible to you right now, but what have we got to lose besides this deep place of misery and pain? It makes perfect sense to be tentative about trusting me to really understand where you are and what you are going through. I don't pretend for a minute to have all the answers or to know exactly how to help you, but I do know the One who can and will. You may find that a portion of this book does not resonate with your circumstances or seems impossible to understand right now, but if you will press on, I am certain you will find the healing your heart is longing for.

Before the crisis, Jesus gave the forecast of difficult times to come. Likewise, we have all been given such a forecast as well. Some of us listen to this forecast and immediately hear bad news. But the good news is that regardless of the storms currently raging or the ones still way out on the horizon, Jesus is here to remind us, "After I have been raised, I will go before you to Galilee." He has a plan to follow every crisis.

YOUR STEPS WITH GOD

As we embark on this journey together I would like to offer this prayer. I hope you will receive this as a blanket of comfort to wrap around your heart as we begin.

> *Dear Lord, I am offering this prayer on behalf of this precious friend. Thank You for allowing us to meet, and please use our time together to be a blessing and encouragement. You are drawing close to listen to our cry because You love us, and if our heart is broken, Yours is also. We need Your help because we are reeling in our circumstances. We are asking You to come into our storm and speak to the wind and the waves threatening to overtake us. Will You be our lifeline today and show us the way to hope and healing? We extend our hand toward You and ask You to comfort and care for us throughout our journey. I'm asking in the name of Jesus, amen.*

2

God's Weather Forecast

It was September 1989, and I had three young children tucked into bed and an exhausted husband sleeping peacefully. After tuning in to the local forecast one more time, I made final rounds upstairs and went to bed. All day the news had been broadcasting about a major hurricane named Hugo, which was moving northward off the coast in the Atlantic. We live in Charlotte, North Carolina, located many miles inland from the coast.

During the late news, the predictions said landfall would occur at the Isle of Palms, just east of Charleston, South Carolina. They seemed very definite. The crazy thing was, there were also tracking patterns taking the storm on a northwest pattern straight to Charlotte. If the predictions were correct, hurricane-force winds and rains would hit Charlotte in the next few hours before continuing on a northward path.

I'd seen and heard the forecast throughout the day, but it was so unusual and so unlikely I didn't take it very seriously. Neither did most of the citizens of Charlotte. We were more than 200 miles from the coast. Every hurricane report I had ever seen included large bodies of water and palm trees swaying in the wind. We had neither. So I went to bed fully informed of the predictions but completely clueless of the effects the storm would wreak if the forecast proved to be accurate.

I was awakened in the early morning by the sound of violent rain beating down and what seemed to be groaning and popping sounds. I made my rounds again to see what was going on and found the windows covered by swirling water mixed with tiny minced pieces of vegetation and sticks. Then I saw water was pouring through the ceiling lights and running down the wall in the main room.

The first light of day brought visibility to what appeared to be a war zone. Huge old oak trees were uprooted by high wind and destroyed everything around them. Power lines were dangling dangerously across the wall and the road, broken glass shards made picking your way across the patio a dangerous risk, roofing materials with shingles and nails were littered across the yards, and pieces of tin were crumpled like notebook paper. Hurricane Hugo had hit Charlotte just as predicted.

Could a Storm Really Happen to Me?

Did you know that in Scripture God has given us a forecast concerning this life? Most of us either have no idea what the warnings are or we don't take them very seriously. It's only in the aftermath that many of us recognize that His warnings were important and applied personally to us.

Why would I listen to the weather forecast and still ignore the predictions for a hurricane to hit my city in the next several hours? In hindsight it seems irresponsible and reckless, but I had no reference point for the devastation of a hurricane, so I couldn't imagine experiencing it, especially 200 miles away from the coast. Yet storms have a path of their own, and we can be caught off guard.

Many things in my life have not gone according to my plans or happened the way I envisioned. We are all encouraged to set goals, have dreams, make a plan, and go after it. My goals were not great in terms of an impressive career or being a radical agent for change, but they were noble in their intention to influence the next generation.

I always wanted to be a wife and a mother. I wanted to be the heart of a happy home where people would come and go and always know they were loved and appreciated, no matter what. I wanted home to be a haven of peace and a comfortable landing place at the end of the long school, work, or play day. I imagined a picture-perfect family and never anticipated anything except my children who thrived, a husband who prospered personally and professionally, and devoted friends and extended family who would always be close and supportive. For several years things seemed to go that way. I foolishly thought I had figured out the formula for a storm-free life.

It is humbling to realize that everyone seems brilliant and accomplished until they have a few unexpected and unanticipated experiences. As long as life goes according to our plan, we can make life look like easy sailing. I desperately desired to build a family on the foundation of faith with deep Christian character and values. I wanted my children to have a standard and a plumb line and know the joys and rewards of walking with the Lord. I wanted them to avoid the problems and pains of neglecting His truth and ignoring His commands. I thought if we took them to church, taught Sunday school, prayed with them and for them, and set a good example, then God would be bound to give us trouble-free years and delightful ease in establishing our family.

I remember one of the first situations that put a slight crack in my perfect picture. I got a phone call from school when James was in kindergarten. (If I had known then how many calls I would eventually get from school, it would have slayed me on the spot!) The teacher loved him and saw all of the positive delights in him. She started there and moved on to the real reason for the call. James seemed to be struggling with the concepts of letters, sounds, blends, and pre-reading skills. He was bright but information seemed to get garbled in his mind. It was the beginning of a lifetime of classroom challenges, failures, and disappointments. Seeds of inadequacy and insufficiency were planted and grew to eventually become tremendous obstacles in his life.

From the very beginning it was a matter of prayer. We prayed through tests, tutors, educational counseling and more testing, teachers, medications, classes to take and avoid, and schools to get into and out of. What I thought would be a typical activity of growing up became a source of great trial and trouble. If you have a child with some sort of learning disability or educational challenge, then you know this battle. Every day was hard, and every day took a tremendous amount of energy.

I remember one day when it snowed enough for school to be closed and everyone was sledding. James was trying to read *Lord of the Flies* and write a paper. After several hours I sent him out to play and finished reading the book for him. I didn't write the paper, but I sat with him and told him everything he needed to know. Trying to do life for someone you love is demanding and hard. I have a feeling many of you know what I'm talking about on numerous different levels.

Many storms and trials later, I have begun to understand that I cannot dictate or tell God how, when, or in what context He chooses to perform His word. He owes me nothing because He has already given me everything I need through Jesus. We have been given fair warning not to set ourselves up with our picture of perfect. Listen to these words from Jesus to His disciples:

> Behold, an hour is coming, and has already come, for you to be scattered, each to his own home, and to leave Me alone; and yet I am not alone, because the Father is with Me. These things I have spoken to you, that in Me you may have peace. In the world you have tribulation, but take courage; I have overcome the world (John 16:32-33).

When we feel scattered and alone, deserted and forgotten, it's good to remember Jesus has felt that way too. But He also reminds us that if we have God, we are never, ever alone. We need to become familiar with the words of warning and the predictions God has given to us in His Word. Remembering and clinging to the truth of Scripture gives us courage. Problems are going to be part of this life and this world. We are going to experience difficulty and disappointment. Our picture of perfect is going to be all messed up—count on it. With Jesus, though, we are stronger than the problem and can take the pressure.

Regardless of when you began to experience life's challenges first-hand, you are no doubt finding the storms or the threat of storms to be disturbing and disrupting. If you are actively engaged with people and listen with any degree of perceptiveness, it becomes clear people everywhere are struggling. Unexpected and unplanned life storms are forecasted.

Are We Holding God Captive?

Almost every single day I am made aware through personal inter-action or secondhand relay of the circumstances in people's lives that threaten to overwhelm them. The more you listen and involve your-self in others' lives, the more the conclusion is clear: No one gets a free pass, and there is no formula to ensure a trouble-free life.

Why does that come as such a shocking surprise and leave us feel-ing betrayed and misled? Could it be because we have listened to the voice of our culture and allowed persuasive language to deceive us of God's truth? Do we believe that if we work hard, do good, and be our best, we will be able to outsmart all the obstacles?

Late one night I was in bed almost asleep when the phone rang. I answered and heard the strained voice of a friend on the other end. She told me she was at the hospital and had just been informed that her sister's recovery from a minor cosmetic procedure had gone terri-bly wrong. Her sister had been young, beautiful, and healthy and was now being kept alive by a ventilator.

My friend had to tell their parents and prepare to make many important decisions. She kept saying, "I can't believe this is happening. There is no reason or explanation that makes sense. I thought if I was a good Christian girl and followed the golden rule that things like this would not happen to me."

Another friend recently expressed similar frustrations. "I worked hard in school, scored well on entrance exams, was accepted into a pres-tigious university, built an impressive resume, and climbed to the top in my profession. How can it be possible to be jobless?"

On a recent flight I sat next to a man who shared his story. "My company was doing well and life was very good for my family until I discovered that my assistant had embezzled everything. It all came crashing down. Now I'm broke, my family is ashamed, I have no friends, and there is nothing I can do but try to scratch my way out of this."

As Christians, many of us can begin to think or act as though we can use God's Word to hold Him captive or twist His arm to do what we want Him to. I've been a part of many prayer circles and have

listened to myself start with, "God, You said in Your Word…" and proceed to try to manipulate His will or dare Him to fail to come through
in the way I thought He had promised. Naive and uninformed, maybe
yes, but not a foreign response to many who grew up in the church.

Many of us are led to believe we are the masters of our own destiny. If we carefully manage our world, methodically plan, and control
the environment, we can keep anything negative or unpleasant from
happening.

Some may ask, "Why bother to be informed of or prepare for the
storms of life? God is going to do what He's going to do, so what difference does it make?" If this is our attitude, it lets us off the hook for
taking responsibility for choices. However, it serves as little comfort
when going through a crisis. I would imagine life begins to feel like a
lounge chair sliding across the deck with every roll of the waves. Having faith is not being fatalistic but is instead being absolutely certain in
the One we believe in.

God Is Always Thinking Ahead

Unpleasant forecasts are disruptions to our plans. They inter-
rupt the carefully crafted dreams and imaginings we have about life.
They are viewed as slightly inconvenient, like rain clouds that force an
alfresco dinner party indoors. This casual perspective will prevent us
from taking the time, making the investment, and becoming familiar
with the forecast God has given in His Word concerning the inevitable storms of this life.

One of the most familiar stories in the Bible is the story of Noah. It
serves as a storm warning for all who will read and heed it. In a world
gone mad with sin and violence, there was one man whose life got
God's attention.

"Noah found favor in the eyes of the LORD…Noah was a righteous
man, blameless in his time; Noah walked with God" (Genesis 6:8-9).
Because Noah was open to the voice of God and had a teachable heart,
as well as a willingness to learn and understand the insights and revelations of God for his own life, God brought Noah into His confidence.

But the forecast was not good. The secret things of God are not always pleasant and sweet.

God told Noah, "The end of all flesh has come before Me; for the earth is filled with violence because of them; and behold, I am about to destroy them with the earth" (Genesis 6:13). Noah could have quit listening then. He could have decided it was so miserable and depressing he didn't want to know any more. He could have ignored the warning and said, "This will never happen." But he continued to listen because he was open to the voice of God. So Noah also heard God say, "Make yourself an ark...I am bringing the flood of water upon the earth, to destroy all flesh in which is the breath of life...everything that is on the earth shall perish...BUT I will establish My covenant with you; and you shall enter the ark—you and your sons and your wife, and your sons' wives with you" (Genesis 6:14-18, emphasis added).

Noah had a relationship with God. As a result of his relationship, he was able to know the plans God had for him. God's plans are not always for ease and comfort; however, they always have an eternal purpose, and God offered Noah an opportunity to be a part of His future plan.

Noah did not have much to go on, but he did have the promise that he would be preserved through the storm by building an ark and his family would come through it with him. It was all he needed.

As I mentioned in the first chapter, God always has a plan for after the storm. He has appointed a place to meet you when this crisis is past. Jesus said, "After I have been raised, I will go before you to Galilee." Likewise, He says to you and me, *You have My word that no matter how dark or difficult the days are, I already see the other side and have a plan for you.*

Confidence and Confidantes

What is the common thread that stretches from Noah in the Old Testament to the disciples in the New Testament? They all had a personal relationship with God. They had invested themselves in knowing and becoming familiar with Him.

Noah had little information, but we know that man is made in the image of God (Genesis 1:26) and God has set eternity in the heart of every person (Ecclesiastes 3:11). A place within each one of us longs to be filled with the Spirit of our Creator. Many times we don't know and cannot recognize what we are hungering for. We have a desire for something that can only be satisfied by Him.

When I was a young woman, I realized I had everything I ever wanted, but I was still restless and dissatisfied. I married my high school sweetheart, and we had one beautiful baby girl with another baby on the way. We were launching our lives together and everything was going well. Why was I discontent deep within?

At this time I was invited to attend a Bible study in my city. I was raised in church, believed the Word, and would have told you I was a Christian. Going to Bible study was not a stretch for me, and so I went in eager anticipation of meeting some other young mothers and doing something meaningful with my time. Within a few short weeks I met Jesus face-to-face in a way I never had before. I realized knowing about Him was not the same as knowing Him personally. I invited Him to come into my heart.

As I listened to the Word of God taught in a relevant way, my eyes were opened and I began to understand that Jesus had created me for companionship with Him. I could know Him through His Word and grow to learn to hear Him speak to me. I deeply desired to have a personal relationship with Him.

I made a decision that if the Bible was true and was the voice of God speaking personally to His people, then I would listen to it. I would learn the promises, the principles, and the warnings and apply them to my life. If God was my Creator and He had given me His Word to be my guide, then I wanted to know it, live it, trust it, and grow in it.

That was 33 years ago. Like the disciples, there are many things I don't understand and many times when I have been uncertain about where to turn and what to do. But I can also tell you that the years invested in learning to listen to God's voice have been honored. He was equipping and preparing me for life. He was guiding and leading me and enlarging my heart for Him.

You and I are the confidants of God.

When our children are small, our role as a parent is to prepare and equip them for the things we know they will need to understand. We have the benefit of experience, and out of love we want to protect and make sure they are not caught in dangerous activities or places. We teach them to never talk to strangers, cross the street without looking both ways, or ride their bikes without a helmet.

Our children depend on us and know that we, their mothers and fathers, are the ones to call on when things are not right. They have confidence we will know what to do and be there for them.

Our heavenly Father wants us to know Him and allow Him to prepare us for the unknown paths ahead. His love for you and me is so great that He wants to take us into confidence and teach us the signs and warnings and give us deep confidence in Him to always know what to do.

God's Unchanging Power

Heeding the forecast for Hurricane Hugo would have drastically changed the days that followed the storm. Being prepared would not have prevented the damage, but it would have made the 17 days without power much easier to bear. As the contents of the thawing freezer seeped in sticky pools across the floor, my husband and I frantically tried to create a semi-safe environment for our three young children. I couldn't help but ask myself, "Why didn't I buy water, get the car filled with gas, gather reserves, and stock up on batteries in anticipation of a power outage?"

There is a natural curiosity to know the future. People are willing to read their horoscope and trust their sign in the zodiac to help them make decisions and choices. Everyone scrambles for a fortune cookie at the close of a meal to see what is predicted for the future. Palm readers, tarot cards, and looking into a crystal ball are desperate attempts to have some idea of what lies ahead. Christians dismiss these acts as foolish, yet how often do we still say, "If I only knew how this would all turn out"?

We have not been left in the dark and unprepared for what lies ahead. We can learn to listen carefully and begin to see the evidence around us that God always has a plan to follow the crisis.

Even if you don't feel this assurance or believe it at this time, God's power to keep what is committed to Him is unchangeable. You may feel as if you are hanging on to a flimsy life raft and the force of your storm may be threatening to pull you under. Even when you are too weak to hang on to Him and your strength is zapped, you need not despair of being lost or forgotten. When you start to sink, God will take hold of you.

In the book of Mark is the story of when Peter and the disciples were in the boat and a storm came up on the Sea of Galilee. The wind and the waves became so fierce that the disciples were straining at the oars and struggling to keep the boat afloat. At that time, they felt threatened and afraid. But Mark 6:48 says Jesus "came to them, walking on the sea." The verse goes on to tell us that He "intended to pass by them." He was walking on top of the storm. He was not threatened or fazed by the wind and the roiling sea. Jesus was headed to the other side to meet them there. But the disciples were afraid, and they cried out, and it says He immediately spoke to them and said, "Take courage; it is I, do not be afraid" (Mark 6:50).

God Holds On

Dear friend, cry out to Jesus today. He is right there in the midst of your storm, and He is urging you to take courage in Him. He is on top of the circumstances in your life, and He is able to hold on to you. If you have weathered a storm, you can be a witness with me that there are times when you don't even realize you have let go. You are so preoccupied with trying to keep the boat of your life from swamping that you cannot reach to take hold of Him. Take heart. He is holding on to you.

YOUR STEPS WITH GOD

I want to share a few of my favorite verses that remind me of God's power during the storms of life. I invite you to turn to these references in your Bible to experience hope and strength. God's Word speaks personally, and there is nothing more calming and reassuring than to allow His Word to wash over you like a warm soothing bath and calm your frayed nerves and anxious heart.

After you record these verses, I want you to ask yourself two simple questions:

What is my part?
What is God's part?

As you discover the power of these verses for yourself, start your own list to build your Christ-confidence for the storm.

- Isaiah 25:1

  My part:

  God's part:

- Isaiah 30:18,21

  My part:

  God's part:

- Proverbs 10:25

  My part:

  God's part:

- Jeremiah 33:3

  My part:

  God's part:

- Nahum 1:7
  My part:

  God's part:

- Habakkuk 3:19
  My part:

  God's part:

- Hebrews 13:5-6
  My part:

  God's part:

- James 1:12
  My part:

  God's part:

3

God's Survival Kit

On that chaotic September morning after Hurricane Hugo tore through Charlotte, the electrical power was knocked out when we awakened. As water poured through our roof, plenty of wishes stormed through our minds. We wished we had flashlights within reach. We certainly wished we had a designated cabinet packed with survival basics, such as a weather radio, plenty of batteries, and a considerable stash of nonperishable snacks. But by the time we realized what we needed, we were scrambling to survive and trying to figure it out in the dark.

We were not alone in our search for supplies. Most of the city's population was on a quest for any number of things: power saws to blaze paths through blocked roads, fuel for cars and generators, ice to keep food from spoiling, cash from lifeless teller machines. Every typically routine task became a daunting challenge. And each struggle seemed worse with the knowledge that had we listened to the warnings and made preparations, the storm recovery would have been more manageable. Everything we needed was readily available the day before, but in the crisis it was difficult to secure necessary items.

Where do you turn to when the winds of adversity begin to blow through your well-planned world? Who has answers that can satisfy or fail-safe instructions to help you navigate your way?

We often attempt to have our inner needs met by outside resources, such as money, education, success, health, beauty, influence, and other people, but most of the time we find that these sources are limited and lacking in our moments of struggle. Not one of these can fully satisfy or supply the needs we have.

What Life Finds in Us

Not long ago I heard it said, "What life does to us depends on what life finds in us."

For the most part, we have very little control over what life does *to* us. We have no influence over who our parents are or what circumstances we are born into. For most of our first dozen years almost every decision concerning our lives is made for us. Little by little we get to make independent decisions and grow in our individuality. What we are becoming on the inside is revealed by our reactions and responses to the things that happen along the way.

Another saying is, "What goes down in the well comes up in the bucket." Jesus said, "Out of the overflow of the heart the mouth speaks" (Matthew 12:34 NIV). No matter what life does to me, if it finds the truth of God's Word inside of me, I will not be a helpless victim or a purposeless wanderer. What comes up from my heart and out of my mouth will be words of life, hope, healing, and redemption.

But why are so many Christians defeated and depleted by life's challenges? Why do so many people who say they know Jesus live with little hope and even less joy and peace? Could it be that we are spending more time trying to dodge and control the storm and less time learning to use the provisions God makes available to us? Because life storms are not preventable, we can prepare in ways to significantly minimize the damage.

God's Survival Kit for the Storm

Being an active, effective participant in an event or happening requires us to show up prepared. Fortunately, most activities we get involved in are organized and come with their own supply list: school, camp, seminars, training sessions, mission trips, and meetings. Without the requested supplies, you are not fully prepared to gain all that is being offered.

You and I would never send one of our children to camp in the woods without a backpack full (and then some) of items necessary for safety and survival. So why do we frequently send ourselves into the wilderness of life without hearts and minds full of the spiritual power and strength necessary for safety and survival? The quality of life after the storm is largely dependent on the attention we give to our spiritual life before the storm. While nobody can guarantee *what* we will encounter today and tomorrow and the next day, I am confident you and I will fare much better if we prepare ourselves with God's supplies now.

I am going to share a spiritual supply list with you. It's one I have tried and found more than sufficient. It's the one given to us by our Creator. He knows us better than we know ourselves because He made us and has every detail of our life in His heart and mind. He knows exactly what we will need. We don't have to try to live life with our resources and strength.

The Red Cross, recognized universally as experts on emergency preparation and response, authored a list of items necessary for survival. Because God is the author of life, He has provided the supply list for our spiritual preparation and response.

Red Cross Supply List	Spiritual Supply List
Water	The Life of Christ
Food	The Word of God
Light	Activated Faith
Emergency Contacts	The Body of Christ
Blanket	Prayer

Let's review these lists together and make preparations to be fully supplied for life.

1. Water—The Life of Christ

The most essential supply for life is water. The human body cannot survive more than a few days without it, so water is the first thing shipped to a disaster area.

The most essential supply for spiritual life is spiritual water. Without it there is no spiritual life. Jesus met a woman sitting at a well in Samaria and asked her for a drink of water. As conversation continued between them, He told her, "If you knew the gift of God, and who it is who says to you, 'Give Me a drink,' you would have asked Him, and He would have given you *living* water" (John 4:10 NKJV, emphasis added). Jesus went on to tell her, "Whoever drinks of this water will thirst again, but whoever drinks of the water that I shall give him will never thirst. But the water that I shall give him will become in him a fountain of water springing up into everlasting life" (John 4:13-14 NKJV).

Living water springs from an unfailing source, Jesus. He is telling the woman how to have her dry, parched, wasteland of weakness, desperation, emptiness, and soul starvation satisfied permanently. The water Jesus offers is not drawn from a well but flows from a fountain. Water wells can dry up or the water can become contaminated and useless, but a fountain is an ever-flowing source of pure, clean, satisfying water. Jesus was using the woman's physical need for water as an object lesson to point her toward her need for spiritual transformation.

There are times when life leads us into desert places—physically, emotionally, and spiritually. Stop with me and rest your weary soul here. Jesus is sitting at the well of your heart and offering His living water to you. He knew that the deepest need within the Samaritan women's heart was to have His life-giving Spirit within her. We are no different. Will you reach out and receive His offer for life?

2. Food—The Word of God

Very few of us have any idea what it means to be truly hungry. We have three meals a day and snacks in between. The real question for most of us is, "What do we have an appetite for? What do we hunger for?" Ask yourself, *Do I have an appetite for spiritual food?* "Oh, taste and see that the LORD is good" (Psalm 34:8 NKJV). *Do I find myself developing a taste for the Word of God and hungry to feed on His truth?* Our soul is nourished and strengthened when we learn to take God's Word and feed ourselves daily. It contains every element we need for vigorous growth and optimum spiritual health.

The Word "will bring health to your body and nourishment to your bones" (Proverbs 3:8 NIV). I am applying this personally and practically as a vital part of my own personal health regimen. The Word will deal clearly and specifically with the many factors of stress, strain, anxiety, worry, and anger that lie at the root of many physical diseases.

The Word of God provides nourishment to sustain and strengthen us for the journey of life. I drank from the well of living water Jesus offered me more than 30 years ago. My appetite and cravings began to change because His Spirit lives inside of me. I started to develop a hunger and thirst for righteousness, and it was satisfied by hearing, reading, studying, and applying the Word of God. Because it is "living and active" (Hebrews 4:12), it changes us from within when we make it a regular staple in our spiritual diet.

I encourage you to stop now and plan your next spiritual meal. Pick up your Bible, any version you have, or download a Bible application. Before you begin, bow your head and thank God for giving you His daily bread. As you begin to read, you are eating spiritual truth. Pray and ask God to sustain, strengthen, and grow you up in Him. If Bible reading is new for you, here is a suggestion:

- Begin with the Gospel of John.
- Read out of the book of Psalms daily, and you will learn to praise and pray.
- Read a Proverb each day, and you will grow in God's wisdom.

3. Light—Activated Faith

A light source is an essential tool for survival. As long as we are in the dark we are fumbling and struggling for clarity and direction.

Darkness is filled with uncertainty and fear, but a flashlight gives us courage to take steps with confidence and certainty. When the switch is on, the flashlight empowers us to move ahead in the path of light.

In the same way, faith is an essential tool for spiritual survival. When a person is steadfast and immovable concerning spiritual matters, we describe them as having strong faith. They seem to continue to move forward with certainty regardless of the circumstances.

Faith is the power that must be activated to move ahead in our spiritual lives. In Hebrews 11 we are given a list of people God used to impact and influence kingdoms and nations. Their lives triumphed over the darkness and difficulty of life storms, and they lived with the power and confidence that comes from activating faith in God's Word. Faith called, enabled, empowered, carried, blessed, strengthened, tested, tried, rewarded, and perfected all those who chose to activate the light and allow God to lead them.

"Faith is the substance of things hoped for, the evidence of things not seen" (Hebrews 11:1 NKJV). By faith, stretch your hand toward Jesus and receive the living water He offers. By faith, a sip of living water becomes a fountain flowing within you. By faith, pick up the Word of God and allow His voice to speak personally into your life and begin to revive you.

Faith is not mystical or mysterious. Faith is a deliberate decision. When we choose to activate faith, our spiritual supply is powerful.

4. Emergency Contacts—The Body of Christ

Isolation is a dangerous position for us to be in when a storm strikes. The most vulnerable and likely to be unaccounted for are those who are unattached to any community.

The same principle is true for all of us who are members of the body of Christ. We were created to need and support one another. Each person is necessary for body health, optimal function, and protection. The Bible says, "Just as we have many members in one body and all the members do not have the same function, so we, who are many, are one body in Christ, and individually members one of another" (1 Corinthians 12:4-5).

A couple of days after receiving the news of James' death, Frank headed to Nairobi to take care of arrangements to bring his body home. A friend accompanied him to help. It was not a time to be alone. Over the course of those initial days, many people who were part of the extended body of Christ—the church universal—stepped forward to help.

Our dear friends Pastor Simon and his wife, Agnes, were some of the first people we talked to. James had lived with them off and on over the last five years of his life and they had loved him as if he had been their own child. On hearing the news of his death, they responded, "We will leave immediately for Nairobi and wait with our son's body until his father arrives." And those loving, godly people headed out from their home in Namanga to be with our James.

Because of deep personal and business relationships, officials from the Coca-Cola Company in Kenya met my husband in the airport. They happened to be three faith-filled businesswomen. Out of love and respect for Frank, one voluntarily witnessed the autopsy herself so she could confirm its accuracy. From the moment she reached James' side, she never left his body. Months later I had the privilege of meeting with these dear women for breakfast. When I thanked them for their love and care, the reply was, "Ma'am, it was my reasonable act of worship unto the Lord."

One of them had even gone shopping so his body would be "properly dressed" when his father arrived. He died in shorts and a T-shirt, and she bought a beautiful light-blue oxford shirt, khaki pants, and a red tie for him to be dressed for burial. It was a tender act of love and kindness performed out of a gentle heart of service to the Lord.

In all of these difficult and trying circumstances, God was there touching us through His people. All of these acts serve as precious reminders that He knows and cares about what we are going through.

There are times when the force of the storm and the weight of the burden are too great to carry alone. If we are going to prevail when the storm is blowing and the opposition is gaining strength, it's imperative we have others in our lives to help. They are our emergency contacts in the day of trouble.

5. Blanket—Prayer

I'm trembling and shaking with cold chills of shock running through me. Someone picks up a blanket and wraps it tightly around me. I whisper, "Please pray for us." At that moment, I can't pray, but I know it's supernatural power that will enable us to survive this storm we've been slammed by. Prayer unfurls God's banner of love and wraps us in His care.

Others begin to pray as soon as the news of James' death begins to spread. First Thessalonians 5:17 says we should "pray without ceasing." As we are bombarded with questions, details, arrangements, and practical decisions, so many members of my church, my Bible study group, family, and friends are praying on our behalf. It's as if layer upon layer of God's truth is being pulled up over our minds and spirits.

"In the same way, the Spirit also helps our weakness; for we do not know how to pray as we should, but the Spirit Himself intercedes with groanings too deep for words; and He who searches the hearts knows what the mind of the Spirit is, because He intercedes for the saints according to the will of God" (Romans 8:26-27). How reassuring and comforting to know Jesus is praying for us, and He knows exactly how to pray and what to pray for.

Finally, I begin to pray for myself, and we gather together as a family and cry out to God, our ever-present help in time of need. I thank God for His provision of prayer.

"Evening and morning and at noon I will pray, and cry aloud, and He shall hear my voice" (Psalm 55:17 NKJV).

Equipped for the Storm

For years my passion has been to teach women to read and apply God's Word to their life. My own journey was changed when I learned the Bible was full of truths and principles that applied to my daily needs, decisions, and hopes.

The years of growing in the truth and then teaching the Word were invaluable to me and to my family. All those days, months, and years were preparation. Every time we applied what we learned, we were storing and updating spiritual supplies. The lessons, principles, promises, and warnings from the Word were being used to equip us for the storms of life. When the headwinds threatened to blow us off course and the waves crashed around us, we knew where to look for help and guidance.

On October 5, 2010, when the personal storm of all time hit us square in the face and threatened to wipe us out, I discovered my supply closet was full and we were prepared in ways I had never realized.

God desires to prepare us and give us grace and strength for tumultuous times. He wants us to be equipped to stand when the tides try to suck us out into a sea of adversity and swirl viciously to drown us in despair.

YOUR STEPS WITH GOD

Now is a good time to take inventory of your spiritual supply list. Let's check the contents carefully for freshness and familiarize ourselves with how to use them.

- Water—Is the fountain of living water, Christ Jesus Himself, flowing freely in your life? If not, ask the Lord to show you what is obstructing your flow. Some possibilities could be: unbelief, unforgiveness, thanklessness, resentment, bitterness, anger, jealousy, or a critical spirit.

- Food—What is your spiritual meal plan?

- Light—Have you activated spiritual power by faith?

- Emergency Contacts—Make a list from the body of Christ. They need to be people who have faith and wisdom.

- Blanket—Do you know people who will pray for you? Are you prayerful on behalf of others?

What part of your inventory is well stocked, and where do you need to strengthen your supply?

4

Shelter from the Storm

My grandmother lived in west Tennessee where farmland stretches for miles and miles over flat, red, dry earth. In this area of the country called Tornado Alley, most farms have a storm cellar where you go for shelter if a funnel cloud is spotted. When the sky grows dark and the atmospheric pressure begins to build, it's time to run for the hatch at ground level and descend the stairs to below the earth's surface and away from the wind's fury. There you find essential provisions stocked and stored to use during the duration of the storm.

Tornados cut an unpredictable and indiscriminate path, leaving destruction and death lying in their wake. In contrast, the storm cellar is a quiet refuge of safety and a dependable place to huddle together for comfort and protection. We never had to go down there when I was visiting, but we knew where it was and the purpose it served.

If you knew a tornado was coming and debris was beginning to tumble around you, would you stand outside in the elements and try to ignore it? If you grabbed on to a nearby tree and closed your eyes, would that effort at denial protect you from ravaging winds and flying debris? Failure to seek shelter leaves us vulnerable and exposed to the imminent threats of the twister. Our survival depends on knowing where we can go to be hidden from the wrath of the storm and then actually going to that shelter.

When our personal storms come whirling on the horizon, we have a similar choice to make. Will we seek shelter or will we refuse protection and stand in the turmoil with our innermost spiritual vulnerabilities exposed and threatened? When life is good, we feel happy with God and the world, and we don't pay much attention to our available shelters. But all it takes is for one piece of bad news to scatter shadows across our lives and decimate our faith and hope. A designated place of shelter allows us to weather trials and prevent them from blowing us apart.

Where do you turn to find shelter when a life storm hits? Do you have a designated shelter that offers genuine peace when circumstances threaten to tear your relationships apart, flood you with unexpected changes, and stir up emotional upheaval? We know God's forecast for our lives includes storms. We can do our part to prepare and assemble our survival kit. But knowing and preparing for a storm is a far cry from surviving one.

When David was king of Israel, he often engaged in battles and crises that threatened him personally and professionally. He not only prepared, but he also sought shelter. In Psalm 61:2-4, he calls out to God, his source of shelter:

> From the end of the earth I call to You when my heart is faint; *Lead me to the rock that is higher than I*. For You have been a refuge for me, a *tower of strength* against the enemy. Let me dwell in your tent forever; let me take refuge in *the shelter of Your wings* (emphasis added).

Hiding Behind Fear

Some disruptions cause us to lose what we have leaned on as our source of security, such as money and relationships or jobs and homes. For example, during the financial crisis of 2008, many people who had considered their lives financially stable were suddenly broke and, in some cases, jobless. You and I can lose or have lost our go-to forms of shelter in other ways. Maybe you went to a routine health appointment only to discover your test results bore signs of abnormalities. Now you live with dread hanging over you like a wrecking ball threatening to demolish your life. You may be a mother who loved, trained, and raised your child as best you could, but today that child is far away, literally or figuratively, and you cannot reach them or change the situation.

You may have slipped slowly into a deep, dark pit of depression and nothing seems to have the power to lift you out. Or you suffer the pain of a relationship failing after you wholeheartedly invested in it, leaving you feeling rejected and discarded. Dreams you have had for a lifetime may be snatched away by the thoughtless, careless, or pointless actions of others. Or you may be standing beside the grave of someone you can't imagine living life without.

When trying to emotionally survive such situations, we tend to cling to anything that is afloat to keep from being dragged under. When your life is being disrupted and waves of fear threaten to carry you out into a bottomless sea of despair, it's easy and natural to be focused on the:

- height of the waves
- force of the wind
- intensity of the pain
- menacing danger or harm
- weight of the burden
- cost of the call

- discomfort of the loss
- silence
- loneliness
- sorrow
- emptiness
- disappointment
- injustice

What you see is not good, and what you feel is threatening to drown you emotionally and spiritually. Fear is a powerful and controlling emotion. It robs, steals, and destroys hope and faith. And while it's founded on the lies whispered into the believer's ear, it disguises itself as necessary for survival. But fear doesn't help us rebuild our foundation or renew our strength; instead, it strips away spiritual power and purpose and leaves us floundering and cowering beneath a flimsy and dilapidated shelter.

God tells us time and time again, "Do not fear." Yet we grab fear, clutch it, and nurse it like a baby. It temporarily soothes but never satisfies because it deceives us into thinking we are being proactive when we are actually avoiding God's protection.

Where Were You, God?

Things feel very out of order when you outlive your child. Nothing can make that feel right. You have so many dreams and desires for your children to live a long, full life. Before James passed away at only 27 years old, I had spent his lifetime praying that God would build him into a mature, strong adult. I prayed that same prayer for all of my children, including my three daughters.

However, James seemed to require a little more frequent prayer and faith. As a young man he struggled to find himself and often felt disillusioned with life and other people. Many parents know the heartache in watching a child struggle to find himself. As a mother, I felt the constant weight of trying to guide James to live his own life and make his own choices.

From the time he was about 13, one of my favorite prayers was based on Psalm 27:13: "I would see the goodness of the Lord in the land of the living." I wanted more than the usual worldly successes for my children. I asked God to do "whatever it takes" to raise up strong and mighty men and women of God in our family. It was a bold prayer voiced out of a sincere desire to see God's best.

But when the news of James' death arrived, I felt timid, afraid, and maybe even a little bit foolish. I lost my son just as he was maturing into adulthood. How in the world could this possibly be God's plan?

Hissing lies of the enemy threatened to drown out the faithful promises of God. Doubts and questions flooded my mind. I wondered, *Why, God? What about all my prayers? Where were You, Lord? Did You forget Your Word? Did I never really hear Your voice in the first place? Was I just going through some ritualistic motions and hoping for things to change? Is it all just a crazy crutch? Is this some sort of payback to me for a mistake I made or a sin I committed? Do You even really care about my family, Lord?*

Each question and doubt felt like a huge wave pounding relentlessly against my heart. I couldn't get this one thought out of my mind: If

God's Word is true and I believed it before James died, how can I just throw it all away now that he's gone? Are God's promises strong enough to endure the agonizing pain I feel?

Crashing Waves Against the Rock of Truth

Jesus spoke to this specific question.

> Therefore everyone who hears these words of Mine and acts on them, may be compared to a wise man who built his house on the rock. And the rain fell, and the floods came, and the winds blew and slammed against that house; and yet it did not fall, for it had been founded on the rock. Everyone who hears these words of Mine and does not act on them, will be like a foolish man, who built his house upon the sand. The rain fell, and the floods came, and the winds blew and slammed against that house; and it fell— and great was its fall (Matthew 7:24-27).

Notice that Jesus mentioned that the storm came against both houses. Being wise and building on the rock does not guarantee storm-free days. Don't allow the enemy or an uninformed believer to deceive you into believing that God's children get a free pass from trials and trouble. Instead, Jesus says the ability to *survive* life's storms is based on these things:

1. Where we build our house—meaning our mental and spiritual foundation.
2. Whom we listen to—meaning the people we allow to give counsel.
3. What we do with the words we hear—meaning our decision to act on God's wisdom or reject it.

God's Word is full of promises that shore up our faith and build up our confidence. We are reminded time and time again that we are never alone and we have nothing to fear. For every scheme or lie the enemy has to undermine and destroy, God has a foundational truth to apply and use to strengthen and support. He is always dependable. But how do we know this is true?

In times of crisis you may feel as if a grueling tug-of-war is going on between your head and your heart. You struggle to look beyond the present circumstances and see only the crashing waves coming at you. The pain is real and your life may forever be scarred by a deep loss. But staring at the pain doesn't stop the wave from washing over us. Once a storm hits, we can't go back in time and remove it. We can, however, take shelter and prevent the crashing wave from wiping us out with lies, fears, and despair. Jesus urges us to seek refuge in Him as a fortified shelter of truth that can withstand the storm.

For example, maybe you're being bombarded right now with a tidal wave of thoughts and emotions, such as:

* * *

My Crashing Wave: "I'm going to fail. There is no point in trying."

The Rock of Truth: "I can do all things through Christ who strengthens me" (Philippians 4:13 NKJV).

* * *

My Crashing Wave: "I'm not worthy and nobody wants me."

The Rock of Truth: "'I know the plans I have for you,' declares the Lord, 'plans to prosper you and not to harm you, plans to give you hope and a future'" (Jeremiah 29:11 NIV).

* * *

My Crashing Wave: "I'm going to run out of money, and there is no one who will take care of me."

The Rock of Truth: "My God shall supply all you need according to His riches in glory by Christ Jesus" (Philippians. 4:19 NKJV).

* * *

My Crashing Wave: "This may never change and I will live with this the rest of my life. I have ruined my life."

The Rock of Truth: "We know that all things work together for the good to those who love God, to those who are the called according to His purpose" (Romans 8:28 NKJV).

* * *

My Crashing Wave: "No one cares about me and I am all alone."

The Rock of Truth: "Those who know Your name will put their trust in You; for You, LORD, have not forsaken those who seek You" (Psalm 9:10 NKJV).

* * *

My Crashing Wave: "I am confused and I have no idea what to do now."

The Rock of Truth: "Trust in the LORD with all your heart, and lean not on your own understanding; in all your ways acknowledge Him, and He shall direct your paths" (Proverbs 3:5-6 NKJV).

* * *

When I received the news of James' death, a great debate between fear and faith began to rage in my mind. But with every fear that crashed over my heart, the Spirit of the living God reminded me of an eternal word of truth. The pain and sorrow were real, yet I could also sense God offering me another option—to take shelter in Him. He had the power to get my family and me through the nightmare we suddenly faced.

Walking by Faith, Not by Sight

My friends Jeremy and Michelle are a beautiful young couple who live in a small, isolated frontier town in Alaska. Their home was built with their hands, and they filled it with three beautiful little girls and three rambunctious boys. If the walls could talk, their home would resound with peals of laughter, echoes of love, screams of delight, and, of course, squeals of frustration. Jeremy is a bush pilot and hunting guide, and Michelle is a full-time mom who works and plays hard.

Several years ago they took the girls on a trip into Anchorage to take care of business, do some shopping, and enjoy time together. There are no roads in and out of their little town, so they fly everywhere. On this particular day, the wind created challenging conditions and snow obscured visibility. Although they were cleared to fly, the conditions became extremely difficult. Halfway into their journey, the weather changed so quickly that Jeremy was forced to make an emergency landing on a frozen lake. As his plane touched down, the ice on the lake underneath gave way. The aircraft spun out of control and crashed into the dark, icy water.

Only Michelle and Jeremy survived. What had started as a routine trip had turned into a literal and figurative storm of life-threatening injuries and unfathomable loss. Nothing could prepare them to face their new, terrifying reality.

It's been almost ten years now. Jeremy and Michelle have lived through the nightmare. They can never get their girls back, and the heart-wrenching memories never fully disappear. If they wanted to rage at God, doubt His Word, or walk away from their faith, no one would blame them. How could anyone find life after a storm of such gut-wrenching tragedy? How could God restore a family who experienced a loss of that magnitude?

In the aftermath, Jeremy and Michelle chose to seek shelter in God. They still battle the lies of the enemy. If they look at their circumstances, they cannot stand in their own power under the pain and the loss. They choose to keep their eyes on Jesus and lean into His strength. When the painful memories threaten to steal their peace and strip them of their joy, they turn to the hope and the truth of God's Word. When they mark what would have been a birthday or a graduation in the lives of their three daughters, they choose to trust in the celebrations they will share in heaven. When the enemy tries to tear them apart as husband and wife, they stand on the rock-solid foundation of God's Word. They sought shelter from the storm in God's truth rather than letting emotions, lies, and painful memories rule their life.

What about you? Are waves of fear and doubt slamming against your mind and threatening to overwhelm you? Do the swirling winds of fear and uncertainty overrule your faith? I don't wish to minimize the force of the waves the enemy is hurling in your direction. There were times in my own life where the overpowering winds of doubt threatened to drown out God's voice of truth. How grateful I am that we don't have to follow the downward spiral created by the force of fear and doubt. Faith is a choice based on the firm foundation of God's truth. You and I can choose to seek God's sure and sturdy shelter.

God's Designated Meeting Spot

We are not the first of His followers to waiver in unbelief when we are fighting to stay afloat in a raging storm. For Jesus' disciples, the fear created by the circumstances surrounding them washed away any remembrance of His words of assurance and care. The events surrounding the last three days in Jerusalem before Christ was crucified swept faith right out from under them and left them holding a bag full of doubts. Shelter was found hiding in a locked room weeping and terrified. At the moment, all they knew was Jesus is dead, and they were utterly disillusioned and disappointed.

If you are feeling disillusioned and disappointed, you are not alone. Jesus knows and understands. But He also says to us, "After I have been raised, I will go before you to Galilee." Don't miss this point! He designated a meeting spot after His death.

Every emergency plan has a designated meeting spot. Jesus was saying, *I will meet you on the other side of this crisis, and I will be there on the other side of the grave.* But fear loomed large, and the disciples were bound by such strong doubts that Jesus had to resend His message to them. He knew they needed a reminder. He had a plan. When Mary Magdalene saw Him after His resurrection, He told her, "Do not be afraid. Go and tell my brothers to go to Galilee; there they will see me" (Matthew 28:10 NIV).

If you have picked up this book and read this far, I have a feeling it's because you or someone close to you is currently experiencing a life storm and the waves are crashing over you. When the wind is roaring, it's hard to hear. When waves of adversity batter us, it's easy to get off course. Allow me to be a voice sending Jesus' reminder to you. I, Jan, am the voice to resend His message. He has gone before you to the other side of the crisis. He is urging you to seek shelter and direction in Him.

YOUR STEPS WITH GOD

Before we move forward, I would like to suggest that you take a few minutes to ask yourself, "What are the crashing waves threatening to take me under? Where do I need to reinforce my mind on the rock of God's truth?"

* * *

My Crashing Wave:

The Rock of Truth:

* * *

My Crashing Wave:

The Rock of Truth:

* * *

My Crashing Wave:

The Rock of Truth:

* * *

My Crashing Wave:

The Rock of Truth:

* * *

Let's ask God to give us ears to hear Him speak, strength to stand to our feet, and faith to head in the direction of the designated meeting spot. He remains the unchanging shelter from the storm.

PART 2

The Storm Strikes

5

The Swirl

*I*n the spring of 2010, my son, James, found himself at a crossroads in his life. He wrestled with the questions many people ask when they are in their twenties: "What am I supposed to do with my life?" During this time of self-examination, he went to Kenya to work with his friend and mentor, Pastor Simon, until he could find a job in Africa.

In Kenya, James spent several months in the small town of Namanga, where he engaged in village life and invested his time, talents, and resources in various improvements. James helped build roads, organized a trash collection system, and constructed hundreds of bricks for building purposes. He felt drawn to the local people and formed deep personal relationships. He began to find a keen sense of purpose in making life easier for others who struggled.

While trying to secure a permanent work visa, he would take odd jobs for a few weeks at a time in Nairobi. Eventually, the working conditions began to take a toll on him physically. He was vulnerable and exposed in the unhealthy environment. During one of these trips to work in Nairobi, he became very sick. Not realizing the danger he was in, he checked into a small hotel to rest. There he died alone of acute pneumonia.

A Fork in the Road

With a quivering voice and tears sliding from her eyes, a dear friend said, "I can't imagine losing my mother. I talk to her every day and she is my very best friend. I need her. I love her so much. But there is no other treatment and her time is short." A strong and committed believer, my friend found herself standing at a new fork in the road.

Another one of my friends ran across an unexpected text on her husband's cell phone that confirmed her suspicions: He was having a relationship with another woman. As my friend tried to comprehend the sickening reality of infidelity, she reeled with a lethal mixture of anger, sadness, and hysteria. This was not supposed to happen in her life. She had been shoved into the center of turmoil that threatened to strip her of her family, her faith, and her future.

No matter how deliberately we may try, life will never be a carefully drawn blueprint. It cannot be calculated in precise measurements and always yield order and perfection. Plans are necessary, but because they involve people they are constantly subject to change. Life is an uncertain journey, and at different intervals along the way we will come to crossroads that require a choice. One path is marked "Surrender" and the other path is marked "Swirl." These paths are not for our eyes to see, but they are the two ways we can follow after a storm enters our life.

The force of your storm may have you slipping toward the edge of turmoil today. It's frightening when you feel yourself losing your grip on your world. You may be frantically grabbing on to a few exposed roots and desperately scrambling to prevent a fall. You may be about to let go because your strength is totally drained. Let's find the way together to navigate this particularly threatening place. We have a Guide who can take us through this valley of decision and lead us to level ground. The challenge is to stop now and unpack the contents in our heart. He can help us gently review our survival contents and show us how to lighten the load. We can choose to surrender to God's care and purpose in the storm, or we can swirl, sometimes for years, trying to escape the pain on our own.

I will be the first to admit my tendency is to avoid surrender because the very word seems to carry an implication of weakness. If you're like me, you may think surrender means we quit working on the problem or make no effort to do anything about the situation. We may see surrender as a sign of giving up something very important to us and releasing something we believe we should have—an unpleasant sacrifice will be required of us. We have dreams and reasonable hopes of decent health, a faithful husband, and the chance to have a family—and those things may not unfold for us. Surrender may feel like throwing in the towel, rolling over, or admitting failure. It sends the message that we will not get our way. The idea of surrender is so misunderstood that I want to talk about it in more detail later. For now, we need to realize we have to make a bigger decision. Do I want to figure this out myself or would surrender be a better way?

The unsettling force of the swirl reminds me of a ride at our state fair called the Tilt-a-Whirl. It's a large disc with double chairs positioned around the circumference. As the ride begins it goes forward and around for a few spins. Then the floor starts to tilt at an angle and each individual chair spins faster and faster on the rotating disc. Eventually, it whirls the occupants around at different angles of high and low, going both frontward and backward. I hate riding it because it's impossible to keep your eyes on a fixed point or find a steady surface on which to ground yourself.

Remaining in a constant swirl and continually living in the spin of unpredictable chaos is destructive and dangerous for us. There is far more at stake than a sick stomach after a four-minute amusement park ride. We run the risk of establishing a debilitating pattern of ineffective coping skills to alleviate the deep longing for inner peace. Yet too many of us choose to enter the swirl and walk that churning path after a storm enters our life. Why do we do this?

For many of us, the crazy-making inner twister entices us toward activity. As long as we keep moving, we feel there is a chance to avoid the power of a storm's slam. We try to live as if we can outmaneuver life's unexpected blows if we take the right steps. "If I'm quick, alert, and willing to fight hard, I can beat this thing."

This is a normal response considering the pain we may feel. But steps that appear good or helpful on the surface can actually lead us into an even deeper pit of despair and destruction. They lead to a life caught in the spin of frustrating activity. We can avoid this situation when we recognize those harmful choices and understand just how they hinder rather than heal.

Some of our common choices stirring the emotional pot are:

- playing the blame game
- taking a denial detour
- being a "fix-it" person
- asking "why me?"

The Blame Game

I watched the horrifying news story of the capsized ferry in South Korea full of high school children going on a class trip. Hundreds were lost in the Yellow Sea. The anguished parents were distraught with rage as they learned of negligence and deception on the part of the crew and ferry owners. The horror and pain are temporarily soothed with blame and cries for justice. Arrests and criminal charges were made, and those responsible will have to pay the penalty. Undoubtedly, law-suits will be filed and monetary restitution will likely be made. All is legally just and fair.

However, no amount of accusing in court will ever bring complete healing and peace for those who lost children. The more the parents focus on someone to blame, the longer they will swirl in misery, anger, and bitterness.

Playing the blame game pins our hurt on someone else so we never have to own our pain and come to terms with our loss. As long as we can turn the attention elsewhere, we don't have to allow ourselves to be vulnerable to the disruptive exposure of our personal storm. Blame is often born out of our own disappointment and resistance to come clean with a basic truth: "This is not the way I pictured my life, and I don't like it. I am uncomfortable and unsatisfied with reality." I discovered this in my own life. Blaming became a way to deflect attention off my own ravaged heart and place the spotlight on someone else or sometimes even on God.

The oldest and most familiar story of the blame game goes back to the beginning of human history. In the Garden of Eden, Adam and Eve were tempted by Satan to eat the forbidden fruit. The serpent planted the seed of blame on God by saying, "Indeed, has God said, 'You shall not eat from *any* tree of the garden'?" Eve answered and said, "From the fruit of the trees of the garden we may eat; but from the fruit of the tree which is in the middle of the garden, God has said, 'You shall not eat from it or *touch* it, or you will die'"(Genesis 3:1-3, emphasis added).

This story reveals two points to consider. First, blame starts with a subtle suggestion. The process begins with a hint that someone has deliberately done something to make things harder for you. The enemy plants the lie in your mind. "God did this to me. He withholds or makes things more difficult for me. This storm is God's fault."

Secondly, blame is contagious. Notice in the Genesis story how Eve adds to God's Word. In Genesis 2:16-17, He never said anything to her about *touching* the fruit. We conclude, "God's expectations are unreasonable and He wants to make my life more difficult."

Blame starts a vicious cycle of finger-pointing and excuses. Adam says to God in Genesis 3:12-13, "The woman whom You gave to be with me, she gave me from the tree, and I ate." In other words, it's God's fault Adam ate the forbidden fruit because God gave him the woman.

"Then the LORD God said to the woman, 'What is this you have done?' And the woman said, 'The serpent deceived me, and I ate'" (Genesis 3:13). She ate the deception and her perspective became contaminated.

When we're feeling the desire to blame other people, we need to ask ourselves, "Have I eaten deception and been contaminated? Am I pointing my finger at someone else or maybe even blaming myself for the pain and struggle I am in?" We mistakenly believe that our quest for comfort and answers is resolved when we can pinpoint a blamable source. "This problem is because of my husband's side of the family." "He's never here and it's his fault things are out of control at home."

"She cares more about her job than her family." "If they hadn't been so strict, this wouldn't have happened."

This can go on forever, and believe me, no one wins in the blame game.

I recently met a couple with a beautiful little girl quietly leaning against her mother's shoulder. I was informed that the daughter was a special-needs child. She was born perfectly normal but suffered a seizure on day five of her life that severely affected her. The girl was about to celebrate her fourth birthday, but she had the neurological development of a five-month-old infant. Both of her parents are strong believers, but they are broken and devastated over the prognosis for their little girl. With tears in her eyes, the mother wondered aloud, "Does God not like us very much? Is this our fault? Are we the ones to blame? Why did He do this to us?"

After James died, I was tempted to blame myself. There were any number of choices and decisions I replayed and questioned. The enemy whispered, "You could have been a better mother…You should have been more aggressive and demanding about some things…You should have made different decisions…You should have never let him go to Africa…You should have gone over there and seen with your own eyes the situation instead of relying on him to tell you…If you had prayed more, this would not have happened. Blame yourself, blame your husband, blame others, blame God, and you can justify this heartache." I even asked God, "Is this payback? Are You that mean or I am I that bad?"

It may be helpful for you to stop here and identify the people you are blaming for your storm. Write them out as I did and name the lies you have listened to. When you name the source of your pain, ask yourself, "Am I spinning around and around or am I at peace?"

Storms leave us swirling for justice, and blame is one way to try to attain it. We operate under the assumption that everything has to square up. Surely there is an explanation for this disruption to my life. The fault must be laid at someone's feet. The more we stir up the blame, the more mixed up and complicated the situation becomes.

Denial Detour

Many times a storm reveals something too difficult to accept or comprehend. We find ourselves dazed by the significance of the after-shock. Naturally, our first reaction is to deny that the situation is out of our control. Because the storm is entirely too painful and the reality so overwhelming, we tell ourselves it cannot be happening. We avoid the fact that the future we envisioned is not going to happen.

The most famous denial of all time comes from the mouth of Peter. Jesus told His disciples that all of them would fall away because being exposed as a follower of His was going to become dangerous, threat-ening, and risky. Jesus knew what would happen. He said, "Before a rooster crows, you will deny Me three times" (Matthew 26:34). Peter adamantly and naively said, "Even if I have to die with You, I will not deny You" (Matthew 26:35).

To Peter, the thought of living without Jesus was too painful. The reality of losing his teacher, rabbi, friend, and leader who represented fulfillment of the promises for Israel was unimaginable. Peter proba-bly thought, *The reality sounds very different from the way we envisioned, and You are not going to really leave us now!*

Denial allows us to sidestep reality for a short time, but eventu-ally the truth has to be dealt with. Of all the disciples, the one who seemed most miserable and most despondent after Jesus was crucified, and even after He was resurrected, was Peter. The burden and shame of having denied knowing Jesus made it difficult for Peter to face the truth and move forward.

If we also deny the truth of our loss, we will find it more difficult to later face the truth and move forward in our own lives. A friend recently told me, "As long as I refused to accept that my marriage would never be the loving relationship I desired, I was refusing to allow God's care and mercy to comfort and complete me." Denial refuses to accept there is anything to surrender. It declares, "Everything is fine." Denial is a game of pretend. It's one way to cope with situations that are over-whelming and seem impossible to change. It can be a reprieve from pain and a temporary way to gather yourself. Denial allows the debris

r heart to continue to pile up and clutter the landscape of our
s. Let's think about how denial may hinder God's healing. Because
He specializes in brokenness, we want to put ourselves in the best possible care.

Pretending to Be a "Fix-It" Person

One of the most efficient ways to try to survive a painful storm is to
kick into the role of Ms. Fix-It, the expert who can repair and remedy
anything. Our culture heaps praises upon problem-solvers and cele-
brates independence and resourcefulness. Such skills are certainly valuable, yet they actually hinder us when we are using them to avoid the
life-changing alterations a life storm creates. In terms of our spiritual
life, we are not the primary source for solutions. Our instant impulse
when something goes wrong is to quickly figure out an alternate plan.

Maybe you can identify with Sarah in the Bible. She decided that
God needed her help to bring the promised heir for her husband, Abram.
After all, more than 20 years lapsed between the time of God's promise
and the answer. Nothing was happening except that her biological clock
was ticking—or had stopped! So Sarah gave her maid, Hagar, to Abram
and she conceived. Sarah's desire to fix the problem brought pain, sorrow, division, and disruption to Abram's household and to the world
afterward through the two nations derived from Isaac and Ishmael.

Let's be honest. Sometimes we don't believe God can do things
without our help. After all, for years you may have been watching or
waiting for some practical proof that your prayers make a difference.
Waiting is wearisome. It's easy to forget that God's plans and purposes
are on His time line and are not bound by our understanding. He's able
to bring His will and work to completion without us. I wonder how
many times our efforts have actually created more pain and problems.
We make phone calls, ask for favors, and pull strings. Rather than learn
to live with consequences and realities, wait for God to open doors,
and trust Him when they close, we often insist on tearing down anything that threatens to obstruct our dreams or expose us as insufficient.

We can never stay ahead of the swirl when we take responsibility
of playing God in our own lives. We will never find the peace and joy

that come from being in the place of gifting and calling that allows His plans to flourish through us. We are not big enough, smart enough, strong enough, or wise enough to be in charge. It's hard to admit, but we don't have what it takes to clean up the mess after the storms of life. This feeling of powerlessness often plunges us into a never-ending swirl. Because God is our Creator, it makes perfect sense that He is the one who knows how to fix us.

Asking "Why Me?"

The nagging need to know "Why?" is a tremendous obstacle that can steer us into the swirl and delay surrender. How many times have you sat at someone's bedside or rallied around someone who has just been slammed with devastating news? A common question pops up: "Why?" It's such a small word—just three letters—but it has the power to hold our healing hostage and lock us in an endless swirl of uncertainty and tension. The lie is that if we only knew why, then we would be satisfied and feel released from the storm.

"Why" creates a figurative rut where we can easily get emotionally and spiritually stuck. The wheels of our mind continue to spin in place. Our wounds cause the ruts to get deeper, miring us down in the broken landscape that is now our life. Countless hours are spent debating, asking, complaining, and fighting against the why of the situation. We consult doctors, lawyers, counselors, and therapists. We spend a great deal of money and time on trying to unearth the answer to why this happened or what can be done to change or correct it. Maybe you've asked yourself:

"Why can't I have children?"
"Why did he get sick and die?"
"Why do I have to live with chronic pain?"
"Why can't I find the right person to marry?"
"Why did it have to rain and ruin my weekend plans?"
"Why this, why now, why me?"

Even if we knew the answer to some of our questions, would we really be satisfied and able to release the disappointment? Do we continue to talk about the situation because we need to validate our feelings of injustice?

Byways and Choices

It's possible you recognize yourself on one or maybe several of the paths we've discussed: blaming, denying, fixing, or asking why. Most of us have resorted to these at some point in life. We entered into the swirl in hopes of outrunning our storm. Now is a good time to determine where we are stuck. I want to challenge you to be very honest with yourself. Pray and ask God to show you the hidden places in your heart. He wants to meet you there and set you free from swirling around and around.

1. Name the person(s) you believe deliberately made life hard for you.

   _____

   A statement of confession: "I am using blame to avoid surrendering my storm."

2. Avoiding truth + sidestepping pain = denial.

   I'm avoiding _____

   and I'm sidestepping _____ .

   A statement of confession: "I'm using denial to avoid surrendering my storm."

3. List the steps you've tried to fix your storm.

   _____

   _____

   _____

   _____

   A statement of confession: "I'm trying to fix it to avoid surrendering it."

4. The "why" that seems to take over my mind and heart the
   most is

   _____

   _____

   A statement of confession: "I'm allowing the 'why' to distract
   me from surrender."

The fourth step we discussed, "Asking 'Why Me?'" is so powerful
that it can override our desire to surrender. That's why we will explore
it together in the next chapter. We can discover how to prevent this
question from stealing our life after the storm.

YOUR STEPS WITH GOD

As you read and pray, ask yourself these questions:

- Do I have peace?
- Are my interpersonal relationships stronger?
- Am I hopeful about the future?
- Is my personal faith growing?

My friend, please understand that there is no exit at the end of the
swirl. It's an unending mode of frenzy that does not lead to healing.
The only way to exit this cycle is to return to that original fork in the
road and choose to surrender.

6

Crucify the "Why?"

*I*t's December 31, 2010, the last day of the deepest, darkest year of our lives. The sound of celebratory fireworks and strains of "Auld Lang Syne" on the radio do nothing to lessen the throbbing ache in my chest. Everything feels strangely distant, as if a thin veil hangs between reality and me. The turn of the calendar page in anticipation of a new year reminds me that time moves on—yet for me and my family it seems to have slowed to a painful crawl.

My immediate family is sitting around the dinner table, and we're trying to look forward, see ahead, and anticipate the future. We are sharing words of faith, and even in our grief we're reminding ourselves that God has a plan and He can be trusted. On the hard days our feelings struggle to align with this truth, but it's what we believe and it's what we know about God.

Then one of my daughters has the courage to speak her doubt. With a trembling voice she says, "You all seem to be accepting this. God doesn't owe me anything, but why did He let this happen to you and Dad?" Her loyalty toward us hits a tender spot, and I want to take her on my lap as if she were a small child and soothe her and myself.

Her question finds the crack in my own fragile faith. Maybe it's still too soon to ask, to accept, to talk about, to approach the doors these questions threatened to open. I'm forced to acknowledge that this question represents one of the many "whys" we each held within our heart as we tried to find a way to guard and protect ourselves and one another. Deep down I have my own questions. Some entered my consciousness immediately after James died and others bubbled up as my mind cleared enough to absorb the circumstances of his death or replayed precious family memories. No matter how they surfaced, once the questions appeared, the decision had to be made to either face them and deal with them or stuff them and avoid the pain.

- Why did he have to die?
- Why didn't he go to the hospital?
- Why did God take our only son?
- Why did we let James go to Africa?
- Why was prayer answered this way?
- Why did God let this happen?

Early on, our minds block the overwhelming emotions of grief. Our list of questions is our attempt to gain perspective and pave the way to accept something we cannot change. We believe an answer to any of them may give us something to hold on to in the grieving process or may unlock an avenue for changing the outcome or circumstances. The questions are attempting to bring:

- order into disorder
- clarity to confusion
- rational thinking to irrational thinking
- justice to offense
- positive to negative

"Why" gives voice to the doubt, the pain, and the loss we are trying to reconcile in our mind and heart. Even when we think there will be no sense of resolution or comfort, something inside us calls out for understanding. *How can this be? How can this be what life looks like now?*

Have you been in this state of why in your own crisis or storm? If your questions seem to be piling up and you feel as if your emotional dam is ready to break, it may be time to voice your personal whys. I know it takes courage to ask the questions because you risk being ignored or misunderstood. Asking why can be perceived as immature or as evidence of an insolent attitude. Others may view it as self-pity or as the cry of someone who doesn't trust God. But asking why is a necessary step to move toward surrender.

We all have longed to know why something happened to us or to a loved one. It's understandable. Behind that why is a deep desire to be shown a bigger picture, an explanation, or an outcome that could remotely be worthy of the loss or worth going on in life bearing that loss.

My own whys stemmed from deep disappointment and sadness. In my mind, this was not the way things were supposed to turn out if we pray and believe in the power of God to change lives. I wondered if my prayers were rejected and if this was punishment for my own mistakes and sin. I never felt mad at God, but I did want to know if a failure on my part as a mother or as a child of God made me somehow responsible.

Holding back your own deep questions or being the listening ear for your closest loved ones as they express their doubts is extremely difficult, but perhaps even more painful is having to take in the questions or explanations of others as the circle of thoughts and opinions grows wider.

When friends and strangers tried to put their spin on what God was doing in our lives through James' death, I couldn't bear it. The loss of my son was so personal, so brutally raw that I felt a fierce need to protect my feelings—and probably James' memory—from opinions, commentaries, judgments, or even well-meaning attempts at comfort.

Maybe, in the beginning, I even feared that those offerings from others would distract me from hearing God's answers to *my* whys. I was straining to hear God's still, small voice as I attempted to take one step at a time. I could not take a chance of anyone or anything derailing my deep desire to trust God with this loss.

Is He There and Does He Care?

When our heart is broken and we are overwhelmed by the disappointment, pain, and loss, one of our first pitfalls is to wonder if God knows about our sorrow or cares. I love Psalm 139 because the verses remind us how well God knows us and how deeply He cares.

> O Lord, You have searched me and known me. You know when I sit down and when I rise up; You understand my thought from afar. You scrutinize my path and my lying down, and are intimately acquainted with all my ways. Even before there is a word on my tongue, behold, O Lord, You know it all. You have enclosed me behind and before, and laid Your hand upon me. Such knowledge is too wonderful for me; it is too high, I cannot attain to it (Psalm 139:1-6).

God knows us so well that He knows our every move. He knows our every question and thought, and even the motive behind them.

Pretending or trying to hide our fears and doubts is pointless because He already knows them. It's a tremendous relief to realize someone really does know and understand me.

> Where can I go from Your Spirit? Or where can I flee from Your presence? If I ascend to heaven, You are there; if I make my bed in Sheol, behold, You are there. If I take the wings of the dawn, if I dwell in the remotest part of the sea, even there Your hand will lead me, and Your right hand will lay hold of me. If I say, "Surely the darkness will overwhelm me, and the light around me will be night," even the darkness is not dark to You, and the night is as bright as the day. Darkness and light are alike to You. For You formed my inward parts; You wove me in my mother's womb. I will give thanks to You, for I am fearfully and wonderfully made; wonderful are Your works, and my soul knows it very well. My frame was not hidden from You, when I was made in secret, and skillfully wrought in the depths of the earth (Psalm 139:7-15).

Here the psalmist reminds us that no matter where we go, no matter how high or low, God is right there.

> Your eyes have seen my unformed substance; and in Your book were all written the days that were ordained *for me*, when as yet there was not one of them (Psalm 139:16, emphasis added).

He has predetermined plans for each of us, and He will accomplish His purposes in our lives. As hard as it is to understand, this crisis is neither pointless nor purposeless. We can take the whys to Him because He knows how to use them and what to do with each and every part of them.

> How precious also are Your thoughts to me, O God! How vast is the sum of them! If I should count them, they would outnumber the sand. When I awake, I am still with You (Psalm 139:17-18).

Don't ever forget, you are always on His mind.

> O that You would slay the wicked, O God; depart from me, therefore, men of bloodshed. For they speak against You wickedly, and Your enemies take Your name in vain. Do I not hate those who hate You, O LORD? And do I not loathe those who rise up against You? I hate them with the utmost hatred; they have become my enemies (Psalm 139:19-22).

Resisting, refusing, and rejecting God's words toward us make us His enemy. Verses 19-22 serve as a strong warning against accusing God of neglecting or not caring about us.

> Search me, O God, and know my heart; try me and know my anxious thoughts; and see if there be any hurtful way in me, and lead me in the everlasting way (Psalm 139:23-24).

This humble invitation of the psalmist serves as our example to welcome God to take a deep look inside our hearts. Let's ask Him to show us where we are harboring hurt or offense and allow Him to lead us out of this dark and difficult place.

How to Go to God

If you are going to talk to a friend, doctor, counselor, or other source of guidance, what do you do?

- schedule a time
- show up
- talk and share your concerns
- listen
- consider opinions and suggestions
- wait for outcome or results
- plan to meet again

We can make the same intentional steps with God.

Schedule time and show up. "Let me hear Your lovingkindness in the morning; for I trust in You; teach me the way in which I should walk; for to You I lift up my soul" (Psalm 143:8).

Talk and share. "I cry aloud with my voice to the LORD; I make supplication with my voice to the LORD. I pour out my complaint before Him; I declare my trouble before Him" (Psalm 142:1-2).

Listen and consider. "Hear my prayer, O LORD, give ear to my supplications! Answer me in Your faithfulness, in Your righteousness" (Psalm 143:1).

Wait and plan. "Because of his strength I will watch for You, for God is my stronghold" (Psalm 59:9).

Now is the time to establish this habit of being in God's presence, listening to His voice speak personally to you, and acting on His truth.

Time and again I would reach for the Bible to receive God's comfort. As I laid my heart bare before Him, His Word would speak gently and tenderly to my spirit. One day I read this verse, "The secret things belong unto the Lord our God, but the things which are revealed belong to us" (Deuteronomy 29:29 AMP).

I wrote in my journal that day: "It is Almighty God's prerogative to keep His ways secret. When whys haunt me and threaten to steal my faith, I will remember, 'The secret of the LORD is with those who fear [are in reverent awe of] Him, and He will show them His covenant'" (Psalm 25:14 NKJV).

If you are struggling with questions and doubts about why you are experiencing this life storm, I want to encourage you to continue taking your questions to God. It may comfort you to know that many of the people God used—Job, David, and others—asked Him why. Because He is our ultimate answer, I believe He is glad to take sincere questions from brokenhearted people. But the more we get to know Him, the more we are able to trust Him if He chooses to withhold answers from us. When He does this, I fully believe it's for my good and His glory.

You may be surprised to know that even Jesus asked why when He was enduring the pain and suffering for all of mankind's sin. In Matthew 27, we have a detailed description of the conversations taking place as people watched the crucified Christ hang on the cross. Roman soldiers, spectators, robbers, and a few followers continued to try to figure Him out and ridiculed Him with insults and taunts. As darkness fell over the earth and God looked away, Jesus cried out in a loud voice, saying, "My God, my God, *why* hast thou forsaken me?" (Matthew 27:46 KJV, emphasis added).

No answer is recorded. God was silent as the sins of the world were atoned for by the perfect life of Christ. Then we are told that "Jesus cried out again with a loud voice, and yielded up His spirit" (Matthew 27:50 NKJV). Jesus yielded. He submitted to the plans and purpose of God.

At that moment, why died.

I have learned a valuable lesson from this and applied it to my own crisis of doubt. Why will always be a snare and continue to trap our faith until we deliberately decide to yield to God. We have to make the decision to take our why and crucify it once and for all.

We are tempted to believe answers will give us knowledge we deserve to have. We want an explanation for the difficulty and struggle.

After all, knowledge is the power to influence and change most things. But in the spiritual realm, yielding is power. God's ways are higher than ours, and He has no responsibility to explain His will and ways to us.

Walking Through Your Why

Your hurt, pain, disappointment, dashed dreams, and ruined plans are very much a part of you. Sharing them requires learning to listen to your own heart. Proverbs 14:10 says, "The heart knows its own bitterness, and a stranger does not share its joy."

Consider the following steps:

1. Write down your why questions. Actually putting words to your feelings can be very helpful in peeling back the layers and getting to the deepest root.

2. Using a concordance or Bible promise book, identify Scripture to speak to your specific questions and doubts. Make a list and keep it handy for reference.

3. Ask yourself, "Will a direct answer or explanation change my circumstances?" Pray and ask God to prove that His Word is stronger than your questions.

4. Listen to praise music. You will find yourself gaining a broader perspective when you look upward instead of always inward.

5. Do something for someone else. Any small act of kindness or care awakens a compassion for others instead of being consumed with self.

Nail Your Why to the Cross

Now may be the time for you to seriously consider letting your why die once and for all. When why dies, faith, hope, and trust rise. You create the opportunity for God to demonstrate resurrection power through your crucified why. Jesus had to yield, give up His spirit, and trust God's judgment to be satisfied through His sacrifice before He could be raised victorious over death, hell, and the grave.

Jesus taught this principle in John 12:24: "Truly, truly, I say to you, unless a grain of wheat falls into the earth and dies, it remains alone; but if it dies, it bears much fruit."

Personally, God gave me great comfort and peace when I yielded these whys: "Why did James have to die? Why did he have to be alone?" He spoke gently and tenderly to me in this verse by saying, "Truly, truly…" I heard Him speak with spiritual ears. *The truth is that this is the way I have chosen to work through James' life, and you can expect to see spiritual fruit.*

Do you remember when I told you about prayers prayed for more than worldly successes? Do you recall that we were asking God to give us generations of Christ influencers? I'm glimpsing the answers to those prayers now that I have crucified the whys. Although the answers do not look at all the way I envisioned when I prayed or have any resemblance to the hopes and dreams we had for our son, God is giving us what we need—the faith to ask, "Now what?"

I don't want to imply that the journey to the place of crucifying your why is smooth or easy. It was not easy for Jesus and certainly not for any of His followers. Sometimes other people want us to stuff our doubts and fears deep down, but God does not. He has a listening ear and an understanding heart. He doesn't expect us to pretend that everything is okay or what we're going through isn't a painful process. All of these struggles show us our need for Him.

Under extreme threat and pressure, the apostle Paul wrote this to the church at Corinth,

> We do not want you to be unaware, brethren, of our affliction which came to us…we were burdened exces-sively, beyond our strength, so that we despaired even of life; indeed, we had the sentence of death within ourselves so that we would not trust in ourselves, but in God who raises the dead…delivered us from so great a peril…and will deliver us (2 Corinthians 1:8-10).

If you are feeling overwhelmed with despair concerning your life, it's important to know you can share your burden with other believers.

This is an example of how important the body of Christ is when we are overwhelmed with life storms. Though Paul poured out his heart and his fears before the church, he knew they were not the ultimate answer. Hope in the crisis was in God alone. He is the only one who can take your crucified why, raise it from the dead, and deliver you from peril. Be willing to share your own burden and be willing to come alongside and carry someone else's. It's part of the crucifying process that leads to life and resurrection.

From Why to Now What

Are you acquainted with two sisters and a brother named Mary, Martha, and Lazarus who were close personal friends of Jesus? In John 11, we get an intimate look into a family in crisis. Lazarus became very sick, and the sisters sent word to Jesus to come. Before He arrived, Lazarus died and the distraught sisters couldn't imagine why Jesus had taken two extra days to respond. When He finally arrived, Martha said, "Lord, if You had been here, my brother would not have died" (John 11:21). That could be interpreted, "Why didn't You come sooner?" Mary said the exact same thing. The sisters were devastated. Many friends were also there mourning Lazarus' death. When Jesus saw their depth of sorrow, the Bible says, "Jesus wept" (John 11:35). When He asked for the stone that closed Lazarus' tomb to be removed, Martha objected. But Jesus said to her, "Did I not say to you that if you believe, you will see the glory of God?" (John 11:40).

When we ask why, we're really saying, "Show me and I will believe." Before the stone was removed, before He called Lazarus out, and before the once-dead man was unbound, Jesus said, "If you believe, you will see the glory of God."

My friend, we are standing together at the place of your loss. Believing He is able to raise your dead dreams and dashed hopes will allow you to see the glory of God in your circumstances. If you will believe first, you will see Him doing greater things than you ever hoped or imagined. Believing is seeing.

It has been more than four years now since James was here and we were all together as a family. Each of us continues along our own individual path of healing. But the one who struggled early with "Why would God let this happen to you and Dad?" has slowly released the question and yielded the right to an answer. God is merciful and full of loving-kindness. He gives us time and tender care. He waits for each of us to bring the load of pain and anguish that are all wrapped up in why and allow Him to take it, nail it, and bury it once and for all. He's waiting to hear you say, "Why no longer preoccupies my thoughts. I'm asking You, 'Now what?'"

YOUR STEPS WITH GOD

Write your "Why me?" question here as a way to surrender it to God. Crucify it to be made into something new.

_____

_____

_____

Now rewrite your question and ask, "God, what now?

7

Surrender

Several years ago, I participated in a mission trip to work with teenagers in the countryside of Mongolia. One of our goals was to build camaraderie, so we scheduled a day of friendly games and competition between the Americans and the Mongolians. The final challenge turned out to be a decisive game of tug-of-war.

As we gathered into teams, I could tell by the look in everyone's eyes that they took the situation seriously. The other team was composed of fierce competitors who had little regard for the fact that my team was older and weaker! Winning was the goal. Period.

Team members strategically positioned themselves on each side of the long rope. The referee blew his whistle and the spectators began to chant, "Pull! Pull! Pull!" The collective strength of each team pulling in opposite directions created incredible tension on the rope. I tried to hang on during the intense battle of back and forth, but my hands started to feel raw and hot. Soon, my strength waned. I felt a throbbing pain in my arms, my knees started to buckle, and my feet began to slide. My teammates and I held out for as long as we could, but after a hard-fought struggle we were overpowered by the other team and yielded to their strength. We had to give up and surrender the tug-of-war.

God Is Pulling for You, Not Against You

When difficult storms blow into our lives, many of us engage in a spiritual tug-of-war with God. We view ourselves on one side of the rope seeking to take charge of our negative circumstances and control the outcome of what has happened. We want to "pull ourselves together" and pull life in the direction we think it should go. We imagine God as the unseen force on the other side of life's rope, pulling us in a direction we don't understand.

But here's the spiritual game changer: There is no tug-of-war with God. He is on the same side of the rope as we are! "If God is for us, who is against us? He who did not spare His own Son, but delivered Him over for us all, how will He not also with Him freely give us all things?" (Romans 8:31-32).

God is for us. He is not playing a sinister power game with our lives. He will not yank or drag us over the line, nor rejoice when we feel crushed and defeated. Instead, He waits patiently and quietly for us to release our grip on the rope. He wants to pull for us as we struggle through life's storms. Surrendering to God *does not* mean giving up. Spiritual surrender is giving over our lifeline to the One who is already the victor.

My friend Lynn and I have spent many hours sharing our struggles and fears. We have walked through deep valleys together and helped each other look at God's Word for our bearings and direction. One day, when my heart was particularly burdened, she kindly reminded me of Colossians 3:15-16, which says, "Let the peace of Christ rule in your hearts, to which indeed you were called in one body; and be thankful. Let the word of Christ richly dwell within you."

The key, Lynn reminded me, is in the word *let*. If I will freely give over my burdens and cares, Christ, who is my peace, will take up the situation for me. Yielding to Christ produces oneness with Him and enables me to recognize that He is for me, not against me. This reality is a cause for thankfulness.

When we release our rope to God, He picks it up on our behalf. Our burdens are His and our cares are in His hands. He reveals what we need to know and guides us in the direction we need to go. I can release the outcome to Him and trust Him to do what is best and right for me. He knows what I need better than I know myself, and He knows what it will take to accomplish His good and perfect will in my life.

The choice to surrender is an intentional one. It's the deliberate act of releasing our lives, hearts, and circumstances to God and asking Him to take over all control. It's tempting to want to use surrender as a bargaining chip when asking for God's help. We suggest an outcome and then offer up a temporary version of agreeing to God's purpose. How often have we thought, *God, get me out of this situation and I will do* (fill in the blank). But this isn't surrender and it certainly isn't a way to experience the freedom of leaning into God's strength and love. It's a halfhearted negotiation. Real surrender is allowing God to be God on His terms, not ours.

I recently read a book by Bob Goff titled *Love Does*. The author is a lawyer, and he tells a beautiful story of an exercise he asks all his clients to do when they are being interviewed for depositions. He instructs them to sit with their hands open, palms up underneath the table while testifying. He says with your hands open and palms up, it's impossible to withhold or clutch anything that needs to be released.

I love that picture. Try it. I suggest you try it while praying. Take your prayer concerns, and with each one spoken turn your hands open, palms up. Surrender is about living with your hands and heart open and your palms and your eyes looking up!

The most powerful picture of surrender is found in Jesus, hanging on the cross. His nail-pierced hands are open as He says, "Father, into Your hands I commit My spirit" (Luke 23:46). Jesus did not give up when He died on the cross. He gave Himself over to the will of the Father.

I'm discovering that living in surrender is a continual process. I'm learning to give my cares and concerns over to Him. Letting go of my rope is not a one-time decision that settles things once and for all. Every single day, I have to consciously decide to give the outcomes, choices, and people in my life over to God.

What difficulties have become fierce competitors on the other end of your rope? What heartache or trial weighs so much that even the strength of your desire for a different outcome is no match for its might? If you allow the pull of temptation to enter that swirl of uncertainty, you will soon lose your footing.

What holds you back from letting God take your end of the rope?

Never Trust a Stranger

As children, we're taught to never trust a stranger. Spiritually speaking, many people never learn to trust God because He is a stranger to them. There are a number of ways to be introduced to Him, but these have little to do with actually developing a personal relationship with Him.

Take a moment to think about a person in your life you genuinely trust. I'm sure this is someone who knows you well. And it's someone you have invested significant time and care getting to know and building a relationship with.

This is how you and I also learn to trust God—we get to know Him intimately.

God already knows you very well because He made you, but you have to take the time to get to know Him and His character and His intentions. You have this opportunity through His remarkable Word. It's a declaration of who He is and what He wants you to know about Him and His great love for you.

Do you remember the thrill of receiving a love letter? There is great delight in reading and rereading the words of someone who knows and loves you so much that he is willing to write it down and proclaim it. The Bible is a love letter God has delivered to you. From start to finish, His words reveal why you can depend on and trust in Him. Read it, cherish it, and hide it away in your heart. Learn it, live it, and let Him prove Himself to you. If you will do that, He will not be a stranger and your personal relationship will grow to be one of deep and abiding trust in Him. Surrender will only happen if you trust the One you're surrendering to.

How Can I Pray for You?

After James died, people frequently asked me, "How can I pray for you?" I know it's a sincere question, but I had a hard time giving an answer. My response depended on how I felt at the moment they asked. The needs were many, and it was difficult to put into words my desperate desire for supernatural help. Most often the honest answer would have been, "It's just too hard to explain."

One thing was and is crystal clear: James is not ever coming back. Losing him will never change, and there will always be a void. As I faced this truth, I realized my prayer and longing was *I want to live with this in a way that brings glory to God.* You may be thinking, *What is that supposed to mean? Is it just some super-spiritual answer offered as a smoke screen to avoid exposing my hurting heart?* For me, it's the ongoing acknowledgment that losing my only son is extremely difficult and that I want to learn to trust God to use it for good in our lives and the lives of others.

I want to surrender the pain rather than clutch on to it and nurse the sorrow. I want to accept the empty place that James' death created in our family and ask God to fill us with faith and strength. And, ultimately, I want to release my unanswered questions to God and believe His redeeming power is greater than all of my circumstances.

Surrendered Expectations

A close friend once said to me, "I am learning that the way to experience peace during this storm is to surrender my expectations." That was good advice for me. Maybe we all need to take a second look at our expectations and willingly lay them down before the Lord. In fact, it's part of our deliberate act of surrender.

Did God promise that all of your expectations would be met and all of your dreams and desires would be fulfilled in the way you envisioned? No. But He did promise that He "is able to make all grace abound to you, so that always having all sufficiency in everything, you may have an abundance for every good deed" (2 Corinthians 9:8).

God alone is able to do this for you. He has given you grace, sufficiency, and abundance. You and I can release our expectations to Him with confidence that He will work through us in ways that demonstrate His overwhelming power to provide *more* than we need in any circumstance or trial.

With His power we can live in a lonely marriage and find meaning and contentment. We can watch grown children make their own choices and willingly release them from our expectations. We can serve failing parents or other demanding relationships with grace and humbly put our own interests and pursuits on hold. None of these scenarios reflect what we envision or hope for our lives, but they are the pieces of our lives that we can surrender to God's will, plan, and purpose. Only when we give our loss to God can we live with that loss in a way that can be used by Him and for His glory.

My friend Amy's husband was recently diagnosed with early onset Alzheimer's disease. It will get progressively worse. When I saw her, she grabbed me with tears in her eyes and said, "I wanted us to get old together and look back on the memories we've shared. I love him so much. Now the reality is he may forget who we are, much less remember our life together." With the grace that only God can give, she whispered, "Whatever comes, I know God will carry me through."

It's easy to be skeptical and wonder how she could make such a statement. How can she be confident this storm won't crush her? Why isn't she angry or railing against God's seeming unfairness or lack of concern? And if we look at her situation in light of our last step in this journey, would we ask how Amy can possibly crucify her whys and give her and her husband's future to God's care?

The answer to all of these questions is that Amy knows that God loves her and her family with everlasting love. She knows that even if strong winds blow or the waves get high, He will be with her in the midst of them.

There may be times when she feels alone and has no idea what to do, but in those dark hours when there seems to be little hope, the Spirit of God will whisper in her heart, *I always have a plan for what happens after the crisis. I have always given My people a way forward. Throughout*

My love letter to you, beginning with the story of Adam and Eve, I reveal how I always make a way. His Word is always the last word.

Jesus told His disciples that after He was raised, He would meet them in Galilee (Matthew 26:32). He knew the days following His death would try their faith. They would have many fears, failures, and personal expectations to let go of. They would struggle to even remember His words of comfort and instruction. It would take reminders from several other witnesses and constant prodding to coax them from a place of utter disappointment and disillusion. With weary and reluctant feet they moved from Jerusalem and started back to Galilee. The appointed meeting place must have seemed far, far away.

When our storm is forcing us to struggle and strain, we are tempted to hold on to what we are familiar with even when it creates misery or exhausts us. Faith is required to open your fist and let God take your expectations. But once He is included, literally anything can happen! Today I want to encourage and prod you to start moving your feet toward Jesus. He is on the same side of your rope…and on the other side of the storm.

If It's Not All Right, Then It's Not Yet the End

The night I received word of James' death, I had a surprise visitor. She was a friend, but I didn't know her well. At least, not well enough for her to be one of the first people I saw. However, she had a reason for coming to see me immediately.

Several years earlier, her only son had died in a plane crash, and she was coming to declare that God is still good. Our isolated, separate circumstances were not good. But when it's all put together with everything else God is doing in our lives, He promises to transform these circumstances for His good purpose. I believe Him. "God causes all things to work together for good to those who love God, to those who are called according to His purpose. For those whom He foreknew, He also predestined to become conformed to the image of His Son" (Romans 8:28-29).

I'm fond of a quote I saw in a newspaper, which said, "Everything will be all right in the end. If it's not all right, then it's not yet the end." Some could say that this idea is merely positive thinking, but because I love God, I believe storms in the believer's life are not the end. What you and I surrender today will ultimately yield eternal and everlasting gain. That's good news!

If It Must Be So

We gain deeper understanding of our own circumstances and faith journeys when we look to the examples God provides in His Word. Our cherished love letter gives us many illustrations of His extraordinary work in the lives of everyday people. To examine the act of surrender, let's look at Jacob. As told in the book of Genesis, he had 12 sons who became the 12 tribes of Israel. However, Jacob showed partiality toward one of his younger sons named Joseph. As you can imagine, Jacob's favoritism created jealousy and strife among the brothers. Eventually, Joseph's brothers sold him into slavery. To cover up their sin, they lied and told their father that a wild animal killed Joseph. The brokenhearted Jacob refused to be comforted and declared, "Surely I will go down to Sheol in mourning for my son" (Genesis 37:35.)

The years that followed this family sorrow were complicated for all. Joseph was a slave who was falsely accused and became a prisoner. His life bore witness to the power of surrender to free you from the emotional bondage of disappointment, unfair treatment, and broken dreams. With every setback he allowed God to take control, and each place of hardship and difficulty became a place where the mercy, favor, and presence of God let Joseph move forward. Ultimately, he was recognized by Pharaoh as one who was informed by God, and Pharaoh said, "There is no one so discerning and wise as you are" (Genesis 41:39). At age 30, what seemed to be lost and forgotten was recovered and exalted as Joseph was placed as second in charge of all Egypt.

Release and surrender your storms, and when God determines you are ready, He will lift you up and out. It is His Word and you can count on it. The sooner we let go and give our storm to Him, the sooner we will come out of our prison of loss and despair.

Back at home, Jacob and his 11 sons suffered under a severe famine.

They heard there was grain available in Egypt, so Jacob sent his 10 oldest sons to buy some. He kept his youngest son, Benjamin, at home. Believing Joseph was dead, the father could not bear the thought of losing Benjamin, his last precious treasure. However, Jacob's attitude set the stage for one of the most intense reconciliation scenes ever recorded.

When Jacob's sons arrived in Egypt, Joseph disguised himself and put his brothers to the test. In order to buy grain, he required them to go home and return with Benjamin. When Jacob heard the news, it was almost more than he could bear. Realizing he was slowly losing his grip of control, Jacob lamented, "All these things are against me" (Genesis 42:36).

Jacob's attempt to hold on to the situation and cling to Benjamin only increased his misery and fear. But his family's desperate need for grain finally forced him to relinquish control. He had no choice but to surrender his last treasure and send Benjamin.

In Genesis 43:11,14, Jacob said, "If it must be so, then do this...may God Almighty grant you compassion...if I am bereaved of my children, I am bereaved." He slid across the tug-of-war line and dropped the rope.

- Jacob allowed his fear of "what if?" to become an attitude of "even if." His decision to release control of his family's circumstances and future set in motion more than he could have ever imagined. What was lost (Joseph) was found.

- Where there was lack (famine) there was plenty (grain).

- Where there was division (lies, guilt, blame, and shame) there was unity and forgiveness.

- Where there was heartbreak (sorrow, grief, and mourning) there was healing, gladness, and rejoicing.

- What was temporary (settle in Goshen) was promised restoration ("God will be with you, and bring you back to the land of your fathers" [Genesis 48:21]).

- What was most broken (Joseph) is given the greatest

blessing. ("Joseph is a fruitful bough, a fruitful bough by a spring; its branches run over a wall" [Genesis 49:22]).

• What man means for evil, God means "for good in order to bring about this present result, to preserve many people alive" (Genesis 50:20).

Jacob's surrender set it all in motion!

What blessings would surrender set in motion in our lives? It is a question worth prayerful consideration.

Moving from "What If" to "Even If"

The enemy of your soul wants to bind you and hold you hostage with the taunting question of "what if?" He can show you multiple scenarios and plant vivid imaginings of how much worse things can get. But God can turn anything, everything, even your storm into something good. Once there were three God-honoring Hebrew young men being held in enemy territory. You probably are familiar with their names: Shadrach, Meshach, and Abed-nego. They were ordered to bow down and worship a golden image set up by King Nebuchadnezzar or be thrown into a furnace of blazing fire. Their answer was bold and clear. "If it be so, our God whom we serve is able to deliver us from the furnace of blazing fire; and He will deliver us out of your hand, O king. But *even if* He does not, let it be known to you, O king, that we are not going to serve your gods or worship the golden image that you have set up" (Daniel 3:17-18, emphasis added).

As these three men faced terrifying threats from an enemy of God, they stood against the "what if" and declared that "even if" their lives were not spared, God was above all and worthy of absolute allegiance. You and I also have this choice as we face threats to our health, our family's well-being, or a future hope. We walk toward the fire in front of us and God may not come through the way we think He should, but He always comes through the best way. And He always is worthy of our faith and allegiance.

You may be in a place in your journey where the enemy is bringing all sorts of "what ifs" to pressure and terrorize your hope and faith.

Releasing those scary possibilities and asking God to help you make them into "even ifs" is a gigantic step toward surrender. He honors and shows His strength on behalf of those who honor Him.

Those three young Hebrew men were bound and cast into the furnace. But when the king checked on them, he said, "Look! I see four men loosed and walking about in the midst of the fire without harm, and the appearance of the fourth is like a son of the gods!" (Daniel 3:25).

Jesus will show up in the midst of your fiery trial. He has the power to loosen the fears and dreads that bind you, and He will walk with you through the fire. Consider this: "The satraps, the prefects, the governors and the king's high officials gathered around and saw in regard to these men that the fire had no effect on the bodies of these men nor was the hair of their head singed, nor were their trousers damaged, nor had the smell of fire even come upon them" (Daniel 3:27).

Seriously, we don't have to wear the side effects of our trials and tests. We don't have to be marked as victims and identified as people scarred by tragedy. You are not damaged goods when you entrust your storm to God's hands. Jesus wants to be with you and bring you through your trial just as He did for Jacob, Joseph, the three Hebrews, His disciples, and all who trust in Him.

I want to repeat the answer I finally learned to give when others offered to pray for me: "I want to live with this in a way that brings glory to God." Even the doubters and the skeptics can't deny God's power and His glory when you come through untouched. Nebuchadnezzar responded and said, "Blessed be the God of Shadrach, Meshach and Abed-nego, who has sent His angel [Jesus] and delivered His servants who put their trust in Him, violating the king's command, and yielded up their bodies so as not to serve or worship any god except their own God" (Daniel 3:28).

YOUR STEPS WITH GOD

Can you take the "what ifs" the enemy is taunting you with and write out an "even if" that will help you release the fear and dread and replace it with God's power and hope? Create reminder statements and declarations of transformation for your journey. List and rewrite those below.

What if:

Even if:

What if:

Even if:

What if:

Even if:

If this is your heart's desire, will you pray this prayer along with me?

> *Blessed be the God of (your name), who has sent His angel,*
> *Jesus, to walk with me. He is delivering me because I trust*
> *in Him and I yield my expectations and all my pain. I will*
> *worship and serve Him alone. In Jesus' name. Amen.*

8

Moving Through Grief

During the days immediately following James' death, the house was full of people coming to offer sympathy and care. In the South it's generally expected to descend on the bereaved family's home with armloads of food, flowers, books about grief, and offers of shoulders to cry on and promises to pray. People are drawn to people in crisis and want to be helpful and encouraging. Because my son's death occurred on the other side of the world, many details were still unknown, and we had many unanswered questions when Frank left Charlotte to go to Nairobi to bring James' body home. We didn't know exactly how long it would take or what all would be involved. The thought of holding an open house for days on end was overwhelming to me.

Most of the time I stayed in my room, but soon I started to feel caged. I wanted to be alone with my girls and a very small circle of close friends. I wanted to be myself, and I had no idea what that meant right then. I didn't want other people to try to explain the ways of God or attempt to figure it out or make sense of it. I was not able to listen to their stories of loss because I was staggering under the weight of my own loss.

On one particular day I ventured out into the living room to speak with a few people, and my pastor and his wife, our spiritual shepherd and close friends, were there. He said something I will always remember because it gave me freedom from the expectations of others and freedom from expectations of myself. He said, "You will get a lot of advice. I am not going to tell you what to do because this is yours and no one else's. No one but the Lord knows what you are feeling and all that is involved in this loss. But remember this. You don't have to do anything you don't want to do. Grief is personal, and there is no right or wrong way to grieve."

I felt a glimmer of hope and said, "Do I have to have a house full of people while I wait in agony to hear from Frank that he is bringing James home?" He responded, "No. Would you like for me to ask everyone to leave?" I nodded and felt great relief.

That gift of wisdom becomes a gift for me to share with you right now for your own personal journey through grief. Our journeys will differ because our way of responding to the demands of grief in a way that is personal and right for us will differ. You may be someone who needs to talk about it over and over to sort the facts in your mind. You may want to have a lot of people around you. Others will want to be quiet and have space alone to try to process the circumstances and absorb the shock. Neither is right or wrong. But I encourage you to remember that God is beside you, and He wants to accompany you through the grief journey. You do not need to live on an isolated island of sorrow while remnants of the storm block your path to healing.

Some of you had some warning and time to anticipate the grief journey that was coming. Others may have found yourselves thrust onto a detour route you never anticipated. Either way, we are acutely aware of our lack of preparedness. It may be helpful to accept that grief's flow is in one direction even if it slows or seems to clog at times. There are many dangers lurking, and sometimes the darkness threatens to overtake us. These are the times we must depend on the supernatural power of God to carry us and His light to lead us. In order to make this journey safely, beware of certain pitfalls threatening to sidetrack you.

Lies from the enemy of your soul are waiting around each corner. They will surprise you in the form of your own twisted thoughts. Sometimes memories will pursue you like a bloodhound. Even your dreams will attempt to drag you into a slimy pit. Remember, the devil is a liar and the father of lies (John 8:44). He wants this sorrow to drain, deplete, and ultimately destroy you. He does not grieve with you; he works tirelessly to ruin you. You must know how your enemy works. "Those who seek my life lay snares for me; and those who seek to injure me have threatened destruction, and they devise treachery all day long" (Psalm 38:12). Grieving hearts are vulnerable prey for enemies.

When this journey becomes hard and long, you will be tempted to turn around and go back. The temptation to live in the past is induced by the lie that you will have no future. We allow fear to steal the hope of tomorrow. We will continue to hit potholes and ditches if we keep gazing in the rearview mirror.

Another obstacle to moving ahead is to search for an alternate route around the pain. Simply said, too many sojourners on this path have warned there are no shortcuts. We would be foolish to believe another lie of the enemy that says we can skip or circumvent grieving.

Grief is defined as mental distress. It's the factual knowledge that we possess intellectually of an intense loss we have suffered. The expression of grief is mourning, and its value may be a well-hidden secret or denied necessity in the grieving process. I have read every Scripture reference on grief and have observed and experienced grief personally. Mourning is the physical and emotional activity that helps me process my pain and loss and learn to accept them. Over and over God gives us examples of people who express their sorrow and distress with outward expressions such as crying, sighing, moaning, loud wailing, writhing in anguish, being sick at heart, experiencing loss of appetite, having aching bones, tearing clothes, and lying in ashes.

Cultural practices and even religious traditions have a great deal of influence over our attitudes of mourning. Grief cannot be denied, but be aware of the lie that discourages you from mourning. In John 11:33-35, Jesus joins Mary, Martha, and family friends mourning the death of Lazarus. "When Jesus therefore saw [Mary] weeping, and the Jews who came with her also weeping, He was deeply moved in spirit and was troubled, and said, 'Where have you laid him?' They said to Him, 'Lord, come and see.' Jesus wept."

My friend, your mourning deeply moves Jesus. He weeps with you. Mourning is a necessary part of grieving. "My soul weeps because of grief; strengthen me according to Your word" (Psalm 119:28).

Listening for Your Shepherd

Many helpful books have been written and a great deal of research has focused on the topic of grief. My only expertise on the subject comes from living with it. Stages of grief have a pattern of relative predictability, but grief is uniquely individual and profoundly personal. Many well-intentioned and sincere friends and others are quick to offer advice and suggestions. Their motive is a genuine desire to help lift the burden and ease the pain. The suggestions range from the absurd and bizarre to the wise and useful. I gained greater insights to the phrase "consider the source." Some common suggestions are listed below, and I'm sure you've heard many of them too:

- see a plastic surgeon
- eat more or eat less
- sleep more or sleep less
- take medication
- get out more, buy yourself a treat, exercise
- plan a marvelous trip
- buy a shiny new car
- get a pet or get a new husband
- have another baby or adopt
- kick him out or let him come back
- get over it or get busy or get involved
- contact a medium*

---

* This one was the most disturbing for me. A woman wrote me after reading James' obituary to share her positive experience of contacting her missing son through a medium. She offered to share her contact. Although she had "successfully" been able to contact him through the medium, he remains missing more than five years later. I'm sorry and sad this is her hope.

We have no control over what others say to us, but we do have control over whose voice we listen to. And there is one voice we are to keep our hearts and minds and ears tuned to. Jesus said, "The sheep hear [the shepherd's] voice...A stranger they simply will not follow, but will flee from him, because they do not know the voice of strangers" (John 10:3,5). We need to be very careful to listen to the words of those who align their advice and give suggestions based on the truth of God's Word. Our counselors and advisors should be people who have a history of prayerfulness and wisdom and whose lives demonstrate they are on solid footing when storm winds blow.

What Keeps You in the Past?

There is only one cure for the pain and sorrow produced by a profound loss, and that is to grieve and move through the grief. Denial or avoidance is the deception that you can figure out a way around or a shortcut path that will allow you to move ahead without feeling or dealing with the loss. The only way to the other side is *through* the grief, through the pain. This isn't so that you dwell in the midst of that grief, but so that you keep on moving all the way through to the side of healing with God's help and presence.

Recently, a mother still in shock after finding her young, adult son dead in her home told me, "I don't like how this feels. I'm a positive person, and I'm going to have to figure something out." It was her desperate attempt to reassure herself the searing pain could be eradicated from her heart quickly.

We're all too familiar with the temptation to come up with plan B. Surely there is a way we can fill the empty space and keep from feeling the void and loss. Often it's as simple as keep busy, keep moving, and keep wearing yourself out doing many good things.

Sometimes our plan B stands for "plan backtrack" because we crank our necks back to keep what we've lost as our only view. Are you making circular trips around and around your circumstances and finding yourself swirling in a whirlpool of defeat and despair that is threatening to take you under? Are you sick and tired of the dizzying emotional roller-coaster ride and ready to go forward?

Years ago my husband and I attended a function with people we went to high school with. We'd moved away from our hometown immediately after college and were not completely on top of local news. In the course of the conversation, my husband asked a woman about her brother. She immediately buried her face in her hands, and through tears she explained that he had died ten years before. The dramatics were definitely a signal of a hypersensitive and unhealed wound.

Small talk can be a land mine for hitting exposed nerves. "Do you have children?" "Are you married?" "What do you do?" When I say I have three daughters, the response is sometimes, "Oh, no boys!" Recently, I was chatting with an acquaintance at a bridal shower who made the statement, "I can't imagine how anyone survives the death of a child. It's just horrible." In neither case did I feel the need to express my personal familiarity with the topic or make them feel ridiculous for making an innocent remark.

I'm not suggesting we forget these things or pretend as if they don't matter, but I am saying conscious decisions must be made to allow God to heal us.

Today, right now, decide to stop going back to the same places and rehashing the same details and chewing on the old memories. Let's agree together to take down the shrines we have erected literally and figuratively. I have a friend who shopped, wrapped, and saved gifts for her deceased sibling for more than ten years. Another person I know rode around with her husband's ashes under the front seat of the car.

If being childless is your heartache, then it's time to stop shopping for a baby and decorating your nursery. Singles, quit seeing a potential mate in every person of the opposite sex. If you're widowed or divorced, quit looking at the empty chair and get up and take the chair away from the circle. Be willing to say, "Now we are one less." If you are brokenhearted, be willing to say you are ready for wholeness and healing in the Lord.

The Cost of Avoidance

In my own personal grief journey, I was keenly sensitive to the danger warnings of trying to avoid or deny grief. I have never been a runner, so the temptation to try to outrun or lose grief by moving ahead quickly never appealed to me. But the thought of being five years down the road and slamming into a brick wall because I had not dealt with the reality of my grief scared me to death. Over and over I have been told there is no way to do it but to go *through* it, so I allowed myself to plunge into grief, heart first.

Can you remember when you were learning to swim or maybe teaching a child how to do that? The fear of the unknown and the inability to touch the bottom are powerful things. The child will cling to the side of the pool or clutch the instructor's neck and climb their body trying to ensure they will not go under. They sometimes scream and flail around with frantic desperation to avoid putting their face under, and in the process of fighting usually drink in water and cause themselves great discomfort.

Avoiding grief looks much like this poolside scene. We hang on to anything to try to avoid getting in. The fear of the pain is so great that all our energy is spent trying to find a way around or over it. If we insist in flailing around in the "whys, what ifs, who, and when," we will soon find ourselves lifeless, listless, and hopeless. A drowning person is dangerous because they may take the rescuer under with them in panic. We can become so preoccupied with our pain and our problems that we become toxic to the people around us.

You have probably been a part of a group where someone monopolized the conversation with their pain. That person is defining herself based on the thing that has happened to her, and she has no emotional capacity left to give anything to others.

After years of being involved with women's groups, I am familiar with the impact we can have when we don't try to move forward. When the name of someone who remains *in* their grief rather than moving *through* it comes up on the list of participants for an event, the leaders go into sincere, earnest prayer. With hearts full of compassion, they pray for that woman and for the other participants who may end up being overwhelmed by that individual's situation.

Often, grieving people want to attach to someone they perceive is strong, and they depend on the other person to carry them through.

It's just too much for me to ask someone else to carry me through the rest of my life. I'm too heavy and it's not their job. The only one who can carry me is the Holy Spirit of God within me. The only time I have ever been able to breathe for two people was when I carried life within me. I can share with you for a limited period of time, but you have to start to breathe for yourself.

This is where spouses often get into trouble. One wants the other to be their source of comfort and healing, and eventually the strain and stress get to be too much. While trying desperately to survive, you actually push the other further and further away. Often it's emotional distance, and sadly sometimes it's a literal physical separation.

An Important Question to Answer

One day Jesus asked a man who was lying on his mat of infirmity, "Do you want to be made well?" Something told Jesus there was a question about his genuine desire to get up and walk. It takes courage and strength to face life after a storm. It takes perseverance and faith to learn to walk in this changed and rearranged life.

Because I care about you, I'm going to ask you the same question. "Do you really want to allow the healing comfort of God to work in your life?" If you say yes, then I must ask you, "Are you are willing to do the work to strengthen spiritually and lean on the truth of God's Word to nourish and reenergize you? Will you choose to release the pain and allow God's healing process to begin?"

Be honest and ask yourself, "What is it I'm really afraid of? Why would I resist being healed?" Let me give you a few starters based on some of my own thoughts and those I have heard from others.

- I'm afraid I will forget.
- It's my fault and I feel guilty
- I don't deserve to be healed.
- I'll always feel like a misfit or less than the person I was.
- I don't think God is fair and I don't trust Him.

At the risk of being offensive, I'm going to ask you to dig a little deeper and ask yourself a few more probing questions.

- Do I like the sympathy and pity others feel for me?
- Does the attention I get because this has happened comfort me?
- Am I comfortable being a victim?
- Do I really want to be made well?

May I share a secret with you? You may not think this sounds sensitive or thoughtful, but I want to say it anyway because I know it's true. Not only will grieving not kill you, it can make you better! I know that sounds crazy, but let me explain what I mean. I've already agreed with you that nothing about grief is pleasant or easy. All of us would choose to skip grieving because we're always trying to plot the course of least resistance. But there are beautiful lessons to be learned when we find ourselves in those inevitable and unchangeable storms. In fact, treasures are in the darkness that have value beyond measure. David expressed it this way, "I call to remembrance my song in the night" (Psalm 77:6 NKJV).

The songs we sing during the night are often sung in a minor key. Night songs are whispered with gravel in our throat and quivering lips. Night songs are usually soaked with tears and brought forth through anguish and travail. They usually begin with a melancholy or mournful melody. Somewhere in the darkness while the night song is being composed from the broken heart, the Father draws near and He joins in the melody. Slowly, in His presence, the tune becomes more hopeful and a lighter note is struck. God is very close in the darkness, and His presence overwhelms the circumstances. He hovers over us to comfort and console. There is no other place where we so personally experience His tender love and care. His presence becomes more prominent than my pain, and my night song is rewritten before I realize it. I begin to lift a song of praise to the One who has brought me through this dark night. "Weeping may last for the night, but a shout of joy comes in the morning" (Psalm 30:5).

In the midst of sorrow upon sorrow and a trail of bitter trials, Job says, "He reveals mysteries from the darkness and brings the deep darkness into light" (Job 12:22).

May I encourage you to go on and don't be afraid of the dark? Now is a time to reach into your survival kit and bring out the light. Activate faith by choosing to believe that God's Word to you is truth over the enemy's lies. In the darkness your hearing is heightened and your senses are fine-tuned. Lean in and listen for the still, small voice of God reminding you of His steadfast love. Remind yourself that "I am convinced that neither death, nor life, nor angels, nor principalities, nor things present, nor things to come, nor powers, nor height, nor depth, nor any other created thing, will be able to separate us from the love of God, which is in Christ Jesus our Lord" (Romans 8:38-39).

YOUR STEPS WITH GOD

Name your pitfalls (the lies you have believed) and then replace those lies from the enemy with truth from God's Word. Use a concordance to help you with topics, if necessary.

If you're currently in a life storm, keep a journal. You're writing your own night song. Remind yourself that joy is coming.

9

Moving into Comfort

The constant activity, decisions, plans, and all of the discussions that accompanied those early days after James' death were over. The steady stream of people coming and going, caring and sharing, was slowing down. Our three daughters returned to their own homes, all out of town. The house settled into its prior quiet and orderly space. But nothing within me felt quiet or orderly.

One particular night, as I lay in bed with my stomach churning and lurching and my head spinning, my heart started to race at lightning speed and I was overcome by anxiety and a palpable sense of dread. It seemed as if I were being chased by a giant tsunami wave, and if I did not get up and run for my life I would be smashed. I headed to the other end of the house because something ugly was about to happen. From an undiscovered cavern deep within my innermost being rose ragged, guttural moans and a wailing sound I did not recognize as my own voice. It terrified me to discover the depth of emotion and overwhelming power of my sorrow. I felt as if I were starting to slide toward a deep, dark, bottomless pit. This threatened to be a free fall into the land of no return. I honestly did not know if I could survive.

After some time of allowing myself to be saturated with the pain, I went to my little office and did the only thing I knew to do. I picked up my Bible and cried, "Lord, I cannot do this. If I am going to make it,

You will have to do it for me." I opened my Bible to the book of Joshua and my eyes fell on these words, "Be strong and courageous! Do not tremble or be dismayed, for the LORD your God is with you wherever you go" (Joshua 1:9).

I had no idea what was ahead or what the grief journey would entail. Like Joshua crossing into Canaan, I had never been this way before. I felt sure it had the potential to be filled with land mines of destruction, depression, and despair. There was no way to plan or to know how to anticipate when these overwhelming fits of sadness and sorrow would surface. What if nothing was ever normal again? What if I couldn't think of anything else but the loss and never recovered my equilibrium? I sat in my chair and trembled with exhaustion as I read those words. "The LORD your God is with you wherever you go." He spoke very quietly to my spirit, saying, *I know every step of this journey. I know where every potential ambush lies. I, the Lord your God, have walked grief's journey, and there is nothing that will catch Me by surprise.*

I marked the margin of my Bible with a pen "10/2010—Grief's journey begins." This would be a memorial stone, a word I would return to many times. A still, small voice whispered to my heart, *Jan, I am your personal tour guide through the valley of the shadow of death. You and yours are safe with Me.* I returned to bed with a calm sense of assurance and rested for the remainder of the night.

Without recognizing it at the time, my healing journey was beginning. It was the first of many times when the presence and power of God prevailed over the pain and sorrow of my loss. The promise of God's Word to be with me wherever I go was impressed in my spirit in a way that slowly but surely gave me strength and encouraged me to watch for joy to return.

The broken heart needs careful and tender care for mending and healing to take place. It requires us to be attentive to the symptoms of grief and patient with ourselves and others. Compassion in steady doses helps to facilitate and invigorate recovery. As each person's heartache is different, so is their path to healing, but the ultimate prognosis for all is that God not only helps us to survive, but He offers the very real hope that we can thrive.

Comfort is offered in the many kind and caring gestures of family and friends. Some send flowers, cards, notes, and food, and they bring their own personal stories and memories to share with you. My two brothers came immediately with my aging mother, who needed to "see me with her own eyes." I am still her child, and she had to see if I was all right.

Friends

Friends can be an important source of understanding and comfort when we are walking through grief. Reading the detailed account of the widespread destruction in the life of Job gives us important insights into the role friends play in the grieving process. Let's see what we can learn from Job's three friends,

> Now when Job's three friends heard of all this adversity that had come upon him, they came each one from his own place...and they made an appointment together to come to sympathize with him and comfort him. When they lifted up their eyes at a distance and did not recognize him, they raised their voices and wept...Then they sat down on the ground with him for seven days and seven nights with no one speaking a word to him, for they saw that his pain was very great (Job 2:11-13).

Love is action, and it prompts us to move toward the source of pain. As my friend Julie poured bowls of homemade soup to the brim, she lovingly crushed a spring of fragrant rosemary on the top and said with tear-filled eyes, "Rosemary is for remembrance." Her sensitivity to share my memories of James soothed my pain.

My take-away from Job's friends (at least when they arrived) is that they recognized there was nothing they could say or do that would lighten the load or speed up the process of grieving. So they sat, stayed, and were silent. They expressed sympathy and comfort in their presence alone.

Often we stay away from a wounded friend because we don't know what to say or we're afraid we'll say the wrong thing. Once a friend, an acquaintance really, did a U-turn with her grocery cart in the middle of the cereal aisle to avoid having to say something to me. It made me feel as if I were a freak or something, but I knew she was painfully unprepared to connect with me. Experience shows that someone's presence is a powerful expression of care, and silence is golden. It's too bad Job's friends didn't keep quiet, and I'm sorry for the times I should have done the same.

I pray these words will empower you to have confidence in your importance in participating in the uncomfortable and difficult companionship of a person in grief and yet free you from the responsibility to say something that will explain, change, or fix the problem. Job's friends did a lot more damage when they started talking and urging him to blame God and blame himself. Friends need to know when to come and when to leave.

Spouses and Family

Those closest to us in our family are often a source of comfort, but they don't have the power or responsibility to fix the source of grief. The very fact that two people have shared life together should give them insight and understanding in how to be a source of comfort to each other, but it's unfair and unrealistic to think you will move through the grief stages at the same pace or in the same way. I was constantly reminded of how different Frank and I are and how necessary it was to give each other the freedom and support to grieve individually. We shared a deep loss, but it was still uniquely individual for each of us.

Our girls were tremendous. Frank nicknamed them "Charlie's Angels" because of the way they stepped up with grace and dignity. They were young women, but they had maturity and strength beyond their years. The greatest lesson has been to accept that I can't manage their grieving or fix it for them. Each one had their own perspective and different relationship with their brother, and each one had to be released to grieve individually. As their mother, my heart was tense and anxious for a while, and I felt some responsibility to try to be aware of what they were going through. I really wanted to keep them from hurting, but I slowly had to acknowledge that this was out of my control. I released them to the only One who could heal their broken hearts and prayed for them to take all their pain to Jesus. He is faithful, and my daughters are deeper, wiser, and more committed to family and to growing in the grace and knowledge of Jesus than ever before.

Your Church Family

Believe me, if you don't already have a church family you are close to, you should find one. Not only will you need it at some point, but also you are needed by them. Most important, Jesus wants His children to be a part of His body. The church family is often the first line of defense, and they serve as a guiding voice initially. After receiving the call notifying us of James' death and coming home to tell me, the first person Frank called was our pastor. Within the hour he and his wife were there. We cried, talked, and prayed, and they helped us begin to make the very first steps as to whom to call, what to do first, what arrangements to start to think about, and what action steps were needed for the next few days.

Over the next months it was not only the pastor but also the entire body of Christ, near and far, who comforted and upheld us in prayer and friendship. Members of my Bible study brought meals for weeks and others came or called often. One beautiful gesture will always be a precious memory. On the date of the first year of James' passing, I came home to find a beautiful bundle of bittersweet wrapped carefully with twine lying on the doorstep. It was indeed a bittersweet day. Our loss was James' eternal gain.

As beautiful and necessary as all these things are, none of them will give lasting peace and rest. There's only one abiding source of comfort because there is only One who knows our deepest needs.

"There is a friend who sticks closer than a brother" (Proverbs 18:24). His name is Jesus, and He is the One who truly knows how to meet the cries in our innermost being. His Spirit is the Comforter, and there are no substitutions for His deep, abiding presence. His Spirit living on the inside is able to fill us from within. "The peace of God, which surpasses all understanding, will guard your hearts and your minds through Christ Jesus" (Philippians 4:7 NKJV).

Notice that God's peace does not come *in* gaining understanding. His peace surpasses, is beyond, and far greater than understanding the answers to our questions and limited comprehension of His eternal wisdom and ways. "Our comfort is abundant through Christ" (2 Corinthians 1:5).

Blessings in the Mourning

One of my dear friends called me a few weeks after James died and said, "I have been praying, and this is what the Lord has given me to share with you." I perked up and listened carefully because when Wendy prays, God speaks to her! I stop right now and praise God for the praying and caring people He has used in my life and for their willingness to listen to Him on my behalf. Now I want to be that person in your life and believe He desires for all of us to be there to help carry one another to Him.

She said, "Jan, I believe the Lord wants me to remind you that there are promises of blessings for you in the mourning. Don't rush, skip over, or avoid mourning because God has very specific blessings in it." She was basing her counsel on words spoken by Jesus. "Blessed are those who mourn, for they shall be comforted" (Matthew 5:4). As I said earlier, when people have advice for you, consider the source. I want to say again, thank you to all those who gave me permission to mourn and the freedom to grieve. Because in doing that, I can declare I am daily comforted in God's truth and care for me.

He is the Great Physician and has the perfect regimen for every individual. He denies no one the opportunity to be made well spiritually. But you and I have to take our meddling hands off, stop talking and start listening, and allow Him to do the work. When healing physically, there's usually a period of discomfort we're required to endure. We have to bear with the pain to get to the other side, and it takes time. Time is such an important part of the process. People say, "Time heals." The truth is God heals and He uses time. We always want to dictate how long the process will be, but God says, "Until I say so." He knows the right time, the ready time, the best time, and the necessary time. Our time is in God's hands when we turn to Him in our storm.

> As for me, I trust in You, O LORD, I say, "You are my God." My times are in Your hand; deliver me from the hand of my enemies and from those who persecute me. Make Your face to shine upon Your servant; save me in Your loving-kindness (Psalm 31:14-16).

Every stage is an opportunity to allow God to pour His strength into us and prepare us for the next step. He is present with us in the process. Visualize yourself in some sort of rehabilitation center and see Jesus holding your hand and giving you grace and power for every painful exercise. "My grace is sufficient for you, for power is perfected in weakness" (2 Corinthians 12:9).

Beauty in the Healing

Every step is moving us toward the destination. You may be wondering, *What is the destination for my life now that it has been utterly disrupted and completely rearranged?* I believe the destination of grief is to reach the place of peace and rest *with* the sorrow and loss. Healing's purpose is not to restore the former ways. You're right if you say, "Things will never be the same again." But there are beautiful blessings and purposeful possibilities in the change if we will genuinely release the pain and trust God's hand to give us glorious gain.

After all, who knows and understands or identifies with suffering and pain more than Jesus? There should be some assurance in His companionship in this journey when you read these words in the book of Isaiah,

> He was despised and forsaken of men, a man of sorrows and acquainted with grief…Surely our griefs He Himself bore, and our sorrows He carried (Isaiah 53:3-4).

Jesus knows full well the depth of your pain and the weight of your sorrow. Remember, He has already gone before you. He knows the sorrow you are struggling with because He already carried your sin and pain to the cross. Before you or I ever existed, He knew we would be broken and our lives would be shattered by the effects of sin in the world. He knew disease would rob us of quality of life and riddle our days with struggle and discomfort. He knew we would be wounded by rejection, betrayal, and desertion. He took all the broken promises and our shattered dreams and carried every shard to the cross on our behalf. He stood in our place and died the death we deserved. Listen,

> He was pierced through for our transgressions, He was crushed for our iniquities; the chastening for our well-being fell upon Him, and by His scourging we are healed (Isaiah 53:5).

Picture Jesus reaching deep into the recesses of time and lifting every person and detail that hurts and causes your grief and making it His personal loss. His heart broke with me the day I lost my son, and He grieves with me as I learn to live in my changed world his death created.

He loves you that much. The deepest and most effective healing agent of all is God's love. He came to save your life and give you quality of life, and now His love is able to renew your life. Although you have suffered loss, Jesus is able to make you whole.

Slowly, without recognizing it at times, you are gaining spiritual and emotional strength. Your steps are growing stronger and your energy is increasing. There may still be days of convalescence, but you know the value of stopping to rest and lean on Jesus. Every time you stretch out your hand to Him, He wraps you in His comfort and care. I wonder if I will ever be fully, completely, and totally healed. I don't think so, but I do know that the Healer's constant comfort means far more to me than the healing.

YOUR STEPS WITH GOD

Make a list of people who were used in your life as sources of comfort and care. Thank them with a call or note no matter how long ago it was.

Make a list of people you can be a source of comfort to. Pray for them and extend practical acts of kindness. Write a note or text, make a call, take a thoughtful remembrance, and pray again.

Thank Jesus for bearing your grief and providing His love on the cross.

PART 3

Life After the Storm

10

Open the Door

*I*t was early fall, and we had just marked the second year since James had gone to heaven. During this time when a deeper understanding of the permanence of the change in our lives was sinking in, I received an email from an acquaintance who had been one of James' elementary schoolteachers. She was now working in women's ministry at the local church where we had worshipped and grown as a young family years ago. She invited me to speak and share *my story* at an annual outreach event in the following spring.

I thanked her and told her I would pray about it. As I hung up the phone, I had a sense of dread in my stomach and felt a resistance in my spirit. I agreed to pray, but I sincerely hoped the Lord would clearly say, "No, not this time."

In the aftermath of an actual storm, there are clear remnants of damage and destruction. Snowdrifts pile up after a blizzard, tornados spawn off of hurricane conditions, and rivers and creeks cresting after torrential rains cause flooding. The storm ceases to dump its contents, but the debris remains for a long time.

The cataclysmic effects on the world from the first flood kept Noah inside the ark for a long time after the rain stopped falling. Calculations say it was around 377 days from the time the door closed until he looked out and saw that the earth was dry. Noah waited and waited, cooped up inside the ark in very close quarters with family and all of those animals.

Waiting is often shunned as boring and useless, but waiting with God is active and productive. Healing is a process that takes place from the inside out. Noah saw the earth's surface and could have interpreted that as his sign to come out. In the same way, our storms may look resolved on the surface of our faces, but genuine healing takes place with time, attention, and proper care. Noah stayed inside the ark long after the rain stopped falling because within the ark there was work to be done.

Eventually, he sent out the raven and the dove. Each served a purpose in God's greater plan. The raven, a scavenger bird, could live on refuse and debris. His return would tell Noah the new creation was not ready for them. But a dove, the purest of birds, would have neither shelter nor food until the renewed world emerged. As he waited for the water to recede and for there to be the nudge from God to step out, Noah had to watch, listen, and discern the work and will of God. Waiting is often a still and quiet time. God did not speak to Noah, and Noah did not make a move. I imagine Noah decided that because God shut him in the ark, He would tell him when to come out. In that time of waiting, he learned an even greater level of trust and patience.

Often we grow impatient and restless while we wait for life to feel normal again. God alone knows what we are facing and what our "new normal" will look like, so He uses waiting to prepare us. While we are waiting, we need to make sure we are allowing the time to be used to train and equip us for the next steps. Waiting time is an opportunity for the healing power of the Word to penetrate deep into our being and for us to actively receive the Spirit to empower us with fresh strength and clear vision.

Readiness was revealed to Noah after he received the dove with the olive leaf, evidence of the water receding and earth emerging. Even then, he waited a bit longer until the dove he sent did *not* return because it had a place to land. God was preparing the way for Noah's safe return to a restored place.

Trust that waiting is divine preparation for His new world for you.

Watching for Your Olive Leaf

God calls us out when He knows we are ready. Will you be ready when He calls? Or will you drag your feet with resistance, the way I did, when you first see your own olive leaf, a sign of a restored land, an emerging life God has prepared?

"Then God said to Noah, 'Come out of the ark, you and your wife and your sons and their wives'" (Genesis 8:15-16 NIV). Remember, Noah faced a brand-new world. He had no idea what it would look like any more. After a life storm we also face a new world and have no idea what it will look like.

Coming out from whatever protective mode of life that has served as our shelter from the storm can be scary. Receding waters signal us that our place of protective covering is no longer necessary for our survival. The day arrived when the ark was not necessary for Noah's survival. The day will come when your current place of shelter from the storm is not necessary. The unknown is intimidating. Even if we are sick of the storm and tired of being cooped up with our sadness, it's often easier and more comforting to hold on to the familiar routine than to step out and trust.

Does change still feel like too much to face right now? If you are tempted to remain where you are, how will you know it is time to come out? You will know it's time to come out when the familiar patterns of comfort and protection are no longer adequate. Here are a few practical examples of what that could look like for you.

- The relationships in our life are strained and stressed. People around us are getting tired of dealing with us.

- We are becoming more and more withdrawn and feel increasingly isolated and disinterested in other people.

- Our life becomes very one dimensional because we are consumed by our storm.

- Death of other relationships and interests indicates we are losing interest in life and becoming preoccupied with what we have lost.

When I began to sense that my storm was over, I felt the fountains of the deep had closed up. My grief was receding slowly but steadily. I caught glimpses of light and felt a faint breeze in my spirit. When the storm breaks, the atmosphere changes literally and spiritually. I was about to enter the calm after the storm. I watched the horizon with patience and listened intently to the voice of God spoken to me in His Word.

During this time, I was reaching out and opening my heart and mind to allow God to show me the next steps He had for me. I knew I was a different person than I was when I entered the storm. The changes it created in my life were evident at every turn. Here I stood at a threshold of the unknown and I sensed His voice saying, "Jan, come out."

Let me take you back to my prayers about the invitation to come and speak. As I prayed, the Lord started to reveal to me why I didn't want to do it. There's that "why" word again. They will rise up in your journey often. Remember that we have the privilege of giving them to God, nailing them to the cross, and waiting for something new.

In being asked to share my story, I knew I was supposed to review the sad and sorrowful events of losing a son and remind people that God is with us. That is all true, but what got my attention was the realization that this was becoming my identity. Would I spend the rest of my life being known as the grieving mother with a testimony of God's power to carry me through sadness? Even in that season of my grief, I recognized this was less than what God wanted from me.

Right now, as I write this, I'm realizing that when I crucified, "Why do I have to be defined this way?" God gave me a clear, new message and filled me with life, hope, and new meaning. I heard Him say to me, *It's time to come out and trust Me to lead you into this new world. I want to trust you with more of Me.*

I reached for my version of the olive leaf and knew it was time to trust God.

This trust resulted in a very big leap of faith. I stood before a large audience on the evening of March 14, 2013, and stepped forward with a new message. It was titled "Life After the Storm." It was a significant time for me because it was on the date of what would have been James' thirtieth birthday. Instead of feeling overwhelming loss and focusing on what would have been a milestone birthday, I felt a sense of life and purpose and was filled with gladness and hope in the new message God had put in my heart. I celebrated what I now call my coming out!

Are You Ready?

Coming out from your shelter is a step of faith. I imagine Noah was a little scared to see what was on the other side of the door. Are you ready to make that step? I am praying you are sensing the presence and call of God to allow Him to lead you out into the new world He has created for you. The only way to get from here to there is to take one step at a time. My steps involved a phone call, a prayer, a time of waiting, more conversations, more prayer, and more waiting.

When a child is learning to walk, it happens in stages and steps before he actually lets go and walks on his own. In the beginning we are unsteady and may falter at times. But slowly and surely, with His hands to steady and guide, confidence grows until we are moving forward one step at a time. The light of life begins to shine from within us, and there is hope for our new world.

God is always present in the darkness, and He uses it to prepare and equip us to move forward to possess the new place He is leading us to. He did it in the lives of all the people who would obey His call to "open the door and come out." To become the father of nations, Abraham had to come out of the familiar and comfortable life in Haran. To deliver the Israelites from slavery in Egypt, Moses had to come out of the wilderness and speak to Pharaoh. To save her people from slaughter, Esther had to come out of the obscurity of the harem and stand before the king. To deliver Israel from the harassment of the Philistines, David had to come out and slay Goliath. To save us from the penalty of sin, Jesus had to leave heaven and come to earth to live and die on the cross to be raised from the dead! To preserve and continue to spread the gospel, the disciples had to leave their place of hiding and go meet Jesus in Galilee.

We are following in the footsteps of all the people who have chosen to allow God to take their life storm and use it for good in their lives and the lives of those they influence. All of the biblical examples mentioned and many more are of ordinary people who were slammed by the issues and disappointments of life in a fallen world. You and I are as important to God as any of these people were, so we can be confident that He desires to do the same in our lives when we yield our storms to Him.

Preparing to Come Out

Sometimes we have to be very literal and practical because in the darkness nothing seems obvious. I want to help you find those next steps and to gain your footing as you wait and listen for the Lord. Here are a few suggestions I either found helpful myself or things other people shared with me. Some of these may help you get ready to open the door.

Get Back into a Schedule

I am not talking about a highly structured regimen without some flexibility. This is about simple, basic habits that may have fallen by the wayside in the darkness. Get out of bed and make it up. Get dressed and eat something at regular mealtimes. Do ordinary and routine tasks that remind you that you are still alive. Slowly add things back. Perhaps make a phone call, schedule an appointment, read the paper, or take a walk.

Get Back into Fellowship with Others

The longer you withdraw and the more you isolate and remove yourself, the easier it is to stay away forever. Get into church and pick some place in which you can engage and participate. One of the most powerful lessons I learned was the one called "show up." If you will show up when you don't feel like it and it doesn't seem important, time and time again God shows up in powerful ways to meet you and encourage your heart.

During my waiting period, a time was scheduled for me to have coffee with the woman who invited me to speak. She wanted to tell me more about the event and share her committee's thoughts and vision with me. I didn't want to go. It wasn't personal. I just knew it was going to require me to show interest in something I was not feeling very excited about. We met and discussed the plans for the event. Then she said, "I'd like to tell you about my last conversation with James." She recounted the recent time she had seen him and the rich conversation they shared together about spiritual things. She had known him as a young boy, and now he was a young man with a heart for Jesus.

I had no idea they had seen each other and never would have guessed they would talk about such personal matters. My heart was filled with thanks and gratitude for one more touch from the Lord when I least expected it. I got in my car and felt the Spirit reminding me, *Just show up and trust Me.*

Choose a Time Not to Talk About Your Storm

Give yourself and every one in your life a break. We wear ourselves out and wear others down when every conversation turns back to the crisis or the effects it has caused. It's okay to say, "I don't want to talk about him/her/it right now. I need a time-out." There are times when your heart and mind need to rest from your circumstances. It's healing and energizing to engage in others' lives and expand our focus. Some-times others forget we have lived with this crisis 24/7 and the biggest gift they can give us is a break from our own thoughts.

I found there were several friends to whom I could say, "Please tell me about you," and they knew this was my signal for a distraction. Human nature naturally turns inward, so we must be intentional about turning our thoughts outward.

I also mentioned that we may need to give others a break. I'm refer-ring to people who may have said or done something to hurt or offend you during your crisis. Remember, they do not share your experience or perspective. We all probably have stories of hurtful or insensitive things people said or did. Examples such as a flippant attitude, thoughtless words and actions, refusal to acknowledge our pain, or insensitive interest in personal details all come to mind. I realized I couldn't move ahead until I released these people and forgave them. Most of them had no intention of hurting me. They were simply unequipped to offer comfort or care. Believe me when I say I have lived this step and it's very important. Even in the case where the actions were deliberate and calculated, forgiveness is the key to unlocking your door.

Make Plans to Do Something You Look Forward To

Engaging in life and looking toward the future may trigger some hard memories or feel like too much effort, but these are signs that healing is taking place. Again, you may have to tell yourself, "I'm making these plans and by faith I believe God will give me grace and strength to carry them through." Jesus could have told His disciples He would meet them in a locked room in Jerusalem. Instead He said, "After I have been raised, I will go before you to Galilee" (Matthew 26:32 NKJV). He knew they would need to get up and come out. He knew they would have to exercise faith to believe He would be there. He knew Galilee would remind them of times when they were fully living life with Him, and that Galilee was a familiar connection for them.

Living in guilt over the past, or remaining closed up with the memories and regrets, doesn't change the past or make way for a future. Regardless of the negative emotions, decisions, and reactions we may have associated with our storm, Jesus always offers forgiveness, grace, and purpose to those who move toward Him.

Spiritual Healing vs. Temporary Relief

True and genuine healing in our innermost being is supernatural work God alone can do. We can find temporary relief and distract ourselves from the pain for a little while, but thankfully God desires so much more for us than Band-Aids and Rolaids. Through His Word and His Spirit He cleans, washes, scrapes, mends, and attends to our broken dreams and fragile heart.

As we yield to His healing touch and take hold of His hand, we slowly begin to discover that His presence is the source of our healing and His touch on our lives is more important to us than relief.

During the earthly ministry of Jesus, multitudes followed Him and desired to be touched with His miraculous power. They wanted physical relief and rescue from their trials and troubles, but few were willing to be identified with Him and suffer with Him. We are often the same. We want the benefits of healing without the responsibility.

I want out of the pain, but am I willing to accept the responsibility that comes with a new plan for my life?

When we are ready to accept the responsibility, He will trust us with His new plan. And although it may not look anything like you thought, it's with a humble and grateful heart you will receive it. Noah came out and God revealed a brand-new world to him. The disciples came out and moved along the road to Galilee, and He was waiting for them with a new plan and purpose.

Knowing Your Part

There were times in the history of Israel when the people had to be reminded of the great and mighty things God had done for them. Sometimes we are so tangled in the present that we forget where God has brought us. Moses had to remind the Israelites when God said, "See, I have begun to deliver…Begin to occupy, that you may possess his land" (Deuteronomy 2:31). If you are impatient because of delay or reluctant because of fear to move out, I see an important lesson for us here. *Action on our part precedes revelation on God's part*. He will reveal His new plan when you are willing to follow Him out. We can trust that when we begin to occupy the place He is calling us to be, our obedience will be used to glorify His name.

YOUR STEPS WITH GOD

Perhaps it's time for you to write down today's date and declare, "This is the day I will follow God through the threshold and trust Him to give me His new plan for my new world."

11

Moved to Worship

*L*et's go back in time for a moment. It is the summer of 2011 and I am part of a short-term mission team in Kenya. We have been sent by my church in Charlotte to partner with a group close to my heart—the With Open Eyes Foundation. It was cofounded by my son, James, and his father after James spent several months in Africa beginning in 2005. The mission of the organization is to come alongside local pastors and provide transportation for them to carry the message of the gospel to remote regions that have never heard about Christ. The short-term mission group plans to assist the local pastors in ministering to the women and children where WOE is supporting ministry in their communities.

It has been ten months since James suddenly passed away. Much of the time I'm still in a hazy fog, and I have no idea if I can handle this trip or if I am ready to face so many painful memories. I am here only because I believe God has prompted me to take this step at this time. Some friends and family fear it may be too soon. Some encourage me and pray for this to be used in my life as a step toward healing. Out of sheer obedience, I go.

May I say to you that if God calls you or leads you to do something in the healing process, you can be sure He will give you supernatural strength and grace to handle the painful memories? I encourage you to be very careful about concocting your own healing potion. Steps not ordered by God could take you into deep, dark places where you will find that you are emotionally in over your head and leave you struggling for spiritual air. He knows when and what we are ready to face.

We are in the small town where James lived, worked, worshipped, and loved the people. They were like family to him, and as hard as it is for me to get my head around this when I look at the dirt, poverty, simplicity, and struggle of life here, I know this is where he found real meaning and purpose for his life. Here he was most comfortable, and here he felt the acceptance and sense of belonging that often eluded him at home.

Our group is in the church led by Pastor Simon Kariuki and his wife, Agnes, and I love them. They have been mentors, friends, pastor, and parents to our whole family through the years. And they invested in James more than any other people on earth besides Frank and me. This couple was the answer to our prayers for God to put spiritual laborers into James' life as a young man.

Our team enters the church on Sunday morning for worship, and I have been asked to share with the congregation. In Kenya a mother is addressed as "Mama" of her firstborn or by the name of her son if she has one. I am Mama James and always will be. I'm prepared with a short message and personal testimony on the faithfulness of God *in* distress. When I am finished, Pastor Simon takes the microphone and calls me to stand next to him. He then asks all who knew and loved James to come and surround me. Many walked to my side and laid hands on me. They began to pray in Swahili, Arabic, English, and their mother tongue. He asks all who were grieved by James' death to join together in the grieving, reminding us that Scripture says, "Weep with those who weep" (Romans 12:15).

Soon our voices are rising together in a mournful sob. Deep groaning in the Spirit and prayers of intersession are offered up for some time. God's Holy Spirit is present, and He is ministering to me and to all of us in a profound, personal way. Slowly the cries in the circle begin to subside, and a peaceful quiet settles over the room and in our hearts. Whispers and praises of adoration tumble unhindered from our lips. Someone starts to clap and many join in. The atmosphere shifts now to one of glorious rejoicing and praise and worship of our great God. Because Jesus is alive, I know James has never been more alive. My sights are lifted above the circumstances, and I am experiencing the ministry of healing through the body of Christ. God is being exalted as the sovereign King of kings, and I begin to worship in spirit and in truth.

Healing Is Not About Erasing the Pain

God used my first trip to Kenya to begin to change my perspective. My heart was bathed in a soothing balm, the balm of Gilead. I caught a vague glimpse of the possibility of God giving me a renewed sense of purpose in my life. I picked up a thin thread of hope and held it tight. A clearer understanding of the genuine healing God offers was being revealed to me. His healing touch does not erase the pain, but rather releases His power and authority into the pain so it can become a place of revival in our life.

As I slowly gained the strength and courage to survey my new environment, I was able to accept and acknowledge all the changes my life storm created. My family was completely rearranged. For twenty years we were a family of six members. The dynamics of each parent to parent, parent to child, child to parent, and sibling to sibling relationship is utterly disrupted when one member is permanently removed. Without James, many of our previous plans and future decisions were profoundly impacted. But maybe most surprising of all was the way this changed each of us individually. My interests, activities, and priorities were changing. At first the greatest priority was to survive. But slowly that desire began to give way to a deep yearning to grow, gain, and thrive in this new environment of a different land.

My outlook for my future was being transformed as I experienced the presence and power of Jesus in intimate and personal ways. The dark clouds of sadness started to lift, and the disorientation subsided as my new reality became more familiar. God was there to give me strength and courage to continue on this journey, and I was lifted as I continued to try to trust His Word to me. An awareness of how much

I had to be thankful for and how blessed I am seeped into the empty places left by James' absence. I could look back and see blessings too numerous to count and the faithfulness of God to sustain and supply when we are in need.

Sharing the sweet and powerful memories of mourning with the African villagers who also loved James reminds me that I am truly in a different place now. God has been with me each step of the way. The storm is over. The pain is not erased, but I am ready to embrace the goodness of God to restore and redeem whatever is lost.

God's Invitation to You

God is holding the door open for you too, my friend. He is inviting you to step out into the new world He has created specifically for you. Are you ready to embrace His wise and gracious plan for your life? You do not have to be defined by the labels you have worn as a result of your storm. He wants to release you from any of these or others you have taken on, been given, or worn by default:

- abandoned wife
- childless woman
- widow
- lonely single
- addict
- unappreciated superstar
- mistreated in-law
- victim
- handicapped

God does not see us as we are; He sees us as He knows we will be. The storm is over and it's time to embrace His hope and healing power and give Him praise. God's presence with me through the storm fills me with awe and wonder for who He is, and I fall in humble adoration and worship Him. Worship turns the focus fully on Him. Acceptable

worship flows freely from a broken heart that is completely surrendered and wholly committed, regardless of feelings and circumstances.

Let's take some of the examples given to us in Scripture and learn
more about true worship that brings pleasure to God.

Worship Is a Choice

After God called Noah and his family and the animals out of the ark,
the Bible says, "Then Noah built an altar to the LORD, and took of every
clean animal and of every clean bird and offered burnt offerings on the
altar" (Genesis 8:20). Worship and sacrifice were Noah's first response
to his new world. When Noah walked across the threshold of the ark,
he was not preoccupied by the daunting responsibility of starting over
in a totally changed and rearranged world. He was not distracted with
the immediate thrill and relief of escaping the discomfort of the ark.
He was preoccupied with and distracted by God Himself.

Let's check our heart. Ask yourself, "Am I afraid to leave this place
because I have no idea what the new world I'm stepping into will
look like?" Or, "Am I so happy to get out of there that I am racing
straight into the easiest and most comfortable place I can find? After all,
I deserve a break." Beware. Both attitudes bypass the One who brought
you to this new place in your life. We don't want to miss the opportunity to worship Him.

David

Second Samuel 12:19-20 contains a detailed account of David's
response to the storm created in his family by his sin of adultery, which
resulted in pregnancy with Bathsheba and the murder of her husband,
Uriah. A prophet of God, Nathan, told David the child would get sick
and die. David fasted and prayed, but the Bible says, "David perceived
that the child was dead; so David...arose from the ground, washed,
anointed himself, and changed his clothes; and he came into the house
of the LORD and *worshiped*" (emphasis added). David placed God over
and above the pain and sorrow of losing the baby boy. Worship gives
God His rightful place as Lord over all.

Heart check: "Will I worship when my prayers are not answered the way I asked them to be?"

Job

Job 1:20-21 is Job's response after receiving one message of bad news after another. He was suddenly stripped of his herds, livestock, servants, and all of his sons and daughters. His reaction is recorded for all eternity. "Job arose and tore his robe and shaved his head, and he fell to the ground and *worshiped.* He said, 'Naked I came from my mother's womb, and naked I shall return there. The LORD gave and the LORD has taken away. Blessed be the name of the LORD'" (emphasis added).

Heart check: "How do I respond when everything is falling apart? Do I bless God and remember that He gave it and He has the right to take it away?"

Did you notice in these examples of true worship that there are no complaints? Neither David nor Job hesitated to bow to the sovereign authority of the Lord God. Their actions demonstrate faith willing to say, "His ways are better than mine, and I will accept that my God makes no mistakes."

The Disciples

In Matthew 28:16 we find others—the disciples—who are willing to turn to worship: "The eleven disciples proceeded to Galilee, to the mountain which Jesus had designated. When they saw Him, they *worshiped Him,* but some were doubtful" (emphasis added). Worship does not depend on our ability to understand our circumstances. Our doubts are safe with Him. Worship is the act of presenting an undivided heart to God.

Heart check: "Do my doubts get in the way of my worship? Am I willing to present all my doubts and all of my heart to God?"

The Samaritan Woman

Jesus met a Samaritan woman at a well, and a conversation followed that led to the subject of true worship. There was confusion on her part about where and whom to worship. Jesus told her, "An hour is coming, and now is, when the true worshipers will worship the Father in spirit and truth; for such people the Father seeks to be His worshipers. God is spirit, and those who worship Him must worship in spirit and truth" (John 4:23-24).

How do you know where and whom to worship? I think we have an insight here if we listen carefully to what Jesus says. He says God is drawn to the places and people who are worshipping Him. He is looking for sincere worshippers. I think that means you can be all alone or you can be with many, and if the Spirit of God is moving and His name is being exalted, the Spirit of God is seeking to spend time with you in the atmosphere of worship. The worship leader, the musicians, and vocalists will not be the main attraction. Your own voice will not be a distraction if your heart is fixed on Him.

Scripture tells us, "You are holy, enthroned in the praises of Israel" (Psalm 22:3 NKJV), so we know He is present when we are praising Him. If you are not familiar with praise and worship, open up the book of Psalms and read the words of the songs David and others wrote to God. Worship has the most sensitive and beautiful way of shifting our focus from our storm to the One who "rebuked the wind and said to the sea, 'Hush, be still.' And the wind died down and it became perfectly calm" (Mark 4:39).

One Sunday many years ago I showed up at church with a heart so heavy I thought for sure I would drown in worry and dread. My emotional boat was filling with burdens faster than I could bail them out, and I was truly about to sink. At some point during the worship the choir began to sing a chorus that repeated over and over the call to magnify the Lord and glorify His name. I moved my lips at first, but my heart and mind were still on my circumstances. The longer we sang, the closer I listened.

Slowly, the Spirit of God began to impress the message on my heart. In my mind I pictured a magnifying glass enlarging the image of Jesus. He began to get bigger and bigger, His presence became clearer and clearer, and my heart shifted to adoration and praise and I became a worshipper. By the time I left I was light in my spirit and my confidence was in the greatness of my God. He was seeking worshippers, and I'm so very thankful He found me that day.

Heart check: "Have I forgotten how to praise the Lord? Will I turn my attention from my pain to His face and glorify His name?"

Just like you and me, all of these people were broken from the storms they endured. God's Spirit ministered in the storm, and ultimately each was moved to genuinely worship Him. The Lord is the object of true worship. Genuine and acceptable worship is demonstrated from a heart that is willing to say, "No matter what, God's ways are right. He is sovereign and I bow my head and accept His will." He owes me no explanation.

As Creator of the universe, it's God's sovereign right to destroy the earth with a flood. As Giver of life, it's His sovereign right to take life away. Only Jesus has the power and authority to walk out of the tomb and conquer death, hell, and the grave. He is worthy of all our worship.

Our worship is genuine and acceptable when we humble our spirit to His Spirit and come under the truth of His Word. Worship is an attitude from our innermost being. It's easy to go through an outward expression of worship but still resist the Holy Spirit and reject the Word of God. Worship is not an expression of how we feel but a choice to accept the sovereignty of God to always do what is right.

Worship Leads to God's Work

From the examples of worshippers, it's clear that true worship always precedes the true work of God. It's possible to start working away on a "God project" but have no blessing or genuine spiritual fruit born from it. True ministry and life care flow from a heart of worship. Look around for evidence of transformed and faith-filled lives. There you will find people who are willing to draw near, listen, abide, wait, glorify, magnify, and yield an undivided heart to Him.

Worship prepares us to step out with faith and begin to receive God's blessings. We don't worship to get the blessing, but He allows worshippers to participate in His work and they are blessed. Let me show you what I mean from the lives of Noah, David, Job, the disciples, and the Samaritan woman. See how their earlier decision to worship led to God's work in and through their lives.

To Noah and his sons, God said, "Be fruitful and multiply, and fill the earth" (Genesis 9:1). David and Bathsheba's son, Solomon, became the king of Israel to build the temple of God. It was the dwelling place of God on earth until Jesus ascended into heaven and sent His Holy Spirit to indwell those who believed on Him. Job's losses were fully restored and his life was a reflection of the redeeming power of God for those who trust in Him.

The disciples met the risen Jesus in Galilee, and He gave them the biggest assignment ever entrusted to men, "Go therefore and make disciples of all nations, baptizing them in the name of the Father and the Son and the Holy Spirit, teaching them to observe all that I commanded you; and lo, I am with you always, even to the end of the age" (Matthew 28:19-20). Those were tall orders for boys who had just blown it as disciples. But He knows what you will become, and He will do amazing things through people who worship Him "in spirit and truth" (John 4:24).

The Samaritan woman shared of her encounter with the Lord and praised Him, and because of that witness, many of her people also believed in Jesus. "Many of the Samaritans of that city believed in Him because of the word of the woman who testified, 'He told me all that I ever did.' So when the Samaritans had come to Him, they urged Him to stay with them; and He stayed there two days. And many more believed because of His own word. Then they said to the woman, 'Now we believe, not because of what you said, for we ourselves have heard Him and we know that this is indeed the Christ, the Savior of the world'" (John 4:39-42).

A Sign for Future Generations

Throughout Scripture we see people stopping to build memorials to remember or commemorate the things God did in their lives. The memorials serve as a physical place of witness and testimony to the prevailing power of God. God instructed Joshua to build a memorial when the Israelites crossed the Jordan River to take possession of the Promised Land. Marking the place where they crossed with stones would serve as a visual sign of this miraculous fulfillment of God's word in their lives for the future generations. God told them that when they repeat the story of what He did there, it was "so all the peoples of the earth may know that the hand of the LORD is mighty, so that you may fear [have reverent awe of] the LORD your God forever" (Joshua 4:24).

Notice that the purpose of the memorial is to lift up His name and point others to the Lord God, who is mighty. When the history of the event being memorialized is recalled, the response of the listener is, "Look at the great thing God has done." In other words, a memorial is not a shrine to the memory of a person. Shrines draw our attention back to the life and loss of a person but do nothing to lift up the power and might of the Lord.

A meaningful way I have found to build a memorial is to gather several smooth stones and a permanent marking pen. Ask God to call to your remembrance the times and places where He has done mighty things in your life. They are the spiritual milestones that you want to always remember and the things you would share as opportunities to lift up His name over your life. They are the times you have been willing to surrender to His sovereign will and wisdom. My memorial stones are marked and dated. Let me share my examples.

- Born-again, 1982
- Decision to make written Word my life guide, 1982
- Trusted His will over testing results, 1990
- Called to teach the Word, 1984, 1990, 1998
- Surrendered to international missions, Mongolia 2010
- Called out from teaching, 2012
- New season of ministry, 2013

My stones are in a small bowl I keep on a shelf, and they serve as a visual reminder of places in my spiritual journey where God's faithfulness to His Word has prevailed in life-changing ways for me. When I look back over my life, my memorial reminds me God is alive and at work in me. When the circumstances are difficult and God seems far away, they encourage me to look up and bow low in humility and worship the One who has brought me through every storm.

There is one other place I build memorials to the Lord. It's in the margins of my Bible. If you opened it, you would find it marked with dates and a few words to remind me of God's personal word spoken to me through the written Word. I have mentioned it throughout our time here together. When God gives me a personal and specific word of comfort, guidance, and direction, I date it and make a short notation in the margin of my Bible. Future generations would be able to pick it up and know "this was a time when the Lord God was mighty on her behalf." This is one way the baton of faith can be passed from one generation to the next. Of course, nothing serves as a memorial more than a life lived for the glory of God, but it will invariably be a life that was saturated in His Word.

My Offering

My time within the storm with Jesus has been a trying but rewarding teacher. He gently reminded me that James was a gift to his father and me. The day he was born, the Creator of life loaned us a beautiful baby boy. He allowed us the privilege and trusted us with the responsibility of loving and molding this gift. We had 27 years and all sorts of incredible experiences to grow and learn with and from James. As an infant we dedicated him to God. We acknowledged we were inadequate as parents and publically declared our dependence was on Him. Not once did God fail to supply and sustain in all the years of raising him. Now I am reminded that James was never ours in life. A true gift worthy of our great God always costs the giver. We need to choose between hanging on to the things lost in our storm and giving an offering back to God with open hearts and hands. Now it's my humble act of worship to gladly offer back to God what belongs to Him and praise Him for His mighty work in my life. It's another memorial stone I place on the altar to the Lord. "As sorrowful yet always rejoicing..." (2 Corinthians 6:10).

As we close this chapter, I want to encourage you to trust God to receive your sincere offering. Our storms become opportunities to share His power to give new life and eternal hope to others. Like the disciples, we may worship with some doubts and uncertainty about the future, but there is no doubt He has proven through us many things so that "the peoples of the earth may know that the hand of the LORD is mighty, so that you may fear [have reverent awe of] the LORD your God forever" (Joshua 4:24).

YOUR STEPS WITH GOD

Make your own memorial of stones to serve as a visual reminder of the goodness of God through your life and your storm. (Nice smooth stones are available at a craft store or floral shop. Light ones are easiest to mark.)

Ask God to help you rewrite your story as an offering back to Him. It's your opportunity to express gratitude for the renewed hope He has given you after the storm.

Consider starting to build memorials to God in the margins of your Bible. Note when and how God is faithful and worthy of your praises.

12

God's Spacious Places

The aftermath of a storm eventually brings cleanup and re-creation. It has been more than 20 years since Hurricane Hugo wiped out my yard and ruined the original landscape. Today, we hardly remember what it was like before as we survey its fullness, maturity, and beauty. Life after the storm may look very different from the vision we had in mind before the winds came, but with His strength our lives can also be full, mature, and beautiful to God. He has a new plan for after the storm.

New Lives, Expanded Borders

Look at David's words in Psalm 31:8, "You have not given me over into the hand of the enemy; You have set my feet in a large place." David knew what it felt like to be pursued relentlessly and to live on the run. He knew the personal pain of being misunderstood and displaced. He knew the reality of suffering at the hands of other people. But he held fast to God's Word and trusted His will. In this verse he declares he is standing in a spacious place. You and I can declare that we have not been given over to the enemy.

I'm sure there were times along the way when you probably doubted if you would make it through your storm, but God has brought you through to give you a spacious place. Pause now to consider how your experiences have expanded your understanding and given you new borders. You, like me, have probably been places and done things you never thought you would. Because of where your life storm has taken you and the new world you live in, you have influence and credibility with people you never could have had before. Your property lines have moved further out and your borders have expanded. That is a blessing out of the storm and a responsibility. There are so many more places we can go for the kingdom of God now.

My family has watched our world expand in unimaginable ways as God continues to use the life of one young man to ignite a ministry that touches countless others with the gospel of Jesus Christ. With Open Eyes is a foundation cofounded by James and his dad to provide transportation to indigenous pastors in Africa. They are enabled to reach remote people groups with the Good News. James' heart for people who are desperate for hope and help would not allow him to forget them when he returned home. Every time I go to Africa and share the experience of traveling alongside one of these pastors we call Mobil Messengers, I am reminded that God redeems and restores.

Only God can turn the emptiness of loss into the fullness of His vision. Your storm and mine allow us to experience His power to multiply anything given into His hand.

Created for Good Works

It's humbling and overwhelming to think God wants to use us to accomplish His purposes. I imagine that is how the 11 disciples felt when they finally got back to Galilee after the resurrection After all, they had to be reminded and prodded to get up and go. They came with doubts and shame. They came wondering "what now?" As long as our focus is on our inadequacy and inability, we will be unable to recognize the spacious place. If I am preoccupied with the changes my storm has created and concentrating on my scars, I will not be able to recognize Jesus.

We hate scars because they remind us everything is not perfect. And one look at a scar can unload an avalanche of painful memories. As I think about it, some of the most beautiful people I know bear deep scars. One person in particular comes to my mind whose childhood was wrought with abandonment, rejection, and neglect. Today, tender kindness and gentleness seep from this person.

I pray my scars no longer need to serve as reminders of my pain from the storm. Instead, they can be signs of the great love and care Jesus has directed toward me. My scars mark me as His dependent, and this moves me to worship Him. I need Him so and love Him so much more.

It's time to surrender our scars to the healing touch of the Great Physician.

When we trust that our life is being shaped and formed by God's hands and our life after the storm is a new plan He sets in motion, we can step into our spacious places knowing there are good works ahead for us…scars and all. It seems that God delights in using us when we have surrendered our scars and allow them to become opportunities to point others to Him. Throughout the Bible, the people God used for His purposes had places of scarring from their struggles and loss. Paul encourages us to remember God's promise, "My grace is sufficient for you, for power is perfected in weakness" (2 Corinthians 12:9).

Jesus has nail-scarred hands and feet. Like Thomas, we are allowed and even encouraged to touch and carefully examine His scars. They are visible reminders of the price His love was willing to pay on the cross and of His resurrection power. Jesus' scars remind us that He is greater than every trial and storm that marks us. There is no question things in our lives will never be the same again. There is no doubt our lives are forever changed. If you are divorced, then your marriage is over. If your final attempt to conceive was unsuccessful, you are childless. I will never again have James with me here on this earth. But as we step into the spacious place God has appointed, our surrendered scars reflect Him. Jesus was dead but now He is alive. Some of my dreams and plans are dead, but He has the power to breathe life into my new world.

In weakness and doubt the disciples worshipped Jesus. Humility is the prerequisite to being called to serve. When we lay our demands, doubts, and excuses down, He will pick us up and set us in spacious places.

The disciples were given an impossible assignment when they were weak and uncertain. Jesus knew their limits just as He knows ours. He told them, "All authority has been given to Me in heaven and on earth. Go therefore and make disciples of all the nations, baptizing them in the name of the Father and the Son and the Holy Spirit, teaching them to observe all that I commanded you; and lo, I am with you always, even to the end of the age" (Matthew 28:18-20).

God has the authority to call and send us. He says we are to get going and make disciples. Disciples are followers of Christ, and people follow when you are an authentic witness. Your life is the testimony that proves Jesus is alive, and He will take you through to the other side. We are the living proof that He is with us and that His power is greater than the scars of the storm. He brings us through so we can turn around and be used to help bring others to Him. It's by His power, through His Spirit. As our faith matures in our new world, we have more opportunities to share the gospel and the message of our own story.

Our Calling

I'm stepping into a spacious place. It's territory filled with hurting and aching people. For a time I detoured around storms and destruction in others' lives because I didn't have the strength to expose my own. Now I'm walking through the door and finding that my borders have expanded. I'm beginning to embrace this as the good work created for me. I never wanted to minister to people who lost children. It is not a club anyone chooses to join. I know you understand because you did not choose your place either. I am beginning to see this as my appointed place in the body of Christ.

I can't just stand by and watch others fight and struggle with their life storms. I know there is hope and want to offer encouragement to them. Sure, people can survive and many do, but I want to thrive. I want the power of resurrected Jesus, who is alive in me, to fill me with strength and power to pour into others. I have been the recipient of His comfort and care in the greatest storm of my life. He brought me through so I could now turn to someone in need. Paul wrote it like this in 2 Corinthians 1:3-4, "Blessed be the God and Father of our Lord Jesus Christ, the Father of mercies and God of all comfort, who comforts us in all our affliction so that we will be able to comfort those who are in any affliction with the comfort with which we ourselves are comforted by God."

Yes, that's what we are called to do. We have a wider border than ever before because we have known varying experiences of affliction. You and I are called to bring the Comforter to those who are aching and choking with pain and sorrow. We are His hands to wrap them in His loving care. We are His feet, willing to move in our expanded, new world to reach those who hunger for comfort. And we give voice to prayers for them to know the sweet blessing of comfort that the "Father of mercies and God of *all* comfort" can give (emphasis added).

It's easy to think, *I don't know what to say* and *I don't know how to minister to others.* But the truth is that it isn't you or me who does the ministering. As we make ourselves available to Him in worship and prayer, He fills us and equips us.

Recently, I was asked if I would speak to a couple whose son had committed suicide a year earlier. I thought, *What do I say that could possibly give them comfort?* Would you believe I later realized I had already prayed for this family at the time of the son's death at the request of a mutual friend? My spirit was acquainted with them before we were ever introduced. That's how God works when we are willing to be used as His vessel to serve His comfort to those within our sphere of influence.

Unexpected Gifts

Just as the beach is always littered with treasure after a storm, I'm still discovering gifts from my personal tempest. At first you may find the treasures buried beneath the debris and rubbish, but if you bend close and look carefully, you will begin to discover the priceless valuables that have been deposited on the shoreline of your new world. My own spacious place considers time more carefully and prayerfully. I realize it's a generous gift from God and doesn't last forever. It's too precious to waste carelessly or misuse. Today's relationships and opportunities will never be this way again, and I don't want to miss a single one.

Words are nuggets of pure gold to be guarded but lavishly spent blessing and encouraging others. I want to share them freely by telling people how much I love and appreciate them and use my words to build up, encourage, and speak life. I want words of thanksgiving to my God to be continually on my lips. Words are the treasures we can use to create a Christlike atmosphere in our new world.

My perspective in this new and spacious place changes how I see everyone and everything. I'm discovering the only frame of reference that matters is from eternity. If my viewpoint is from God's heart, my attitudes and actions will serve to enlarge my borders further and continue to create spaciousness in this new land He has brought me to. Look carefully, and the gifts will be more significant than the scars.

- I am in awe of the power of Christ in my life.
- My weakness has caused me to learn a deeper dependence on His strength.
- My immediate family is even more precious because of this journey. We appreciate and cherish one another because we know the meaning of loss.
- I know who I can trust to be there for me.
- I know God is always there, and that makes the future a little less scary.
- Love is deeper because we have shared each other's pain.
- Grieving gives the unique opportunity to experience God's limitless love.
- Christ-confidence is strengthened.
- I am able to embrace this new place and thank God for it.

Spacious places give us room to spread out and space to grow into. They are wide-open spaces free from clutter and junk. The most valuable treasure of all is a spacious heart. By that I mean a heart that is open to the things of God and available to grow, give, and go in His name.

Throughout this journey, you and I have shared a lot of ways to cultivate a spacious heart. It seems my heart is most productive spiritually when it's broken by His love, emptied for His glory, and filled with His power. When we yield ourselves to Him, renewal is His promise to us.

> For this reason also, since the day we heard of it, we have not ceased to pray for you and to ask that you may be filled with the knowledge of His will in all spiritual wisdom and understanding, so that you will walk in a manner worthy of the Lord, to please Him in all respects, bearing fruit in every good work and increasing in the knowledge of God; strengthened with all power, according to His glorious might, for the attaining of all steadfastness and patience, joyously giving thanks to the Father, who has qualified us to share in the inheritance of the saints in Light (Colossians 1:9-12).

Because of the storm, I have a new heart and am aware of His Spirit within me in greater ways. He has given me sensitivity for the things that concern Him and a deeper love for the things He loves. Needless to say, on the other side of the storm I'm realizing I'm the one who has been profoundly changed, and I pray the process is making me into a clearer reflection of the image of Jesus. Perhaps that is the greatest unexpected gift of all from life after the storm.

I marvel at God's ability to take the rubble from devastating storms and create something beautiful. It's the touch of His Spirit literally, figuratively, and spiritually. The ultimate gift is awakening to the transformation taking place within myself. As I have allowed Him to speak to the winds and quiet the waves, my heart is finally hushed and still. It's on this still surface that I can see the reflection of His beautiful face.

I'm going to close by sharing a list with you. It's a list my family has kept over the last four years. It's personal to our circumstances, but maybe it will encourage you to start your own list. Ask God to show you the treasures, hidden and obvious, revealed as a result of your storm.

Because of James...

- We all are changed.
- Ministry has been born in all of us.
- We are all filled with care and compassion for people who struggle in all sorts of ways.
- Countless connections have been made to people from many walks of life.
- I'm going places I never dreamed and doing things I never imagined.
- Mission trips are taken to remote and removed places to preach the gospel and lift up the downcast.
- We have been honored to go and give to "the least of these."
- Namanga Baptist Church is built.
- James' House is finished and opened in Kenya as a place to refresh and minister.
- With Open Eyes Foundation is growing, thriving, and multiplying.
- God has raised up new leaders in our family to be used for Him.
- Heaven is more precious and fills us with hope.
- We're watching for Jesus to come.
- Everything is different—life, love, and loss.

David was a poet and inspired by the Holy Spirit, so I can't improve on his words. But, I can personalize them, because they beautifully share the thoughts on my heart as I stand back and see the goodness of God to my family and me.

> He caused [our] storm to be still, so that the waves of the sea were hushed. Then [we] were glad because they were quiet, so He guided [our family] to [our] desired haven. Let [us] give thanks to the LORD for His lovingkindness, and for His wonders to [us] (Psalm 107:29-31).

God wants to give us new dreams. The vacancy created by the life storm is not to leave us empty and incomplete. God is a Giver and He is a Redeemer. He is able to take the losses and use them for good and give us new opportunities and places of joy and purpose.

Your journey has brought you to a new place of discovery. The possibilities are countless when you give yourself to be used by God. He has all authority to send you to a new and spacious place of growth and influence. He is not expecting you to know exactly where you are going or to be prepared for the task. He has used the storm to equip you with a deeper dependence on Him and a certain confidence that He will guide you and lead you in the way you should go. He sends you out with clearer vision, keener hearing, and a more tender heart. He gives you His Spirit, His Word, and wisdom to move ahead. Your new and spacious place is filled with people who need the love and touch of Jesus in their lives.

Before Joshua led the Israelites into the new land God had promised them, he told them, "Consecrate yourselves, for tomorrow the LORD will do wonders among you" (Joshua 3:5).

My friend, by consecrating yourself you can anticipate that your new and spacious place will witness God's wonders to and through you. Will you open your heart, your mind, and your hands to the new place of calling God wants to give you now? It's time to look toward the horizon and watch for the dawning of a new day.

YOUR STEPS WITH GOD

If you are still searching for treasures from your storm, I want to encourage you to be patient and persistent. Remember, it's not about finding what we are looking for; it's about discovering what He wants to reveal. Faithfully return to the shore and pray for eyes to see treasures from the darkness.

If you are ready to follow Him to your new and spacious land, take this opportunity to consecrate yourself. Will you dedicate your life to be used to glorify and magnify God? It's an act of worship given from a changed heart.

13

This Is Not the End

The time is April 2011, six months since James went to heaven. Pastor Simon and Agnes are sitting at my kitchen table, and we are remembering and sharing insights and memories about James. My heart is heavy, and as I ask the question on my mind, my voice breaks and I begin to sob. It hurts so bad that I wonder how long I can take the pain. "Did he know how much we loved him?" I knew the answer in my head, but I needed to hear it from the last people who had personal conversations and time with him.

Simon replied, "Yes, Mama James. He knew." Then he opened the Bible sitting on the table in front of us and read these words from the book of Isaiah:

> Do not call to mind the former things, or ponder things of the past. Behold, I will do something new, now it will spring forth; will you not be aware of it? I will even make a roadway in the wilderness, rivers in the desert (Isaiah 43:18-19).

The margin in my Bible next to this reference is dated "04/08/11—Simon to me."

I confess it took time for me to receive these words into my spirit. Now, the former things have begun to settle into their natural place in time, and although I cannot forget, it's no longer necessary to go over and over details of the past. I believe wholeheartedly that God is doing something new in me. It finally sank in that I would miss the new life He is unfolding in front of me if I stayed busy and preoccupied with the past. This realization reminds me of several places in Scripture where looking back was warned against. When Sodom was burning, Lot's wife looked back against God's instruction and was turned into a pillar of salt. Jesus said, "No one, after putting his hand to the plow and looking back, is fit for the kingdom of God" (Luke 9:62). If we become fixated on the past and always wish for the former days, we will miss what God wants to give us now.

Look Ahead

I understand your storm and its aftermath may cause you to feel abandoned in the wilderness, but this is not the end. That is worth repeating. This is not the end, my friend. This is not where God will leave you. He can and will make inroads into impossible situations to show us the way through and then out of the old life.

Look forward. Look up. Look ahead. The time is now!

We may be tempted to focus on the difficulties we've experienced because we are becoming familiar with our suffering and loss. The danger in lingering too long in our season of sorrow is that God's spacious place of renewal becomes more distant. When we release the old, the closer we will move toward the new season of life God has prepared for us. New life begins to blossom out of the healing environment of faith and trust in God.

An entire book of the Bible was written about a man called Job. His name is synonymous with suffering, but his suffering and loss were not the end of the story. "The LORD blessed the latter days of Job more than his beginning" (Job 42:12).

Suffering and loss are not the end of the story when they are given over to God's hand. Earlier, I confided how I spent a very long while marking time in my life as either before or after James' death. From now on, time is going to be marked as my beginning and latter days.

I'm watching for God's blessings to multiply and His goodness to be revealed in the latter days of my life. I'm on the other side of this turbulent and destructive storm. He has brought me to this spacious place to experience latter days of blessings. The true blessings of the storm are peace that surpasses understanding and confidence in His ever-present help. I'm thankful for my former days, but I have hope my latter days will be filled with new blessings. I could have never gotten here without the storm.

From Loss to Abundance

No matter what the storm has wiped out of your life, God is able to fill every void. My friend who was never able to have children and whose life dream of family looks very different says, "It's not at all the way I imagined, but it is good." God has filled the void with His peace to accept the things she cannot change. He has given her new interests and places of growth and challenge.

The couple who lost their little girls in the plane crash has added three more children to their home. There are six boys now! God doesn't replace the people lost; He does something brand new. He fills the empty places with new revelations of His character and deeper awareness of His presence. There is a profound sense of blessing in every gift and opportunity.

In my life I experience insight into places and situations where I was blind. I am empowered to walk in places I previously refused to go. God is continually adding and filling my spirit with a new dependence on Him. My latter days are being filled with new opportunities to grow, learn, bless, give, forgive, and understand.

All of these things are examples of the abundant life Jesus gives. They are the benefits of His abiding presence. He wants us to experience and enjoy His life in us in our present life. Abundant life is a supernatural quality of life that has nothing to do with the circumstances we are in. It's life filled with the attitude and perspective of eternity even when our natural life is full of disappointment, pain, and loss.

You and I can genuinely experience the abundant life Jesus intended for us to have. The storm threatened to ruin me, but when the winds were hushed and the waves were calmed, I realized Jesus was with me, filling me the whole way.

A Better Day

There is one final storm for all of us. Its conditions will look different for every soul, but there is no one who will escape it. It's that final journey we make from this life. No one knows their day or hour, but the wise person heeds the forecast and prepares for the other side of this life. One day I was reading my Bible, and I came across a verse I had never seen before. It was one of those times when the Word seemed to jump off the page and the Holy Spirit witnessed to my spirit. His impressed message was, *This is God's personal word to you today.* Because it was close to the third anniversary of James' final journey, you will understand why it arrested my attention.

> A good name is better than a good ointment, and the day of one's death is better than the day of one's birth (Ecclesiastes 7:1).

I wrote in the margin of my Bible "10/05/10 a *better* day than 03/14/83."

I remembered the day my son was born to a young and clueless couple. We were thrilled when the doctor flipped him over and we saw he was a boy! It was in the years before ultrasound and life was still full of surprises. We gave him the name of the three generations before him and almost immediately we began to deposit hopes, dreams, and prayers into him. It was thrilling to call family and friends and share this wonderful and exciting blessing. If you are a parent, you share the memory and the joy.

A *better* day, the day we had to call family and friends and tell them James was gone?

"Lord, how can this be true?" I had to ask Him to show me the truth. Slowly, as I meditated on eternal truth and allowed the memories and the scene of the day of his birth to settle, God started to reveal truth from His Word. All of us are born into a lost and dying world. We are born in sin and separated from the One who knows us intimately and created us for His glory. All of life is a strain and a struggle for us to release the natural man and put on the spiritual man. We're bound by all of the limits and shortcomings of this fallen world. We are born to die. As long as we live we strive for acceptance, security, peace, freedom, contentment, and satisfaction. These are worthy things and worth our energy and attention, but we know they will never completely fulfill us. In fact, they will often elude and disappoint us.

I thought of all of James' personal and particular struggles and the constant energy spent trying to reconcile and redirect himself. The world and many others would say, "James has it made," but we knew that was not so. During different periods of his life, storms raged and he was battered and bruised by them. But this was the final storm, and I had no doubt this time he was not battered or bruised. He is whole, healthy, and walking in the light of the glory of God, safe on the other side.

"Yes, Lord, I bow my heart under the sovereign wisdom of Your Word and I agree, it is a *better* day." This is only possible because I know where James is and I know I will see him again. It's not just wishful thinking or a way to reconcile my loss. This is the gospel. James prayed to receive Christ as his Lord and Savior as a young boy. "As many as received Him, to them He gave the right to become children of God, even to those who believe in His name" (John 1:12). He was always keenly aware of his need for a Savior. "God so loved the world, that he gave His only begotten Son, that whoever believes in Him shall not perish, but have eternal life" (John 3:16). James fully recognized he did not deserve forgiveness based on anything he could do. "By grace you have been saved through faith; and that not of yourselves, it is the gift of God, not a result of works, so that no one may boast" (Ephesians 2:8-9).

Through all the ups and downs, James kept a strong faith in the goodness of God and His amazing grace. Five days before his death, he had his last conversation with us by phone. It ended the way our conversations often did—we prayed together. His last words were words of thanks to God "for always being there and giving us daily needs." We said, "I love you," and hung up for what would be the last time I would hear his deep voice.

My pastor is a very direct man. He tells it like it is. For those who need ecclesiastical words spoken in hushed tones, he's probably not the shepherd for you. But we will never forget him looking us square in the eyes and reminding us with absolute certainty that "James was in London, James was in Charlotte, James was in Kenya. James is in heaven. It's as real as any of those other places. You know exactly where he is and he's never going anywhere else! So what's the problem?" His statement gave me a great sense of assurance. The reminder of heaven's literal space helped me physically place James in my mind's eye. Because he was prone to wanderlust, I smiled at the thought that he was finally relocated to his place of permanent residency.

The Final Storm

We have spent quite a few hours together now on this very personal journey through our storms. I've shared thoughts and realizations with you that I've never said out loud before. Through each chapter I have prayed for you. I've asked God to allow me to encourage you and be a companion to you as you walk through your storm. I cannot leave without asking you one more very important question: Where will you live eternally after your final storm?

"There is salvation in no one else; for there is no other name under heaven that has been given among men by which we must be saved" (Acts 4:12).

Jesus is the only one who can forgive us from sin and present us to a holy God, washed in His blood and clothed in His righteousness. For years I thought my church membership and interest in spiritual things were all I needed, but I had no peace and assurance my eternal destiny was safe and secure. I was convinced making it to heaven depended on being a good person and working hard. Relief flooded my heart when I realized my salvation did not depend on me!

Your spiritual journey uniquely belongs to you. One amazing thing about Jesus is His ability to meet each of us where we are and tenderly call us by name. His love never excludes but is always reaching out to include everyone. There is no one else who knows us, understands, cares, loves, and forgives forever but Jesus. Belonging to Jesus is full

of advantages, and it's His heart's desire for all of us to enjoy the benefits of a personal relationship with Him. If you have been able to recognize His comfort and care for you during your storm, will you stop
now and simply say, "Thank You"?

If you would like to know Him in this personal way, it's a simple act
of faith. Although we don't understand everything about life in Christ,
if we receive His offer by faith and through His Word, we will begin the
journey of eternal companionship and abundant life in Him.

The Good News declares that "if you confess with your mouth
Jesus as Lord, and believe in your heart that God raised Him from the
dead, you will be saved; for with the heart a person believes, resulting
in righteousness, and with the mouth he confesses, resulting in salvation" (Romans 10:9-10).

Before we close I want you to have the opportunity to pray and ask
Jesus to be your Lord and Savior.

> *Dear Lord Jesus,*
>
> *I confess I am a sinner but You are the Savior. Thank You for
> dying on the cross for me. I choose to walk away from my self-
> centered and selfish ways and turn toward You and the abun-
> dant life You came to give me. I believe Jesus is "the way, and
> the truth, and the life; no one comes to the father but through
> [Him]" (John 14:6). I confess with my mouth that Jesus is "the
> resurrection and the life; he who believes in [Him] will live
> even if he dies" (John 11:25). By faith I receive Him as my Lord
> and my Savior this day. In His name, I pray. Amen.*
>
> Today, _____ (date), I accepted the gracious
> invitation to belong to Christ, and I am eternally secure in
> Him. "These things I have written to you who believe in
> the name of the Son of God, so that you may know that
> you have eternal life" (1 John 5:13).

This calls for a celebration! You started this journey sick at heart and
reeling from circumstances. Your circumstances no longer rule you
because with Jesus as Lord He is present to guide and lead you through

every step of the journey called life. Your perspective is no longer limited to this world, but you now have a clearer perspective through His eyes. The ground underneath may shift, but you are standing on the solid rock!

Your Lifeline

If you know your final storm will take you into the presence of Jesus, it softens the blow of all the other storms we encounter on this side. Once Christ's life lives within, the Holy Spirit is present to guide and lead you through the storm-tossed trials and difficulties you face. The Captain of your salvation will show you how to navigate the way through all the disturbances and turbulence of life. No matter what threatens to wipe you out or tear you apart, you have a lifeline to hold on to.

> We know that God causes all things to work together for good to those who love God, to those who are called according to His purpose. For those whom He foreknew, he also predestined to become conformed to the image of His Son (Romans 8:28-29).

If you love God, you can be sure none of your storms are wasted and nothing in your life is useless. It's all being used together. Alone and isolated as a single event or situation—that is not good. But when all things are put together in God's wise and perfect plan, they will be used to display God's power and ability to make everything right in His time. I want you to be able to trust that your storm will produce God's good plan for your life. I want you to have the comfort and confidence of knowing your pain and struggle are not wasted and everything will be used to conform you to His image.

God's Truth Remains

Our circumstances are constantly shifting, and the seasons of life create an ever-flowing current of change. At times the natural order is disrupted by situations we didn't anticipate, and the unpredictability of life casts us into turbulent waters. It's here we must learn to reach toward the one true, constant, unchanging person of Christ. How comforting to know He is always reliable and dependable. "Jesus Christ is the same yesterday and today and forever" (Hebrews 13:8).

Jesus takes every step of the journey with us. In my yesterdays, when my clouds began to gather, He was there. During the ferocious winds and destructive waves, He was there. Today, as the rays of sunlight are breaking through and a new day is dawning, He is here. I'm confident this is not the end because He has promised to be with me forever. Listen to these beautiful words from the book of Lamentations, "The Lord's lovingkindnesses indeed never cease, for His compassions never fail. They are new every morning; great is Your faithfulness. 'The LORD is my portion,' says my soul, 'therefore I have hope in Him'" (Lamentations 3:22-24).

Take these words and hide them in the treasury of your heart. When you encounter new storms and places of uncertainty, draw on the character of your closest Companion, who never changes. His faithfulness endures forever. Set your hope on Him to carry you through to His spacious places.

YOUR STEPS WITH GOD

Thank you for allowing me to come alongside you during this journey. I pray you have received encouragement. As we continue on our way, I would like to offer this prayer for you from my heart to the heart of our heavenly Father.

Dear Lord,

We started this journey together sick at heart and reeling in our personal circumstances, but You have shown us that sorrow and suffering are never wasted when we surrender them to You. We believe You have life and blessings for us from our storms. Help us to keep the spiritual supply of our heart well stocked with Your fresh provisions. Thank You for bringing us to a spacious place and for showing us this is not the end. If heaven is our final destination, we can be confident nothing can wreck us from now and through eternity. You are Lord over every storm and we praise and thank You.

In Jesus' name.

Amen.

GOING DEEPER—

Personal Reflection and Study

God Carries You

*F*riend, thank you for allowing me to walk alongside you. Even though I don't know what storm has changed or is changing the landscape of your life, I pray you wholly trust that God is with you—and that He will carry you through.

This section provides a deeper exploration of truths we've gathered during our shared journey. It's a place to linger awhile and sink deeper into God's promises and hope. Give yourself the luxury of leaning more deeply into His presence. Here, I believe you will find comfort in words that fill your heart, mind, and spirit with assurances of a loving God who sees you, understands you, and cares greatly about your healing.

Each offering explores a "Going Deeper" quote from its featured chapter. I have chosen quotes that illuminate how God is carrying you and me. Then we will walk through evidence of His character and mercy in Scripture and close with a gentle prayer or exercise to help you experience His abiding presence and love more fully.

Take the time you need with each portion so that you will begin to stand in Christ-confidence. His words have supernatural power. As you allow them to saturate your life, faith will grow. "Faith comes by hearing, and hearing by the word of God" (Romans 10:17 NKJV). I believe there's great value in doing this either on your own or with a group of caring people.

Most of all, I pray this time of reflection will strengthen the reality of God's hands embracing you, holding your every need, and carrying you…now and always.

Going Deeper – 1

Regardless of the storms currently raging or the ones still way out on the horizon, Jesus is here to remind us, "After I have been raised, I will go before you to Galilee" (Matthew 26:32 NKJV). He has a plan to follow every crisis.

—*from "My Storm Strikes"*

There are times in life when the circumstances are so unfamiliar we find ourselves at an utter loss for direction. We have no prior experience to help us handle the situation because it's completely foreign to us. We may have turned to others to help us make sense of our struggle or to express our deepest pain only to receive a response that leaves us feeling more alone. We need to be able to cry out to the Lord.

Have you cried out these words, "Oh my God, what are we going to do?" He hears your desperate plea for help. Maybe your question is different during your storm. Make it a cry to God to express what is happening in your life and what your heart needs from your Lord right now.

When you cry out to God, do you have confidence in His understanding or knowledge of your circumstances? He is the One who has all the insights and understanding no matter what your need is and no matter how dark your storm has become.

In the following three Scriptures, God invites us to turn to Him. Read them carefully. Meditate on them. Allow yourself this opportunity to take a long warm soak in His words and He will minister to you here.

1. "Call to Me and I will answer you, and I will tell you great and mighty things, which you do not know" (Jeremiah 33:3).

> How does this invitation make you feel?

> How does this invitation help you in this moment?

> Are you aware of mighty things God is revealing to you even now?

2. "Therefore the LORD longs to be gracious to you, and therefore He waits on high to have compassion on you. For the LORD is a God of justice; how blessed are those who long for Him" (Isaiah 30:18).

> How have you experienced God's compassion in the past and in this circumstance?

> What do you long for most as you seek God's help and presence?

3. "If any of you lacks wisdom, let him ask of God, who gives to all men generously and without reproach, and it will be given to him" (James 1:5).

> What specifically do you need wisdom for right now?

> What has become your greatest lack during this storm? Write it down and ask God for His abundance to fill that need.

* * *

The verses we just explored are God's words of truth for anyone who will take Him at His word. It does take that leap of faith to embrace

His words and believe they are for you. *They are for you.* How does that feel? Has it sunk in?

How do you feel about allowing God to be your guide through this unknown place in your life? If one of these verses sparked hope and gave you confidence that you are not alone in this, consider writing it out in your journal or typing it up and printing it out. Then you can place it where you will see it throughout your daily routine. Friend, believe me, there is great comfort and hope that fills us when God's words, promises, and hopes become a part of our thought patterns.

If you want to read further about someone who found himself in a very difficult situation with no clue what to do when surrounded by his enemy, read 2 Chronicles 20:1-30. The man's name is Jehoshaphat. You will find some literal and practical steps he took and see how God directed his steps through the crisis. You will be encouraged by God's willingness to direct your steps through your crisis when you seek Him.

Deeper into His Presence

One of the most humbling and simple prayers prayed in Scripture is one we can pray together today. With no clear answer or certain direction to take, Jehoshaphat prayed these words, "Oh our God…we are powerless before this great multitude [of decisions and problems that] are coming against us; nor do we know what to do, but our eyes are on You" (2 Chronicles 20:12).

Pray this verse and list those needs, problems, decisions, and obstacles that seem to be countering your healing and your hope right now. Turn each of them over to God's care and spend time resting in the knowledge that God has heard each cry and He is with you.

God has a plan. And while you may not see it or even feel it right now, you can call out to Him with complete confidence that He sees your storm, He is right there with you, and He is unfolding a path of healing. Rest in this mighty, wondrous truth: God longs to be gracious to you. He awaits your prayers, your trust, and your cry for help. Even before you utter the words, He knows your heart. By lifting up your storm and your grief journey to Him, you are partnering with God in His plan and His hope for your future.

Going Deeper - 2

Problems are going to be part of this life and this world. We are going to experience difficulty and disappointment. Our picture of perfect is going to be all messed up—count on it. With Jesus, though, we are stronger than the problem and can take the pressure.

—from "God's Weather Forecast"

L ife's hardships can cast a shadow on our picturesque dreams and desires. But looking ahead is not meant to be overwhelming or defeating. God longs for us to be ready for those times when we encounter challenges. He has given us His truth and His forecast—including its warnings and wisdom—and He gives us the hope of His presence and power to bring us through.

When David was being pursued by his enemies, rejected by his own people, and threatened by his captors, he had nothing tangible to hold on to, so he held fast to his hope and trust in the Lord and wrote a psalm of praise and thanks. "The eyes of the LORD are toward the righteous and His ears are open to their cry. The face of the LORD is against evildoers, to cut off the memory of them from the earth. The righteous cry, and the LORD hears and delivers them out of all their troubles. The LORD is near to the brokenhearted and saves those who are crushed in spirit" (Psalm 34:15-18).

When you have nothing to hold on to but the Word of God, you can choose to praise and thank Him. And you can cry out with a desperate plea for help and He will hear you. He's present and will deliver you. He's near and will save you from your trouble. Deliverance is not a magic act that picks us up and places us somewhere far out of the reach of our storm. Rather, He uses each affliction to strengthen you and enable you to walk *through* the circumstances of your storm.

My friend, when your eyes are swollen closed from tears you may find it difficult to see Jesus. But remember that His presence is not based on what we can see with our eyes or feel emotionally. His presence is guaranteed because of His Word.

God is looking straight at you today and is listening to you. Cry out to Him.

* * *

I encourage you to take your Bible and read Psalm 34. Using David's pattern, rewrite this psalm as your own personal song of praise and thanks to God.

Use words of blessing, praise, boasting in Him, and exaltation to place Him above your circumstances. (verses 1-3)

What happens when we seek the Lord and no one else? (verse 4)

What flees when I seek Him?

What changes about me? (verse 5)

What does God do for you? (verses 6-7)

What happens within you when you begin to take Him into your life and experience Him? (verses 8-14)

How does the Lord actively engage in your life circumstances? (verses 15-19)

When we make Him our refuge, we are always…(verses 20-22)

I pray this exercise lifts your heart and fans the flame of faith within your innermost being. God's children are never doomed to destruction no matter the circumstances of this life. The outlook is neither depressing nor defeating when we put our trust in Him.

Deeper into His Presence

Knowing God's character helps us to withstand the pressure from without because He makes us strong within. He is our Deliverer in every storm. His presence makes us stronger than the afflictions. That, my friend, is a cause for praise! Write a prayer to God as Deliverer. Take time to feel the comfort of His presence as He strengthens you in this storm.

Going Deeper - 3

The quality of life after the storm is largely dependent on the attention we give to our spiritual life before the storm.

—*from "God's Survival Kit"*

The specifics of our challenges are not nearly as important as our own spiritual readiness to endure storms and to experience wholeness after them. But spiritual preparation requires that we invest time, energy, and resources. No one experiences a real victory without engaging in a struggle of some sort. And we're all engaged in a spiritual battle whether we recognize it or not.

While many people live as spectators and simply follow the winning team, those who follow Jesus recognize the opponent and are called to engage and win. I must admit that I'd rather experience wins without having to experience a struggle. But if Jesus had to prepare for the opposition He faced, why would I think I could wing it?

So how do we train for spiritual battles? Let's take a look at six practical steps we would follow if training for a competition of any kind.

1. *Identify your interest.* Is spiritual life a priority for you? If so, make a commitment to be spiritually equipped so you always view challenges and blessings through the lens of faith.

2. *Find someone to train you.* I like to start my day with Jesus. It means some days begin very early, but it's my concentrated time alone with Him. My friend who swam throughout her college years was in the pool every morning at 5:30. Our spiritual training requires this same

discipline. When you love something, you are eager to embrace it no matter the sacrifice.

3. *Hone your skill.* The most important spiritual skill is to learn to read God's Word and listen to His voice. I've said this many times, but it's the truth: God speaks personally to you. The Bible is a love letter written from God to you. He wants to "bring [you] into the wilderness and speak kindly to [you] there" (Hosea 2:14).

4. *Build your strength.* Prayer is our way to access the deep well of God's strength, so learn to pray. Read the prayers found in Scripture, pray for yourself and for your ears to hear Him speak, and pray for others. In time you'll live with a strengthened attitude of prayer.

5. *Increase your endurance.* Knowing the fundamentals isn't enough to secure victory. We have to consistently practice them in daily life to proficiently apply the truth of the Word. "Prove yourselves doers of the word, and not merely hearers who delude themselves" (James 1:22).

6. *Compete with an opponent.* We live out spiritual strength through our daily actions and interactions to prove it's changing us within. We don't know what a day will bring, but if we're developing in our faith walk, we'll discover that we have what we need for the day's adversity.

Peter is a great example of someone who tried to wing it in his own power and found himself totally ill equipped for the trials of following Jesus. He's the disciple who denied Jesus, although he swore it would never happen. It usually takes a wipeout (or two) for us to realize we don't have the inner strength to stand when the winds of adversity begin to howl. As an older man with many life experiences behind him, Peter knows and shares the importance of spiritual priorities. He wants us to develop our inner man with the provisions God supplies.

Read Peter's prayer for believers and experience this as the Holy

Spirit's voice praying over you today. Read it out loud and linger over the words of hope and blessing.

> Grace and peace be multiplied to you in the knowledge of God and of Jesus our Lord; seeing that His divine power has granted to us everything pertaining to life and godliness, through the true knowledge of Him who called us by His own glory and excellence. For by these He has granted to us His precious and magnificent promises, so that by them you may become partakers of the divine nature, having escaped the corruption that is in the world by lust (2 Peter 1:2-4).

Now consider these thoughts as you read, apply, and pray these words.

- What do you gain when you grow in the knowledge of God and of Jesus?
- What have you been given to live life in Christ?
- Who called you to belong to Him and by what authority or power?
- What has He supplied us with?
- What is His purpose for giving these to us?

My friend, our generous Father has supplied all we need to overcome the threats against us. Now it is our choice whether or not we prepare and develop His abundant provisions for us. With Him, we can be prepared with supplies for a victorious life regardless of our circumstances!

Deeper into His Presence

If you've had a wipeout along the way and find yourself utterly unprepared, please allow this to encourage you. It's never too late to get started, and God honors the one who is willing to say, "I can't do life without You." He's always willing to take our failures and turn us into spiritual winners.

Pray today with intention and with listening ears. Take time to confess your failings, to acknowledge that you need God, and to ask for His wisdom as you depend on His spiritual supplies.

Going Deeper – 4

> Our survival depends on knowing where we
> can go to be hidden from the wrath of the
> storm and then actually going to that shelter.
>
> —*from "Shelter from the Storm"*

There was a time in my life when I was homeless. That may come as a surprise to you, but it's true. Oh, I'm not talking about the literal sense of having no physical space to call home. I'm talking about having no place to go where I knew I was always safe, secure, and accepted no matter what was happening in my life. I had all the usual signs of a homeless person. I was restless and always in search of something to make me feel connected. I had nowhere to go that gave me peace. And no matter what or whom I had, I was lonely and empty. I tried to satisfy my inner needs by holding tightly to possessions, accomplishments, and anything that gave me a sense of significance.

I always had a gnawing hunger in my spirit that nothing could satisfy. I was dirty; covered with guilt and shame. I was unhealthy, sick at heart, demanding, needy, and begging for attention. I was angry, resentful, offended, and misunderstood. I had everything the world offered but was without a permanent shelter for comfort and protection.

Even though I had much to be grateful for, I was becoming more and more aware of what I was missing. Because we're created in the image of God, we have a void within us that only He can fill and satisfy. Religion, goodness, church membership, relationships, and a nice home will not fill it. I had all of those, but still I was empty.

Then one day a man stopped and noticed me. He reached into the deep recesses of my heart and touched me with His love and kindness. He reached out to take my hand and offered me forgiveness for my sins.

He met me where I was and made eternal life in Him available to me. The man's name is Jesus, and needless to say I accepted His gracious invitation to become His child.

Now He feeds me daily with His living Word and I never hunger or thirst. He gives me living water that springs up into a well of everlasting life. I am washed in His blood and I'm cleansed whiter than snow. I am robed in His righteousness. He gave me a new identity, and He is my soul's satisfaction. I'm never lonely because He is with me always. Jesus has a plan and a purpose for me, and it's to prosper me and give me hope and a future. He has good works already prepared for me to do and has given me spiritual gifts to use to accomplish His appointed works through me. I have an eternal inheritance with all the saints and He has prepared a place for me.

Now when storms rise, I'm reminded of the years when I had nowhere to go and am grateful for my eternal shelter.

* * *

Would this simple prayer from Psalm 61 be something you could say from your heart to God? If yes, will you stop right here to say, "Thank You, Lord"?

> You have been a refuge for me, a tower of strength against the enemy. Let me dwell in Your tent forever; let me take refuge in the shelter of Your wings (Psalm 61:3-4).

Have you been looking for a dwelling place? I'm not talking about a new house or a vacation home or a change in location. A real estate agent or Zillow.com can't help you with this search. Let me share the details with you.

He is the foundation. "No man can lay a foundation other than the one which is laid, which is Jesus Christ" (1 Corinthians 3:11).

He is the cornerstone. "So then you are no longer strangers and aliens, but you are fellow citizens with the saints and are of God's household, having been built on the foundation of the apostles and prophets, Christ Jesus Himself being the corner stone, in whom the whole building, being fitted together, is growing into a holy temple in the Lord; whom you also are being built together into a dwelling of God in the Spirit" (Ephesians 2:19-22).

He is the door. "I am the door; if anyone enters through Me, he will be saved, and will go in and out and find pasture" (John 10:9).

He is our hiding place. "Behold, a king will reign righteously and princes will rule justly. Each will be like a refuge from the wind, and a shelter from the storm, like streams of water in a dry country, like the shade of a huge rock in a parched land" (Isaiah 32:1-2).

He is our habitation. "You have made the LORD, my refuge, even the Most High your dwelling place" (Psalm 91:9).

Deeper into His Presence

My friend, the offer for a safe and secure shelter from the storm is always open. There will always be room for more to settle in and the light of life is always on. Jesus is holding the door open wide and inviting us to step into life with Him. Will you join me there? We could be members of the same household of faith, and I would really like to be kin to you!

Dear Lord, I am grateful and thankful for the place of safety and security I have in You. Even when I am in the midst of raging storms, I am huddled down and safely tucked up against Your heart. Your everlasting arms are circled around me, and I am relieved to be sheltered in Your love. I am confident the foundation will not cave because my life is built on You, my Cornerstone. Whatever comes...thank You for being my shelter. In Jesus' name I pray and praise, amen.

Going Deeper – 5

> Life is an uncertain journey, and at different intervals along the way we will come to crossroads that require a choice.
>
> —*from "The Swirl"*

*C*hoices present themselves virtually every minute of the day. Choices give us the impression we are in control because we can have a say-so. But they also can require an overwhelming overload of decisions that can leave us more confused and out of control than we were before we started. This is the junction where fear and faith intersect. This is the place where we deliberately choose to accept or reject the reality of our own painful storm and either run toward or run away from the truth of God's Word. God longs to guide you in the way that you should go. He has declared Himself to be a light in the darkness and a voice in the wilderness. All we have to do is call out to Him. He wants to relieve us of the weight of our excuses and deliver us from the exhausting effort expended in trying to outrun or outsmart the storm's devastation. "In returning and rest you will be saved, in quietness and trust is your strength" (Isaiah 30:15).

If you find yourself standing at a crossroads, please listen carefully to the promise offered to anyone who will stop spinning and scheming and just be still in the presence of God. "Your ears will hear a word behind you, 'This is the way, walk in it,' whenever you turn to the right or to the left" (Isaiah 30:21).

Jesus is the answer. He is the source of all wisdom and knowledge, and nothing is hidden from Him. He is able to shed His divine light on our path. Wherever we go, He is present to illumine our insights and understanding. His knowledge stands above all, and His directions never fail. His Spirit resides within us as an internal GPS system to guide us safely through this storm.

* * *

While waiting in a prison cell, the apostle Paul wrote a letter to Timothy, his son in the faith and fellow minister of the gospel. Paul was facing the last of his many personal life storms. He was awaiting trial before Emperor Nero. Knowing his end was eminent, he wrote these words: "For this reason I also suffer these things; nevertheless I am not ashamed, for I know whom I have believed and am persuaded that He is able to keep what I have committed to Him until that Day" (2 Timothy 1:12 NKJV).

Whom have you believed in?

When have you believed in someone or something that has not been able to come through for you?

When you have no idea how to explain what's happening in your life and your choices or explanations seem to be falling through, you need to know *whom* it is you can believe. The most important issue is not what to believe but whom to believe. No other religion besides Christianity invites you to know God the Father, Son, and Holy Spirit in a personal and relational way. Only through Jesus' life, words, and teachings are we able to truly know God. Jesus said, "He who has seen me has seen the Father" (John 14:9). God came to be with us through Jesus—Immanuel.

The situation in your life right now may have no obvious or logical explanation. You may be in a place you could never have prepared for in a practical sense. I want to encourage you to choose to cry out to the One who is prepared and equipped to carry you through anything.

Has this place of disappointment or loss in your life revealed your need for someone who is able? Jesus is able to do for you what you cannot do for yourself. He is able to do what no other person or philosophy or religion can ever do for you. He is able to bring peace, joy, hope, and faith because He is the source of peace, joy, hope, and faith...even in the bleakest situations.

During the darkest days of my storm, I possessed a deep abiding sense of peace because I knew Jesus was with me. I couldn't hold on to Him in my own strength or determination. I had none. But His Spirit within me was exerting His strength on my behalf. That strength is in each of us when we choose Jesus.

May I suggest there is no time like the present for you to decide to become persuaded about the person of Jesus? Don't seek to find resolutions or relief. Simply find relationship with Him. When that happens, He will give you resolutions to your choices and questions. He will give you relief from your anxiety and fear. This can be your personal assurance today: "I love those who love me; and those who diligently seek me will find me" (Proverbs 8:17).

Throughout my children's years growing up we ended our days with what became affectionately known as worship time. Don't get the wrong idea that everyone came piously or enthusiastically—especially as they grew older. But it was great time as a family to seek God together. When they were small, we always read a Bible story and then asked questions to see who had listening ears. Children love to show what they know. One night as the questions were being asked, James gave his little sister a tip. "The right answer is always Jesus no matter what the question is." So many years later I am struck at how profound that statement is. Jesus is always the right answer.

Deeper into His Presence

Maybe it would be helpful to you to make a column of the questions your storm has stirred up. In prayer, commit this list to Him. Now beside each item, write His name, JESUS. Today that may feel too simple and vague, but as you grow to know Him your faith will grow to know whom you believed, and you will be persuaded that He is able to keep that which you have committed to Him until that day.

Behind that why is a deep desire to be shown a
bigger picture, an explanation, or an outcome
that could remotely be worthy of the loss or
worth going on in life bearing that loss.

—from "Crucify the 'Why?'"

*W*hen life is disrupted by storms and crises, it's hard to imagine there is any purpose apart from ruin. The definition of a storm suggests a violent disturbance that creates commotion, turmoil, and turbulence in our lives. We can heed storm warnings and secure storm supplies, but when the storm actually descends on us, there seems no purpose other than to destroy us. This is when we often find ourselves in personal conflict and even offended by God. Why would He allow this?

I honestly thought I understood the situation and knew what was best or right in my personal storm. I prayed and believed. I took promises and pleaded with God to fulfill them in our lives. I didn't waiver with unbelief or falter along the long and often bumpy road of life with James. I saw promises fulfilled at times and dreams dashed at others. I witnessed victories in some seasons and overwhelming defeat in others. But I was not prepared for the sudden death of my son. I was offended that God would seem to quit on me—on us—now!

You may know exactly what I mean. Maybe you have believed for healing and prayed for it in the lives of others. You may have actually seen miracles in the natural realm, and yet you or someone you love is struggling with physical pain and sickness. You may have lost your loved one through divorce after you prayed and believed for a healed marriage. You are wondering if you missed the truth and totally

misunderstood the Scriptures, but in the end you really wonder why
God did this to you.

* * *

I find the words of Paul to be a source of insight and comfort, and I
pray you will too. These verses are often chosen as the text read at a wed-
ding because they speak of the excellence of love, but Paul is referring
to the perfect love of God. He has this insight for us, "Now we see in a
mirror dimly, but then face to face; now I know in part, but then I shall
know fully just as I also have been fully known" (1 Corinthians 13:12).

Today, as you survey the devastation of your storm, you may be able
to see only a distorted portion of the full story. This view can distort
your sense of God's love. But when we are with Him and viewing the
whole picture with divine clarity, we will see our storm through His
lens. What I know and understand now is partial and incomplete, but
there will be a time when I will see the whole completed product just
as God sees it now.

God is operating outside of time and space because He is omnip-
otent and omniscient. We are bound by time and limited by space
because we are not yet complete. Our perspective is obscured. Our
vision is imperfect. Up close things get very blurry at times, and when
things are far away, we cannot make out important details. But one
day—when we stand in the presence of Jesus, in the light of His glory—
all things will become perfectly clear. We will see the things that seem
out of place and unfair now as He sees them. We will have His perspective and His clarity. It's going to be amazing. I suspect I will be ashamed
or at least greatly humbled for doubting His goodness and demanding
His explanation for why it is this way now.

Would you like to join me to bow before the One who loves us
perfectly and tell Him, "I'm sorry for underestimating Your goodness
toward me"? Now let's thank Him that one day we will see Him face-
to-face and see things as they truly are. Until then, I'm asking Him for
strength and grace to wait and believe.

I recently revisited a familiar passage of Scripture while preparing a devotional. I want to share it with you because it was a blessing that ministered to my heart. Luke 2:19 holds these familiar words, "Mary treasured up all these things, pondering them in her heart." I went back to see what "all these things" were and found they were the parts and pieces of understanding she was given by Gabriel, by the Holy Spirit, by her cousin Elizabeth, by Joseph, by the shepherds, and by Simeon and Anna in the temple. Things were not completely clear or fully understood by Mary. She was part of the greatest story ever told but would endure deep loss and sorrow.

Personally, I saw our life storms and disruptions as partial fragments and portions of God's story in our lives. Though some parts seem random and unwelcome, each part is precious and valued for completing His perfecting work in all of us.

I thought of all the broken and ragged pieces in my life that I have been unsure what to do with. I saw them all being swept up together, and I took them as precious treasures instead of sharp, harmful offenses. I have decided to keep them close to my heart and trust that God will use them all in His own good time to piece together His redemption story in my life. Over every crack and seam I will be able to trace His hand, and it will be a beautiful whole one sweet day.

Deeper into His Presence

Maybe you would like to gather up your fragmented pieces and place them in His hands. Write them down and then pray to release each one of those fragments to God's care. There they will become the treasures of your heart that you can ponder over.

Let this prayer express and strengthen your belief in God's power, mercy, and understanding.

> *Thank You, Jesus, for Your great love for me. Only You can turn these broken pieces into beautiful treasures. You are the Redeemer. I trust You with my circumstances, my needs, and with my future. I trust You with my big picture. Amen.*

Going Deeper – 7

The choice to surrender is an intentional one.
It's the deliberate act of releasing our lives,
hearts, and circumstances to God and asking
Him to take over all control...Real surrender is
allowing God to be God on His terms, not ours.

—from "Surrender"

For some reason my problem with surrender is that I'm always afraid God's terms will be unfair and painful. It boils down to the question of trusting Him to be for me and not against me. Recently, I found myself extremely stressed. I had invited my mother to come and visit before I knew about an extended assignment with a shortened deadline. I tried desperately to control the situation. It was stressful, frustrating, and futile. The more I tried to manage the details, the more tension I felt.

Then I remembered that God is for me. He wants to help me. Deliberately, I took my meddling hands off the situation and placed the conflict in His. It was an intentional act of surrender in my daily life. He reminded me that when I allow Him to control my time and attention I have perfect peace. I set the project aside and turned my full attention to this special time with my mother. He honored my surrender with one of the most meaningful visits she and I have shared in a long time. And He gave me peace to trust Him with the outcome of the assignment. This wasn't a crisis of tremendous proportion, but the lessons in allowing Him to take charge were tremendous.

The practice of surrendering daily equips us for the surprises that come our way through storms and crises. It reminds us that God not only is able, but He is ready to take control of our struggles for us. Jesus said, "Come to Me, all you who labor and are heavy laden, and I will give you rest" (Matthew 11:28 NKJV). Does this invitation give you a sense of relief and hope? Why do you need this invitation right now in your life?

Come to Jesus. Your doctor, counselor, pastor, or friends cannot carry your load. We are invited to come to Jesus first because He is the only one who can take the weight from us and give us rest. All other sources and resources are limited. They can give you advice, ideas, sympathy, and opinions, but they cannot give you spiritual rest. Sometimes we try to reinforce our side of the tug-of-war rope with all the other resources in our lives and forget that all we need to do is to put it in the hands of Jesus.

Surrender doesn't mean we quit. Quitting is disengaging and walking away in defeat. Surrender is staying completely engaged with God in control. Jesus invited us to follow Him. He leads and we follow, but we're working together to accomplish His good and perfect will. Not because He can't do it without us, but because He allows us the opportunity to participate with Him.

* * *

I've noticed over the years in women's ministry that it's acceptable and common to state, "I'm a control freak." Our culture embraces the concept of micromanaging our lives and everyone else's too. Christlike culture embraces the position of being a follower and surrendering control to Him.

Spend time reflecting on the following three verses while you examine your attitude about surrender.

1. "Search me, O God, and know my heart; try me and know my anxious thoughts; and see if there be any hurtful way in me, and lead me in the everlasting way" (Psalm 139:23-24).

   Ask the Holy Spirit to show you your own heart. When we're willing, He will use these insights to strengthen and heal us not strip and harm us. What insights are you given?

Have you ever taken pride in being a control freak or found it very difficult to release control of your life to Him?

2. "Even before there is a word on my tongue, behold, O LORD, You know it all" (Psalm 139:4).

Remember, He knows us better than we know ourselves. There is no reason to be defensive or to try to justify ourselves in His presence. Are you insulted or made uncomfortable by being asked to be a follower instead of the leader? If your answer is yes, this is an opportunity to ask God to forgive and free you from self-pride. He is for you.

3. "The eyes of the LORD move to and fro throughout the earth that He may strongly support those whose heart is completely His" (2 Chronicles 16:9).

Would God say your heart belongs completely to Him?

Deeper into His Presence

Does your life seem fractured, scattered, and in hopeless disorder? We don't have the intellectual, emotional, or spiritual capacity to repair the damage. This realization can lead us to the invitation to surrender all the broken pieces of our lives to the Lord.

My prayer for you is to be filled with hope as you read the words of Psalm 68. David speaks of God as our burden-bearer and the one who gives us deliverance from our enemies. They build our confidence that He is more than able to take over our lives. "Blessed be the Lord, who daily bears our burden, the God who is our salvation. God is to us a God of deliverances; and to GOD the Lord belong escapes from death" (Psalm 68:19-20).

Write or say a prayer of surrender to the Lord. Give Him your daily burdens with peace and confidence.

I encourage you to remember that God is beside
you, and He wants to accompany you through
the grief journey. You do not need to live on an
isolated island of sorrow while remnants of the
storm block your path to healing.

—*from "Moving Through Grief"*

*P*art of the challenge in grieving is the unpredictable nature
of where and when the emotions and expressions of mourning will show up. Grief leaves us feeling vulnerable and emotionally
exposed, and others rarely know how to respond to that raw expression
of our wounds. Today's cultural practices have little time or patience
with the grieving process, and few know how to embrace mourning as
healthy and necessary.

Do you sense friends and family feeling unsure of what to do and
how to help you? Try to remember that for many of them it's not
because they don't care. They simply don't know how. The lack of
understanding from others adds to the aloneness of the grief journey.
It's already isolating because it's a solitary experience. No one else can
grieve for you, and you can't grieve for anyone else.

This can be discouraging until we are assured we are not utterly
abandoned and isolated from God's solace and care. When I feel
alone or am immersed in sorrow, these facts from God's Word give
me security:

- God is with me because He is still Immanuel (Matthew 1:23).

- God goes before me the way the pillar of cloud by day and
  the pillar of fire by night did for the children of Israel in

the wilderness. God knows I'm in a wilderness and need help (Exodus 13:21).

- God watches over me. He is the Guardian of my soul (1 Peter 2:25).

- Underneath me are His everlasting arms. They are always there to catch me when I stumble and fall (Deuteronomy 33:27).

For those who belong to Him, no place, no matter how dark, can ever cut us off or deny us the loving care of the One who loves us unconditionally and whose eye is always on us. When you have the feeling that no one understands or could possibly know how you feel, remember there is one exception, and His name is Jesus.

How fortunate we are to be in the comfort of the Lord's presence during our storms.

How would it help you if people around you could understand your need for time and space? What else do you wish others understood about your grief journey?

* * *

Take a close look at the three wonderful promises God gives to Hezekiah, a king in Israel who was in deep trouble. These are promises for us too. "I have heard your prayer, I have seen your tears; behold, I will heal you" (2 Kings 20:5).

1. *I have heard your prayer.* God is always listening to His children cry. He invites us to cry out to Him and pour out our hearts in His presence. Your thoughts, fears, cares, and concerns all matter to Him. That is what prayer is—heart cries to the most alert and attentive listener you could ever have. He will never ever respond with, "Not now," "I'm too busy," "Can you call later?" or "I don't know how to help you."

   What do you need God to hear from your heart today?

2. *I have seen your tears.* What a relief to know our tears are noticed and that they matter to our heavenly Father. He is not uncomfortable with them or oblivious to them. David made this request to Him, "Put my tears in Your bottle. Are they not in Your book?" A record of every single tear is being kept, and they are stored away with Him. They count. There is no need to hide your hurt and pain. Cry tears of sorrow and sadness freely and openly, and remember that God's loving hand is gathering every single one.

What pain or burden do you need God to see and take from you?

3. *I will heal you.* Hezekiah was physically ill, but prayers and tears surrendered to God brought forth healing. We can also anticipate that our prayers and tears surrendered to Him will bring healing to our broken heart. No matter the source or the reason behind your tears, they are worthy offerings honored by God. Remember, in the quietness of your dark place He is listening carefully and wiping your face so gently you may not have realized it was Him.

How have you experienced healing so far?

How do these three promises change your perspective and your sense of hope for your grief journey?

Which promise do you hold especially tight today?

Deeper into His Presence

At all times, know that God is beside you. He is holding your heart, your hurt, and your hope in His hands. It's also true that He is holding your healing. Do not believe for a moment, even in the dark, that you are alone in this journey. Repeat the promises that were given to Hezekiah in the past and to you, again, today and every day. They will breathe hope into your life.

Do you feel lonely and misunderstood? Let God be your companion. He is able and He is loving. And He will not let the debris of the storm block your path to wholeness. May this prayer lift up your need to God and remind you of your hope in His ever-present comfort.

> *Lord, help me to feel Your presence. When the impatience or distance of others leads me deeper into sorrow, lead me to the shelter of Your love, forgiveness, care, and understanding. In this shelter You hear me, see me, and heal me. Thank You for always knowing who I am, what I face, and what I need even when I cannot find the words to express it. In Jesus' name, amen.*

Going Deeper - 9

His Spirit is the Comforter, and there are no
substitutions for His deep, abiding presence.

—*from "Moving into Comfort"*

*L*ife storms can create significant discomfort in our lives. The changes and disruptions, the sadness and sorrow, and the strain and stress wear us down and empty us out. Our stability is threatened and our faith is taunted and tested.

Would you consider this idea? Our afflictions are not something that have been done to us but have been allowed by God for us. It's hard to imagine how this could be true, but I want to give you a real-life example that may serve as a comforting insight for you. After a long life filled with struggles and personal life storms, David gave us these words, "I know, O LORD, that Your judgments are righteous, and that in faithfulness You have afflicted me. O may Your lovingkindness comfort me, according to Your word to Your servant. May Your compassion come to me that I may live, for Your law is my delight" (Psalm 119:75-77).

If afflictions are expressions of God's faithfulness to us, then His comfort is a demonstration of His loving-kindness directed toward our lives. It's the assurance of His unchanging and unconditional love that allows us to know and believe we are under His care in all circumstances. Like David, you may have felt that your affliction would drain life from you, and you are desperate for comfort that will soothe and heal you. God is the source of that comfort.

Can you believe that nothing in your life is deeper, greater, or too hard for Him to fill with His comfort? Has anything in your grief journey made this difficult to embrace? Take a moment to let the truth wash over you and fill you.

During times of affliction and sorrow, I have learned utter dependence on God. In the hard and painful realities of my life, I have been pressed to Jesus. And that is where I have experienced His grace, love, and comfort in supernatural ways. It's in these moments I recognize that my affliction is a tender blessing because comfort comes through Christ alone.

This is not a simple or easy place or perspective to reach. We must spend time in the wilderness of affliction before we long for the kind and depth of comfort God gives. When running from and resenting the changes our storms have created, we reach a state of emotional upheaval. We become desperate for something or someone to lessen the pain and ease the ache in our heart. The usual expressions of comfort from people all around us are needed and appreciated, but they never last in a way that can sustain or carry us through. People eventually forget as pressing storms break in their lives, words are lost, and flowers fade. Then we're left feeling vulnerable and alone. This is when each of us might wonder, "Who is available to comfort and care for me?"

If your storm surge is behind you, think for a few minutes about the things that linger in your heart that brought you comfort when you were being tossed and torn. I still marvel at God's loving touch through people. I have shared some of mine with you throughout this book, and many of those memories continue to give me a deep sense of being cared for and loved. Take a minute to allow your memories to bless and encourage you. They are gifts. Yet even with those words and gestures from others, our void and pain remain because the most thoughtful expressions of human care are only temporary measures of comfort. They show us an example of God's love, but they are not substitutions for the lasting balm that only God provides.

* * *

Jesus knew our needs would always exceed our ability to fulfill them. The world will never be able to provide a lasting state of ease or an abiding sense of comfort. When His disciples—His closest friends on earth—were facing uncertainty and were uneasy about the future, He assured them with these words, "I will ask the Father, and He will give you another Helper, that He may be with you forever; that is the Spirit of truth, whom the world cannot receive, because it does not see Him or know Him, but you know Him because He abides with you and will be in you" (John 14:16-17).

There is the difference. There is the cure instead of a temporary fix. He remains permanently with me and is in me! Would you like to pray along with me? *Welcome, Holy Spirit. I know how much I need You! I open myself to Your abiding presence and thank You for living within me. Amen.*

If you're like me, your afflictions have taught you that your need for help is around the clock and forever. I'm talking about the need for the resident Comforter and Helper who never goes off duty. This is the security Jesus gives us when we allow His Spirit to have access and control of our lives. His presence is abiding and His comfort is limitless. He is able to comfort in the most complete way because He knows and sees everything. He sees in secret and yet He meets our needs in an obvious and open way. We become outward evidence of His abiding presence in us when we are filled with the ease of His supernatural comfort and care.

Jesus knew life would be overwhelming at times, and by asking His Father to give us His Spirit, He provided what no one else could. What a blessing to be a recipient of God's love and care.

Take time to meditate on the fact that He sees into the deep crevices of your heart. He meets each one of us where we are and offers His abiding presence. Now receive the Father's open reward of comfort and allow Him to lift your head and flood your heart with rest and peace. Thank Him.

Deeper into His Presence

As he prays for the believers in Thessalonica, the apostle Paul gives us this prayer as a way to connect our heavy hearts to the heart of God. Receive these words into your spirit and as a prayer prayed over you. "Now may our Lord Jesus Christ Himself, and our God and Father, who has loved us and given us everlasting consolation and good hope by grace, comfort your hearts and establish you in every good word and work" (2 Thessalonians 2:16-17 NKJV).

Allow these sincere words of truth to fill you with strength and hope.

Going Deeper – 10

The waiting time is an opportunity for the
healing power of the Word to penetrate deep
into our being and for us to actively receive the
Spirit to empower us with fresh strength and
clear vision.

—from "Open the Door"

Few things agitate human nature quite the way waiting does. We
spend a tremendous amount of time trying to avoid the day-to-
day episodes of waiting. We wait in line, wait for our turn, wait for the
bus, the train, the elevator, the light to turn. We wait for phone calls to
be returned, test results to be delivered, payday, one day, someday! We
wait for an opportunity, wait for prayers to be answered, wait for God
to open the door. Because waiting is an inevitable part of life, maybe
it's time to learn how to wait in a way that is positive and productive.

Is this period of waiting in your journey beginning to frustrate
you? Are you climbing the walls trying to find a way to break out of
the uncomfortable place you are in? Can I encourage you to consider
that this waiting room God has placed you in can be productive and
purposeful? This place can be used to strengthen and empower you for
the rest of the journey. While we wait, God works; and if we will allow
Him to, He will make it worth the wait.

"Wait on the LORD; be of good courage, and He shall strengthen
your heart; wait, I say, on the LORD!" (Psalm 27:14 NKJV). When the
focus of waiting shifts from our discomfort to the Lord, we are filled
with His courage. Instead of merely hoping for relief and reprieve, we
can eagerly anticipate Him. When we open our hearts to hear from

Him, we are filled with His strength. The waiting room has the potential to become a place of preparation instead of agitation.

* * *

Let me share a few examples from Scripture of people who waited
and who were moved forward by God in their season of waiting. These
stories spoke personally to me. If one of these resonates in your heart,
get your Bible and a notebook and make your own journal of lessons
that give you strength and courage.

- Noah waited while wickedness increased. Waited to go
  into the ark. Waited for rain to fall. Waited for the rains
  to stop falling. Waited for the waters to recede. Waited for
  the raven to return. Waited for the dove to return. Waited
  to be called out. (Genesis 6:8–9:29)

- Abraham waited for the promise of descendants. Waited
  for the promised son for 25 years. (Genesis 12–22)

- Joseph waited for his dreams to be fulfilled. Waited to be
  rescued from the pit. Waited to be released from prison.
  Waited for the baker to remember him. Waited to meet
  Benjamin and to see his father again. (Genesis 37–50)

- Moses waited in a basket to be rescued from a death threat
  against all Hebrew baby boys. Waited 40 years in the wilderness to return to Egypt. Waited for Pharaoh to let the
  people go out from Egypt. Waited 40 years circling in the
  desert with stubborn and rebellious people. (Exodus 2–40)

Your heart will be renewed with courage and strength as you explore
the many powerful stories in the Old Testament about the waiting
rooms of others. Daniel waited in the lions' den. His three Hebrew
friends waited in the furnace of fire. John the Baptist waited in Herod's
prison. Mary and Martha waited for Jesus to come. The apostles waited
in public jail. Peter waited in prison. Paul waited in a basket, in prison,

in chains, and in the hold of a ship. The apostle John waited in exile on Patmos.

God moved in these people's lives while they waited in their dark and difficult places. They sang and prayed and waited. They witnessed and wrote, worked and won converts, and waited. They allowed God to use the waiting room as preparation for the next step.

Your waiting room may be a result of different circumstances from these examples. Maybe you are in a waiting place created by small children, aging parents, sickness, depression, sorrow, grief, financial burdens, habits, attitudes, past memories, regrets, poor choices, loneliness, desertion, abuse, neglect, or a thousand other possibilities. No matter the origin, I want to encourage you to surrender this waiting place to God's hands so you can be strengthened and encouraged.

Right now, will you bow your heart and give this place to Jesus? Will you focus on Him and ask Him to give you His strength to see the plans and visions He has for you? *Lord Jesus, I surrender this place of waiting to You. I'm going to wait for You here and believe You will give me courage and strengthen my heart.* (See Psalm 27:14.)

When we're ready, God will open the door. He allowed us to be closed in and He will bring us out. Jesus said, "I am the door; if anyone enters through Me, he will be saved, and will go in and out and find pasture" (John 10:9). He is our entrance to the things of God, and where He leads there is always growth in our inner being. In the darkness of the waiting room we can grow, and when the door opens we can go on to greater growth.

Deeper into His Presence

I pray the waiting room of your journey has become a new place of hope and possibility to you. I know beautiful plans with eternal possibilities are waiting for all of us when we allow God to prepare us for the open door. Let's lift each other up and wait with eager expectation for these words to become our life testimony. They may be familiar to you, but they take on a whole new meaning when we take them personally for our lives. "Those who wait for the LORD will gain new strength; they will mount up *with* wings like eagles, they will run and not get tired, they will walk and not become weary" (Isaiah 40:31). Waiting never felt more promising! I will declare that He makes it worth the wait.

Here is a prayer of thanksgiving and hope.

> *Thank You, Lord, for strengthening my heart and giving me courage today through the promises in Your Word. I wait here knowing You are working in my circumstances and You are leading me toward Your promises. In Jesus' name, amen.*

Going Deeper – 11

His healing touch does not erase the pain, but rather releases His power and authority into the pain so it can become a place of revival in our life… The storm is over. The pain is not erased, but I am ready to embrace the goodness of God to restore and redeem whatever is lost.

—from "Moved to Worship"

For so long, all I have wanted is for the pain to go away. I hurt so bad I wondered if the throbbing and aching would ever stop. My heartache and sadness diminish the most intense physical pain I have ever experienced. Interestingly enough, my most intense physical pain in this life has been childbirth. But now the pain of child loss is much more profound. The lifeline that connected me to my child has been severed. This time it's forever. The joy that erases the physical pain of childbirth is not present. The pain continues on and on. I'm drained, exhausted, and depleted, and my spirit is anemic. I'm suffering from faith-poor blood instead of iron-poor blood. What am I to do and where am I to go?

My heart is encouraged and my spirit is lifted when I remember another woman who was weary and weak. Her story is found in Mark 5:25-34. She is known as the woman with the issue of blood who was healed when she touched the hem of Jesus' robe. Take time now to read these verses and allow the words recorded for you by the Holy Spirit to minister to you today. She was desperate for help, and the Bible says, "She thought, 'If I just touch His garments, I will get well.' Immediately the flow of her blood was dried up; and she felt in her body that she was healed of her affliction" (Mark 5:28-29).

Your life storm and the pain of your losses may be draining you of spiritual blood and depleting you of strength and energy. Take a lesson from this woman who risked it all to reach for His hem. Press through the obstacles that stand between you and Jesus. Stop and think for a minute what those are at this point in your journey. Putting names to them can be helpful in determining what keeps us from moving on.

Now, do you believe in His power to heal and revive you? I am learning every day that I need to reach toward Him to renew my strength. My pain is not erased, but each time I touch Him in faith His healing power is released and my spirit is revived. I fall down in His presence and worship the One who meets all of my needs through His shed blood and supplies my spirit with His life to restore and revive me. I hear His voice whisper personally to me, *"Daughter, your faith has made you well; go in peace and be healed of your affliction"* (Mark 5:34).

Do you live with some lingering pain or chronic ache because of a loss or upheaval in your life? When I look around at believers, I see a lot of people who are exhausted, depleted, and spiritually anemic. Many seem to be lost in the crowd, hidden from Him by the obstacles in their way. Have you grown sick and tired of being sick and tired spiritually?

* * *

Many of the followers of Jesus began to fall away from Him when the pressure increased and the opposition within the religious circles started to mount. People are fickle, and there is nothing like trial and difficulty to sort out those who are uncertain of their convictions. Jesus turned to His 12 disciples and asked them, "You do not want to go away also, do you?" Simon Peter answered, with a very reasonable response, "Lord, to whom shall we go? You have the words of eternal life" (John 6:67-68).

If we are asked the same question, what is our answer? Where else is there to go and who else has the power to release revival into your pain, fill your spirit with His eternal life, and restore your strength and hope?

List the places and people you have looked to for healing during or after your storm. Have they been able to restore and revive your faith? Are you going forward with the peace He bestows on those who reach to Him?

When God calls us out into the changed world of our life after the storm, He is opening another door. He is leading us deeper and deeper into His heart and allowing us to glimpse another facet of His character. His ways are beyond discovery, but His overwhelming love in the midst of our pain gives us clearer revelations than we could have ever gained had we not discovered our powerlessness without Him. As I draw closer to His throne I am overwhelmed by the privilege I have as His child to stand in His presence. I'm there because the pure, perfect blood of the Lamb has washed and cleansed me.

The transfusion of everlasting life has taken place at the foot of the cross. His blood redeems and revives us. We can call out the words of Psalm 51:12 with assurance that He hears us. "Restore to me the joy of Your salvation, and sustain me with a willing spirit."

Deeper into His Presence

Let's turn to Psalm 71:20 and read it as a statement of faith to declare over our lives. Read it aloud and draw strength and hope to believe its powerful truth. "You who have shown me many troubles and distresses will revive me again, and will bring me up again from the depths of the earth."

Consider the troubles and distresses God has shown you. Now rest in the truth that He will revive you and bring you back up from the depths. If you are in the deep waters of struggle or are finally reaching the shore of life after the storm, may this statement of faith give you courage and clear the obstacles that stand between you and the healing power of Jesus. Reach out to Him.

I invite you to pray this prayer.

Thank You, Lord, for being completely open and honest about the trials and troubles I face. You never promised life would be easy or trouble-free when I became Yours, but

You are there to heal and give me peace. My answer to Your question in the aftermath of trial and opposition is that I don't want to go away from You! You alone have the answers to eternal life. I am looking to You to revive my spirit and fill my heart with love and devotion to follow You all the days of my life. In Jesus' name, amen.

Going Deeper – 12

Your journey has brought you to a new place of discovery. The possibilities are countless when you give yourself over to be used by God.

—from "God's Spacious Places"

When we are taking our first, tentative steps into our new world, we can breathe a sigh of relief knowing this is not enemy territory. Jesus always leads us into spacious places.

When I need assurance, I remember these timeless words of wisdom from the book of Proverbs: "Trust in the LORD with all your heart and do not lean on your own understanding. In all your ways acknowledge Him, and He will make your paths straight" (Proverbs 3:5-6). As we rest in this truth, we can believe that any place—every place—the winds of adversity take us can become spacious places for occupation. Sometimes they are actual physical places, but they are always spiritual places of possibility.

God's spacious places have no boundaries around them to keep people in or shut God out. There are no limitations set on what He is able to do in or through your life. When we say, "He can lead me anywhere, at any time, to do anything He wants me to do," we surrender the where, when, and what and make ourselves available to be used for His glory. Let me share a beautiful example with you.

I recently attended the funeral for my dear friend Julie's mom. She was a beautiful vessel inside and out who poured the love of Jesus on everyone she met. The last two years of her life had been spent in a grueling battle with ovarian cancer. In the face of death she poured life into everyone in her path. The doctors, nurses, other patients, friends, family, and strangers became recipients of Jesus' words of healing and hope. For Bobbi, the walk through the valley of the shadow of death was never about her. She made it about the Shepherd and Guardian of her soul. She wanted everyone to know Him. She allowed God to make her dying days and final moments a spacious place of blessing for her daughters and her husband. Now generations celebrate her life and mourn the loss of her daily doses of love and prayer, but as they step into this new land, they embrace the opportunity to make life a spacious place for others to know Him. What more could we give to the One who brought us through this storm?

* * *

The possibilities are endless when we embrace our new place and say, "God can lead me anywhere, at any time, and to do anything He desires for me to do." Think about the life of Abraham. Read about his willingness to respond to God's call in Genesis 12–13. He moved forward in obedience. "By faith Abraham, when he was called, obeyed by going out to a place which he was to receive for an inheritance; and he went out, not knowing where he was going" (Hebrews 11:8).

We don't have to know where we are going because God knows where He wants to lead us. I never anticipated I would be called to teach and minister in Africa. I never imagined I would have a love and compassion I cannot explain for the people there. It's a benefit of the spacious place God has taken me to since James' death. Would you be willing to say, "Lord I will obey whatever You ask of me? I will release the desire to have a detailed plan and will move when You say." If you're willing to see this place as your appointed place, He will show you when to move ahead.

Think about the children of Israel when they followed Moses out of Egypt. The Red Sea stretched out before them and the Egyptian army was bearing down from behind. They appeared to be caught, trapped, at a dead end. But God made a way through the middle of the sea. Read the story again in Exodus 14 and be reminded of His awesome power. See what He is willing to do on your behalf to accomplish His plans. Remember, He does not change. "Jesus Christ is the same

yesterday and today and forever" (Hebrews 13:8). When He determines it's time for you to move ahead, He will make a way. Keep your
eyes on Him.

Often I hear people say, "I don't know what I'm supposed to do for
God." I wonder if we stumble over *what* because it doesn't look like we
thought it would or should. Just because we don't recognize it doesn't
mean this is not God's spacious place for us. We usually throw up our
hands with a sigh of exasperation and mutter, "Whatever," when we are
frustrated and ready to quit. Perhaps we need to say, in a different way,
"Whatever You have for me, Lord, I'm willing." I'm thinking of the
example of a young girl preparing to be married, whose life was entirely
interrupted and disrupted with the news that she would be with child
by the Holy Spirit. When she was reminded that the impossible is possible with God, listen to her response. "Behold, the bondslave of the
Lord; may it be done to me according to your word" (Luke 1:38).

Are you willing to trust God to use the unwelcome situations and
circumstances in your life and make them spacious places of opportunity? If the thing you are being prompted to do is too hard for you
or too far outside of your experience or skill set, or if it makes you
uncomfortable and more dependent on Him, the chances are that's
God's assignment for your new territory. "Whatever!"

Deeper into His Presence

Together let's celebrate the goodness of God that has brought us
this far. He puts hope in our hearts and a new song on our lips. We are
beginning to realize the beautiful spiritual treasures we have accumulated as a result of our storms. Let's agree together to continue to pray
the words of Paul for ourselves and for one another.

> [I] do not cease to give thanks for you while making men-
> tion of you in my prayers; that the God of our Lord Jesus
> Christ, the Father of glory, may give to you a spirit of wis-
> dom and revelation in the knowledge of Him. I pray that
> the eyes of your heart may be enlightened, so that you may
> know what is the hope of His calling, what are the riches

of the glory of His inheritance in the saints, and what is the surpassing greatness of His power toward us who believe (Ephesians 1:16-19).

Our desire to know what to do and where to go is found in the knowledge of Him. Seek Him. Wisdom and revelation are found in Jesus. With Him, every place can become a spacious place! Write or speak a prayer through Ephesians 1:16-19 and ask God for the vision to see this as new land from which you can praise Him.

Going Deeper – 13

This is not the end, my friend. This is not where
God will leave you. He can and will make
inroads into impossible situations to show us the
way through and then out of the old life. Look
forward. Look up. Look ahead. The time is now!

—from "This Is Not the End"

Times and circumstances can be so overwhelming and disruptive to
our present life that the only place to look is to the future. And, my
friend, that is the right direction. I know it can be really hard to look
forward, but we need to look past the devastation and debris piling up
around us so we can be reminded of the bigger picture. We need to fix
our sights on the hope of heaven. For believers, this is not escape mentality but a reality check. Wanting to encourage and help the people
he had ministered to in Thessalonica, Paul said, "We do not want you
to be uninformed, brethren, about those who have fallen asleep, so
that you will not grieve as do the rest who have no hope" (1 Thessalonians 4:13).

How do we grieve with hope? What does the future hold for
believers?

I want to share something I wrote in my journal on the morning of
October 5, 2013. It had been three years since James had fallen "asleep"
in the Lord. I realized that on the day we lost our son from our lives,
many of the things I believed and prayed for in James' life were completed. It was a startling yet incredibly hopeful revelation. It filled me
with gladness as I wrote an alphabet of all that had been fulfilled.

> James is now…Accepted, Beloved, Complete, Delivered, Eternal, Forgiven and Fulfilled, Glorified and Glad, Healed, Immortal, Justified, Kept, Loved, Made New, Never Alone, Overcomer, at Perfect Peace, Quiet, Redeemed, Saved, Transferred, Understood, Victorious, Worthy…(XYZ) *everything and more* than I could ask or think!

This is surely a reminder of the hope we have in eternal life.

As I continued reading that morning, I read from Psalm 116:15. "Precious in the sight of the LORD is the death of His godly ones." I prayed and asked for God's perspective, for faith to believe that death is not tragic from His point of view; it is precious. Reviewing my list of the heavenly exchange that takes place in His presence, I had to agree.

I read on. "Who has known the mind of the Lord, that he will instruct Him? But we have the mind of Christ" (1 Corinthians 2:16). There are no accidents, mistakes, or uninformed decisions with Him. If I have the mind of Christ, then I can see things from His perspective *and* I can have His vision for the future. And so can you.

It's still a mystery to me. There are times after the storm that you and I will grieve. We may cry, feel great anguish, or even fall back into some earlier thought and doubt patterns. But I want you to know and believe in this truth: When we grieve with hope, a peace deep within our spirit reminds us there is every reason to look ahead with hope as well.

* * *

This is our last time of reflection together, so I want to walk with you through the above three steps that I experienced not so long ago. My prayer in this very moment is that a shift will happen in your spirit, and you will begin to see that grieving the life you had before the storm can become an exercise in and a witness of hope. Because when you grieve with hope, you can then face the future with hope.

1. *Create your own alphabet of faith.* This can become a list of hopes and needs fulfilled (or even questions answered) in and through your storm. Thank God for each of these, for they will remain evidences of His presence.

2. *See your circumstance, your storm from God's perspective.* My storm centered on the death of my son, so my verse of hope was one about God's view of death. Spend time in His Word to find a verse of hope and perspective relevant to your loss, challenge, change, or pain.

3. *View your future with the mind of Christ.* Spend time in prayer asking for a clear view of the hope ahead.

How have these three steps changed your perspective?

What hope do you have now, at this time in your storm, that you didn't have weeks ago, months ago?

As you receive glimpses of the hope and healing ahead, what do you see? How is God revealing a future of hope to you?

Deeper into His Presence

F.B. Meyer, an international evangelist in the early twentieth century, said, "God's hard words are never his last words. The woe and the waste and the tears of life belong to the interlude and not the finale." My dear friend, this time of grief that you're in is not the final word from God. Allow Him to tilt your chin up to look into His beautiful face. There you will see eyes of compassion filled with love for you today. Allow Him to wipe the tears and place them carefully in a bottle so none are lost. Can you whisper back to Him, "Thank You, Jesus, for the hope that this is not Your final word to me. I love You."

In the days to follow, write or speak a prayer of praise and hope for your future in God's capable hands. Start your morning or close your day by giving to Him any remnants of the storm's debris so nothing becomes an obstacle to His plan for your healing and wholeness. The time is now.

I'd like to close our time together in prayer.

> *Lord, give us the courage to look up and look ahead. Let us see beyond the heartache we have endured so that the path of healing You have shaped is in clear view. Relieve us of the burdens we have carried for too long in our limited strength. As we give You our wounds, we believe You will*

transform them into evidences of Your healing power. Teach us to rehearse our alphabet of faith so that we dwell on Your promises fulfilled already…and on those that will be fulfilled in the future. We praise You, Lord, for Your presence in the darkness and for always leading us toward a future of hope. In Jesus' healing name, amen.

INSPIRATIONS FOR

My Healing Heart

These pages are here for you to record insights, verses of meaning for this season of life, experiences of healing, times of feeling God's presence, your needs, and your prayers for your ongoing healing journey.

It can be a great encouragement to look back at notes you take and realize how faithful God was and is and to rest in His eternal promises.

Acknowledgments

I never thought about writing a book. This project has been a step of faith ignited by God and fanned into being through the encouragement and support of many people. To all I want to say thank you for being here for me and somehow knowing when to push, when to pull, and when to pray. Your willingness to share the load, lead the blind, and lift me up has allowed me to see Jesus in practical and personal ways.

Thank you, Frank, for seeing God's potential and patiently pushing me out of my comfort zone. Without your kind and consistent encouragement I would have never had the courage to try.

Morgan, Caroline, and Carter, you are the most awesome cheerleaders a mom could ever have on her team. Your constant and consistent encouragement and care give me strength and energy to carry on. I'm so thankful for you and proud of Jesus in you. Watching you grow and mature in Him is one of my life's greatest joys.

Jimmy McBride, you are one of the most unselfish people I have ever met. Thank you for being a pastor, mentor, and friend to my family and me. You have guided me through this process from start to finish. Your knowledge and experience never trumped God's wisdom and grace in you.

Stacy McKenzie, you are the reason the dream became a reality in the literal sense of the word. No one executes like Stacy, and without her gifts of administration this book would have never been done. Thank you for your reliability, dependability, and for being a sensitive sounding board for many thoughts and ideas.

Hope Lyda, gifted editor, you are a breath of gentle, cleansing air when I thought I would choke on words. For always offering a path through the thicket and a clear view toward the horizon, thank you. Your gifts shared are continually multiplied.

Prayer partners, too numerous to mention all by name but you know who you are. A special thanks goes to my prayer partner Margaret. You are one of God's rare gifts in life. To my precious sisters at Women of the Word, you carried me when the storm raged. I'm eternally grateful. To the prayer group at With Open Eyes, your example and commitment challenge and bless me. Countless others have prayed for me throughout this project and heaven has heard you!

To my pastor and spiritual shepherd, Loran Livingston, thank you for charging us to "read and pray, pray and read." It works! Sandra, his wife, I thank you for standing beside me in some of the hardest moments of my life and covering me with prayer.

Pastor Simon and Agnes, "where would we be without you?" Thank God for being the "laborers" we prayed for in James' life. I love you.

About the Author

Jan Harrison has been inspiring women for more than 20 years as a Bible teacher and speaker at women's conferences and retreats. She served on the leadership committee for Anne Graham Lotz's *Just Give Me Jesus* revivals, held in 30 cities, 12 countries, and for hundreds of thousands of attendees.

She wrote *Life After the Storm* to share how the unexpected death of her son transformed her life and tested her faith, and to offer readers hope and the tools to stop living in fear and experience the transforming faith that only a storm can unveil.

Jan and her husband, Frank, live in Charlotte, North Carolina. They are involved in the local and global faith community and are leaders in an international ministry, With Open Eyes, founded by their late son, James F. Harrison IV. They have three grown daughters and two grandsons.

For more information or to contact Jan for a speaking engagement, visit www.JanHarrison.com.

With Open Eyes

Founded in 2008 by the late James F. Harrison IV and his father, Frank, With Open Eyes is an international ministry working to introduce the message of Jesus Christ and establish self-sustaining and reproducing churches in remote areas of the world. The organization partners with local ministries and international missions agencies to identify, train, and equip messengers of the gospel as they seek to access unreached and underserved people groups. Jan Harrison, James' mother, serves as vice chairman of the board of directors.

Visit www.WithOpenEyes.net for more information.

It is the intention of the author to commit 100 percent of her royalties from *Life After the Storm* to With Open Eyes.

To learn more about Harvest House books and
to read sample chapters, visit our website:

www.harvesthousepublishers.com

HARVEST HOUSE PUBLISHERS
EUGENE, OREGON